THE ANGLO-SAXON CONQUEST OF ENGLAND

Frederick Arthur Storr
1902–1987

Maurice Arthur Storr
1925–2004

John Arthur Storr
1953–2009

The Anglo-Saxon Conquest of England

Jim Storr

Helion & Company Limited

Helion & Company Limited
Unit 8 Amherst Business Centre
Budbrooke Road
Warwick
CV34 5WE
England
Tel. 01926 499 619
Email: info@helion.co.uk
Website: www.helion.co.uk
Twitter: @helionbooks
blog.helion.co.uk

Published by Helion & Company 2016. Published with revised and amended text as
The Anglo-Saxon Conquest of England 2023
Designed and typeset by Mach 3 Solutions Ltd, Bussage, Gloucestershire
Cover designed by Paul Hewitt, Battlefield Design (www.battlefield-design.co.uk)

Text & figures © Jim Storr 2016, 2018, 2023
Images © as individually credited
Front cover: The medal, or disk, is in the collection of the Department of Coins, Medals
and Antiques of the Bibliotheque nationale de France. Image © Dominique Hollard.
Rear cover: Photo © Jim Storr.

ISBN 978-1-804512-98-2

British Library Cataloguing-in-Publication Data.
A catalogue record for this book is available from the British Library.

For details of other military history titles published by Helion & Company Limited contact
the above address, or visit our website: http://www.helion.co.uk.

We always welcome receiving book proposals from prospective authors.

Contents

List of Figures

Legend

	Marsh, swamp, fen etc.
	Woodland. Note: marsh, swamp, fen and woodland are not shown on all figures. In most cases they are only shown to illustrate a particular point.
◆--⌇--◆	Ford over a river.
■ CALLEVA (Silchester)	Roman town, etc, with modern name.
■ Dorchester	Roman town, etc, (Latin name unknown, or not shown).
● (Swindon)	Name of other town, etc (eg, a town not known to have existed in Roman times).
Summergill Brook ⟶	Name of watercourse, with direction of flow.
△ .259	Summit of hill, with spot height (in metres above sea level).

Ermine Street	Roman road.
- - - - - - - - - - - - - -	Presumed course of Roman road.
Devil's Ditch	Name of earthwork.
▬▬▬▬▬	Linear Earthwork. The thick line represents the bank; the thin line represents the ditch. Hence this earthwork faces up the page (see Figure 1.2).
▬▬▬▬	Linear Earthwork of uncertain orientation. In this case the earthwork is assesed to face up the page.
▬▬▬	Presumed course of earthwork.
◆	Place with name ending with '-ing' or '-ings' (see Chapter Four).
✚	Place with name containing 'Tye' or 'Tey' (see Chapter Four).

List of Plates

In Colour Section

Acknowledgements

I am grateful to several people for their help in the research for, and preparation of, this book.

Four academics gave most useful help and advice in the early stages. They were: Dr Catherine Hills, Dr David Pratt and Dr Carl Watkins of Cambridge University; and Dr John Pearce of King's College, London. In particular: were it not for Catherine Hills, this book would never have been written.

My friends and colleagues at Birmingham University sat through a presentation of some of my early findings. Their deep knowledge of many aspects of war studies provided useful insight, both then and subsequently. They suggested several avenues for further work. More importantly, their verdict was that the broad gist of those early findings was credible. That gave me the impetus to continue.

Many friends, and many members of my extended family, provided a meal and a bed for the night whilst I did my field research. Their hospitality was often accompanied by perceptive questions and critical insights. Several came with me on my field trips; providing company, asking questions, and obliging me to explain my ideas simply and clearly. One was a highly experienced military surveyor. One was an infantry officer for over 30 years. One couple are both very capable horsemen. One of my brothers read medieval history and English at university. The other was an infantry officer and a deeply knowledgeable student of military history. But sometimes the most innocent of questions resulted in the greatest insight.

My research has taken me across the length and breadth of England. I have come across a great number of people, complete strangers for the most part. Their many simple acts of kindness have been most welcome.

I thank them all.

Introduction

How did Roman Britain become Anglo-Saxon England?

The answer matters. This book is written in English. Not Scots Gaelic, nor Latin. Before the Anglo-Saxon conquest there was no 'English'. Anglo-Saxons gave the world the English language (the language of Shakespeare, Keats, Byron and Shelley); parliaments; trial by jury; and (perhaps unfortunately) cricket and warm beer. Every time you get into a passenger aircraft, anywhere in the world, the air traffic controllers will be speaking English. So it does matter. It's not just about re-writing a chapter of the history of England. It's about how the English became the English and, to that extent, much about the modern world.

We do not, however, really know the answer. There are very few historical sources from the period. There are also a few intriguing but garbled and confused oral sources, which were written down centuries later. The archaeology of the period is scant, confusing, and at times contradictory.

What we understand of the period today is a mosaic of facts, half truths and myths. Some of the biggest myths are surprisingly recent. There is not really any one single, coherent account. What little we do know shows huge gaps and some surprising inconsistencies. This book attempts to shed light on that simple question: how did Roman Britain become Anglo-Saxon England?

The book takes what we know of archaeology and history and adds a few more ingredients. They generally relate to the landscape. What did it look like at the time? What can that tell us? One ingredient is an aspect of place-name study: asking what the name of a place can tell us about what it looked like in historic times. Another ingredient is an extensive and thorough look at the terrain and the landscape today. That involved weeks of map study, months of personal reconnaissance, and employing a soldier's eye for ground. Soldiers are trained to look for things which other people are not. They may see things which archaeologists and historians, for example, have not. In addition, just having a fresh pair of eyes looking at a problem may reveal things that others have missed.

The real impetus to write this book, however, was the identification of a major series of archaeological anomalies. That is, things which simply shouldn't be there. Alternatively, since they *are* there (they do exist), they are effectively unexplained. What they are, and what they imply, will become apparent as we progress through this book.

The Anglo-Saxon Conquest of England was originally published, in 2016, as *King Arthur's Wars*. Since then three things have affected the way in which very-early-mediaeval England has been understood.

Firstly, there has been a growing awareness of the period, in Britain at least, related to the discovery of the Staffordshire Gold Hoard. The Hoard has undoubtedly drawn attention to the period. However it has, if anything, highlighted how little we really know. Who made the items in the hoard? Who owned them? Why was the hoard hidden? Why was it hidden where it was?

The Hoard has been linked in a very concrete manner to a major uplift in the visitor facilities at Sutton Hoo in Suffolk: the Hoard was probably hidden around the same time that the Sutton Hoo ship was buried. The new visitor centre at Sutton Hoo was opened in 2019 at a cost of £4m. In the summer of 2022 part of the Hoard was displayed in that centre, under the banner of 'Swords of the Kingdoms'. It was clearly intended to evoke synergies between the Hoard and the ship burial. That synergy was increased by the film 'The Dig', which describes the discovery of the Sutton Hoo ship in 1939 and stars Ralph Fiennes.

Secondly, in 2018 Dr Eric Grigg published *Warfare, Raiding and Defence*, which seems to be based on his doctoral research.[1] Grigg appears to be an historian by training. The strength of his work lies in a combination of high-quality analysis of written archaeological records and extensive fieldwork. Grigg's main findings relate to a series of linear earthworks distributed throughout England (and, in a few cases, beyond its borders). He concludes that they generally relate to the period of the transition from Roman Britain to Anglo-Saxon England, and that they are military in purpose and defensive in nature. In that, Grigg's findings agree entirely with the contents of this book. The only substantive disagreement is that Grigg contends that those earthworks were defences against raiding. This book contends that they had a more general defensive purpose. It is hard to see that, say, a defensive system 60 miles long was intended merely to stop raiders.

The third development was the publication of a *Sunday Times* Bestseller: Marc Morris' *The Anglo-Saxons*.[2] Any listed bestseller which throws light into this aspect of British history is welcome, if only for doing just that. Regrettably Morris' book tells us little that is new. It tells us a lot about ecclesiastical history, because that is what the principle sources (notably Bede) do. In consequence the book tells us little about the 99 per cent of people who were neither priests, saints nor bishops. It tends to largely ignore geography, as many historians do. Its writing falls into the 'must have' fallacy, described in Chapter 1 of this book. However, Morris' book does at least recognise the existence of long linear earthworks. It accepts that they were military in nature and relate to post-Roman Britain. That tells us that established historians, at least, are beginning to look at the Anglo-Saxon conquest of England in a subtly different way.

1   Dr Eric Grigg, *Warfare, Raiding and Defence in Early Medieval Britain*. Marlborough: Robert Hale, 2018.
2   Marc Morris, *The Anglo-Saxons. A History of the Beginnings of England*. London: Penguin Random House, 2022.

Memorial: On the Banks of the Tamar

He stood on a hill overlooking the river. He was Egbyrth son of Egfrith son of Aethelwald, earldorman of Wessex. The river was the Tamar. Across the river was Cornwall, the last refuge of the British.

Aethelwald, his father's father, had marched north with the king of Wessex to fight the Mercians at the great battle of Ellandun. *His* father's father's father's father's father had been with the king when they marched into Winchester, and he was there when the next king was crowned.

His father had fought at the Broad Ford, when the men of the West Saxons had beaten the Welsh and gone on to conquer the shires of Wiltshire, Dorset, Somerset and finally Devon.

It is said that *his* father had been there when the holy Birinus first preached to the West Saxons, and thus brought the love of Christ to the Companions.

They were Saxons; they were West Saxons; but before Saint Birinus they had just called themselves 'the Companions'. *His* father had fought with the mighty Ceawlin at Bedcanford, and when they seized the towns of Limbury, Aylesbury, Benson and Eynsham.

And it is said that *his* father's father's father was one of the few to escape from the massacre at Badon, when the accursed Arthur had brought his cavalry down from the north and slain hundreds of the north folk and the south folk. Never again did the men of Norfolk and Suffolk rise against the British.

All those kinsmen had lived in Britain for many years. But it is said that *his* father's father's father had sworn an oath, under a German chieftain, to fight for the Romans, in Colonia Augusta on the mighty River Rhine in Germany.

He was Egbyrth son of Egfrith son of Aethelwald, earldoman of Wessex. From him to that day in Cologne were fifteen sons and fathers. It is said that one day his king, Aelfraed of Wessex, would be king of all England; or perhaps his son; or his son's son. And Egbyrth was proud. For was he not, himself, a true Saxon?

1

The Anglo-Saxon Conquest of England

By the late fourth century, England and Wales had been part of the Roman Empire for about 350 years. Roman Britain had many towns and about 30 cities, connected by an extensive and well-built road network. Most of the population spoke a Celtic language, but some spoke and wrote in Latin. Society was organised, government functioned, and trade was conducted using Roman law. England, Wales and much of both Scotland and Ireland were part of a continent-wide trade system. Goods from places as far away as Turkey and Egypt were traded for tin, corn and other cargoes from Britain.

By the mid-ninth century, Britain was very different. Most of the people in what had become England spoke an entirely different language. Roman law had disappeared. It had been replaced by a rapidly-developing system based on Germanic tribal custom. The towns and cities had been largely abandoned, but were slowly being redeveloped. In simple terms, in the year 400 AD most people thought of themselves as Roman citizens. By 850 they did not.

Those changes had been accompanied by several wars. Many of them were fought between the descendants of the Romano-British inhabitants and people who were, or were descended from, Germanic invaders. We now call those people Anglo-Saxons and we know that, broadly, they won. However, that was by no means inevitable. For more than a century it seemed unlikely. We know very little about those wars.

The change from Roman Britain to Anglo-Saxon England was not just a matter of warfare. There was major social, political, economic and cultural change as well. But war was a major factor. War can, and has, changed the fate of continents; and can do so astonishingly quickly. War was hugely important in this period. It was a period of much violence, brutality and main force. The wars by which Roman Britain became Anglo-Saxon England are the main subject of this book.

If there was someone called Arthur, someone who we now know as 'King' Arthur, what role did he play? It does seem that he, and others like him, were key figures in those wars. That is why we shall sometimes call those conflicts 'King Arthur's wars'. But no matter what role he played, no one man could be responsible for the course and outcome of a series of wars which stretched over 450 years.

The English have forgotten. They remember the Norman Conquest. There were only about 7,000 Norman invaders; perhaps as many as 10,000. With their families and retainers, the total may have been 20-30,000 people. They took over England in roughly 20 years. They had a major impact on society. Within a generation, over 70% of all men had names of French origin: Roberts, Williams, Hughs, Johns and so on. Arguably, however, the Normans had little impact on the law or the language. Today the English speak English, not Norman French. The Normans made several laws, but did not change the underlying basis of the law. The Anglo-Saxon conquest (if conquest it was) took far longer: about 450 years. 450 years from the Norman Conquest would take England into the reign of Henry the Eighth, arguably England's first post-medieval king.

The English are unlike many other Europeans. They do not, like most of western Europe, have a Roman law code. A law code is the basis for the way society is run, government is conducted, and trade takes place. Laws and legal systems are written statements of observed and enforceable social, political and economic norms. So the fundamental basis for the way in which England is run is very different from that of much of Europe. That difference has had major implications; for example, in Britain's relationship with the European Union.

Roman law triumphed elsewhere, for several reasons. Most of them did not apply in a society which, like post-Roman Britain, had largely collapsed. Britain is the only major region of the former western Roman empire which did not develop a Latin-based language. England is different. The Germanic takeover of England took centuries and had a major impact. The use of a Germanic language (which is closer to Frisian Dutch than any other similar language) suggests that Roman structures of law and society largely disappeared. They were rebuilt by Germanic incomers and their successors. The difference is important. Without the Germanic takeover, Britain might still be called Britain, as it was in Roman times. But England would not be the land of the English. The English language would probably not exist. The United States, the Commonwealth, and several other countries would not exist as they do now. Many million people around the world would not speak English. America might be 'the Land of the Free', but its constitution would be very, very different.

Terminology is highly important in this area. Terms like 'Dark Age', 'Celtic', 'Anglo-Saxon' and 'British' are often used loosely. That can be a problem. In this book they will have fairly specific meanings. 'Britain' will be taken to mean the whole of the British Isles, whilst 'Roman Britain' will mean that part of Britain which the Romans conquered. Put simply, that means England south of Hadrian's Wall (thus excluding much of Northumberland), and Wales. Southern Scotland was an important part of the Roman Imperial system and will be discussed later.

The question of what 'Celtic' means is important. Here it is used very narrowly to describe culture and language. Before the Roman conquests, much of western Europe had something broadly described as Celtic culture and spoke Celtic languages. So when we refer to 'Celtic' in Britain, we mean the language and culture that underlay Latin and Roman culture. By extension, 'Romano-British' is a general term to describe the largely Celtic-speaking people who lived in Britain at the end of imperial Roman rule. They didn't go away or disappear. By and large they were conquered, or taken over, by what we now call the Anglo-Saxons.

The origins of the Anglo-Saxons were Germanic. Many of the original invaders came from what is now north Germany, the Netherlands (especially Frisia) or Denmark. They are described in historical sources as Angles, Saxons and Jutes. By the tenth century or so, the term 'Anglo-Saxon' had been coined to differentiate their successors from the Romano-British. By then, however, almost none of the 'Anglo-Saxons' had ever been to Germany. Their ancestors had lived in England for centuries.

'Saxon' requires very careful consideration. The Romans used it fairly loosely, in the way the we might now say 'German' or perhaps 'Germanic'. Many people who we now think of as having Saxon origins (such as the people of Wessex) never used the term to refer to themselves. To reduce ambiguity, we will use 'Saxon' in one of two specific ways. The first, and least important, is to refer to people who come from the region of north Germany around Hannover: Saxony. The second is to refer to the people of what became the kingdoms of the East, South and West Saxons: Essex, Sussex and Wessex respectively.

'Welsh' requires even more careful use. The word is derived from a Germanic word for 'foreigner'. The word has developed to describe several peoples who lived beyond the borders of where Germanic people lived. Hence 'Wallis' (the German name for the French-speaking canton of Valais in Switzerland); 'Wallachia' in Romania (the principality beyond Transylvania, where many Germanic people had settled); and 'Wales'. Unfortunately for us, the Anglo-Saxons called the Romano-British 'foreigners', hence 'Welsh'. That leads to confusion because, for example, a Germanic warrior in Kent in the fifth century (who was by origin possibly a Jute from Jutland) might call the Romano-British inhabitants of London or Surrey 'Welsh'. To avoid that confusion we shall call those people 'Romano-British', and keep the word 'Welsh' for the inhabitants of Wales. They are, after all, inhabitants of what we now call Wales. They are descended from the Romano-British, and still what the Anglo-Saxons would have called 'foreigners' (hence to that extent 'Welsh'). Modern Wales is, essentially, the part of Roman Britain which the Anglo-Saxons never conquered.

The inhabitants of Ireland had a Celtic culture and language, as did most of Scotland. Some confusion arose in the past because there are broadly two main forms of Celtic language in Britain. They are known as 'p' and 'q' Celtic, or alternatively 'Brythonic' and 'Goidelic'. The boundary of where those languages were spoken was not well understood, and there was some movement of tribes. Hence, confusingly, a tribe called the 'Scotti' were considered to be Irish. We shall use the term 'Irish' only to refer to people who lived in Ireland, and 'Scottish' to refer to people who lived in modern Scotland. The term 'Picts' or 'Pictish' will be taken to mean Scots who lived north of the River Firth, where the Romans never settled. The Romans used the term *Picti* ('the painted ones') to describe them from about 300 or 310 AD.

The modern Welsh word for Wales is 'Cymru', which is derived from the Romano-British word for 'companions'. The late Romano-British used it to describe themselves, as opposed to the Anglo-Saxons. One form of it was '*Cumbroges*', hence Cumbria as a region of the Romano-British. Cumbria was one of the last areas to become Anglo-Saxon. The Romano-British called themselves '*Britones*' (hence 'British') when they wrote in Latin, which they continued to do until after the Norman Conquest. Thus when a Welshman today says he is British, he is absolutely correct.

When were the Dark Ages? The term is used loosely and can mean different things to different people. There is very little if any written record between the end of Imperial Roman Britain and, for example, the writings of the Venerable Bede. The period in between is 'dark 'to the extent that little or no historical record illuminates it. We will use the term 'Dark Ages' to mean the period from about 400 to about 730 AD. Historians tend to use the term 'early medieval', but that can include the period up to the Norman Conquest.

The broad sequence of the Anglo-Saxon conquest of England is quite simple, although the dates are vague (for reasons which we will discuss later). Imperial rule in Britain seems to have ended soon after 400 AD. Some Germanic people were already settled in Britain by then. Increasing numbers arrived in the fifth century, often as warriors to protect the east coast and (to some extent) to replace Roman forces. In the middle of that century (about 450) some of them rebelled. The rebellion was put down, and by about 500 the Germanic element was contained in what we now call East Anglia, Essex, Kent and Sussex. Strictly, East Anglia is the land of the East Anglians. It was divided between the land of the North Folk and the South Folk, hence Norfolk and Suffolk. It does not include the land of the East Saxons, namely Essex. There were probably also groups of Germanic settlers in Lindsey (the area around Lincoln), East Yorkshire, Northumberland, and some other smaller pockets.

That situation lasted for about fifty years. Then, in the middle of the sixth century, separate groups began to fight the Romano-British again, and conquer further territory. The Kingdom of Wessex developed from about 550 AD. Germanic kingdoms developed in Essex, East Anglia, the Midlands, Yorkshire and Northumberland from about 570 AD. By no means all of the fighting was against the Romano-British. The Yorkshire and Northumberland kingdoms fought each other until one man ruled both, as the king of Northumbria. Mercia, the midland kingdom, fought against Northumbria and Wessex for centuries. At times any or all of them were allied to Romano-British kingdoms, whose names are often wrapped in mystery. By about 850 AD Northumbria, Mercia and Wessex had conquered most of modern England, swallowing up the smaller kingdoms of Kent, Essex, Sussex and East Anglia on the way. It was a slow and fitful process. In some areas no progress was made against the Roman-British for a century or so.

King Alfred, the only king in English history be called 'The Great', ruled from 871 to 899 AD. He was a king of Wessex and never ruled England. Viking raids had started in 793. Alfred and his contemporaries spent far more time and effort fighting the Vikings than the remaining Romano-British. His son Edward the Elder united England under one throne, not least due to the Viking invasions. England was not free of Viking incursions until after the Norman conquest of 1066. It can, however, reasonably be said that Alfred's descendants ruled a unified Anglo-Saxon kingdom. The advent of Alfred, and the Vikings incursions, can be seen as the end of the Anglo-Saxon conquest of England.

There are many problems in trying to understand this period. There is almost no historical record and little archaeology. Both disciplines present problems when looking at the Dark Ages. History books tend to describe one of two views of the period, which we can call 'Edwardian' and 'Modernist'. 'Edwardian' writers tended to take works such as Bede's largely at face value. They believed that Britain was invaded by waves of Germanic invaders, who felled the mighty oak forests, ploughed the land, rapidly disposed of the effete and decadent Romano-British, became Christian, and brought democracy and parliamentary government to England. That, of course, is a great simplification, but it exposes two things: the attitudes of the Edwardians, and the relative absence of archaeological evidence in Edwardian times.

According to the 'Modernist' view, there were no invasions; just migrations. The cultural shift from Romano-British to Anglo-Saxon was largely peaceful and cultural. Key archaeological issues (such as the fact that many of the Germanic migrants cremated their dead, rather than burying them intact) are taken to reflect peaceful cultural transition rather than conquest. Men started to carry weapons in public as fashion statements, to reflect a peace-loving society(!) The mighty forests were not hewn down: they did not exist, because Britain had been deforested in the Iron Age. That is also a parody, but each of its elements is taken from recent books on the 'Dark Ages'.

The great works on the subject tend to come from mid- to late-twentieth century. They are the standard text books used at universities. They tend towards the Edwardian rather than the modernist view. The volumes of the Oxford (University) History of England are important amongst them. The first volume, originally written in 1936, was entitled 'Roman Britain and the English Settlements', by R. G. Collingwood and J. N. L. (Nowell) Myres. Myres wrote the piece most relevant to us, namely the final five chapters on post-Roman Britain. When the book was re-written fifty years later, Myres re-wrote his work as a separate volume simply called 'The English Settlements'. He was then 84 years old and it was a mistake to ask him to write it. His thinking had not moved on. The Roman part of the original book was re-written in 1981 by Peter Salway. The succeeding volume, 'Anglo-Saxon England', was written by Sir Frank Stenton in 1943.

There is no good, modern, standard reference book which covers our period in general, and the wars between the Romano-British and the Anglo-Saxons in detail. That causes several problems. For example, there may have been a major incursion against Britain by Picts, Saxons and others in or about the year 367 AD. As a result several archaeologists in the early twentieth century dated sites or finds to 367. Some recent writers took that at face value. Indeed much early dating is now considered to be wrong, but there is no way to get writers who only read the Oxford History to understand what is now thought to be right. A related problem is that Bede, who is almost the only (and certainly the most reliable) writer who lived close to the period, only dated nine events relevant to our subject in a period of several centuries. So there is little or no chronological backbone on which to hang events. The fifth and sixth centuries are a critical period, in which Bede provides no useful dates at all.

The Edwardian approach tends to largely overlook the Romano-British, not least because Bede did. It also tends to dwell extensively on the advent of Christianity among the Anglo-Saxons. Well, the Anglo-Saxons may have adopted Christianity much as Bede described it. After all, he was a monk and became a saint. However, the Romano-British were already extensively Christianised. They had churches and bishops long before the end of Imperial Roman Britain, and they survived long after.

Earlier historians tended to cling to the notion of a conquest, and a large migration of Germanic warriors. Newer generations, and particularly archaeologists, increasingly reject that view. Some of them are definitely in the 'modernist' camp. The reason is fairly easy to see. History tends to be written by the winners, and from the top down. It looks at kings and the view from the throne. Conversely archaeology tends to look from the bottom up. It often looks at things like huts, farming, and cooking implements. The archaeology shows little direct sign of wars. The two views can be reconciled, but for this period that has not yet happened.

A further problem is that of place names. The names of the locations of events such as battles are known to us from works such as Bede's or the Anglo-Saxon Chronicle. Early historians made educated guesses as to where those places were. They then joined those places together to form a picture of how wars took place. Unfortunately the locations are often flawed. They are perhaps wrong; not credible; or lead to seriously misleading conclusions. Unfortunately many writers do not check the original texts against what we now know of the origins of place names. As a result some fairly major myths exist, and will persist unless corrected. A further tendency is to wrap a few place names up with a fairly superficial understanding of warfare. The result is a simplistic view of the strategy of the wars of the Dark Ages.

The two main ways of shining light into the Dark Ages are through history and archaeology. Since the early 20th century, history has been increasingly concerned with the study of documents and other recorded material. To that extent it is not 'the study of the past' but 'insight into what happened in the past, based on what has been written, and what we can say about that'. Some people believe that history can tell us 'what actually happened.' That, however, is impossible. The historian cannot do more than collect, assess and interpret evidence. He should then come to some opinion or judgement.

That point is critical. In a criminal trial, the jury must believe that the evidence is convincing 'beyond all reasonable doubt'. In a civil trial, however, the evidence is only required to be 'more likely than unlikely'. For the Dark Ages, we cannot be certain 'beyond all reasonable doubt'. For this book we shall normally make judgements based on evidence that we think is 'more likely that unlikely'.

The original historical sources, and most modern history books, have great gaps in them. For example: we know that, soon after the Roman invasion, the *Iceni* revolted in about 61 AD. We know that the *Iceni* were a tribe based in what is now East Anglia.

We also know that, by 500 or so, East Anglia was extensively settled by Anglians. 'Angeln', where they came from, is a region of Denmark. How did that happen? What happened to the *Iceni*? When did it happen? We simply do not know. That is a major gap in our knowledge. There are many others.

Most of the original, historical, source documents we know of are made up of half-truths. They were sometimes collected from lost original texts, or distorted by the interests or ignorance of their authors. The only contemporary source written in England is Gildas' 'The Ruin of Britain'. We don't really know who Gildas was; when or where he was writing; what his occupation was; nor when the events he described took place. He probably wrote in about 540 AD, and he was not writing a history. His main purpose was a religious tirade against the un-Christian behaviour of the rulers of post-Roman Britain. Reading his work today, he comes across as a religious fanatic. He tells us a fair amount about the life and social attitudes of the times, but relatively little about what took place. Even though we believe he wrote in the sixth century, the earliest copy we have is from the tenth. Two other copies are from the twelfth and thirteenth centuries. They all show some evidence of amendment from the presumed original.

The next source, in terms of date, is the *Historia Britonnum*, or 'History of the British'. It is often referred to by the name of its supposed author, Nennius. One version contains a version of the *Annales Cambriae* or 'Welsh Annals'. There are many problems with the use of these works as historic sources. The Medieval and Celtic expert Professor David Dumville strongly criticised any reliance on Nennius and similar Welsh sources, not least because they were written down about 250-300 years after the events to which they relate. In the interim a lot of the material was probably changed by being passed down verbally. The *Historia Britonnum* has very little detail in the sixth century after the events of Arthur, who probably died in about 530 AD or so. It is of little use as a historical document. If it is not reliable, then there is no way of validating the events described in Welsh legendary poems such as 'The Book of Taliesin' and 'The Book of Aneirin'. Such sources are a good example of what happened when medieval authors tried to marry legendary, narrative material with a dated record. So, apart from Gildas, there is *no* contemporary British written source from before the ninth century, and later sources are unreliable.

Professor Dumville's remarks, published in the highly respected journal 'History', also had the effect of discouraging respectable academic historians from looking specifically at 'The Age of Arthur' (say, 400-550 AD). There had been two quite good books in the 1970s, but nothing of that quality since.

The much-venerated Bede wrote his 'History of the English Church and People' in the early 730s AD. Bede was a monk at the monastery at Jarrow. He enjoyed the patronage of the King of Northumbria. He was not British. He was an Anglo-Saxon, which strongly affected what he wrote. Bede paraphrased Gildas for the critical early chapters of his book, which has two main effects. Firstly, it tells us nothing useful about the period up to 550 AD or so which is not mentioned in Gildas. Secondly, several modern writers do not realise that, and have drawn false conclusions. For example, it has been suggested that Bede 'corroborates' Gildas. He doesn't. He *repeats* Gildas. Bede's story of the arrival of the Germans in Britain was: not his; written 300 years after the event; and does not actually describe a mass migration, as Edwardian historians tended to assume. His story of the two Germanic leaders Hengest and Horsa is almost definitely legendary. The two names mean something like 'stallion' and 'mare' respectively. A Germanic warrior quite possibly had the name of nickname of 'the stallion'. It stretches belief to think that another warrior was called 'the mare'.

Bede was undoubtedly very pious, and his work is hugely valuable. However, we would now say that 'he didn't get out much'. He entered the monastery as a boy and almost never left it until he died aged about 62. Almost anything he wrote came to him, at best, from second hand.

The chronological background to this period comes to us largely from the Anglo-Saxon Chronicle, which was composed over several centuries in the courts of various Anglo-Saxon Kings. It continues well after the Norman Conquest, to 1158. Several versions exist. There are errors, discrepancies and omissions in, or between, all of them. None is the original, and none are particularly early. Some of the early parts are based on Bede, which is of course based on Gildas. Some of it has obviously been made up. For example, in the period 556-592 AD it lists eleven events. Two can be corroborated from other sources, but six of the others fall on leap years. Statistically, that is incredibly unlikely. By probably no coincidence, that section of the Chronicle refers to the foundation of the Kingdom of Wessex. For a long time the Chronicle appears to have been composed in the court of Wessex.

The Chronicle also weaves together what are clearly two different stories of the origins of Wessex. Were the chroniclers trying to get the best of both? It is unlikely that both are true. They are often taken at face value even today, but to academic historians they are obviously a concoction. Researching the wars of the periods reveals only 12 relevant events in a period of 300 to 350 years. Most of them are described in a sentence or two. They tell us some names, actions and places. However, we rarely know who the people were, nor how they were related. Today we have often got the places wrong as well. Several of the references come from outside Britain, and are only of passing relevance. Overall, as Professor Dumville put it, '[t]he basic fact is that we have no written English evidence … which pre-dates the seventh century.'

Then, as now, the ownership of pieces of land was recorded in written documents. These land charters were only written for major land transfers. They were typically transfers (grants) from the king to major noblemen, or from the king to the Church. Church charters have generally survived better than the others. A total of about 1600 charters are known to exist, but many relate to the later Anglo-Saxon period. Some are forgeries. Some are copies. Some have been altered in part. There is no clear overall pattern as to which are authentic, and many of them are irrelevant to our purpose. The variation in quality allows for a lot of interpretation, and hence difference of opinion as to what they mean to us.

One other work broadly pre-dates the period, but is hugely relevant. Called the *Notitia Dignatatum*, it is an official Roman document which can be described as the Master Organisation Table of the Roman Army, worldwide. (It is actually a list of major government officials, but it describes all military unit and formation commanders, and they dominate the list.) Its date is the subject of much discussion. We will look at it in detail in Chapter Two.

Probably the biggest single problem in this area of history is the story of the Rescript of Honorius. A rescript was an official Roman document which recorded the emperor's personal judgement in response to a petition. Rescripts had the status of law. The Emperor Honorius probably issued hundreds of rescripts during his reign as Emperor from 395 to 423 AD. However, only one is important to us. The story goes that Honorius, in a rescript, ordered the Roman legions to leave Britain (which would then be undefended) in about 410. That, then, was the end of Roman Britain.

This story is hugely important. According to the Edwardian view, one can almost see the *Primus Pilus* (senior centurion) of the 20th Legion (*Valeria Victrix*) saluting, turning to the right and jumping on board the last ship to leave Dover, leaving Britain to its fate. That is highly unlikely. The story comes to us from an Eastern Roman (Byzantine) court official called Zosimus. He wrote in the early sixth century, a hundred years after the events he described. He wrote in Greek, not Latin. The relevant passage comes amidst a discussion of the province of Aemilia, which lies around Ravenna where Honorius held his court for several years. It appears to say that Honorius wrote to the cities of Britain, telling them to 'look to their own defence', or similar.

That does not say that Honorius ordered the Roman army to leave. Nor does it mention a rescript. Victorian or Edwardian historians invented that, on the grounds that that was what Roman emperors did. The context is questionable, and the original Greek text may have said 'the city called Bruttia' or 'the city of Bruttia', or similar, rather than 'the cities of Britain'. Using the word 'Britain' is out of context. If a modern academic researcher proposed that the end of Imperial Roman Britain took place that way, on that evidence, he would be laughed at. It is simply not credible by modern academic standards. But, critically, it has long been an accepted statement of fact. The problem arises because our whole understanding of the end of Roman Britain and the origins of Anglo-Saxon England hang around the alleged Rescript of Honorius. Zosimus might even be referring to people in the Roman province of Armorica (Brittany). This problem has many aspects. For example, Zosimus wrote about 100 years after the event. He could, at best, use Byzantine (not Roman, nor Ravenna) court archives. The only corroboration is Gildas, and Gildas is not entirely dependable. The corroboration in Gildas is weak: for example, he does not refer to any writing from Honorius on this subject, let alone a rescript. Zosimus' account contradicts both the *Notitia Dignatatum* and the Anglo-Saxon Chronicle. 'Bruttia' may refer to a city in Italy.

The *Notitia Dignatatum* appears to date from well after 410 AD, and includes the names of all the units in Britain. There were about 60 of them, totalling about 30,000 troops. But the Rescript suggests that all the Roman forces had left in about 410. So was the *Notitia* wrong, or a fake, or was the part referring to Britain out of date?

Historians have jumped through intellectual hoops to explain the *Notitia* based on the alleged 'fact' of the Rescript. Yet it seems more reasonable to believe that the *Notitia* is correct and that there never was a Rescript. That is, Honorius did not order the Roman Army to leave Britain in or about 410. If that is the case, we have no date for the end of Roman Imperial rule in Britain. It could be anything between, say, 400 and 450 AD. There is actually no good evidence of the Roman Army leaving. What actually happened to it will be discussed later. Regrettably, even highly reputable historians cling to the alleged Rescript as an article of faith.

About a hundred years ago, archaeologists' and historians' work overlapped. Both could be described as 'antiquarians'. However, just as historians came to focus on the analysis of documentary sources, archaeologists came to see themselves as a branch of anthropology (the study of human culture). That is a fascinating area, but not necessarily related to the study of actual events in the past. Indeed, at least one archaeologist has said that his colleagues examine and analyse what they find, leaving it for others to ascribe relevance. Not least, relevance is always (to some extent) subject to the viewpoint of the beholder. Some historians have criticised that approach, complaining of a tendency to ignore the historical (that is, documentary) evidence. Archaeologists may not be particularly concerned with actual events much at all. They don't necessarily see it as their job.

By and large, archaeologists don't study wars: there is very little physical evidence. Some archaeologists study battlefields, and their work can help correct some completely wrong assumptions. An example is the recent discovery of cannon balls and shot on the site of the Battle of Bosworth in 1485 AD. That corrected the assertion (strongly held until then) that the battle had taken place on a different site, a couple of miles away. Archaeologists do consider 'conflict', although often in a somewhat bland and general way. Without the historical context, such study is inevitably general. But between conflict in general and individual weapons or battlefields in particular, they cannot tell us much about the conduct of a whole series of wars. For example, we do not know the precise location of a single Dark Age battlefield in England.

Dates are a particular problem. Archaeologists cannot normally specify a precise date without a cast-iron historical link. Such links are rare in the Dark Ages. Archaeologists can provide 'not before' and 'not after' dates. That can be used to construct quite sophisticated chronologies. Some seem to be quite accurate, but the overall result is only as accurate as the assumptions made in putting it together. For the Dark Ages the result is much less precise than a non-specialist would suspect.

Burials are a major source of evidence for the Dark Ages. The terminology needs to be explained. If the ashes of a cremated body are scattered, there is no way of detecting what happened. However, the ashes of many cremated bodies were buried in small, crude pots. Both the pots and their contents can be analysed. However, the word 'burial' strictly refers to both burying ashes in pots and to burying whole bodies (typically in shrouds, coffins or both). Archaeologists use the word 'inhumation' to refer to the burial of uncremated bodies. However, for simplicity, we will use the terms 'cremation' and 'burial' respectively.

Traditionally it was assumed that late-Roman practice was for burials with few, if any, grave goods. Germanic bodies were typically buried aligned north-south with many grave goods, or cremated. Christian burials were normally aligned east-west with the head facing west and no grave goods, and in those days Christians did not cremate their dead. As the Anglo-Saxons adopted Christianity both pagan funeral practices (north-south burials with grave goods, and cremations) died out. So, within a given kingdom, a pagan cemetery can be assumed to pre-date the time when its king adopted Christianity. That picture may be broadly true, but in real life the picture is not that simple. Burial patterns cannot, as some historians have believed, fill in all the gaps in the historical record. Archaeologists are now far less certain of a close and definite link between burial pattern and the ethnicity of the local population. A type of hut known as the 'Grubenhaus' or 'sunken–floored building' has also been associated with Germanic settlers or migrants. The design is, most probably, imported from the Continent. That does not necessarily tell us that the people who built them were Germanic migrants.

There is a limit to what an archaeologist can tells us. He can stare at brooches as long as he likes, but they will never speak Celtic to him. A brooch will never tell us what language its wearer spoke. Importantly, we cannot be sure of his ethnicity, nor that of his rulers. Some techniques, such as enamelling, were developed *in England* by Anglo-Saxons. Some weaving techniques were adopted by the Anglo-Saxons from the Romano-British. Artefacts such as brooches might be dated to within 30-40 years, but we cannot know for certain it was a novelty or an antique when it was buried. There is no direct relationship between (say,) pots and people; just general trends.

Similarly with well-preserved bodies found in bogs. Modern scientific methods can tell you where they were born and where they reached puberty. They cannot tell you much about their political affiliation. We cannot know what language they spoke. In any case, language can be a status symbol rather than evidence of race. It is reasonable to believe that in 1080 AD many people in England spoke French or Latin if they could, regardless of where they were born. It is most rare for archaeology to be able to tell us definitively who a person was, what language he or she spoke, nor who his or her ruler was.

Technical breakthroughs in archaeological technique occur from time to time. Carbon dating, pollen analysis and ground-penetrating radar are examples. What follows has been described as a somewhat childlike rush to grasp the new technology and cling to its findings, overlooking anything that contradicts it. There is probably no single magic bullet. Archaeology works slowly, gradually, and sometimes along blind alleys. In general, archaeologists come across as the expert forensic scientists, but not the detectives. Sometimes the detectives are the historians. For the Dark Ages, the historians cannot contribute much.

As we have seen, the written sources were often written well after the event. So, if one says that King 'X' reigned for 'N' years, how can we be sure? Such statements are not a safe basis for sequencing. We can compare the dates given in the Anglo-Saxon and Welsh chronicles. For the period 600-800 AD just 12 entries can be compared. They only agree in one instance. In that case it refers to an external event which could be validated elsewhere. The dates of only two events differ by five years or more. Sometimes the date in the Anglo-Saxon Chronicle is earlier than that in the Welsh Annals. In other cases it is the other way around. Thus there is anything up to ten years of possible error. Neither source can be considered to be entirely reliable. From a statistical perspective, each is equally poor. At best, we can generally believe that a given date is probably correct to within five years. In general the two chronicles, and other sources, give us some confidence that given events did take place, but not necessarily as described. They give us some confidence that the sequence is correct, as long as the intervals are not particularly short. They give us less confidence that the stated interval between them is correct. They give us very little confidence as to the precise date, other than probably within plus or minus five years.

There are written genealogies for many Anglo-Saxon royal dynasties. Most of them contain precisely 14 generations and claim descent from a god, typically Wotan. The eighth on the list is typically the first recorded ruler of that kingdom. Comparing pairs of genealogies can give rise to impossible consequences: they cannot both be true. The pattern is typical of the Old Testament. That suggests that the genealogies were concocted by monks, after the adoption of Christianity. That in turn implies that they were not even *pagan* oral tradition, so we can have very little confidence in them. They are fairly obviously invented, and hence unreliable. Their main purpose may have been political. That is, to give legitimacy to a dynastic succession. Yet it is astonishing that many of them have been used to calculate seemingly precise chronologies for early Anglo-Saxon dynasties.

Many coins can be dated to their year of minting. Tens, if not hundreds, of thousands of Roman coins have been found in Britain. However two major problems face anyone trying to use coins for dating in Dark Age Britain. Firstly, almost no Roman coins were brought to Britain after 407 AD, and the Anglo-Saxons did not start minting coins until the seventh or even eighth centuries. Any coin must have been lost or buried *after* it was minted, that is 'not before' the minting date. All that really means for Dark Age Britain is 'not before 407'. That could be, say, 408; 508; or even 608.

The condition of a coin can tell us something. Coins are generally usable for about 50 years after minting. They wear with use. However, that is a gradual process. Dating by wear or condition is not very precise. Any Roman coins *in use* would not have been usable after about 460 AD. After that there is no reliable way of using coins for dating until roughly the eighth century. Genealogies, pottery, coin evidence and the like have given rise to an amazing pseudoscience of dating for the events of the Dark Ages. The results sometime appear to far be more precise than they deserve.

So much for 'when?' What about 'where?' In general, historians do not dwell very much on geography. There are several possible reasons for that. However, as we shall see, the business of warfare is much about the lie of the land and the relationship between places on the map. Peter Heylyn, a 17th-century English writer, made the point with commendable clarity: 'Historie without Geographie like a dead carkasse hath neither life nor motion at all.'

Some historians are notoriously bad at geography. An historian was once televised talking about the Staffordshire Gold Hoard. He talked about the location of the find as being near an important junction in post-Roman Britain. He said that it was near where Watling Street crossed the Fosse Way, both of which were major Roman roads. He said that it was equivalent to the junction of the M1 and the M6. Now, Watling Street did cross the Fosse Way. Unfortunately, that was 26 miles away from where the gold was found, in Warwickshire. He was describing the wrong junction.

Some of the books published about Dark Age Britain are of very dubious quality. The standard academic works were described earlier. Even some of the best books sometimes fall for what can be described as the "possibly' – 'probably'- 'must have" school of reasoning. They first introduce an idea quite tentatively. Later in the book they use that to corroborate another idea, which then seems to be proven; or they accept the initial idea as fact, rather than suggestion. Well before the end of the book, the idea is accepted as proven. It is not clear whether the writer is trying too hard to convince the reader; whether he is deluding himself; whether he genuinely does not realise what he is doing; or whether he is just being dishonest.

Another literary device which is greatly overused for this period is the 'must have …' and 'no doubt …' process. An example is 'whatever the truth of Boudicca's rebellion, one thing is certain …' No, it isn't. We can say absolutely nothing *with certainty* about an event over 1500 years ago about which we know almost nothing. There are many, many examples of this. Logically, it is simply not good enough. It could be suggested that it is a literary device which is not intended to be taken literally. It is, perhaps, given some legitimacy when used by an Oxford professor. But we should have difficulty with a literary device which brings the writer to say things he does not actually mean. It is, unfortunately, insidious

The situation is even worse when known facts are incorrect. There is a village in Wiltshire called Baydon, astride a Roman Road. Myres wrote that there are no earthworks at Baydon. In fact earthworks were shown on the one inch to the mile Ordnance Survey map which was current when Myres first wrote in the 1930s, and on the 1:50,000 scale map current when he revised the work in the 1980s. Even more earthworks are visible on the larger-scale 1:25,000 map. It seems that Myres did not check the map on either occasion. Even worse, another author writing in 2000 repeated the same error. He simply didn't check. There are several other examples of where the standard reference books available at the time would have provided the facts, if the writer bothered to check. The problem is not simply that of minor errors of fact. It extends to interpretation, which can have major consequences. Even seemingly minor facts can have huge implications, as we shall see.

Sociological claptrap also rears its ugly head. When one reads that (for example) 'Dark Age leaders sought re-validation through the extensive reuse of Iron-Age hill forts', or similar, one has to question what the writer was smoking. Dark Age leaders may have sought *protection* through the extensive reuse of Iron-Age hill forts. But they wouldn't chose to live in high, waterless, windswept and cold hilltops just to 'revalidate' themselves.

Some of the very few historical records refer to three main Romano-British characters: Vortigern, Ambrosius (perhaps Ambrosius Aurelianus) and Arthur. Yet, according to some authors, there were two different Vortigerns, two Ambrosiuses (more properly *Ambrosii*) and anything up to four Arthurs! Some of that is probably due to fundamental weaknesses in dating, which the writers didn't either understand or acknowledge.

One archaeologist, in a book of about 350 pages, scarcely mentions wars at all, and virtually nothing about war between the Anglo-Saxons and the Romano-British. There are, however, some excellent books. They tend to be written by experts for experts. They are not easily available to the public. David Dumville's works on early texts, Catherine Hills' work on the Anglo-Saxon migrations, and several others are clearly well-written and reflect very thorough and professional research. They tend to be fairly cautious in their observations and deductions, because they do not go further than the evidence allows. But elsewhere there is a lot of speculation. Some writers tend to take the experts' works as fact, where the original writers see the same issue as one of conjecture rather than conclusion.

There is a good reason why some of the books on this subject are poor. A glance at their cover will often tell you that the author has a degree in this, or that, subject. That's good, but not nearly as good as having a master's degree or a doctorate. This is not intellectual snobbery. Higher degrees do not just teach people more things. They also give them a deeper understanding of the approach to the subject and, critically, train them in advanced research methods. In this field, people with first degrees often simply don't have the knowledge nor the research skills to make a serious contribution. They may well be able to write very good English. That does not of itself mean that what they write is significant. Overall, what we see today on library and bookshop shelves is a real mixture. There is much reliance on secondary works, consensus, and a reluctance to contradict others.

A sense of time is also often missing from this period. Dates are not just figures. They have meaning. Take two alleged dates of battles, say 552 and 596 AD. The two battles may have been fought by the armies of the same kingdoms. But it is unlikely that anybody fought at both battles, because they were over 40 years apart. Observations like that have significant implications for the sorts of armies involved and the likely progress of the battle. It is alleged that Arthur fought in over a dozen battles. If so, he was an extremely experienced soldier by any standards. But if no-one fought a battle for over 40 years, then everybody at the later battle was a novice.

We will look at Dark Age warfare in the next chapter. We should, however, note that it was an exceptionally human phenomenon. It was dominated by emotions such as courage, fear, shock and panic. The way in which battles were fought and wars were waged reflected deeply-held values; often poorly enunciated, and never written down. It is very hard to know how they were actually fought, and much of the archaeology and history for this period doesn't help.

Intellectual disciplines have systemic biases. Their practitioners tend to look at things in a certain way. This can lead to a build-up of belief which is not supported by evidence. There are fashions in thought. Ideas come and go. This is largely subconscious. Overall, and despite much enthusiasm by some and much careful work by a few, much of our understanding of the period is a mess. In such cases we should wield Occam's Razor. We should relentlessly seek the simplest explanation that fits the known facts. Several writers have tied themselves in intellectual knots because they can't, or won't, see the simplest explanation. As a result, they end up with astonishingly convoluted explanations which don't seem plausible. The real world is complex. But at the distance we are looking at it, the main issues should seem simple and clear.

The legend of Camelot is a prime example. Camelot was first mentioned by a French romantic poet, Chrétien de Troyes, in the 12th century. The various poems and legends of Arthur mention several places where he held court. Most of them are easily recognisable, such as Gloucester, London or Bath. But then there is Camelot. In the 16th century the English writer John Leland asked where the legendary Camelot might be. He started a search which continues to this day.

Ask a different question. Why might a medieval French poet think that Arthur held his court at a place called Camelot? He may have made it up, or he may have heard the name of a real place and recorded it as best he could. The Roman *Londinium* was London. *Lindum Colonia* was Lincoln. *Lutetia Parisorum* was Paris. And so on. In Latin, Colchester was *Camulodunum*. Camulod. Camelot. So the issue is not that there was a mythical, legendary, fabulous castle where King Arthur held his court. It is that simply Colchester was one of the places where someone (possibly Arthur) held court (or set up his command post, or whatever). It is probably that simple. Writers have been on a wild goose chase since the early 16th century simply because one antiquarian asked the wrong question. To that extent, there never was a 'Camelot'.

History requires us to make judgements. To make judgements, we need evidence. Evidence which we consider to be conclusive is called 'proof'. In this area we will accept evidence that is 'more likely than unlikely'. In a criminal court that would not be proof. That is very important. For Dark Age Britain there is, today, probably no proof. We are seeking evidence that is *probably* true, and we shall make deductions or inferences from that.

As far as possible, we will be rigorous about probability. To a statistician, probability ranges from 0 to 1, or 0% to 100%. If something is 'probable', it has a probability of more than 50%. If it is 'unlikely' or 'improbable' it has a probability of less than 50%. If it is 'almost definite' it has a probability close to 100%. If it is 'most unlikely', its probability is close to 0%. Expressions like 'there is little doubt' mean the same as 'almost certain' or 'highly likely'. See Figure 1.1.

The sum of all probabilities in a given case is 1; that is, 100%. This has some fairly important yet simple consequences. Think of a long earthwork. Assume it is part of a defensive structure, so it was built to defend something or somebody. It was built to face one way. Figure 1.2 is a sketch of the profile of a simple earthwork which faces to the right.

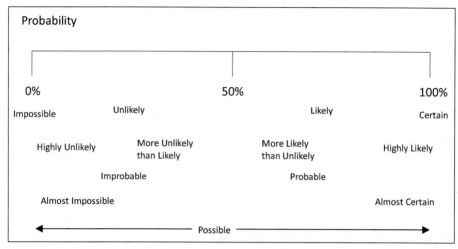

Figure 1.1 Probability.

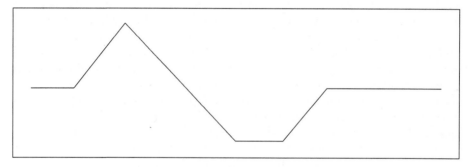

Figure 1.2 A Defensive Earthwork.

The defender stands on or behind the bank. The attacker has to fight across the ditch and up the bank. Now, 1500 years later, it is badly eroded. If we can see what we think is a ditch on the right and a bank on the left, we can be fairly sure that it faces right, as on the diagram. It is probable, or 'likely'; and 'more likely than unlikely'. If we can only see a ditch *or* a bank, then we cannot say. It must face one way, but the probability of it facing either left of right is about 50%. In general, with a dyke (ditch and bank) like this, if the bank *seems* to be on the left and the ditch on the right, then it *probably* faces right. The probability that it faces right is more than 50%. Conversely the probability that that dyke faces left is less than 50%. This example is intended to be simple and clear. Many real examples are neither as simple nor as clear as that.

This book describes what I believe was the broad sequence of the Anglo-Saxon conquest of England. It is written as 'did happen', not 'may have happened'. It is the result of much research and analysis. Much of it is conjecture, based on reasoning and assessment. In some cases probability and statistics underpins it. For example, in one important area something occurs in at least 41 out of 43 cases. It is 'highly likely' that that is no coincidence. One might actually say 'almost definite'. I haven't laid out all the reasoning and the argumentation behind my findings. We shall see why in Chapter 14.

In broad terms, the story looks something like this. The Anglo-Saxon conquest was not an 'elite takeover', like in France, where the Franks effectively took over the existing Gallo-Roman society and government in one generation. Nor was it a massive migration of hundreds of thousands of blond warriors, their wives and families. Instead, Germanic war bands, who had been settled in Britain by Roman or Romano-British leaders, revolted and gradually conquered or took over new territory. They often married Romano-British women. They imposed their language and laws on those who they conquered. Their children thought of themselves as Germanic. A similar pattern repeated itself in subsequent generations. There was some further migration of Germanic settlers, over three or four centuries. There were setbacks, some of which were massive, but it was generally successful.

There were many battles and much slaughter, but the result was not the extermination nor the expulsion of the Romano-British. They were assimilated, initially as little more than slaves (and in many cases actually as slaves). There is considerable evidence of intermarriage: several Anglo-Saxon kings had British, rather than Germanic, names. In the long run the disappearance of British language, culture and laws was not the extermination of the Romano-British. It was the result of the total political, military and economic domination of the Anglo-Saxons. The British were not suddenly defeated. They went into a long, gradual social and economic decline, until they were little more than a few wretched survivors living in the far west. For those who became the Welsh, the British were little more than a memory to be celebrated in heroic poems.

2

Seen Through a Soldier's Eyes

In order to understand how the wars of Dark Age Britain were fought, we need to understand what the countryside looked like at the time. We must also try to understand what that meant to a soldier, and particularly a commander, at the time. It clearly meant different things to a late-Roman general or a Germanic tribesman. It may have meant different things again to warriors of, say, the eighth century. Certain things, however, would have stayed the same. The landscape was different then, but it may not have changed much between the fifth and eighth centuries.

The landscape is real. It affects life in very real ways, particularly without the benefit of internal combustion engines. A hill which we might not even think about today might be impassable to a horse-drawn cart. Today a typical car can develop about 100 horsepower. A Dark Age cart may have benefitted from one or two horsepower, and horses were quite rare. If the ground was wet or muddy the problem became much, much worse. We rarely even think about that today.

The terrain and the landscape affect warfare in hard, physical ways. It is hard and tiring to fight uphill. Swamps and bogs are largely impassable on foot. Woods are difficult to navigate and very hard to keep formation in. Rivers may be impassable, and typically can only be crossed at a few places. Those places can be predictable, and can be good sites for ambushes. To really understand the ground, you need to get out and look at it. (When a soldier uses the term 'ground' today, he means what an archaeologist or historian would normally call the 'landscape' or the 'terrain'.) You need to study maps, and try to understand how the terrain looked at the time. It is even harder to understand what that meant to a late-Roman, or Romano-British, or Germanic warrior. But most of all, you must go out and look at the ground. The British Army still adheres to the Duke of Wellington's maxim, that time spent on reconnaissance is seldom wasted. It is hard to really understand the ground from even the best maps. I spent more than 90 separate days out in the countryside (and occasionally in large built-up areas) looking at the landscape in order to research this book. Many of the insights I came to were fascinating, and could not have been gained in any other way. The landscape affects which battles are fought; how; why; and where. Understanding those processes can tell us a lot.

I am in good company. When he first wrote the chapters of 'The English Settlements', Nowell Myres wrote 'I have always thought that an essential prerequisite to this age must lie in an attempt to see the countryside ... from the same point of view as that which presented itself to the newcomers from the Continent. ... [This] can only be achieved by detailed personal inspection undertaken on foot or horseback.' Myres had spent a lot of time as a young man doing just that. Ironically he was wrong about some of the things he might have seen, such as the earthworks at Baydon. His general approach, however, was spot on. Modern technology, such as satellite imagery available through applications such as Google Earth or relatively cheap three-dimensional mapping, helps enormously. But they are no substitute for personal reconnaissance.

The ground affects how battles are fought. The conduct and outcome of battles affect the ways that campaigns are waged. Campaigns are, effectively, the building blocks of wars. The landscape also affects decisions such as where to invade the enemy's territory and which routes to advance on: that is, the planning of campaigns. So the ground and the geography have a major impact on the conduct and the outcome of wars in many ways.

It is critically important to understand the ground as it was, not as it is; and how a soldier of the time would have seen it. I was trained as an infantry officer in the late 1970s and the 1980s. We were trained to think out to about two kilometres in front of our position. That was due to the ranges of the weapons which infantry battalions had (and broadly still do). So, to some extent, soldiers of my generation tend to look and therefore to think out to about two kilometres. A Dark Age warrior could only dream of weapons that were effective out to 2,000 metres. Few if any of his weapons had a range of more than about 40 yards. None were effective at more than 200 metres or so. It would typically take him about 40 minutes or more to cross 2,000 metres (or yards). In an armoured personnel carrier we can now do that in about four minutes. The critical factors of time and space were very different in the Dark Ages. We see the terrain through different prisms. It takes a lot to re-focus and see it like they did.

The phrase 'inherent military probability' is sometimes bandied about by military men looking at old battlefields or historic campaigns. They will look at a situation and say that it is inherently probable, in their experienced military judgement, that 'X' happened at place 'Y'. Well, that is scarcely rigorous and often wrong, as the story of the Bosworth battlefield tells us. Not least, we should be explicitly aware whether something is actually 'more likely than unlikely'. We should have sound, demonstrable reasons for thinking so.

Many people have difficulty understanding the terrain, even when standing looking at it. Some soldiers, even quite senior commanders, never do. Building up a feel for the ground can takes years of experience in peacetime, although probably rather less time in war. In war it seems to become instinctive: that is, implicit and hard to explain. Years ago I was out in Suffolk following a fox hunt. There were about 40 followers looking on. A fox came into sight some distance away. Three of us saw it. One was a 60-year old farmhand. The other two were my brother and myself. We were both soldiers. The three of us saw the fox more than a minute before anyone else. It wasn't a coincidence.

Such an implicit feel for the terrain is, however, typically very specific to the current conditions of warfare. That is hard to step out of. Someone writing about Dark Age earthworks near Cambridge in Victorian times remarked about them 'having command of' something else. In modern parlance that would mean 'being in charge of' something. The writer, however, meant 'being higher than', hence 'being able to overlook' something. 'Having command' in that sense was a technical term taken from siegecraft. It is not used today. However, the writer was probably wrong. He was definitely *not* wrong about it being higher: I have checked. He *was* probably wrong to see the situation in terms of 18th and 19th century siegecraft, not Dark Age warfare.

There is more to battlefields than what can be seen. They are also about what can be heard, felt and smelt. In much of northern Europe there is often a mist that burns through in mid or late morning. Not only can you seen more, but it suddenly becomes considerably warmer. Mist tends hang over rivers and lakes. Mist and fog also deadens sound. Freshly-turned earth also has a particular smell, as anyone who keeps a garden will know. For infantrymen digging trenches, that smell is very familiar. It also accompanies cavalry galloping across damp turf. A large force of cavalry galloping can be felt through the ground. Fresh blood can be smelt, and has a metallic taste (due to the iron in the haemoglobin). That is the reality of the countryside in war, and that is what we have to understand. Battlefields would have stunk of sweat, shit and piss. 'Sweat' and 'shit' are Anglo-Saxon words. 'Piss' comes to us from Norman French. Sweat gets in your eyes. It stings. Some soldiers foul and wet themselves in fear. Horses have their own particular smells, as does the leather of harness and soldiers' equipment.

Have you ever walked uphill across a ploughed field? Imagine what it would be like if it had been raining for days. Imagine what it would be like if everyone was carrying 40lbs of arms and equipment. Now imagine what would happen if the enemy were waiting at the top to kill you. Then imagine why Dark Age commanders would be cautious about how and where they attacked.

I once witnessed a group of horsed cavalry riding at full gallop more-or-less straight towards me from a couple of hundred yards away. They were up to us, and gone by, in seconds. It was the best demonstration I have ever seen as to how dangerous horsed cavalry could be to dismounted infantry, It showed very clearly how the realities of time and space were very different in times gone by.

Incidentally, in this book I tend to use imperial or metric measurements as required. A good reason for using miles is that distances in Britain were, and still are, given in miles. A good reason to give elevations (heights) in metres is that, nowadays, almost every map gives heights in metres. I also tend to give equivalents to the degree of accuracy required. To most people a mile is a bit more than one and half kilometres, and that is generally good enough here. A highway engineer needs to know that a Imperial (Statute) mile is 1.609344 kilometres (or 1760 yards). A Roman mile was about 1617 yards. Readers won't generally need that degree of accuracy.

The countryside used to look very different. I was once looking out across the Blackmoor Vale in Dorset with some old maps. What we see now is a patchwork of fields, with many mature trees in the hedgerows. Most of those hedges are marked on a map from the 1830s. So are several orchards that have long since been grubbed out. Most of those hedgerows, and hence many of the trees, were not there in the 1780s. The map from that period showed that the fields had not been enclosed, and that the land was mostly common grazing. What we see in the landscape is greatly shaped by nature, but also enormously affected by the use to which man puts the land. To that extent, the English landscape is not natural to any significant degree. It has not been 'natural' for over two thousand years.

The land is formed around the topography, the physical shape of the ground. In much of northern Europe the topography is dominated by the results of the last Ice Age, about 10,000 years ago. That sits on the results of the formation and movements of the earth's crust, a process of millions of years. Clearly the 1500 or so years since the Dark Ages have not seen much change, in geological or glacial terms. However, we need to consider the topography in order to understand the landscape. Much of England lies on layers of rock that have been raised, lowered or tilted since they were first formed. In several places this has resulted in ridges which are asymmetric when seen today. Figure 2.1 is an idealised section through a typical ridge.

Viewed from the left this ridge appears as an escarpment, hence the name of the steeper 'scarp' slope. The other slope is generally much gentler and dips away, perhaps for several miles. As an example, travelling down the M40 past Aylesbury towards London you soon see the scarp slope of the Chilterns, which rises about 140 metres (well over 500 feet) in a mile or so. As you carry on, past the ridge, you can sometimes glimpse the dip slope stretching for miles, all the way to central London. Dip and scarp slopes are drained in different ways. Scarp slopes usually have short, steep streams which typically run into a river running parallel to the crest of the ridge, perhaps at right angles to the slope. On the other side the streams run gently down the dip slope and join together to form rivers some distance away. Occasionally, perhaps due to glacial action, streams and rivers rise on the side of the scarp slope, cut through the escarpment, and join those on the dip slope. There are a few examples in the Chilterns. The Bulbourne Valley, in which Berkhamsted lies, is one.

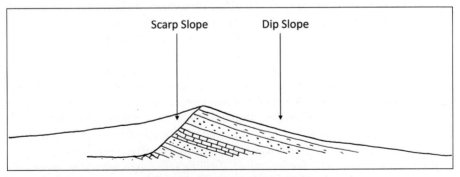

Figure 2.1 Section through a Ridge.

The geology may not have changed, but the surface features (the vegetation and the watercourses) generally have. How can we know what the landscape looked like 1500 years ago? Several things can help us. The most important clues come to us from a useful coincidence. By and large, when the Anglo-Saxons arrived in an area they did not adopt the names of places from the Romano-British. They named what they saw, in their own language. The study of the meaning of places names is called toponymy. It is very useful to us because the great majority of place names in England are Anglo-Saxon, and they come to us from the very period which we are studying. Toponymy is a wonderful tool for shining light into Dark Age England. It is less useful for Wales, where the great majority of place names are Celtic.

However, woe to the unwary! As Myres put it, 'no subject has attracted more misguided enthusiasts and ignorant amateurs than the study of place names.' In order to decipher a place name, you first have to find the earliest recorded version of the name. That might be from the Domesday Book of 1086 AD or perhaps an Anglo-Saxon land charter. You also need to be able to translate Old English, in the case of Anglo-Saxon place names; or Old Norse or Old French for Viking or Norman names. A place name in the Domesday Book might never have been written down before 1086, and might have changed significantly from its original meaning. If it was never written down, how would anyone know?

Place names fall into two broad categories: habitative and descriptive. Habitative names are the names of settlements. The simplest Anglo-Saxon place names typically end in '-ing' and denote the followers of a person. Reading, Goring, Angmering and Hastings are examples. The first part of the name refers to the name of the leader, say 'Reada' or 'Gara'. '-Hams' and '-tons' or '-tuns' are villages or other settlements. '-Wich' often denotes a Roman settlement (a *vicus* in Latin) which the Anglo-Saxons found and renamed in their own language. 'Wickhams' are 'hams' at, or near, a *vicus*. '-Ingtons' or '-inghams' are 'settlements named after the followers of', or similar. I am delighted to say that there is a Storrington in Sussex, although in this case the original meaning of the name ('*Storgetune*' or similar) was 'the storks' farm').

Habitative place names can be useful to us. Not least, '-wickhams' may well be the oldest Anglo-Saxon settlements in a given area, while a group of '-ings', such as those on the Sussex coast, often denotes the oldest settlement of Germanic tribesman in that region. A 'Newton' is a 'new settlement' (at some stage), and so on

Descriptive place names are even more useful. In the 1950s and 1960s an expert Anglo-Saxon linguist, Margaret Gelling, noticed that many of them related to similar landscape features. She then collaborated with a physical geographer, Ann Cole, to correlate place names with topography. They proved conclusively that the Anglo-Saxons used the same terms for the same geographical features, be they in Dorset or Northumberland, Essex or Cheshire. Thus descriptive place names can be deciphered, with a bit of difficulty, to tell us what the Anglo Saxons found when they got there. That may have changed. They tell us what *was* there, not what *is* there now.

Place name study was revolutionised. Gelling's findings were not necessarily welcome, because they dismantled old certainties. Unfortunately several recent books do not reflect modern toponymy. Much of England has been surveyed by the English Place Name Survey, county by county. Their surveys cover the old, pre-1974 county boundaries, as does this book. The surveys do so because of the effort that would be required to revise the volumes produced before 1974. This book does so because the old county boundaries are mostly Anglo-Saxon and can tell us quite a lot. The pre-1974 counties are shown at Figure 2.2.

An example of poor toponymy is the site of the Battle of Wilton in 823 AD. The Anglo-Saxon Chronicle actually records a battle at a place called 'Ellandun'. Place

Key:

(1) Nottinghamshire
(2) Rutland
(3) Worcestershire
(4) Northamptonshire
(5) Huntingdonshire
(6) Cambridgeshire
(7) Bedfordshire
(8) Buckinghamshire
(9) Hertfordshire
(10) Middlesex

Figure 2.2 County Names in England before 1974.

names change over time. There is no 'Ellandun' in England today. Somebody, somewhere took a guess at 'Wilton', the former county town of Wiltshire (fairly close to Salisbury). Unfortunately nothing in the history of the name of Wilton is anything like 'Ellandun'. Its name has always started with 'wil', not 'ell-', and never had a middle syllable with an 'n' in it. In fact it has never had three syllables. There is no record of it ever being Ellandon, Ellanton or similar. There are some much closer matches, but they are not near Salisbury. Yet the myth persists that the battle in 823 was fought at Wilton; for no good reason.

A bigger myth is that of King Arthur's great battle at Badon. Gildas tells us (in Latin) that there was a battle there. Nennius tells us that Arthur fought there. The date was about 500-510 AD. One of the copies of Gildas tells us 'Badon, that is Bath'. That addition was probably made in the 11th or 12th centuries. Unfortunately the Latin name for Bath is *Aquae Sulis*, and Gildas would probably have known it as that. The Anglo-Saxons initially called Bath 'Akemanceaster', and only later 'Aet Baeth'. They knew of the hot baths. Since Gildas wrote in the 540s or thereabouts, it is unlikely that anybody called it 'Bath' at the time, or anything like that (the word 'bath' is Germanic). Wherever the (first) battle of Badon took place, it was most probably not at Bath. The assumption that it was has seriously coloured our views of events.

Some key words are useful. Words ending in '-leigh', '-lea' or '-ley' typically describe a clearing in a wood. That is hugely important. Several other words relate to woodland, or the use of it. '-Ley' words (and similar) rarely pre-date 730 AD in documents. Words ending in '-ey' such as Anglesey, Guernsey, Jersey and Alderney are islands, but '-ey' places can be islands in marshes. Ironically 'Anglesey' *may* mean 'the island of the English', but today almost all the place names on Anglesey are resoundingly Welsh. Anglesey is not the 'Island of the English'. It probably never was. Confusingly '-ey's might originally have been '-ley's, so a bit of detective work on the map is sometimes needed. Was it a clearing in a wood, or an island in a marsh, or both?

Several place names begin with 'Ambros-', or similar. That may recall the name of Ambrosius Aurelianus. Amesbury in Wiltshire may be 'Ambrosius' town or fortress'. Ambrosden, near Bicester in Oxfordshire, may be 'Ambrosius' hill or clearing'. Unfortunately the 'amber-' in 'Ambersham' in Sussex may, or may not, mean something to do with a species of small birds (buntings).

As you move west, you find more place names which have Celtic origins. The names for large features, such as rivers, are more likely to be Celtic. 'Afon' or 'avon' means 'river'. There are many examples in Wales, and four different River Avons in England: the Devon, Hampshire, Gloucestershire and Warwickshire Avons.

Studying maps can tell us a great deal. The present location and shape of woods can tell us a little, particularly in conjunction with place names. Streams and rivers do not naturally run straight. So when watercourses *are* straight, they are man-made and often drainage channels. That tells us that the land was boggy, marshy or swampy before it was drained (why drain dry land?) The shape of the contours can tell us much about the topography, but generally only with a great amount of detailed study for most people. After years of practice I can visualise a piece of ground from the map, having seen it first. I only know of one man who can really visualise terrain from the map. He was a military surveyor for over 30 years and at one time the senior instructor at the Royal School of Military Survey. Most people cannot. There is no substitute for going and looking at the ground. The Duke of Wellington's maxim still holds. In addition, you should not criticize other peoples' understanding of the ground unless you have seen it yourself.

Much of the terrain in England is fairly flat or gently rolling, and native trees commonly grow up to 40 feet high. That means that the extent of tree cover is a crucial factor in how the terrain looks from a distance. Not least, a general canopy of trees, or even just one row of trees, can completely disguise the shape of a hill or ridge. The question of how much of England was woodland is very important for our study. The Edwardian view was that England was either a mighty forest which the Anglo-Saxons cleared, or that it had grown back after the Romans left (and the Anglo-Saxons then cleared it).

In the 1980s landscape historians challenged that, but they seem to have gone too far. They pointed out that much of England had been deforested before the Romans arrived, and that there was not much evidence of reforestation ('growback'). We should start with the premise that, left to itself, about 85% of Britain would be mature, deciduous, woodland. It was, after the last Ice Age. There are only 35 native woodland species; almost all of them have simple common names: 'oak', 'ash', 'birch', 'elm', 'beech' etc. They belong to just 17 genuses. Much of Britain was, probably, deforested in the Iron Age and kept clear through the Roman period. Then the evidence becomes less clear. In the fourth century, most of the trees chopped down (and, say, used for furniture or house building) has be shown by archaeologists to have been quite young. However, in the sixth to the eighth centuries, much of the timber used had started to grow in the fifth century. That suggests that people largely stopped chopping trees down in the fifth century, and for centuries afterwards there was plenty of mature timber.

The site of a fifth century Germanic settlement in Suffolk suggests that the people there occasionally ate bear. Bears live in woods. Farming evidence across England suggests that, in the fifth and sixth centuries, people abandoned thick, heavy clay soils and concentrated on land which was easier to plough. If you abandon English countryside the trees grow back. The Domesday Book tells us that in 1086 about 15% of England was woodland. In some counties the total was 30%. Today it averages about 8%. That's about half what it was in 1086. But the woodland was not evenly distributed. There were great belts of woodland, but they were not necessarily continuous. The Wealden forest ran west from near Folkestone for about 130 miles, perhaps as far as the New Forest. One wood south of Taunton (the forest of Nerode) covered 15,000 acres. (There are 640 acres in a square mile, so that is about 23 or 24 square miles.) It has gone now. There were 260 woods in Somerset of more than 35 acres. Cranborne Chase on the Wiltshire/Hampshire/Dorset border is now just a few square miles of wooded ridge. Today it is about 5 miles from the village of Cranborne. Assuming that the village was in or near its edge, it would have been perhaps eight to ten times its present size in the Dark Age.

The word 'forest' is a problem. It is a Norman word which did not exist in England before 1066. It means a royal, or noble, hunting reserve; typically for deer but also wild boar. Forests were not necessarily wooded, and especially not *continuously* wooded. However, deer and boar like woodland. So it is fair to say that much of what we now call forests were extensively wooded.

Landscape historians seem to have gone too far to prove that England was not one mighty (oak) forest in the Dark Ages. There does seem to have been a lot more woodland. It might not have been continuous. Some numbers are useful. Germany is currently about 30% woodland. Some of its woods go on for dozens of miles. The Teutoburger Wald, the site of Varus' defeat in 9 AD, is over 80 kilometres long today. In that area it is quite possible to walk for well over 100km and almost never leave continuous woodland. The Black Forest is about 100km long. To this day much of it is only crossed by a tarmac road every ten kilometres or so. It provides a useful military example. In the Ulm Campaign of 1805, Napoleon's cavalry (commanded by Murat) made a massive feint from the west along the roads through the Black Forest. The Austrians were deceived into thinking that Napoleon was attempting to force the routes through the Forest. They concentrated at Ulm, intending to engage him as he emerged on the east side. In a huge encirclement, Napoleon cut the Austrians off from the roads to Vienna and captured most of them. The Black Forest had been used as part of a massive deception plan. That is a marvellous demonstration of how thick woodland can affect the conduct of a campaign. See Figure 2.3.

We don't have to believe that England was completely reforested in the Dark Ages; nor entirely deforested. We have evidence that it was much more wooded than now; that there were some very big woods; and that that may have affected warfare. We can, however, go further. In the United States, most of New England was deforested in the 180 years or so from about 1650 to 1830, using broadly the same tools as were available in the Dark Ages. Then, due to industrialization, much of the land was abandoned. By 1900 most of it was mature woodland again. Studies of the initial deforestation show that one settler can clear one to three acres per year whilst farming the land he has already cleared. Let us apply that to Britain. Assume that we have 1,000 settlers, and each clears an average of two acres per year. Assume also that there is one able-bodied man in five of the population (accounting for women, children and a few elderly). There are about 32.3 million acres in total in England. A quick calculation suggests that those 1,000 settlers could clear about 3% of England every year. So, theoretically, they could clear the whole of England in about 35 years. 1,000 settlers, or 5,000 people in total, would have been about half of one percent of the million or so inhabitants of England. We know that in 1086 only 15% of England was forest. But our calculations suggest that even if England had become entirely covered with trees by, say, 600 AD, the population could very easily have deforested it again by 1086.

If you abandon English countryside the trees grow back. Within five to seven years, chalk downland (like Salisbury Plain) would be a thick impenetrable scrub of bramble, hawthorn, alder and so on. However, within 20 years a canopy of straight-growing hardwoods (oak, ash, beech, elm etc) would have grown up through the scrub and

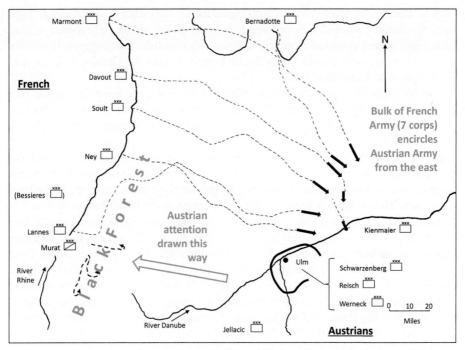

Figure 2.3 The Ulm Campaign of 1805.

started to choke it out. After 40 or 50 years the woodland floor would be fairly clear of undergrowth and relatively easy to traverse. Germanic tribesmen cleared woodland by herding pigs. Pigs will clear the undergrowth and, if left unattended, start damaging the trees as well. At that stage the trees are cut down, the stumps cleared out and the land planted with crops. It is hard, unrelenting work, year after year; but it moves the woodland back decade by decade. By the time of the Domesday Book, woodland was being managed. Pigs were only taken into the woods, to forage for acorns and beech mast, in the autumn. But that was 500 years or so after our period.

In modern Britain much of the landscape is kept clear by grazing, mostly with sheep. Before the advent of refrigeration, however, sheep had to be slaughtered and eaten locally. Without a long-distance trade in wool, (such as developed in England after the Norman conquest), there was a limit to the number of sheep which the population could, or would, support. If there were too many sheep the wolves would get fat. Then the trees would grow back.

The Anglo-Saxons named what they found. The Germanic word 'wald' means 'wood' or perhaps 'forest'. When the Anglo-Saxons came to Lincolnshire, East Yorkshire, Oxfordshire and parts of Leicestershire they found large woods. That's why they named the Lincolnshire and Yorkshire Wolds, the Cotswolds, and places such as 'Stanton-on-the-Wolds' in Nottinghamshire. They didn't name them as high, open farmland. They had different words for that. Those 'wolds' only appear to have been high, rolling farmland from the 13th century onwards. That suggests that those areas were extensively wooded from the fifth century until the Domesday Book, and for a century or more after that.

The 30 Years' War of 1618-48 was, relatively speaking, the most destructive ever fought in Germany. Over four million people died from a population of about 20 million. The trees grew back. Whole areas were reforested. Some are still abandoned, more than 300 years later. In northern Europe it is, generally, population pressure that holds the woodland at bay (through activities such as grazing and growing crops). All this evidence points to a significant population decline in England in the fifth and sixth centuries. We don't know how much, and we don't know how much the trees grew back. The evidence is indirect. But for our purposes we don't really need to.

Soldiers traditionally dislike woodland. It is a place of surprise and ambush. It is easy to get lost in woodland. It is hard to keep together as a group and fight together, shoulder to shoulder, as they did. It is easy to find tight, narrow places where a few can hold off a multitude. It is easy to block, simply by felling trees. That makes it practically impenetrable if the defenders are at all determined. If there were tracks through them which the defenders blocked with trees, we would not know today. If the defenders dug short earthworks, as the German tribes did when they ambushed Varus and his legions in the Teutoburger Wald, it would be very hard for us to know what those earthworks meant. If that woodland has been cleared, we might find a short section of dyke with nothing at either end and be puzzled. If the woodland has not been cleared, we would find a short section of earthwork in a wood and no other context. Fighting in woodland would probably have been rare, and would probably leave little trace today.

We do not need to believe that all this woodland was impenetrable. We only need to accept that commanders would avoid using woodland for anything more than occasional raiding. Additionally, in the fifth to eighth centuries moving through woodland could have major negative consequences if the enemy could march faster around the woods; not least, by using roads.

Woodland can be difficult for soldiers to traverse. Rivers, bogs and swamps may be practically impossible. Walking on the central plateaus of Norway today reveals a post-glacial terrain in which ponds, lakes, streams, bogs and swamps are far more common than in England. Few scholars seem to realise that the English landscape is the product of centuries of drainage. Many places have names ending 'in the Marsh', '-mere', '- Fen', or perhaps begin with 'Fen -'. Margaret Gelling pointed out that many fen names did not exist before later medieval times, which strongly suggests that those areas had previously been too swampy to be used by human beings. There are also several less obvious place-name clues. Time and time again straight, narrow blue lines on the map represent drainage ditches. Streams and rivers generally flow faster and straighter today, and their banks are far less boggy, because of centuries of improvement. Crossing marshy and boggy areas is very difficult on foot and completely impractical for formed bodies of soldiers. Horses are heavier: the effect on cavalry is even more marked.

There is some evidence of land drainage during Roman times, but also good evidence of it breaking down in the Dark Ages. Almost any reasonably flat piece of land more than a few yards across in England may have been boggy and swampy. Although valley bottoms may have been the boggiest, flattish areas higher up (or valley sides) might also have been swampy. It takes weeks or months for some thick, clayey soils to drain. In a land of relatively frequent rain, that may never happen without artificial drainage.

Marshes could extend over large areas. We shall see that much of Oxfordshire and south Yorkshire had extensive marshes or swamps. In each case they extended for tens of miles. That would have significantly affected where, and how, commanders could lead their forces.

It is difficult to know where the sea level lay in the Dark Ages. There is some evidence that in some areas, such as the Somerset Levels, it was lower in Roman times than at present. Some of the forts of the Saxon Shore from Suffolk to Portsmouth, which are now two miles from the sea, were originally on the coast. However, the sea level may be almost irrelevant. Figure 2.4 shows the area around Cambridge as it is today. A close examination suggests that 'fen' names occur below the 10 metre contour line in that area. If we assume that any land below that was in practice swampy or boggy, then the usable land would now like Figure 2.5.

The 20m contour has been added, dashed, to show the overall shape of the ground. Similarly, Figure 2.6 shows the land around the Saxon Shore fort at Pevensey as it today. There are, however, several '-ey' place names in the land to the north and east. They tend to lie above the five metre contour. If we assume that the land below that was swampy and boggy, then at high tide the usable land might look like Figure 2.7.

Fords on rivers and major streams were very important. By definition, crossing those rivers elsewhere is difficult. There are thousands of '-ford' names in England. It is reasonable to believe that every usable ford on a river was named, so that people knew which ford they were talking about. The name '-lade' typically means a place where a river can be crossed with some difficulty. 'Lechlade' and 'Cricklade' are examples. The lowest ford on a river is often the highest place a coastal boat or ship can get inland to without grounding (on the ford). In addition, travellers or armies moving along the coast have to go inland up a river as far as the first ford. For all those reasons the lowest ford on a river was often an important place. Markets, towns and bridges often developed there. Forts were often placed to guard them. London, Gloucester and York (some of the oldest cities in Britain) are among them. They ford some of the most important rivers in England: the Thames, the Severn and the Yorkshire Ouse. The Ouse flows out of the Vale of York, which for centuries was some of the best farmland in northern England. It flows into the Humber.

The landscape which a Romano-British or Anglo-Saxon soldier saw had been extensively affected by Roman engineers. They were astonishingly skilful. In the years just before the birth of Christ they build an underground tunnel to bring water to

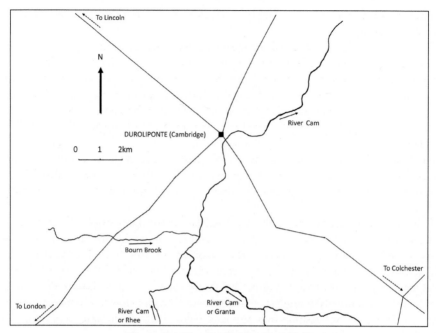

Figure 2.4 The Cambridge Area Today.

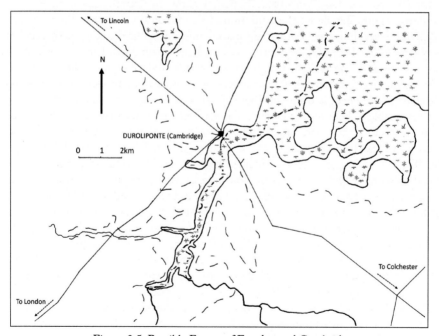

Figure 2.5 Possible Extent of Fen Around Cambridge.

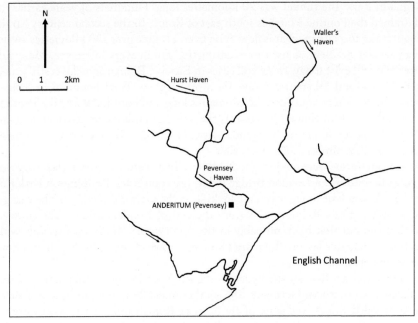

Figure 2.6 The Pevensey Area Today.

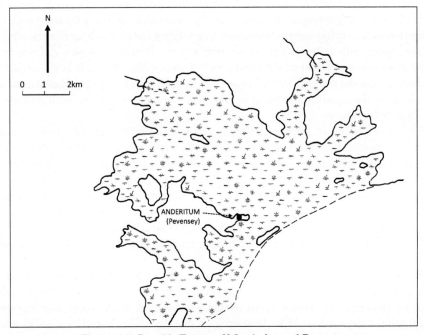

Figure 2.7 Possible Extent of Marsh Around Pevensey.

Bologna in Italy. The tunnel was 20 kilometres long. Hundreds of years earlier they had drained the Pontine Marshes south east of Rome. In the second century AD they brought water to a city in what is now Syria from a source over 130 kilometres away. It had an average gradient of just three centimetres' fall in every kilometre. Many kilometres of it still exist today. In several cities in Europe, Roman aqueducts still provide water from several kilometres away. The world-famous Trevi Fountain in Rome is supplied by the Virgo aqueduct, 22 kilometres long and built in 19 BC. The Pantheon in Rome was built in about 126 AD. It is the world's first large mass-concrete domed building. It is over 40 metres high and is visited by thousands of tourists, in complete safety, every day: almost 2,000 years later.

Roman engineers were not just good builders. They were also world-class surveyors. If you walk south from London Bridge today, you soon reach Kennington Park Road (the A3). As you look along it you are looking in the precise direction of the east gate of Chichester, 59.84 Roman miles from the end of London Bridge. The surveyors who first laid out that road, probably in the first century AD, knew precisely which direction Chichester lay in. There are two major rows of hills (the North and South Downs) in between.

In about 155 AD Roman surveyors re-aligned a section of 82 kilometres of frontier defences in southern Germany. The southernmost 29 kilometres ran over several heavily wooded ridges, yet none of the forts (a Roman mile apart, with turrets in between) is off the direct line between start and finish by more than 1.9 metres. That is a deviation of less than five minutes of arc (five sixtieths of a degree). The accuracy which Roman surveyors achieved was phenomenal. It was only bettered with the invention of surveying instruments with magnifying optics (such as the theodolite) in the seventeenth century. Yet, as far as is known, Roman surveyors did not even have an instrument for observing and copying angles directly (such as a protractor). However, by about the year 500 AD or so nobody in England could even build in stone, let alone lay out aqueducts or build in concrete. Concrete only came back into use in the late 18th century.

The most significant impact of Roman engineering on the life of a late- or post-Roman soldier in England was that of the roads. They were originally built for military purposes and were hugely important. Walking on a track or path, it is fairly easy for a single man to walk three miles in an hour. It is quite difficult for a formed body, or any large group of people. Fences, hedges, streams, fallen logs and any number of minor obstacles hold up their progress in a way which is almost impossible for someone who has not experienced it to understand. It is not uncommon for progress to fall to one mile per hour, or even less. Many medieval armies only managed to move about ten miles per day.

Roman roads allowed units and formations to move 20 miles a day as a matter of course. Imperial Roman Army units were required to train by marching 20 miles a day on three days in every month. Some of that was to be off-road. Forced marches were of 30 miles a day, and could be kept up for a few days. The Anglo-Saxon Chronicle reports how King Harold's Army marched from London to York in August 1066 to engage a Viking army. They travelled up Ermine Street (the Roman road from London to York via Lincoln) or the Old North Road, which follows much the same route. The details are not clear. One interpretation is that they reached Tadcaster, ten miles from York, on the evening of the fourth day. That seems impossible: Tadcaster is 192 miles from London; that would require them to march about 45 miles per day. A different analysis suggests six days. That is about 30 miles per day, every day for six days. They were not too tired: on the seventh day they marched straight through York, then met and defeated the Viking army at Stamford Bridge. It was quite a feat.

Cavalry could move even faster. Roman cavalry units (called 'wings', or *alae* in Latin; the singular is *ala*) could march at 30 miles a day for months without breaking their horses. The legend of Dick Turpin, the 18th-century highwayman, is insightful. The story has it that Turpin robbed and killed a man on Surrey Heath early one morning. He then rode at great speed north through London and reached York that night. When arrested, he successfully avoided conviction on the grounds that he was seen drinking in a pub in York that evening. Surely he could not possibly have been on Surrey Heath in the morning and York that night?

What makes the story remarkable is that he is supposed to have done so on his own horse, Black Bess. That is not impossible, but few horses could do that. The Romans had a network of inns and stables at regular intervals along all the important roads, throughout the Empire. Couriers on official business changed horses, and official travellers were put up, at the public expense. This system, the '*Cursus publicus*', was still functioning in much of the Continent in the early to mid-fifth century. We do not know when it fell apart in Britain. Roman couriers normally covered 50 miles a day.

The roads allowed astonishingly rapid travel. The Emperor Theodosius is known to have travelled more than 200 miles on one day. That means that, for example, in times of dire emergency a message from York could reach London the same day. A cavalry unit in York could reach London comfortably in seven days at 30 miles per day, and probably in four (at 50 miles a day) if required. On foot, the 200 miles or so would normally take a Roman infantry cohort (of about 5-600 men at full strength) about 10 days; 6-7 in an emergency.

That enabled the Romans to concentrate forces over great distances. Imagine that a Roman commander had cohorts at York, London, Lincoln and Colchester. That would mean that, if he had to, he could assemble them all at any of those places in a week in an emergency; or about 10 or 11 days fairly easily. Four cohorts would have been an enormous force by the standards of post-Roman armies in Britain. The roads played an important part. The training, the organisation and the discipline were just as important as the roads, if not more so. King Arthur is thought by some to have fought separate battles in the Scottish Lowlands one year and near Bath the next. One historian considered that to be impossible. A Roman commander could have done it in a fortnight. The roads made such rapid movement possible. They also made it predictable and calculable.

According to the *Notitia Dignatatum*, there were 16 *alae* of cavalry in late-Roman Britain. The road system would have given an army with cavalry a huge advantage over an army which had none; particularly if it also did not have the training, organisation and discipline to march at 20 or more miles a day. It is clear that using Roman roads would have significantly affected the conduct and outcome of warfare in the Dark Ages; if they were still in use and still used. It is also clear that an army with no cavalry would have been at a great disadvantage. They might have gone to great lengths to overcome that disadvantage. A force of half a dozen cavalry units would have been able to exert a major influence over the whole of Roman Britain.

Moving such large distances also depended on effective logistics, primarily a supply of food. Roman armies *could*, and *did*, organise adequate food (and fodder) supplies. However it has been shown that without an organised food supply it is difficult to keep an armed force together for more than about three days. As the organisation of the Roman army fell apart, the ability of commanders to concentrate forces over large distances would have got less and less.

Historians and archaeologists make repeated references to Anglo-Saxons advancing, and colonising, up the line of river valleys. They make occasional remarks about them being good sailors, and imply that the two are related. Neither is necessarily true and the two are not necessarily linked. I served in Germany for years but I was no seaman. Clearly the original Germanic warriors had to travel from the Continent, and had to do so by boat. But they had to do so only once in their lives. And there is little, if any, evidence of the early Anglo-Saxons using rivers. There are a number of instances of them colonising valleys from one end to another, but there always seems to be a Roman road close to the line of the river. The valley of the Warwickshire Avon is a good example. The Fosse Way (the Roman road from Lincoln to Exeter) runs broadly parallel with it.

Villages ending in '-wickham' or similar may have been among the earliest Anglo-Saxon settlements. Margaret Gelling showed that 20 or the 23 known to exist lie within 3 miles of a Roman road. It seems 'more likely than unlikely' that there is a connection between those settlements and Roman roads.

Maps (such as the Ordnance Survey series) and gazetteers of Roman roads show obvious gaps. That is, areas where a Roman road starts, runs to nowhere, and then reappears near a town or junction some miles further on. Those are areas where the road went out of use so extensively that no trace can be found today. It may be in areas where the land was abandoned: some run through areas of thick, heavy soils. It may be because the area was abandoned for other reasons, such as a frontier which had almost no traffic across it. During the Cold War, the areas on both sides of the Iron Curtain suffered serious economic decline. Most of the roads across it went out of use. Something like that may have happened in some areas in Dark Age Britain. If it did, the trees would have grown back. Root growth may have broken up the road surface, making it unrecognisable today.

We will look at details of the road network later, but here we should make one important observation. Only two Roman roads went generally west out of London, through or past the Chilterns and the Weald. One, Akeman Street, went north west to *Verulamium* (very near to modern St Albans). It then went on a more westerly course along the Bulbourne Valley through the Chilterns, past modern Berkhamsted, and on into the South Midlands. The second road ran west south west, south of the Thames, to *Calleva Atrebatum* (now called Silchester) near Basingstoke. Roman roads then fanned out south and west from Silchester. Both *Verulamium* and *Calleva* were deserted but their walls still stand, up to twenty feet high, today.

Fortifications are another aspect of the military engineer's craft. Britain was unusual in that almost all of its major Roman towns were walled. The walls were not particularly high, but were built (or re-built) with fairly large round towers which could support artillery. The artillery of the day did not, of course, use gunpowder. Roman artillery was, however, almost as effective as early cannon. Catapults could throw large stones accurately over a few hundred metres, whilst *ballistae* (like large crossbows) could fire a large spear-type missile that would go right through a man at a similar distance. Such weapons were fearsome, and very few of the enemies that the Romans ever fought against could besiege Roman fortifications.

Victorian and Edwardian antiquarians often associated the Romano-British and Anglo-Saxons with hill forts. That may have been because they did not know that the hill forts were mostly built in pre-Roman times. It was only in the 1920s and 1930s that they were investigated thoroughly. Unfortunately the association has stuck, in some quarters. The Anglo-Saxons almost never used hill forts. Some were taken back into use in the Dark Ages, and some of them were rebuilt on a very substantial scale. One, at South Cadbury in Somerset, had its ramparts rebuilt with heavy timber framing. About 20,000 yards (well over ten miles) of heavy timber baulks were used in the building. The hill forts that were re-used were generally occupied for a short time (perhaps a generation or so) and are almost exclusively in the south and west. That suggests that they were taken back into use by the Romano-British.

The real legacy of that mistake, however, lies in place names. Victorian and Edwardian antiquarians made a number of educated guesses as to where, for example, battles took place. They often associated them with hill-forts. That was sometimes just because they knew that there was something historic at that site. Unfortunately, more recent place-name study has shown several of them to be wrong. However, the association with both wrong locations in general, and hill forts in particular, persists. One modern historian associated 12 and possibly 13 out of 28 known place names with locations such as hill forts. His deduction was that they were important sites which attracted military commanders' attention. A better deduction is that they had resulted from poor toponymy. Another group of those 28 place names relates to rivers and fords. As we have seen, they may well have been important militarily, but we do not know where most of them were. Several appear to refer to the British (ie Celtic) names of rivers which the Anglo-Saxons renamed, so we do not know which river or ford was referred to.

There may also have been errors in place names in the historical sources. For example, Bede mentions almost no places west of a line from the Isle of Wight north through the Midlands and on through the Pennines. He had no real idea of the geography of

Britain. There were no maps. He also recorded several events centuries after they took place. We should expect some error.

So much for the terrain that a soldier would have seen. What use did he make of it? At the individual and small group level, warfare was a brutally short-range affair. Late Roman, Romano-British and Anglo-Saxon armies made little use of archers. Most of the weapons recovered from the period were spears, with a few swords and knives. Axes were rarely used in war, except by the Franks. Large round shields were common. They were usually made of wood with a circular boss (and maybe a band around the edge) of metal. Armour was not common. Roman soldiers had extensive body armour and helmets, but the amount of armour in use fell away rapidly during the Dark Ages. Few warriors wore helmets.

Close-quarter fighting is bloody and dangerous. Fear and panic is infectious. When soldiers turn and run, the result is often a rout and butchery on a large scale. There was therefore a great premium on staying together and facing the enemy. Physical and social cohesion were vitally important. They could be inculcated through training and discipline (as in the Roman Army), through social and cultural norms (not least, in later armies), or through hard and vicious experience. There is a continuing historical debate about cavalry in this period. The stirrup was not yet in widespread use. That limited the ability of cavalrymen to charge home against a foot soldiers who were sufficiently brave or determined to stick close together. However, few doubt the effectiveness of cavalry, with or without stirrups, to butcher a broken enemy fleeing across open ground. In many circumstances a foot soldier's life may literally have depended in him staying close together, physically, with his companions.

Some modern terminology is useful to avoid confusion. Many writers bandy terms around without being particularly accurate in their meaning (and perhaps not even realising that specific meanings exist). Strategy is the conduct of wars: the application of violence for the purposes of the state. Wars are normally conducted by the planning and execution of a series of campaigns in theatres of war. Until perhaps the late 19th century, most campaigns were the fighting of one season. That often took place in the short period after the crops had been harvested and before the advent of winter (although winter and spring campaigns did happen occasionally). One modern writer wrote of Arthur's 12-year 'campaign' against the Saxons. He was using the term 'campaign' loosely, to say the least. He meant 'war'. Campaigning is sometimes referred to today as 'operational art'. The terms 'campaign' and 'operational' are used as adjectives to mean the same thing. Tactics is the planning and conduct of individual battles or engagement. They are what happens on a battlefield, or during a siege. 'Tactical' therefore implies a lower level than 'campaign', or 'operational;' which in turn are a level lower than 'strategic'.

Those are the terms used in this book. We should be careful, however, about projecting modern meaning onto Dark-Age usage. What might we expect of commanders and soldiers in those days? The Romans had a good grasp of strategy and how war could be used for the purposes of the Empire. They certainly had a very good grasp of tactics. They could, and did, alter their tactics to suit the ground and their enemies. They planned wars as a series of campaigns, and they planned those campaigns in some detail. They also taught tactics to their subordinates (who became their successors), and had several military textbooks.

It is reasonable to assume that, say, the Kingdom of Wessex had some grasp of strategy, often in terms of the purposes or intentions of the King of Wessex. Given the size of armies, the shortcomings of logistics and the inability to do much fighting over the winter, Dark Age strategy seems to have been intermittent and spasmodic. It consisted of occasional campaigns with some general theme (such as, say, the conquest of the south west, or a dynastic struggle against Mercia). However, if we go back to the fifth century and think about a Germanic tribe somewhere in, say, the Yorkshire Wolds which could muster a war band of perhaps a few hundred warriors, it is questionable whether it really had a strategy. It could probably enunciate simple long-term goals (such as, perhaps, to defeat the local Romano-British), and link that to the purpose of a campaign. In turn that campaign might only consist of one major operation; perhaps an attack on a neighbouring location, and its consequences. The strategic horizon, in modern terms, might be very low.

Equally the tactics in use might be very simple and very traditional. They fought that way because, as far as they knew, they always had; or they had learned the hard way that they had to; or both. We should be careful, however, of underestimating Dark-Age warriors. They may have learnt a lot from the Romans, and necessity is the mother of invention. In practice much about warfare is a tension between traditionalism (soldiers tend to be very conservative about what they have found to work, because the cost of failure is often death) and innovation (the value of success is also high).

The extreme physicality of Dark Age warfare was discussed above. The realities of warfare often come down to issues of the ground (what is it like, and where are things located?); time and space (where are people and things located, and how long does it take to get from one place to another?); and the enemy (who and where is he, how many troops does he have, what weapons do they use, and how do they fight?) Some of those factors do not much change over time. For example, the nature of the enemy may not change over decades. Some factors, however, do change and deserve continuous reconsideration. There is some evidence that Roman commanders thought in those, or similar, terms. There is evidence that even today some commanders don't think about them enough.

Warfare was very different without maps. A commander could only really understand the ground if he, or someone he trusted, had been there. That placed a great premium on reconnaissance. It also gave a considerable advantage to someone defending his own land. Good commanders used the ground to their advantage, almost by definition. The specifics vary from time to time. Nowadays we train soldiers to fire antitank guided missiles in enfilade: that is, across the battlefield at targets approaching one's neighbour, rather than head on. We also train them to fire from positions in defilade: tucked in behind a fold in the ground or a wood, so that the weapon cannot be seen and engaged from its front. Ironically that often results, on Salisbury Plain, on siting them (on exercises) behind Iron-Age tumuli or Dark Age dykes. The specifics of how ground was used at the tactical level would have been very different in the Dark Ages, but there would have been common habits and patterns of use.

Landscape features can have strategic and operational (campaign-level) consequences. The ridge of the Chilterns was described earlier. It is reasonable to believe that a feature of that scale may have materially affected the whole shape of wars and campaigns, and would have been a constant feature for many years. Similarly the shape and terrain of, say, East Anglia would have affected how armies could move in and out of it, and hence how wars and campaigns could take place.

One specific terrain issue needs explanation. It is that of forward and reverse slopes. Imagine that you are standing on top of a long ridge, looking downhill towards the enemy. The slope in front of you is the forward slope. The slope behind you is the reverse slope. You may, and several armies have, chosen to defend on the reverse slope, rather than on the crest or the forward slope. There might be several reasons for that. Those reasons would depend on the current situation and the weapons in use.

Occam's Razor should be employed in thinking about warfare. It can cut very cleanly, because the cost of failure is so high. Some archaeologists have come up with astonishingly complex theories to explain things which may in practice be very simple. Large numbers of swords have sometimes been found in bogs. Occasionally they number in the thousands. This is described as 'sacrificial' or 'religious'. Let us think again. Weapons are heavy and dangerous. After a massacre, an army might have taken hundreds or even thousands of swords from the dead and the fled. They had to be got rid of. Swords are valuable and can be sold, but on that scale the market will be glutted. They can be melted down and the metal re-used, but that takes time and may require transport. They shouldn't be left lying around: they are dangerous. The simplest way of getting rid of them is possibly to throw them into a bog, where they would be hard to find and even harder to retrieve. Spears are easier: the iron heads can be broken off and carried away quite easily, as can shield bosses and so on. That seems fairly simple and self-evident. It is surely simpler explanation than the idea that a large number of weapons be collected in order to be discarded as part of some arcane ceremony. The Staffordshire Gold Hoard appears to be just the valuable elements of a stash of weapons, regalia and equipment taken from a beaten enemy. Some pretty fanciful alternative explanations have been dreamt up.

Warfare sometimes also leaves behind what can be termed 'fossilised frontiers'. There are many of them. During the Crusades, the Crusaders built a chain of castles to protect the Holy Land. After they left, the castles became largely irrelevant. Today they look much as they did when they were built. In the later Middle Ages, King Edward the First built a ring of castles around Wales as part of his strategy of conquest. They reflect the castle-building styles of the time and can still be seen today. In the late 17th and early 18th centuries the French engineer Vauban developed a network of star-shaped bastioned fortresses around France, and particularly on the northern and north-eastern borders. They reflect developments in siegecraft intended to resist attack by gunpowder artillery, and can still be seen in large numbers today. In

1942-4 the German Army and Navy built the Atlantic Wall to repel the forthcoming Allied invasion. Its bunkers and pillboxes were designed to withstand high explosive attack. Many can still be seen today. There are many other examples. The Duchy of Brittany did not become part of the Kingdom of France until its duchess married the French King in the 15th century. Brittany and France had been at war spasmodically for centuries. The towns and castles along the border today reflect the fortification styles of the late-medieval period. To the experienced eye they are very, very '15th century'. The point is that regions often display a fossilised skeleton of the warfare, and therefore the kingdoms or states, of the times. Just like on a skeleton or fossil, we cannot see the flesh and blood: the living tissue. We can, however, infer or conjecture a lot about it.

Much of what we shall discuss later is conjecture. It is written in the style of 'what happened' rather than 'what may have happened', for reasons to be discussed in Chapter 14. But it is conjecture based on the balance of evidence, as far as that can be seen. In Chapter Three we are on fairly firm ground. But as we then progress deeper into the Dark Ages we can be less certain.

3

The End of Roman Britain

The decline of Roman Britain seems fairly clear if we ignore the alleged Rescript of Honorius and apply Occam's Razor to what few historical sources we have. After 407 AD no new coinage was shipped to Britain, limiting the money supply. In 418 or so the Imperial treasuries in Britain were emptied to help pay for a ruinous period of wars on the Continent. As a short-term measure, emptying the treasuries wasn't a great problem. In the long term it would cause major difficulties.

In 429 AD St Germanus, bishop of Auxerre and a former imperial duke, visited Britain. The story of his visit tells a lot about everyday life in what seems like any other part of the late Roman Empire. A few years later, in 436, the Visigoths besieged Narbonne in southern Gaul. Aetius, the Roman commander-in-chief of the western Empire, ordered reinforcements from Britain to help raise the siege. Those units probably never returned. In addition, the imperial court had stopped appointing officials to posts in Britain. Roman civil life was slowly unravelling. Just a few years later, in 446, Romano-British officials invited a Germanic war band to help defend the critical area of eastern Kent. That story forms the beginning of the next chapter of this book.

In late Roman Britain there were about 30 cities and several dozen towns. Some *vici* were almost as large as the smaller towns. There were hundreds of villas. By 550 AD or so, or 600 at the latest, the great majority of those settlements had been abandoned. Some life continued in some of the larger towns and cities, but that was often no more than a hamlet or a farmstead inside a circuit of Roman walls. The Edwardian view was that they were all abandoned when the Romans left, and that the Anglo-Saxons didn't use them. That now seems a bit simplistic.

The old view of desertion of towns stems in part from the fact that evidence from those centuries is fragile and hard to detect. The sites of houses and villas which have been excavated show almost no durable household goods. However, all major Roman sites show some use into the fifth century. It is rarely monumental, and normally reflects decline. That applies to both towns and villas. Sometimes stone buildings were knocked down and rebuilt, but perhaps in wood. In York the site of one house revealed that a tiled roof collapsed and fell on top of a layer of earth which contained Roman pottery. Archaeologists believe that it was the site of a house, was a then garden or a farm plot for a while, and was then built over again.

This decline may have partly resulted from changes to the structure of Roman society. Town councils originally consisted of local dignitaries who raised taxes and spent a proportion of them on local public works. That system was replaced by one of civil servants who largely followed orders from provincial and imperial governments. Spending on local public works such as amphitheatres and market places fell. The rich increasingly lived out of town in their villas. This was so much of a problem in the later Empire that new laws were made to prevent it. Nonetheless, the rich increasingly spent their money on their villas, which became steadily more elaborate through much of the fourth century. The towns and cities appear to have gone into decline well before then.

The villas generally reached a peak of development in the late fourth century and then went into gradual decline. Some show signs of what seems like squatter occupation in the fifth century, with (for example) evidence of cooking directly on top of mosaic tiled floors. There is, however, literary evidence of at least one fifth-century villa owner who kept his bath house in use, although he only used it at weekends.

Walls were typically built around Roman towns in Britain in the period from 150 to 180 AD, and rebuilt in stone about a century later. Many of the forts in northern Britain were extensively rebuilt in the early fourth century. Artillery towers were built on town walls in the mid to late fourth century; that is, about the period of the troubles around 370. Even quite small British towns had walls. They were built to a broadly common plan, which implies some degree of official (Imperial) control, but local construction. The fortifications were repaired in some places well into the fifth century, which suggests habitation. The forts on Hadrian's Wall were in regular occupation in the early fifth century, and in some cases considerably later. There was some sign of decay in towns and cities as early as the second century. That might imply that the cost of building and repairing town walls contributed to the decay in public works. Even in London considerable areas of land inside the walls were used for gardens or agriculture quite early in the imperial period.

Outside the towns, a typical pre-Roman house was circular. That gave way to rectangular buildings with internal partitions and hence rooms. In some cases such dwellings were rebuilt in stone. This process was one of gradual and not very deep cultural change at the lowest level of society. It was abandoned fairly quickly after the end of Roman rule.

The Roman military garrison was not very large (about 25-30,000 soldiers in a population of perhaps four to six million). What it did, or did not do, is important to the story of Dark Age warfare. It played some role in the period after the end of imperial rule. The names of some units of the *Notitia*, for example those named after the emperor Honorius, suggest that they were present in Britain well after that date.

The old structure of large (5,000-man) legions had long since gone. The army was now made up of named cohorts of infantry and *alae* of cavalry, although the designations of some differed. For example, there were some '*numeri*' of infantry, roughly a 'unit', and even '*cunei*' (a *cuneus* was literally a wedge; the word refers to a particular battlefield formation). Most cohorts and *alae* were nominally of 500 men. Some were of 1,000. The names of several of the old legions had survived as cohort-sized units, and were clearly considered to be special. Late-Roman and Byzantine writers refer specifically to legions being moved, but rarely to other cohorts.

Roman Britain was one diocese of four (or perhaps five) provinces. A 'diocese' was a Roman administrative region. The Church borrowed the term to refer to the district of a bishop. In each diocese the army was divided into *limitanei* and *comitatenses*. *Limitanei* were border defence forces, but were not necessarily deployed actually on the front line. *Comitatenses* were the regional reserves. In Britain there were three major commanders. The *Dux Britanniarum*, or Duke of the Britons, commanded 23 units along Hadrian's Wall and 14 units in reserve throughout northern England. The Count of the Saxon Shore commanded nine units garrisoned in the Saxon Shore forts. Confusingly, and contrary to later practice, a *Dux* or Duke (literally a leader) was junior to a *Comes* or Count (a 'companion' of the emperor). The term '*comitatenses*' literally means 'of the count', so we have the anomaly of a group of coastal defence forces ('*limitanei*') commanded by a count. That was unusual in the Roman Empire. It suggests that, in Britain, the Saxon Shore was an important command. The Count of the Saxon Shore was at least nominally the same rank as his boss, the Count of the Britons. The latter personally commanded the operational reserve of ten units.

The division of units between infantry and cavalry is interesting and important. It is shown at Figure 3.1.

Commander:	Cavalry Alae	Infantry Cohorts	Total	Remarks
Count of the Britons	6	4	10	Strategic or operational reserves
Count of the Saxon Shore	2	7	9	
Duke of the Britons				
(along Hadrian's Wall)	(5)	(18)	(23)	
(tactical reserves)	(3)	(11)	(14)	Based up to 100 miles south of the Wall
Total	8	29	37	
Totals	16	40	56	

Figure 3.1 Roman Cavalry and Infantry Units in Britain.

Note that five cavalry units were used to patrol along or in front of Hadrian's Wall, but there were also three more cavalry and 11 infantry units in reserve. Some of them were actually stationed on the coast, such as *Numerus Barcariorum Tigrisiensium* ('The Battalion of Boatmen from the River Tigris') stationed at South Shields near Newcastle. The Saxon Shore command was mostly infantry, but both of its two cavalry units were stationed on the East Anglian coast. The operational reserve, however, had just four infantry units and six of cavalry. That constitutes almost half of all the cavalry in Britain. The late-Roman Empire clearly viewed cavalry as an important part of its mobile reserves.

The name of a unit often reflected where its soldiers originally came from, but not where they were currently recruited from. Some had been in Britain for centuries. *Cohors Secundae Daciorum* (the second cohort of Dacians, from modern Romania) were in Britain for over two hundred years. Importantly, three Legions remained in the garrison: *Legio Secunda Augusta; Legio Secunda Britannica;* and *Legio Sixta*, sometimes referred to as *Victrix* ('the Victorious Sixth'). *II Augusta* had arrived in Britain in the invasion of 43 AD and seems to have never left (but see below). Little is known of *II Britannica*, but in the *Notitia* it was one of only four cohorts in the *Comitatenses* (and the only legion). *VI Victrix* was based at York. It had served in Britain since 119. It formed part of Hadrian's' forces when he pacified the north and built the Wall. York was the Duke of the Britons' headquarters and the main military base in northern England.

By the late fourth century the old distinction between legionaries and auxiliaries had long since gone. All troops were 'regular', wherever they came from in the Empire. Troops were no longer required to live in barracks, and could be married. Typically they lived in *vici* which were effectively suburbs of the major garrison towns or forts. Some soldiers may have been detached as town guards; either permanently, or by rotation (that is, for a few weeks or months at a time).

There were many Germans in the garrison. There had been Roman troops of Germanic origins in Britain for centuries. The *Notitia* list several such units. Batavians and Tungrians had taken part in the invasion of 43 AD. Sarmatian cavalry had arrived in about 160-180, Burgundians and Vandals in about 270-80, and Allemani in about 372. Some had originally arrived as auxiliaries, or as *foederati* (allied troops). By the late Empire, however, such distinctions no longer had their original meanings.

These were the days, as the British Army now puts it, when a Centurion was a rank, not a tank. Roman society had three broad classes: the plebs (commoners), the equestrian (roughly 'knightly') and the senatorial (roughly 'noble') classes. Cohorts and *alae* were typically commanded by officers from the equestrian class, whilst more senior officers generally held senatorial status. Centuries of infantry were commanded by centurions. *Turmae* (troops) of cavalry were commanded by decurions. Both can be translated as 'captains', but the way they behaved suggests something more like sergeant majors. They were either promoted from the ranks or commissioned directly from what we would now call educated middle-class applicants.

There was a recognised career progression throughout the army. It was quite possible for a very senior centurion to be granted equestrian status on retirement. The Romans increasingly allowed soldiers to reach the highest ranks of society. Several came from families of Germanic origin, but we should be careful what this means. The son of a senior centurion, himself born of Germanic parents, might have had a formal, 'classical' education. In turn his son may well have been born into, educated in, and married into the equestrian classes, and spoken Latin as his first language.

A cohort had six centuries of about 80 men each. A century typically formed up for battle in eight ranks of 10 men. Each soldier originally had 2 throwing spears (*pila*), a sword, a large (oblong) shield, a helmet and body armour. The century was drilled to attack like a well-oiled machine. It advanced in step. At about 40 yards from the enemy, each man would take one javelin from his left hand to his right, reach back and throw in a volley. He would then take the second, reach back and throw, all the time keeping in formation and marching forward in step. He then drew his sword and rushed the last few yards to the enemy.

The few dozen enemy immediately facing the century had just had about 160 heavy javelins hurled at them. Some would have been injured or perhaps killed outright. Many would have tried to fend off the *pila* with their shields. Some *pila* would stick into those shields, making them very unwieldy and almost useless. Some of the enemy would react by throwing their shields away: a mistake they would probably not survive to make twice. The cohesion of the enemy formation was probably broken in the confusion. Then, within seconds, ranks of heavily-armoured legionaries were in and amongst them. A legionary's first job was to push with his shield, knock his opponent over or back, and then thrust with his sword. He was not interested in sword fighting or fencing. He kept his shield up, pushed forward and thrust at any exposed flesh. The ranks behind stabbed anybody on the ground, pushed past anybody wounded in the front rank, and kept going. A century was a well-drilled killing machine intended to break the ranks of the enemy in front of it. When the enemies' front was broken and they lost their cohesion, they would turn and run. Then the slaughter would start.

Each Roman soldier was allocated a frontage of one yard, so a cohort in eight ranks would have a frontage of just 60 yards. However, every second century deployed back about 30 yards from the front. Each century had a depth of about two yards per man, so about 15 yards in total. A cohort had a total depth of about 45-50 yards. Forces of several cohorts were typically assembled in line with no gaps between them, into longer and longer frontages. However, in very big battles cohorts were drawn up in two, three or even four lines. The overall effect was that of a chequer board of centuries. A man's shoulders are typically about 20-24 inches wide, so a frontage of one yard per man allowed a foot or so between them. That is just enough to allow him to use his weapons (so long as he does not slash about), but close enough to be protected by men to the left and right. See Figure 3.2

This formation had been developed fighting against Hannibal's elephants, centuries before. It had two main advantages. One was that it was good at breaking the enemy's line into pieces; the enemy force rapidly lost its cohesion and broke. Centuries in the second and any subsequent line guarded the flanks of those in front of them and acted as reserves. The second advantage was the opposite of the first. If one century broke under enemy attack, the others were independent and would not get swept away themselves. This degree of tactical articulation was unique, a battle-winner, and not repeated until perhaps the 18th century in Europe.

Cavalry were used far more flexibly, and in shallower formations. There is not much point in deploying cavalry more than a couple of ranks deep. They were often used

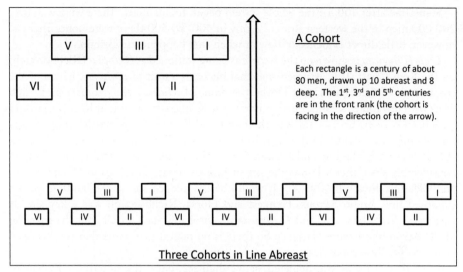

Figure 3.2 Imperial Roman Infantry Battle Formation.

for scouting, screening or pursuing a broken enemy. The names of some cavalry units in the *Notitia* suggests that they were, at least originally, heavily armoured. None of those were on the Saxon Shore or in the forts along Hadrian's Wall. They were part of the reserves.

By the fourth century, equipment and training had evolved. Shields were round rather than oblong, and there is less evidence for the use of *pila*. Historians disagree about the relative quality of *Limitanei* and *Comitatenses*. Much of it is inferred or conjectured without much evidence. The *comitatenses* were supposedly generally better, and the *limitanei* supposedly became little more than a militia. Furthermore, there is evidence that after major disasters (such as the Battle of Adrianople in 378 AD), some units were promoted from the *limitanei* to the *comitatenses*. There is also evidence that some units were 'doubled'. That is, they were split into two and brought up to the strength of two separate units with new recruits. Both actions are supposed to have diluted the quality of the units involved.

There are, however, no bad soldiers, only bad officers. Time and time again, respectable units have been created by taking poor material and injecting good commanders. In the Roman case that would mean a new commander (typically a tribune or a prefect) and some good centurions. They would also need equipment and, particularly, time to train. But, given a few months, there is no particular reason to believe that such units were not, at least, respectable. By analogy, British Territorial Army units were doubled in both the First and Second World Wars. Many fought with distinction. Such units might not be 'first rate' until they had a bit of battle experience. They could, of course, suffer a crushing defeat before or even after that happened.

Sometime after 400 AD the whole system began to fall apart. There were well over 200,000 men in the western Roman Army in 400. By 500 there were none. There is, however, little direct evidence of how or when that happened in Britain.

Legio II Augusta is shown on the *Notitia* as being stationed at *Rutupiae* (Richborough) on the Kent Coast. It is assumed that that makes it a unit of *limitanei*. Much of the coast south of there (such as at Dover, the home of *Militum Tungrecanorum),* is high cliffs with few routes inland. Further north, the Kent coast (such as at Reculver) would have been marshy. So was much of the Essex and East Anglian coast. *II Augusta* was one of only three legions in the army in Britain. Richborough was on a good landing site. It was fairly shallow and sheltered from the winds (the coastline has changed considerably since then). It was the site of Julius Caesar's landings in 55 and 54 BC, and Claudius' invasion of 43 AD. It would be the alleged site of the landings of the supposed first Anglo-Saxons, Hengest and Horsa. Richborough was a key site. It deserved a first-class unit, and *II Augusta* was probably such a unit. But the garrison of the Saxon Shore were *limitanei.* So there is no reason to assume that the *limitanei* were necessarily second-class.

The Army probably was depleted, as we shall see, but it did not all go. By way of comparison, units of the Roman army in Egypt were still recruiting the sons of legionaries around 580 AD, and their grandsons fought the invading Arabs when Islamic armies conquered Egypt around 640. Several Roman forts in Britain are known to have been occupied by bands of soldiers well into the fifth, if not sixth, centuries. All but two of the forts in the north belonging to the Duke of the Britons were occupied in the fifth century. So were some of the Saxon Shore forts.

A later romantic poem, 'The Gododdin', relates a tale of a force of cavalry who fought against the Anglo-Saxon, reputedly at Catterick, around the year 600 AD. The narrator, Aneirin, says that he was the only (or perhaps almost the only) survivor. The language of The Gododdin can be interpreted as saying that they were a regular, full-time unit which was barracked and stabled much as, say, the Household Cavalry are today. If so, then perhaps Aneirin was the last recorded 'Roman' soldier in Britain. The real impact of that may not have been the outcome of the battle of Catterick, but that for centuries afterwards people still had a folk memory of Roman cavalry and, particularly, of Arthur fighting on horseback. The Red Dragon emblem of Wales is probably a copy of a Roman cavalry standard.

The Roman Army did, however, decline. It eventually disappeared from Britain. After 407 AD no new coinage was brought to pay the soldiers. There would still have been a lot of money in circulation until the treasuries were emptied in 418. The money supply started to break down. Soldiers would increasingly have been paid in kind, and probably farmed their own plots. Regular training would have been increasingly rare, not least if the soldiers had to produce their own food. They might, for example, only train in the afternoon, then only on a few days per month, then scarcely at all. The centralised production and distribution of arms and equipment would have broken down. For a long time they could maintain what they had, and produce their own copies; but over years the standards would slip.

There are no bad soldiers, only bad officers. Therefore the real problem in the long-term may have been a lack of educated, motivated men to be officers. Sons may have followed fathers; but be increasingly less well educated, less experienced, and more parochial in outlook. Ambrosius was reputedly of senatorial rank. Arthur may have been the son or grandson of a senior commander; perhaps a count or duke of the Britons. But no further individuals of that status are known to us.

Gildas reported significant fighting in the fifth century. However, it is possible that Britain in the early part of that century was reasonably peaceful. It may be that, in the long run, the late-Roman army in Britain fell apart through lack of interest, lack of funding and lack of enemies to give either incentive or practice.

All was not entirely in order, however. Piracy had long been a problem in the Channel. The Romans had previously kept a fleet there. They seem to have reorganised that into the system of the Saxon Shore, with forts and commanders on both the British and Continental (Gallic) coasts. That was a recognition that chasing pirates (who were perhaps in smaller and faster boats) at sea was a waste of effort. The identity of the pirates is a mystery. They may have been Scottish, Irish or Germanic. They are often described as 'Saxon', but that may mean no more than 'Germanic'. Today we might call them Danish, Dutch or Norwegian. The problem of pirates did eventually go away, but we don't know why. It may be because they were Germanic and that, after the initial Germanic settlements on the east coast, they stopped raiding. Alternatively those settlers may have been the pirates, or the settlers dealt with them. They may have been Scottish or Irish; and either the Germanic settlers dealt with them, or they didn't, but we no longer hear of them (not least because they were all illiterate.) They may have been the precursors of the Vikings. It is quite possible that they were all of those things. After all, if the British and Gallic Coasts were prosperous and poorly defended, anybody with a sea-going boat could 'have a go' if he wanted.

The problem was sufficiently serious that from about 270 or 280 AD the Romans rebuilt and refortified the coastal forts and town walls along the east coast. There seems to have been a major, organised enemy incursion in about the period 367-70. Count Theodosius, the father of a later emperor, was sent to Britain with a small force of reinforcements (of four cohorts or *alae*). He re-established law and order, and withdrew units that had been deployed as outposts north of Hadrian's wall. Some gates in the Wall were closed, and some suburbs were abandoned. However, about this time an entirely new system of defence was put in place.

Theodosius disbanded the *Areani*, a unit of irregular scouts. They, and other forces north of the Wall, were replaced by inserting Roman-educated dignitaries as the hereditary leaders of the local Scottish tribes. A series of watch towers up to a hundred feet high was built along the north east coast as far south as the River Humber. It was linked by roads and signal beacons to units inland. For example, the watchtower at Scarborough was linked by beacons to the *Numerus Superuenientium Petueriensium* at Derwent, and hence to the Sixth Legion about a day's march further inland at York. The Saxon Shore was also refurbished, and the last fort in the chain, at Pevensey, was built. The fort at Pevensey is the least regular in plan.

A glance at the maps shows that something appears to be missing. What about the section in between? Further investigation reveals a major and hitherto unexplained defence, albeit in an unusual place. The Lincolnshire coast is low-lying and wind-swept. It would have been a most unattractive place. Inland lay the extensive wooded area of the Lincolnshire Wolds, with only two towns, both walled, and one road. Inland from there, however, lay the Lincolnshire fens and then the rich hinterland: first Lindsey and then the Midlands. The Lincolnshire Fens drain south into the Wash. There was little to stop small boats slipping up or down the coast and into the Wash. They could then move up the rivers, creeks and streams over a wide area. Once on dry land, or perhaps with a camp established on an island in the marshes, the pirates could raid pretty much at will.

The Romans dug a defensive earthwork along the edge of the dry land from Lincoln to what is now Peterborough. They may have linked that to other inland waterways to the area of Cambridge. There is evidence of major earthworks for a few

Figure 3.3 The Late-Roman Defences of Britain.

miles northwards from Waterbeach, five miles down the river Cam from Cambridge. Cambridge is the lowest place at which the Cam could be crossed. The major section of the defences, however, ran for 57 miles from Peterborough to Lincoln. It is like nothing else that the Romans ever built, anywhere in the Empire.

Today it is called the Car Dyke. It was between 11 and 14 feet deep and up to 50 feet wide. It had a flat bottom and sloping sides. There was little or no berm on either side; that is, the spoil from the excavation was banked up on both sides immediately next to the ditch. It ran broadly along the five metre contour, but was not continuous. There were perhaps five short breaks in it. Traces of earthwork forts were found in, or near, the gaps. There was a break, and a fort, roughly every six to seven miles in the northern section. The dyke was full of water. Archaeologists had to pump out water seeping into it as soon as they started to excavate.

The strategic and operational siting is obvious. The Romans did not attempt to defend the whole of the coast. They protected the area inland. Strategically, Ermine Street ran from London to York through Lincoln. Protecting Lindsey also protected major communication, trade and reinforcement routes. Tactically, the siting of the Car Dyke is superb. It shows an expert eye for ground. Over much of its length it hugs the bottom of the high ground. In several places the streams above it are winding and sinuous. Immediately below they are straight. That is, the ground below has been drained at some point since Roman times. The fenside (as opposed to upslope) bank is no more than couple of feet above the level of the fen as a whole. That would ensure that the Dyke would remain full of water. The upslope bank, however, would remain

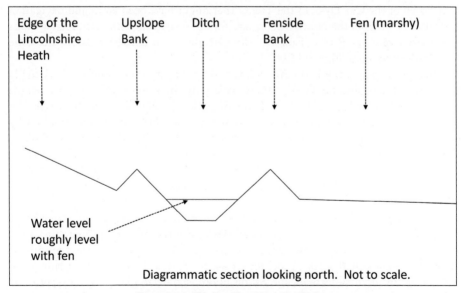

Figure 3.4 The Profile of the Car Dyke.

dry and actually be drained by the ditch, making it easier for Roman forces to move along it.

In the area of the River Slea the Dyke cuts straight across the low ground. That avoids both a long detour inland and presenting a salient to any raiders. Pirates or raiders are primarily motivated by robbery. Imagine that they had sailed up a creek in a boat. They beach their boat and come to a steep bank right across their path. They clamber over the bank and find a ditch full of water several metres wide in front of them. There is a further, higher bank on the far side. Now, if there are no enemy about they can get across, go inland, raid and return with their loot, perhaps including livestock.

It is difficult to persuade livestock to swim, let alone clamber up a steep bank out of a stream or river. The banks are occasionally patrolled, and Roman units are sited a few miles away. They Romans may have cavalry, and can move up and down the main road very quickly. The raiders are not numerous. They do not want to stand and fight. Not least, with a bit of thought the defenders might attack and burn the boat. The Dyke could not be continuous: the Slea, and several other streams, had to flow through it. But would you wish to raid deep inland in your boat, and pass between the point where fortifications overlook the river on both sides? Not least, the defenders would know that you had to pass back through there. In passing, the extension of the Car Dyke south from Peterborough is called Cnut's (that is, King Canute's) Dike today.

Lincoln lies at the junction of the Till and Witham Rivers. It overlooks the area where the Witham flows east into the Fens. Those fens drain south eastwards into the Wash. Only a few miles west, a major river (the Trent) flows north to join the Ouse and becomes the Humber. Another dyke, the Fosdyke, ran from very close to the north end of the Car Dyke to the Trent. That might have been an inland navigation (to allow boats from the North Sea or, say, York to reach Lincoln). Inland navigations were very rare in the Roman Empire. Alternatively, it may have been part of the same defensive system (see Figure 3.5).

North of Lincoln, the River Ancholme flows north into the Humber. It virtually cuts off the Lincolnshire Wolds. There were only three fords across it in a length of about 50km (at Snarford, Pilford and Brigg (originally 'Glenford Bridge')). The valley of the Ancholme was a marsh up to 5km across. That begs the question of why something like the Car Dyke wasn't built north of Lincoln, west of the Ancholme. The answer lies in place names. Whereas the valley of the Witham is largely described as 'fen', the valley of the Ancholme is largely 'carr': wooded marsh. It would have been much less attractive to pirates. In addition a Roman cohort was stationed at Wintringham, less than two miles from the mouth of the Ancholme.

There were nine forts on the Saxon Shore. Most are far too big: about two or three times too big. The Romans had standard sizes for forts. Temporary marching forts were smaller than permanent ones. A permanent fort for a cohort was typically of about three and a half acres. A fort for a cavalry *ala* was about five and a half acres. Of the seven infantry forts on the Saxon Shore, six are too large. The exception is Richborough, which was probably the oldest. None show a *vicus* (suburb), and the

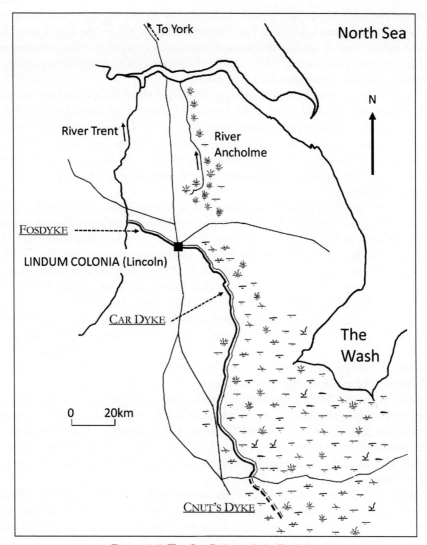

Figure 3.5 The Car Dyke and the Fosdyke.

internal layouts of some had show an irregular street pattern. It seems that the Romans built them large enough to include space for families and dependants. Eventually the occupants reorganised the internal space as they wanted. They were not so much forts as defended settlements. This is not the traditional view of the forts of the Saxon Shore.

The two cavalry forts are about the right size. Cavalry units require more space for stabling. They also need access to grazing, or at least fodder, all year round. Those two forts are about 50 miles apart, whilst all the rest are 35 miles apart or less (except for the westernmost stretch across to Portchester: see below) Given the broad, low-lying East Anglian coast, it appears that some of the *turmae* (troops) of those two *alae* were not based there permanently. They may have operated away from there; perhaps in rotation, as infantry centuries did in the towns.

Units along the Saxon Shore had been redeployed there from elsewhere. *Cohors I Baetasiorum* had originally been at Maryport in Cumbria, but moved to Reculver. *I Aquitanum* was at Brancaster for some time, having also moved there from northern England. It was then replaced at Brancaster by *Equites Dalmatarum Branadunensium,* a cavalry unit. The fort at Pevensey was the last to be built. Before it was there, the gap from Lympne in Kent to Portchester (near Portsmouth) would have been almost a hundred miles.

Not long after Theodosius' reorganisation, a Roman leader from Britain called Magnus Maximus rebelled. In trying to become emperor, he may have taken some of the garrison of Britain with him to the Continent. Magnus Maximus was killed in about 388 AD. There was further trouble in Britain in about 396. Stilicho the Vandal, a leading Roman general, ordered (and may have led) an expedition to Britain to restore order, just as Theodosius did about 20 years earlier. In 406, the Year of the Three Pretenders, the Army in Britain rebelled again. One of the three, later known as Constantine III, emerged as its leader. He led some of the British garrison across to the Continent. Honorius was the western Roman emperor at the time. At one stage Honorius recognized Constantine as a sub-emperor and had Stilicho executed. However, on the last day of 406 vast numbers of Germanic tribesmen broke across the frozen Rhine: mostly Allemani, Burgundians and Vandals. It was the beginning of large-scale Germanic migrations into the Empire. For a while imperial attention was focussed on stabilising the situation. They never quite succeeded. The Goths sacked Rome in 410. Germanic tribes continued to roam the western Roman Empire. The Vandals dismantled the western Empire in 467. Deferentially, they sent the imperial regalia to the Byzantine emperor in Constantinople.

Flavius Constantius, the Roman commander-in-chief in the west like Stilicho before him, had re-established some semblance of control. Constantine III had been executed in 411 AD. Constantine and Stilicho may have removed troops from Britain. One legion is reported to have been removed in 401. There may have been a major barbarian attack on Britain in 408. It was during Constantine's revolt that the Romans stopped sending new coinage to Britain, or minting it there. In about 418, with the imperial coffers severely depleted due to loss of revenue and constant war, the Romans removed the remaining money reserves from the treasuries in Britain. Constant war in Gaul made it harder and harder to administer such a far-flung province (Britain was the most northerly diocese of the Empire). In 436 a Roman army was besieged in Narbonne. Aetius summoned troops from Britain, for what was probably the last time, in order to relieve Narbonne. Those troops probably never returned. By this time the Emperor had stopped appointing new officials to Britain.

There is some intriguing evidence. Some centuries ago a decorative bronze disk was found in northern France. From its style, it appears to come from this period. The decoration shows units of late-Roman soldiers. The inscription suggests that it was made to celebrate an occasion when two legions, *II Augusta* and *XX Valeria Victrix*, were camped together. The disk was presented to their commander-in-chief. *II Augusta* is shown in the *Notitia* as being based in Richborough. It may finally have been ordered to Gaul in 436 AD by Aetius. *XX Valeria Victrix* had, like *II Augusta*, arrived in Britain in 43 and stayed for a long time, but there is no record of it at all after about 293. It is not shown in the *Notitia*. (The disk is shown on the cover of this book.)

On the disk, the soldiers are carrying round shields, which generally came into use after 300 AD or so. At or about that time the old legionary structure was finally abandoned. So the disk shows a meeting of the two legions – not detachments – sometime after 300. It shows *XX Valeria Victrix,* which clearly existed at the time the event recorded on the disk took place. So:

a.   The event took place sometime after 300, but before the *Notitia* was written (since *XX Valeria Victrix* is not shown in the *Notitia*).
b.   The *Notitia* shows several units created during Honorius' time, and named in his honour. Therefore it was written after 395 AD, and probably several years after that date. It may have been as late as 423.
c.   *We can conclude that* the *Notitia* was written some time after 395 AD, and the meeting took place some time before then.

Frustratingly, none of this proves that the *Notitia* was written after 409 AD. But it does seem more plausible than an imaginary Rescript which does not exist and has only ever been presumed.

Britain was a diocese of four, or perhaps five, provinces. There was a 'vicar' (governor-general) of Britain and four, or perhaps five, provincial governors. At some stage in the fifth century, they were not replaced from Rome (or Ravenna) when they retired or died. Local aristocrats were appointed to replace them, and the Roman governmental structure persisted for some time. The degree of Roman activity in the fifth and early sixth century is often understated. Gildas implies, or even asserts, a period of relative prosperity. Taxes may have been low for decades, because money was not sent to Rome or Ravenna.

The visit of St Germanus to Britain in 429 AD suggests a continuing Roman lifestyle, although the story of his visit clutters a reasonable narrative with ecclesiastical detail and miraculous tales. Similarly, St Patrick was a real historical person who was brought up in Britain in this period. His father had wanted him to enter public life. That implies that civil society still functioned, and that a career in local or national government was still attractive to a well-bred Romano-Briton. The *Notitia* implies that there were about 1,000 salaried civil servants in Britain. They, and their families' lifestyles, were supported by locally-raised taxes. The system eventually broke down.

A century later Gildas decried that the nobles had become 'tyrants', in a sense that we would understand as 'dictators'. Their appointments had become hereditary.

Buildings were being re-built in the same styles, but increasingly in wood rather than stone. The money supply did break down. However, for example, St Patrick never mentioned a lack of coinage. A very few coins of Constantine III, minted on the Continent, have been found in Britain; but almost nothing later. Luxury goods such as olives, wine and tableware were being imported into Britain in the fifth and even sixth centuries, but they may have been paid for by barter. We don't know what happened to the use of coins. It didn't suddenly stop. Some coins may have remained in use to the end of the fifth century. Some villas continued to function through this period. Overall, however, it appears that it was the economic basis of everyday life, namely the growing and selling of surplus crops and livestock for cash, which declined. Britain had become a barter (and largely a non-urban, subsistence) economy by 500 or perhaps 550 AD.

The civilian population was predominantly Christian. British bishops had attended councils at Arles in 314 AD and Rimini in 359. There were four British bishops in 431. One of the most important theological disputes of the fifth century centred around a British cleric called Pelagius who, admittedly, lived in Rome. Speculation about ecclesiastical matters in general, and Pelagianism in particular, hugely colours accounts of the period. St Germanus was sent to Britain in 429 to make sure that the diocese did not succumb to Pelagianism. It seems to be more important to some modern writers that Vortigern 'must have been' (sic) a Pelagian than who he was, or what he did. ('Vortigern' is a title or nickname.) The visit of St Germanus is more useful to us for what it says about life at the time than what he may, or may not, have done as a priest.

Germanus visited the shrine of St Alban outside *Verulamium* and was greeted by a local magistrate. There is evidence of life in *Verulamium* until the year 500 AD or so. The Welsh Book of Llandaff describes two bishops alive around 600 or so. (Llandaff Cathedral is near Cardiff). There seems to have been some continuity of Christianity in South Wales from Roman times until then, and from then until now. Gildas describes much about an organised church which is familiar to us from medieval times. Much of the Romano-British religious evidence available to us from the fifth century is Christian, rather than pagan. (Some pagan shrines, however, seem to have remained in use.) St Patrick was a protégé of St Germanus. He was appointed bishop in about 433. There had been some Christians in Ireland for about 50 years by then.

Urban life, however, depended or trade. Trade declined and, with it, urban and villa life. Cross-channel trade declined in volume and worth. Items like wine, olives and tableware became luxuries and status symbols of the rich and powerful. That may, or may not, have been anything to do with piracy or Germanic depredations. The Roman economy needed three things to work together: money, urban markets, and the organisation of transport. All three broke down, in what may have been a cycle of decline.

There was a general decline of living standards. Under the Empire, imported Samian crockery was relatively common. It was good, cheap, and mass-produced in factories. As trade declined so did the use of Samian tableware. It was replaced by increasingly crude locally-produced substitutes. The owner of one villa was reduced to repairing broken crockery with soft copper rivets. Oysters had been popular throughout Roman Britain. If they are to be safe to eat, oysters must be delivered either quickly or in barrels of brine. The former requires very quick transport, the latter the safe transport of relatively heavy barrels on carts. The eating of oysters died out.

Cut stone, such as gravestones, was increasingly re-used to repair buildings. Eventually buildings were repaired or replaced in wood, if at all. Many Roman households cooked on charcoal suspended on flat salvers hung below a bronze tripod. The Romano-British lost the ability to repair bronze tripods, and then cooked directly on the floor. These processes, however, happened over decades, not years. By analogy, a colleague of mine spent some time working in Saddam Hussein's former palace in Basrah sometime after 2003. Many of the original rich trappings, such as the expensive gilt chairs, wore out and broke with use. An NCO went down to the local supermarket and bought plastic chairs to replace them. My colleague was very much aware that something vaguely similar may have happened in Romano-British villas, whether the occupiers were British or Anglo-Saxon.

There is no direct evidence of a dip in population, but it does seem to have declined. Famine and disease may have been a possible and partial explanation. The population of Britain under the Empire was probably between four and six million. By Domesday it was perhaps one and half million. In the late 14th century, just before the Black Death, it was between four and half and six million. The population could, and did, grow back quite quickly. Tree-ring evidence points to a major global cooling in the period 536-540 AD. That may have caused crop failure, which might have devastated a subsistence economy. A plague also struck the Empire a few years later (the Plague of Justinian), and may have come to Britain. There is some evidence of plague in Cirencester. The Plague of Justinian may have been devastating. By comparison, the Black Death killed between a quarter and a third of the population of England in eighteen months from June 1348. Reforestation does not necessarily mean that the population has declined: it may have moved away. The evidence for population loss is indirect. But, intriguingly, in 1086 the densest areas of population were in the centres of the original Germanic settlement: East Anglia, Kent, Sussex, the Lincolnshire Wolds and around Lindsey. There were also pockets around places such as Abingdon in Oxfordshire.

St Germanus and Gildas painted a picture of relative prosperity in the fifth century, which Bede (relying on Gildas) did not contradict. However, by the mid-sixth century Britain had slipped back into an heroic, tribal, non-urban society. Roman civilisation had collapsed. But it had been a gradual process. Gildas was somewhat alarmist, but was taken largely at face value by the Edwardian school. Archaeological evidence of urban life in the fifth century often indicates refurbishment and fortification: blocking up gateways and reoccupying hill forts. The evidence is of gradual decay and decline. Many of the educated Roman classes were dead or had fled, perhaps to Brittany.

Under the *Pax Romana* of the Empire, civilians were forbidden to carry arms. The prohibition was enforced. By 600 AD or so Britain was reduced to warring tribalism.

The names of every single roman villa in Britain disappeared. Conversely, in France many of them can still be identified in village names today. The field boundaries which they used were often the same, but the patterns of landowning had changed significantly.

There was some, limited continuity. The names of Cymru and Cumbria persist. 'Cornwall' may reflect the last remaining tribal name, the *Cornovii*, perhaps with the suffix for 'welsh'. Trade in England was almost nonexistent in the sixth and seventh centuries; slight before the ninth or tenth; and not considerable until the 12th. By the late sixth century Britain had slipped into a dark age.

4

The Germans Arrive

There are many traces of Germanic people in Britain before the end of Imperial rule in Britain. Confusingly, some supposedly 'Romano-Saxon' pottery is now thought to have been simply Roman. Many sites which were thought to be early Anglo-Saxon settlements now need to be re-assessed. The dating may be correct, but attributing them to Germanic migrants may not.

For example, the area around Abingdon in Oxfordshire was long thought to have been a major and early area of Germanic settlement. That skewed the picture of what the Anglo-Saxons conquered; where; and when. A cemetery excavated at Querford Farm, near a Roman town at Dorchester (on Thames) a few miles east of Abingdon, contained at least 200 graves from our period. All but two were buried lying east-west with no grave goods. That does not suggest a strong Germanic presence. 212 graves have been excavated at Frilford, near another Roman road a few miles further west. 13 were cremations and 28 seem to be Germanic burials. That means that over 80% were not.

At Dorchester, a Germanic-style brooch was found of a style that seems to have gone out of fashion *before* 500 AD. Some pottery from the early fifth century was found at Sutton Courtenay, five miles away. A late fourth or early fifth century belt buckle was found at Cassington. An early Germanic *Grubenhaus* which was occupied *well into* the fifth century was excavated at Dorchester. Overall, there is little sign of Germanic settlement in the area *during* the fifth century. So what was thought for decades to be a major Germanic enclave shows little real sign that it was. Its proximity to Oxford, its University and its department of archaeology may tell us more about its apparent importance.

We have already noted that many early Germanic sites are near Romano-British sites. Many show signs of being occupied at the same time. The identity of the 'wickhams' as some of the earliest Germanic settlements is further evidence of early Germanic presence *alongside* functioning Romano-British towns and villages.

Bede and Gildas suggest that some major events took place in the middle of the fifth century: perhaps in 446-7 and 450-455 AD. However, although those are the first datable events we have, that does not mean that they are the dates of the first arrival of the Anglo-Saxons. It seems that some Germans arrived as Roman soldiers, some as mercenaries, some as conquerors, and some as settlers. They came in separate groups or as individuals. Some came under their own leaders, but there was no political unity amongst them. We shall look at that process in this chapter. The events it describes generally took place in the fifth century, and so this chapter partly overlaps with previous and subsequent chapters.

The major historical events can be described quite quickly. St Germanus visited what seems to have been a largely peaceful post-Imperial country in 429 AD or so. Some of the army was ordered to the Continent to assist in raising the siege of Narbonne in 436 and probably did not return. According to Gildas the British wrote to Aetius, the Roman Commander-in-Chief in Gaul, in 446 AD asking for help in resisting the attacks of pirates and raiders. No help was forthcoming. A Romano-British ruler known as Vortigern invited a Jutish warband to Britain a year or so later. The Jutes rebelled a few years afterwards and formed the kingdom of Kent. Another Romano-British leader, Ambrosius Aurelianus, emerged and led a struggle against Picts and Germans which continued on and off for decades. He seems to have been replaced by Arthur, who continued the struggle through to his death in the 520s or 530s. Several different Germanic groups became established on the eastern and southern coasts during this period. Those were the origins of the kingdoms of East Anglia, Essex, Sussex and Wessex. Archaeology suggests that the largest migrations started in the early fifth century and were centred around the Wash, particularly in Norfolk.

There is considerable evidence that many of these Germans were originally mercenaries invited to defend post-Roman Britain. Their main enemies seem to have been Pictish; occasionally Irish; but sometimes other Germanic raiders. These warbands were not classless. They had a hereditary class of leaders, usually related by blood to the band's commander or leader. He had a close group of 'gesiths', or companions, who ate and slept in his hall. Other members of the band, known as 'ceorls' (hence our modern word 'churl', as in 'churlish') had individual rights and were, to that extent, free men. There were also slaves who had no rights. Numbers were never very large: King Harold had perhaps 8,000 men at Hastings in 1066. That was a very large army by the standards of the times. Armies of a few thousand would have been rare, and a few hundred perhaps more normal.

The weapons they used were fairly basic. Analysis of post-Imperial graves shows that the use of spears was quite widespread. They were generally stabbing spears up to seven feet long, with heads 12 to 16 inches long. A few javelins (throwing spears) have been found. Swords in graves are rare. They are almost always associated with high-status graves, as denoted by other finds such as jewellery. Very little armour has been found, and very few helmets. Whilst Germanic warbands may have been fairly well-equipped, we should remember that the areas they came from survived on little more than a subsistence economy. Metal was scarce, expensive, and tended to be re-used. The typical image of an Anglo-Saxon warrior may be accurate but should be restricted to a relatively few *gesiths*. Most Anglo-Saxon men were not full-time warriors. They may have had a spear to hunt with, or protect themselves from wild animals. Germans were still hunting boar with spears in the 19th century. Anglo-Saxon men probably also had a knife. Some also had, or could make, a shield. But few had any need for, nor could afford, any other specifically military equipment.

Warfare amongst Germanic tribes was originally simple and brutal. The opening sequences of the film 'Gladiator', starring Russell Crowe, catch the idea quite well. Germanic armies drew up opposite each other, perhaps a few hundred yards apart. The best equipped were in the front rank. After a certain amount of posturing and working up courage and morale, one side or the other (and sometimes both) would charge. The first impact could be bloody and decisive. The first side to give way would be routed and butchered. If neither did, there would then be a bloody, sweaty, brutal hacking match.

'Gladiator' suggested that such tactics didn't work too well against organised Roman armies. They worked particularly badly against a commander who could carry out something as simple as a surprise attack by cavalry on the enemy's rear. Yet the tactics of the charge persisted. Perhaps the last time it was used in Western Europe was at the Battle of Culloden in April 1746.

German tribesmen were not stupid. There is evidence that they learned a lot from fighting against, and in some cases with, the Romans. They did not perhaps have the discipline of Roman cohorts. They learned to keep together, shoulder to shoulder. They learnt not to charge headlong, but rather to advance at a walk; keeping some semblance of formation. As a result, battles might not have finished quite so quickly and dramatically. But they would be brutal, sweaty and vicious. Tactics would be fairly simple, but if one side did break and lose its cohesion the result might still be a disaster.

Roman discipline and tactics would still have been a great advantage; if, and only if, they had survived. That may have depended largely on the presence of leaders who could organise and train the human material at hand. Any cavalry with even a semblance of the effectiveness of Roman *alae* would have provided a massive advantage.

We know little of the real origins of the early Germanic settlers: neither who they were, where they came from, or when they did so. Some may have arrived as raiders in the troubles of 367 AD, or as Roman troops in the events of 372. Some seem to have been invited by Romano-British leaders. We can be moderately sure that that was what happened with the Jutes in Kent. But we cannot be particularly certain about the rest. There seems to have been four broad, overlapping categories of warriors. Firstly, that they were (or were descended from) Roman units, under regular officers and with recruits from within the Empire. Secondly, that they were formed from drafts from tribes outside the Empire, typically as part of a treaty obligation, and formed into Roman units with Roman equipment. Thirdly, that they were organised to some extent as formed units but under their own tribal leaders. Their organisation and training would only broadly resemble that of a normal Roman army unit. Lastly, they might be a warband co-opted under their own leaders.

These latter categories could be termed '*foederati*'. Another term, '*laeti*', has a similar but slightly different connotation. Such troops would tend to be more Germanic, less integrated during their service, and less Romanised after discharge. That would tend to show up in the material artefacts that they left behind. Did they receive pensions? Were they given land? Were they settled into villages? What kind of pottery did they use? Did they build *grubenhäuser*? The details would vary from group to group. As we shall see, some rebelled and seized land. That cannot be detected in the archaeological record alone. Nor is it possible to separate them from others who might be invaders; migrants; or raiders who settled.

If some of the Germans arrived by negotiation with the Romano-British, the collapse of the money economy would have affected how any agreement was met. Cash would have to be replaced with goods in kind. That may have caused disagreement; for example, over the value of the goods provided. Gildas said that Germans warbands were invited. The terms that the Romans used in these circumstances included '*hospitalitas*' (which could mean 'billeting'), '*annona*' ('grain tax') and '*epimenia*' ('rations'). But any process which the Romano-British many have used in, say, the 420s AD might be different from practice 20 years later; or 60; or 80.

Gildas describes the Jutes in Kent revolting. This process, of *foederati* revolting, taking advantage of their local monopoly of arms and military skills and seizing land, may have been repeated elsewhere. In other places pirates may have turned into raiders who then stayed and settled. They may have interbred with local women, or sent back to their homelands for their wives. In either event there were probably very few of them at first, but they were followed in increasing numbers. Those who were invited would have generally been warriors. Subsequent waves of migrants would increasingly not be.

Some Germanic warbands had experienced fighting with, and for, the Romans. That raises the intriguing question of how much knowledge of engineering they picked up. It may have been relatively little. However, the engineering we discussed in Chapter Two doesn't require many skilled engineers. It requires a few, who direct large amounts of unskilled labour. We shall return to that issue later.

The Edwardian school of Anglo-Saxon history dwelt at great length on the rulers of the various kingdoms which developed through the Dark Ages. There has been a lengthy academic debate about the nature of kingship. Terms such as 'sub-kings', 'under-kings' and 'kinglets' have been bandied about. One academic wrote that the kingship was 'a personal, not an hereditary office, and any male member of the royal kindred was eligible'. Another spoke of a 'cousin's right to participate in kingship'. Such high-falutant language is common in these discussions.

Much of the discussion comes from translation of sources such as Gildas, translating the Latin word '*rex*' (plural '*reges*') as 'king'. That summons up images of, say Henry the Eighth or the French Louis the Fourteenth. However, my Latin dictionary, which dates from 1899, does not translate *rex* as 'king'. It uses 'ruler' or 'prince' (as in 'principal', a leading figure). A king is a ruler and to that extent a prince, but it seems that writers have translated the Latin over-literally. So when Gildas pointed out that the Germanic migrants had many *reges*, he did not necessarily mean that they had many kings. He probably meant that they had many rulers. No written source originating before the seventh century describes Anglo-Saxon kings at all. It was Bede who first used the term widely. He wrote in the early eighth century, by which time kingship was well-established. Bede was probably describing what he knew from first hand; not what happened three centuries earlier.

The use of the term *rex* in Latin sources in relation to Britain had died out soon after the Roman invasion of 43 AD. It only re-emerged in the fifth century. As we shall see, most of the Anglo-Saxon kingdoms only emerged after about 520, and slowly even then. This is another case of the need for Occam's razor. The amount of ink that has been spilt analysing the nature of early Anglo-Saxon kingship is remarkable. In practice Germanic government was pretty simple and pretty personal. Society was tribal. A ruler ruled. When he died, or was killed, someone else took over. That person needed legitimacy. If he was the son of the last ruler, so much the better. If he was the son of the last ruler but he wasn't very effective, he might be killed and replaced fairly soon. Family connection to a strong, good or famous ruler gave someone legitimacy. That stood for very little in the barbarous, violent and butcherous conditions of early Anglo-Saxon settlement. Of course rulers employed bards to construct elaborate tales of descent which sought to support their legitimacy. Naturally, over time those tales became very elaborate. Naturally, they were re-used by subsequent generations to support their own legitimacy. Several of those genealogies have come down to us. Several of them were elaborate fakes.

Succession was important not just to someone coming to the throne, but also to the holder. Without a clear succession, old age could become lethal. As a ruler became old and feeble, unless he had an obvious successor who would support him (in the expectation of ruling in due course), he would be easy prey for an ambitious younger man. Legitimacy, succession, and hence genealogy were important in simple but violent times. The best known genealogies relate to the rulers of the West Saxons, who claimed legitimacy as descendants from the first of them, Cerdic. From Alfred the Great onwards almost all English sovereigns could claim descent from Cerdic. That includes the present Queen, Elizabeth the Second. As we shall see, there is a very good reason why descent from Cerdic was an important prop to legitimacy.

There is a great and unspoken myth about the Anglo-Saxons being great sea-farers. There is also very little evidence. Yes, the original settlers crossed the sea: once. So did the Romans. The Romans also came by ship. We know that their ships were far more sophisticated than those of the Germanic settlers, but we do not think of the Romans as great seamen. Anglo-Saxon seamanship is largely an Edwardian myth. It is not supported, as it is with the Vikings, by epic sagas of exploration and heroic deeds at sea.

The Sutton Hoo ship burial is important for many reasons, but it is in fact one of only two Anglo-Saxon ship burials which we know of. It may have been the grave of an East Anglian king, possibly Raedwald, showing off how rich he was. Furthermore there is very little evidence of seafarers in the North Sea having ships with masts and sails during the fifth and sixth centuries. The Sutton Hoo burial seems to be from the early seventh century. There is no direct evidence that it had a mast. It was about

90 feet long; not much longer than a cricket pitch. It is roughly as large as any other North Sea ship from the period. Sails seem to have come into use from about 500 AD, well after the initial Germanic arrivals. Even if the Sutton Hoo ship did have a mast, it was not the sort of ship in which to go on epic voyages; particularly not with 30 or so people in it. Ships like that were mostly rowed, not sailed, and needed about 30 oarsmen.

The early accounts of the arrival of Germanic warriors (such as Hengest and Horsa, Cerdic and his son Cynric, or Aella of the South Saxons) tell of those leaders coming ashore 'in three keels': that is, with three shiploads of followers. Sometimes there were five, or a similarly small number. Those accounts have a mythical ring to them. Some are obviously fakes. Yet, even if taken at face value, they relate to successful warband leaders who started out with only 100 or so warriors. Post-Roman Britain may well have been a fairly peaceful place, occasionally troubled by pirates and raiders, but where the presence of a hundred or so well-armed men could cause serious trouble.

Just a few decades later, early Germanic society in Britain was tribal and violent. Of six known rulers of East Anglia in a 46 year period, five died violently. We don't know how the sixth died. 12 of the 27 recorded battles in seventh-century England resulted in the death of at least one royal figure. The short reigns of such kings, and the resulting lack of dynastic continuity, was a big factor in the history of certain kingdoms. Some suffered from a series of very short reigns, whilst their opponents enjoyed long periods of stable (although not necessarily peaceful) rule. Early Anglo-Saxon rulers were all pagan. They showed little sign of piety or morality as we would understand them (in stark comparison with the life of, say, Edward the Confessor).

Feuds and blood loyalty weighed heavily in this Dark Age society. The first recorded Anglo-Saxon law codes are based on how to manage feuds without breaking the peace. Warriors initially earned land through service to their leader, which shows that this was a society of migration and conquest. Land only became inheritable later, and then only after three generations. So it could not have applied to the first few generations of migrants and settlers. The normal unit of local government was not the village or the district but the 'hundred', a group of 100 freemen settled on land over which they had some rights. Again, this strongly indicates the settlement of warbands and other migrants. Formal, written law codes developed from the beginning of the seventh century. They are the basis of the Common Law in use today. They stressed the everyday realities of a tribal population: individual's ('folk') rights; keeping the peace; and the common wealth (that is, communal behaviour for the common good). Those laws reflected a tribal society which was very different from Roman civilisation. 'Civilisation' is derived from 'civis', a town. Early Anglo-Saxon society was still pre-urban.

Knowing broadly where the Germans arrived is easy. Knowing what sequence they arrived in is not. The earliest migrations of any significance may have been Angles coming to what is now East Anglia. There were some Anglians in Norfolk from the late fourth century. As we shall see, Saxons (and other Germans) were settled to defend against them. Other Saxons settled, or were settled, on the south coast in what became Sussex. We don't know whether they were originally *foederati* or raiders. Some Jutes settled on the Isle of Wight and some other Saxons in southern Hampshire. These two groups became intermingled to some extent. The arrival of Hengest, Horsa and their Jutish followers in Kent may have been the *last* major arrival. However, if the arrivals of Cerdic of the West Saxons and Aella of the South Saxons are taken literally from the Anglo-Saxon Chronicle, they arrived later in the fifth century. More of that in due course. Smaller groups of Angles settled in Lincolnshire, east Yorkshire and Northumberland. They became the kingdoms of Mercia, Deira and Bernicia respectively. They may have been splinter groups from those in East Anglia. Although we call such groups 'Anglian', 'Saxon' or 'Jutish', the archaeological record is not clear cut. To some extent burials, artefacts and other evidence are intermingled.

The first known leaders of those groups emerged over a period of more than a hundred years. Hengest and Horsa, the first leaders of the Jutes in Kent, are known of from the 450s AD. Aella of Sussex is dated from 477 or so. Cerdic is known of from about 495, but started to rule in about 519. The first rulers of the kingdoms of the East Saxons, Mercia and Bernicia are known from the 520s. Deira only emerged as a recognisable kingdom in the 560s, and we know of the first ruler of East Anglia only from the 570s. So about four generations passed from the establishment of the Jutish kingdom of Kent to the point at which we know of a kingdom of East Anglia.

The balance of evidence, despite the high profile of Kent, is that most immigration in the fifth century was Anglian. We know little of the Germanic settlers except that they spoke Germanic languages, were pagan, had lived outside the Roman empire, and came to hate the Romano-British. 'Saxon' was initially a generic name, broadly meaning 'Germanic'. It was Bede who first differentiated between Angles, Saxons and Jutes.

Deira and Bernicia were united to become the kingdom of Northumbria in about 604 AD, completing what became known as the 'Heptarchy' or 'Seven Kingdoms': Kent, Essex, (East) Anglia, Sussex, Wessex, Mercia and Northumbria. The term was first used in the twelfth century by Henry of Huntingdon. There was little or no sign of the Heptarchy in 500. There were also a series of other shadowy groups whose existence is doubtful. For example, there probably never was a kingdom of the Middle Saxons (hence Middlesex), but equally there might have been a kingdom of the Middle Angles in what is now southern Lincolnshire, Huntingdonshire, Leicestershire and Northamptonshire.

The story of Hengest and Horsa is moderately well known, and is the only tale of the arrival of the Germanic settlers that can be dated with confidence. Ironically those Jutes may have been the last of the major groups to arrive, but the first to revolt. They do seem to have been invited as *foederati* from beyond the Empire. It may be that they were invited to Kent because, strategically, Kent was important for cross-Channel links to the rest of the Empire. That suggests that, until the 440s AD, Kent was reasonably secure. Why or how, and what happened to the Saxon Shore garrisons of Lympne, Dover, Richborough and Reculver, we don't know. Some of them may have been moved to France to France to help raise the siege of Narbonne in 436, and never returned. There are traces of Germanic settlers in Kent before the Jutes, but the picture is confused because what had been thought to be 'Romano-Saxon' artefacts are now thought to be simply late-Roman.

It is notable that Dover, Reculver and Lympne kept what were broadly their Roman names (*Portus Dubris*, *Regulbium* and *Portus Lemanis* respectively). Similarly Canterbury is unique in keeping a vestige of its pre-Roman tribal name. That suggests a fairly orderly transition from Roman to Germanic governance, as in much of Gaul. The towns broadly kept their former significance and hence their former names. The fact that three of them were Saxon Shore forts draws attention to the fact that the name of Richborough does not seem to reflect its Roman name (*Rutupiae*). However, a detailed analysis suggests that it is actually derived from '*Rutupiae*'.

Place-names ending with '-ing' (or '-ings') seem to be among the first places where Germanic settlers built their own villages. There are about 70 '-ings' (or similar) in Kent today. Over half of them (about 37) are within a mile of a Roman road or the prehistoric Pilgrim's Way. 18 more are within three miles. There is a group of 10 more along the Medway. That accounts for 65 of the 70 or so. This pattern is not really surprising. It suggests that the settlers used the Roman roads, or the Pilgrims' Way, and settled near to them where they could. '-Ings' are marked with a diamond on Figure 4.1.

There are archaeological traces of Jutes living in Canterbury in the fifth century, and Jutish cemeteries along Watling Street between Canterbury and the Surrey border. That is almost as far as London. This all suggests that the Jutes were actively settled by the Romano-British.

The story in the Anglo Saxon Chronicle is, briefly, that Vortigern invited the Jutes to Britain once the request to Aetius for help had been turned down. The letter to

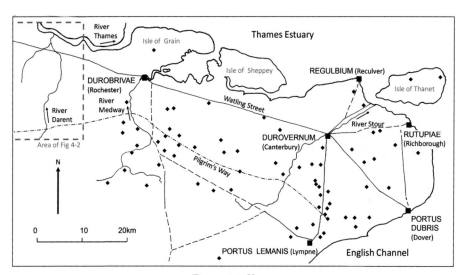

Figure 4.1 Kent.

Aetius was sent in 446 AD and the invitation to the Jutes in 447. Those dates are quite reliable. They can be corroborated with other historic sources, which discuss Aetius but do not mention the British request. As we have seen, we should not give too much credence to a warband whose leaders were called 'the Stallion' and 'the Mare'. Some of the tale is mythical. But it does appear that the Jutes rebelled within a few years, in 455 or so. They fought battles against the Romano-British at Aylesford in 455, Crayford in 457 and Wippedfleet in 465.

Aylesford is the lowest ford on the River Medway (although the Romans had built a bridge further downstream, at Rochester). Crayford is on the River Cray, which flows into the River Darent just below Dartford. Both Crayford and Dartford are the lowest fords. The Darent is about a dozen miles west of Medway. Wippedfleet is possibly Ebbsfleet near Richborough, which suggests that the Jutes had been pushed back almost as far as the Channel. They may have been defending the Isle of Thanet, which was surrounded by marshes in the Dark Ages (and there are two '-ings' on Thanet). Naturally, the Anglo-Saxon Chronicle says that the Jutes were victorious. It also describes how, in a monumental act of treachery, they pretended to negotiate with the Romano-British. They lured their leaders into a massacre. They slaughtered most of them and captured Vortigern.

A look at the archaeology of west Kent tells a different story. There were only two land routes west out of Kent in late Roman times. Watling Street was the main route. The Jutes built a dyke crossing it on the high ground between the Cray and the Darent. It wasn't continuous. There is evidence that it was not dug across marshy re-entrants. The ditch was about 24 feet wide, which makes it one of the biggest Dark Age dykes in England. There is some evidence that the bank had a gravel path along the top, presumably as a patrol route for the defenders. Today the total height of the remains (from the bottom of the ditch to the top of the bank) is about four or five feet in places. The dyke, called the 'Faesten Dic' or 'strong dyke', faced west. The Jutes were trying to keep the Romano-British out.

Only a few miles further south, the ridge of the North Downs rises up to about 240m above sea level. On its south side the ground drops dramatically by over 100 metres down an escarpment. An ancient trackway called the Pilgrim's Way runs along the bottom of the escarpment. The Pilgrim's Way is the second route westwards out of Kent. (Crayford is where Watling Street crosses the River Cray; Aylesford is the ford where a traveller on the Pilgrim's way would have to cross the Medway. Hence the battles in 455 and 457 AD respectively). Near Westerham, about 10 miles south of the Faesten Dic and a few miles further west, the Jutes built another dyke. Today it has no name. It was originally about 20 feet high. Today it is eight or nine feet high in places. It cuts across the narrow valley which the modern A25 runs through. We don't know how far it extended, nor how much of the area was woodland. But it faced west. The Jutes were trying to keep the Romano-British out. See Figure 4.2.

The second dyke is just east of the easternmost of the three Roman roads that led south from London into the Weald. Further north, Saxon burials have been found at Orpington, Croydon and Beddington. Each burial ground lay relatively close to one

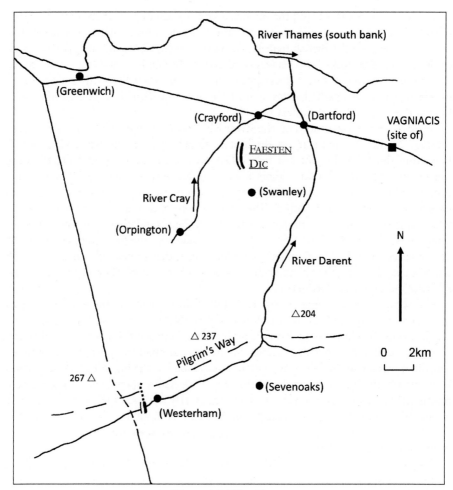

Figure 4.2 West Kent.

of those roads. Those Saxons may have been settled in response to the Jutish revolt. So it appears that the Anglo-Saxon Chronicle did not tell the whole story. The Jutes won a defensive campaign that gave them a homeland. But that was all. The *Faesten Dic* lies within a few hundred yards of the western boundary of Kent. The dike near Westerham lies right on it. The Romano-British bottled the Jutes up in the land which they held. There is no record of Kent ever conquering land beyond those borders. Over 1500 years later, the boundaries which they fixed are broadly the same. Not perfect, perhaps, but strategically quite a good outcome for the Romano-British.

What, then, had been happening in post-Roman Britain, from the British perspective? Gildas describes a broadly peaceful state interrupted by pirates and then Germanic incursions. We know of Vortigern, one of the more successful of a series of dictators, who fought an important battle in 437 AD in some form of civil war. We don't know who he fought or where the battle was. The name used translates today as 'Wallop'. Most writers assume that that means the villages called the Wallops in west Hampshire. All we really know about the battle of Wallop was that Vortigern won.

It was during this period that the British appealed to Aetius, commander of the Roman armies in Gaul. They asked for help against the pirates and Germanic invaders. This seems reasonable: only a few years before, Britain had sent troops to Gaul to help raise the siege of Narbonne. This time, however, no help was forthcoming. We should understand why. Ever since 409 AD the Roman Army had been fighting against a bewildering series of mostly Germanic enemies inside the Empire. The Goths had divided into two main groups: the Eastern, or Ostrogoths; and the Western, or Visigoths. Other Germanic groups such as the Vandals, the Burgundians, the Allemani and the Franks were sometimes allies of Rome, and sometimes its enemies. In 440, the Huns had crossed the Danube into the Eastern Empire. Attila became their king in 445. Throughout the 440s the Romans fought mostly against, but sometimes with, the Huns. The decisive battle would be fought in 451 at the Catelaunian Fields in the Champagne region east of Paris: well inside the Empire. On that occasion the Visigoths were fighting alongside Aetius. Events in Gaul meant that, for several years, neither Aetius nor any other senior Roman commander would have been able to send troops to help Britain.

Aetius subsequently clashed with Ricimer, commander-in-chief of the Roman armies in the West and the power behind a series of puppet emperors. Ricimer was of royal German descent. As imperial rule gradually collapsed, Aetius established himself as ruler (king?) of an area of northern Gaul. He was succeeded by his son Syagrius. Another German, Odovacer, emerged as king of Rome and effectively abolished the western Roman empire in 476. He sent the imperial regalia to the Emperor Zeno in Constantinople, saying it was no longer required. Syagrius ruled in Gaul until 486 AD when he was defeated by Clovis, king of the Franks. In 507 Clovis converted to Christianity and was recognised by the Byzantine emperor. That set in train the emergence of the Franks as rulers of France, and Charlemagne's crowning as Holy Roman Emperor in 800. All this has little direct bearing on events in Britain. But it does explain why there was no-one else to turn to after the appeal to Aetius was turned down.

We don't know Vortigern's real name. 'Vortigern' means 'overking' or similar. There is some reason to believe that he was a Pelagian, but the whole issue of the Pelagian Heresy dominates accounts of the mid-fifth century to the point where we know little of practical value. It is an example of early church history dominating the search for what actually happened. Vortigern fought the Jutes at Aylesford. He had a son, Vortimer, of whom we know little and who did not succeed him for long. Vortigern is reported to have feared Ambrosius Aurelianus, who seems to have taken over from him as the overall leader of the Romano-British in the later fifth century.

Ambrosius seems to have been of noble parentage, which would have been rare in Britain by then. That would have given him considerable legitimacy. He also seems to have been an effective leader. Welsh epic poetry still celebrated his life and deeds many centuries later. He seems to have been responsible for settling Saxons on the Essex-Suffolk border and in northern Sussex, as witnessed by 'ambros' place names. As far as we can tell he was the leader of some, most, or perhaps all the Romano-British in the mid to late fifth century. He was, in some way, succeeded by Arthur.

Many Romano-Britons seem to have fled Britain to the Roman province of Armorica. That is why it is called 'Brittany' today. The migration appears to have started in the 450s AD. There is a historical mention of a British leader called Riothamus active in Gaul in the 460s. He might have been one of those who had moved to Armorica. He may have died in Burgundy, near the Roman town of *Aballo,* modern Avallon. That may be the origin of the myths which describe Arthur dying 'on the Isle of Avalon'. There may have been several waves of British migration to Brittany, well into the sixth century. Many place names in modern Brittany reflect British origins. Several semi-mythical early Breton saints seem to have had British origins. The Breton language shows many similarities to Cornish, but that may simply be because both are effectively remnants of Celtic. Perhaps more importantly, stories of Arthur appeared in later medieval French sources, having originated in Brittany. They seem to have been exploited by Plantagenet propagandists in order to legitimise what was, in effect, rule by Frenchmen over England.

History tells us that the Romans found a people called the *Iceni* in what is now East Anglia. It tells us that the Iceni revolted under Boudicca, their queen, in about 61 AD. They were suppressed. Archaeology tells us that the Romans built them a town as their tribal and regional capitol, called *Venta Icenorum* ('the market of the *Iceni*'). It was walled. Surprisingly, two Saxon cemeteries have been found near the site of *Venta*. Remains in the later cemetery show some fusion of Anglian and Saxon styles. Archaeology has detected military activity in *Venta*. Interestingly, it suggests not late-Roman imperial troops from the fourth century, but *foederati* from the fifth. *Venta* was completely deserted in the later fifth or sixth centuries, although the walls are more or less intact today. They are just outside the village of Caistor St Edmund, near Norwich. Human remains suggest that the town may have been attacked. We know that the two Saxon Shore forts in Norfolk, Brancaster and Burgh Castle, had housed Roman cavalry units. The two units were the *Equites Dalmatarum* and the *Equites Stablesianorum*. We know that there were Anglians in East Anglia in the early fifth century. We know little more than that.

It is tempting to think that those two *alae* were withdrawn, perhaps sometime after 410 AD or so, and that Anglian *foederati* were settled to cover that area of coast. That may have happened. There are two collections of '-ings' in East Anglia. The first, of about 11 places with names ending in '-ing' or '-ings', lies mostly just north of the valley of the River Waveney. The Waveney flows east to the North Sea. It rises in the same boggy area from which the Little Ouse river flows west, eventually draining through the Fens into the Wash. The Waveney valley is effectively the heartland of East Anglia. Today there are very few dairy farms in East Anglia. Two of them lie in the Waveney valley. It is rich meadowland. The rest of East Anglia is mostly arable. The Waveney valley was occupied by Anglians by the early- to mid-fifth century.

Whether *foederati* or raiders, those Anglians soon caused trouble. The Romano-British built a chain of dykes – defensive earthworks – to the west to keep the Anglians contained. Those earthworks (called Bunn's Bank, the Devil's Ditch and The Grundle) lie on a shallow crescent from near Attleborough in the north to near Stanton further south. From the bottom of the ditch to the top of the bank they were at least 12 feet high. Detailed reconnaissance and map analysis suggests that they linked a series of shallow, marshy valleys, and that they faced east. That is, they were built by the Romano-British to keep the Anglians in.

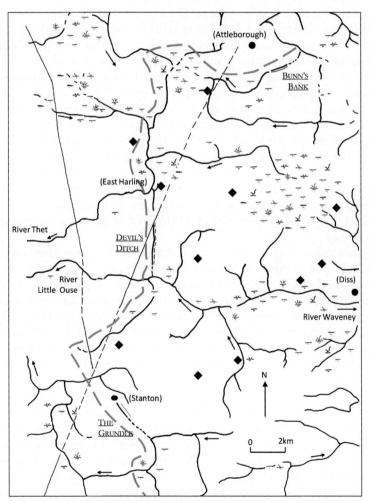

Figure 4.3 Dykes in Central East Anglia.

On Figure 4.3, the general course of the line of streams, marsh and earthworks which enclosed the Anglians in or near the Waveney Valley is shown as a grey dashed line. When those dykes were built, or how long they were kept in use, we cannot tell. The second group of '–ings', about seven of them, lie about 15 miles further north, just west of the River Wensum and clustered around modern Dereham. Swaffham, 'the settlement of the Swabians' lies a few miles west. It is in a very odd place. Most old towns or villages in Norfolk lie along river valleys. Occasionally they are tucked into a fold in the (low) hills, just above a stream. Unusually, Swaffham is on top of a hill (an unnamed 70m ring contour) and not near any stream. It is within a couple of miles of three Roman roads. That suggests that it was a military settlement sited to keep watch over the Anglians in the '-ings' a few miles further east.

There was some trouble here, witnessed by a couple of short dykes facing west (the Launditch, and the Panworth Ditch near Ashill). These were relatively small: not much more than six or seven feet high. Both appear to cut across spurs of dry land, with what were probably marshy streams to the north and south. The Launditch cut a Roman road. About three miles to the north west, at Spong Hill, is the site of the largest early Anglo-Saxon cemetery ever found. 2,259 cremations have been identified. Burial activity started well before the middle of the fifth century. We can be reasonably sure that these Anglian settlers were initially peaceful, given the orientation of Bunn's Bank, which lies to the south and faces almost due south. However, trouble did break out. The northern group of Anglians built dykes (the Launditch and Panworth Ditch) to defend themselves from the Romano-British (and perhaps their Swabian *Foederati*). At a theatre level, however, the Romano-British had a problem. They now had a second group of hostile Anglians behind their initial line of earthworks. (The first group of '-ings' is not shown on Figure 4.4 for clarity.)

The Romano-British built another series of dykes further west. They can be traced over about 15 miles from near Marham (close to Swaffham) to near Brandon. The dykes ran from the valley of the River Nar in the north down to the marshy valley of the River Wissey, and then on to the valley of the Little Ouse. They were originally at least nine feet high. They also face east. The sections are called the Devil's Dyke and the Fossditch. What happens further south is not obvious. There is a further section roughly half a mile long, about 10 miles to the south east near Ampton. It is not obvious which way it faces, so it is not obvious whether it is related to the Marham-Brandon section or not.

In order to understand what happened further south, we need to look at the geography of southern Suffolk and northern Essex. The rivers Lark and Kennet flow north and west. The Colne, Stour, Brett, Gipping and Deben flow south and east. The headwaters of those seven rivers form a network of interlinked streams across an area which runs more or less east-west. Historically the county boundary has run along the Stour.

When the Germanic settlers started to name places, some areas were heavily wooded. '-Leigh', '-lea' and particularly '-ley' place names are quite common, but more common in some areas than others. Woodland place names such as 'Ardleigh'

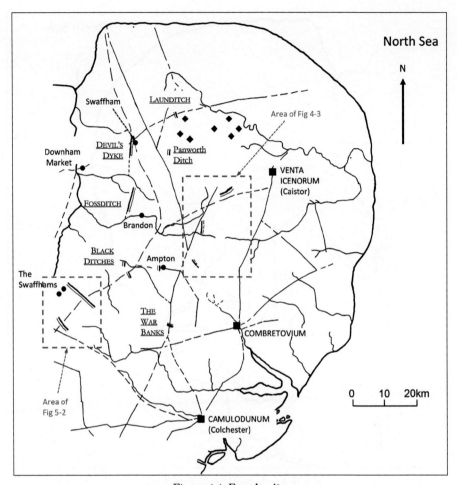

Figure 4.4 East Anglia.

(where my great-grandfather mustered his troop of the Essex Yeomanry for war in August 1914), 'Mistley' (where one of my aunts had a small farm) and 'Hadleigh' are common. The whole area is a patchwork of old, irregular mixed woods which is typical of old forest broken up over centuries of woodland clearance. West Essex was generally more heavily wooded than the rest of the area. There are fords roughly every five or six miles on the major rivers. Most of the fords were not close to wooded areas. That implies that the areas near fords had been deforested. There are some inland '-wicks' and '-wickhams'. The biggest concentration is in the headwaters of the rivers, which suggests that some early Germanic arrivals were allowed to settle in moderately remote inland areas.

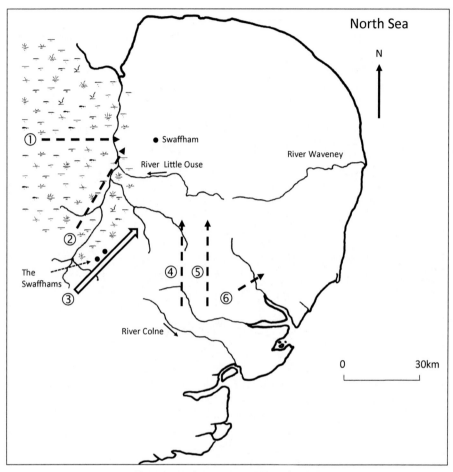

Figure 4.5 Approaches to East Anglia.

'-Ing' place names fall into two main groups. There are a reasonable number in southern Suffolk. They would appear to be Anglian. There are several in western Essex, which appear to be Saxon. There are two more smaller groups, which we will look at later.

The region contains about 30 pairs of settlement that can be identified as 'Great' and 'Little'. 'Great ~' and 'Little Bentley' would be an example. Two pairs are '-ing's. Nine are '-ham's, five are '-ley's, three are '-fords' and two are '-field's. Geographically most pairs are a mile or so apart and typically lie on different streams; often tributaries of the same river. Many were called 'Great' and 'Little' (or equivalent) before Doomsday. The 'Great's tend to have parish churches, the 'Little's do not. Several are among areas of '-leys'. The 'Greats' and 'Littles' identify areas that were gradually cleared for cultivation, by the same groups of people, at some stage after initial place names (such as the -ings, -hams, -leys, -fords and -fields) had emerged.

Hundreds of farms and other small habitations in the area have moats. There are also many moats which are no longer associated with a habitation. Many are quite small, but some enclose areas as much as two or three hundred yards across. Most are moderately narrow: the ditches are rarely more than five yards across. Archaeologists tend to say that they were a medieval fashion statement. That overlooks the fact that their geographical distribution is very specific. Why should Suffolk people living east of the River Fynn (a tributary of the Deben) build moats, when people just across the river did not? Why would people living amongst the headwaters build hundreds of moats, when those a few miles south build almost none?

Virtually none of the 'Greats' and 'Littles' contain moats. That suggests that the period of woodland clearance, indicated above, took place after the moats were built but before the Norman Conquest. So, just as with dykes: who built them? Why did they build them? Why did they build them *there*?

To a Roman or Romano-British commander, there were six good routes in or out of East Anglia. They are numbered '1' to '6' on Figure 4.5 above. Route 1 ran from *Durobrivae*, Water Newton near Peterborough, eastwards across the Fen Causeway to dry land just west of Marham. It was joined near there by another fen route (2) coming up from *Duroliponte*, Cambridge, to the south west. In either case, this approach required crossing fenland to reach dry land near Marham.

Route 3 was the Icknield Way. That was a pre-Roman long-distance route which was not a single track, but a series of alternative paths used depending on the time of year, depth of water in the fords, and so on. It ran from somewhere near the north Norfolk coast down towards Cambridge, then on (just north of the Chilterns) to cross the Thames near Goring. As the Ridgeway, it passed south of Oxford and on to Amesbury. From there, related routes ran on into the West Country. For much of its length, and particularly the section from east of Newmarket (where it crossed the River Kennet) to southwest of Cambridge, it ran on dry chalkland slightly above the fenland. That is the section shown by the broad arrow '3' on Figure 4.5. That route would have been relatively easy to deforest, and skirted south of the Fens. So, although the Icknield Way is shown as a defined path on modern maps, in historic times it represented little more than the use of the belt of chalkland to pass from the Amesbury area into East Anglia (or vice versa). The Romans did not build a road along it, but did use it as part of their transport network.

South east of the Cambridge area was a heavily wooded area which ran south into western Essex. Further east, the Romans built two roads (Routes 4 and 5) north into what is now Suffolk. They branched off an east-west road which ran across to the site of a fort at *Combretovium*, Baylham, just north of Ipswich on the River Gipping (Route 6). That road split: north to *Venta Icenorum*, and northeast towards the coast at the mouth of the River Blyth. These routes cross an area of rivers, streams and relatively few fords.

So, at a theatre level, a Romano-British commander could defend, or attack, along three broad axes. The first was across the Fens, either from Cambridge or Peterborough to the Marham area (Routes 1 and 2). The second, and the only really good approach, was the Icknield Way (Route 3). The third was from the south: either across the Gipping at *Combretovium*, or by either of the two north-south roads (Routes 4, 5 and 6).

At some stage the Romano-British responded to events in East Anglia by engaging two further groups of *foederati*. Unusually, they were south Germans. The Swabian tribes had originally lived outside the Empire, but the great Germanic migration across the Rhine in the first decade of the fifth century carried many Swabians into Gaul. Swabians were deployed, and settled, to cover two of the major routes into (or out of) East Anglia. One group was deployed to cover the eastern end of the Fen Causeway and gave their name to Swaffham in Norfolk (as above). The other was deployed to cover the Icknield Way east of *Duroliponte* (Cambridge). They gave their name to the twin villages of Swaffham Prior and Swaffham Bulbeck, about a mile apart on the edge of the fens in Cambridgeshire (covering Route 3). We should remember that the word 'fen' was not used there until after the Norman Conquest. Before that date the fens were generally uninhabitable.

The Romano-British countered the Anglian threat south from East Anglia (Routes 4, 5 and 6) by organising Saxons into the defences of what is now northern Essex. The area was fought over for several years. The evidence falls into four parts. See Figure 4.6

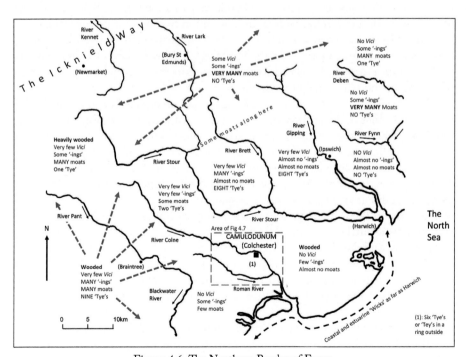

Figure 4.6 The Northern Border of Essex.

The first piece of evidence is the distribution of moats. There are, for example, over a hundred in the area of the headwaters. The second piece of evidence is the Tyes. 29 place names in this region have 'Tye' as the second word. There are also three 'Teys', of which the biggest is Mark's Tey. One Tye is just within Hertfordshire. One is just east of the Deben. Sixteen lie between the Stour and the Gipping. Six lie in a ring around Colchester. Tyes and Teys are very rare outside Essex.

Some of the Tyes are close enough together to relate to the same feature, and one or two can be discounted for other reasons. Detailed analysis shows that almost all are sited on a ring contour (isolated hill) or spur, sited to look in a certain direction. Today most Tyes are either single farms or small hamlets. Most of them look northeast. Isolated hills and exposed spurs are not typical sites for habitation. They are much easier to understand as a series of occupied outposts which form part of a defensive system.

The word 'tye' basically means 'a part' or 'a section', as in a piece of land. In modern German the nearest equivalent is 'teil' (pronounced as in the English word 'tile'), which sounds quite similar. Several of the 'tyes' (and 'Mark's Tey') are compound names which are possessives. In simple terms 'Mark's Tey' does mean something like 'Mark's section'. 'Nedging Tye' means the section belonging to the followers of Hnydda, or similar. So the Tyes and the Teys were inhabited outposts, typically named after the Saxon warriors appointed to command them. 22 of them were sited to defend the border with the Anglians to the north and protect *Camulodunum*. Note that, unlike in Kent, these settlements ('-ings' and Tyes) are not primarily along the line of the roads.

The third piece of place-name evidence is that of four villages: Saxon Street, Saxham Street and Great and Little Saxham. Saxham means 'the settlement of the Saxons'. Saxon Street means 'the road of the Saxons'. That is quite unusual: Anglo-Saxons usually used 'street' to mean a paved road, typically one which the Romans had built. There does not seem to have been Roman roads at Saxon, nor Saxham, Street. So the term seems to mean a road or path that the Saxons used, or where they lived. All four villages are east and a little south of Cambridge.

The fourth piece of evidence is a cluster of place-names which appear to refer to Ambrosius Aurelianus. Of the perhaps a dozen or so places in Britain that meet that bill, three are roughly in a line from Cambridge to Colchester. Taken together, the place-name evidence strongly suggests the deliberate siting of Saxon warriors in a band across the southern edge of East Anglia.

Camulodunum was originally a legionary garrison, the capital of Roman Britain, and then a colony for army pensioners. Even in the late Empire it was probably one of the half dozen most important cities in Britain. *Camulodunum* would have been the regional headquarters for defence against the Anglians. It was occupied in the fifth, sixth and into the seventh centuries. There is a series of dykes around Colchester. They enclose an area of several square miles. Julius Caesar had described earthworks at Colchester, so it is not clear which are pre-Roman and which were first dug (or re-dug) in the Dark Ages. See Figure 4-7.

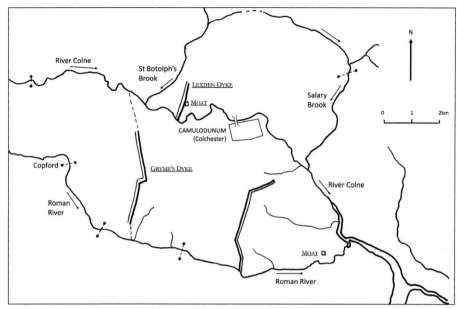

Figure 4.7 The Colchester Area.

We should not see Colchester as a walled town or city. It is, in effect, a pair of fortified islands. The main promontory or 'island' is formed by the River Colne and the Roman River. Below Copford (where the Roman road from London crossed the Roman River) there were just two fords. Below the lowest, the valley was marshy and tidal. A set of rectilinear dykes, facing west, walled off the neck of the promontory. A second dyke, facing east, defended against raiders getting across the marshes. The only moated habitation in this 'island' is right at the east end, overlooking the marshes.

(In passing, place-name experts seem to have almost fallen over backwards to demonstrate that the name 'Roman River' does not mean 'Roman River'.)

A Roman bridge crossed the Colne just north of *Camulodunum*. The area immediately north of the bridge is bounded by two brooks, St Botolph's and Salary Brook. They both rise in the same area and hence enclose an area of five or six square miles. Both brooks flow through relatively narrow and steep-sided valleys, except where St Botolph's Brook flows into the Colne. Another straight dyke closed off that route, and a Roman fort had been built just east of it. The site of the fort became the only moated habitation in the northern 'island'.

The two 'islands' form an area which is unique in the region. There are no 'ing's. There is just one 'ley' and one 'tye'. Both they and three 'wicks' (see below) are sited to look outwards. The two moats are right on the edge of the area. The 'islands' enclose an area that is far too large an area to be explained as infantry fortifications. It suggests (as do some other locations in Britain) that the site was big enough to protect large numbers of grazing horses against raids by Germanic warriors. Cavalry would have given the Romano-British huge advantages, but had to be based somewhere. If that base was vulnerable to raiding, the horses could have been stolen or killed quite easily and the cavalry destroyed as a fighting force. By analogy, there is good evidence that in the 1880s Apache Indians deliberately targeted US Army cavalry horses for similar reasons.

As an aside, the area noth and east of Colchester (between the Colne and the Stour) was initially wooded, has a few '-ings', had no inland 'wicks', virtually no moats (two, in fact), and the one Tye is obviously part of the ring around Colchester. However, it is the pattern of 'Greats' and 'Littles' which provokes interest. There are four pairs, of which three are '-ley's. Unusually, they are much further apart than normal: up to three miles. There are no other substantial settlements between a 'Great' and its corresponding 'Little'. It suggests an extensive period of land clearance in an area with few settlements.

The almost complete absence of moats indicates that the period of moat digging was over before the clearance got underway. The moats were not 'medieval'. They were Dark Age. Furthermore, those three pairs of '-ley's, and two more nearby, show a radial pattern spreading outwards from Colchester. *Camulodunum* remained a significant place.

Putting the evidence together, the operational picture in the late fifth or early sixth century was as follows. Angles had settled as far south as the headwaters. Saxons had settled in west Essex, but had then been organised by Romano-British commanders to defend against the Angles. The southerly rivers ran generally south-east, and there were fairly few fords. Not surprisingly, the Tyes in the north were generally sited to look north east. They are often sited on high ground above a named ford. Further west, the land was more heavily wooded. Angles could raid through the woods southwards into much of west Essex. Tyes there generally look northwards. The Saxons responded by building moats around their farmsteads.

Cavalry based in *Camulodunum*, linked to a border defence force of Saxon *laeti* (or similar), would have been a serious threat to the Anglians. The cavalry could pick their way around the rivers (or perhaps use an unguarded ford) to attack into southern Suffolk. The Anglians responded by building moats around hundreds of their farmsteads in the area of the headwaters; and in lesser numbers further north. The northern group of Tyes served as outposts for the Romano-British. Large groups of Anglian raiders would have caused the Saxons to 'call for the cavalry', who could typically have been on the scene from Colchester in a few hours. Using Roman roads, however, the cavalry could have been as far away as Cambridge (*Duroliponte*) in about a day, and in the Peterborough region (say *Durorbrivae*) in about two. A large raid might have prompted a call for reinforcement from further afield: perhaps Lincoln, York or London. But it might also have prompted a theatre-level counterattack. With many of the Anglian warriors fighting along the border and being held up by the Saxons, a bold cavalry commander could take his troopers across to the Icknield Way, ride into the Anglian heartlands, and burn villages with impunity. Doing that even once would give the Anglians a major lesson which they would not wish to repeat. Unsurprisingly, the Roman road to Great Chesterford was blocked by a dyke just north of Saffron Walden. It faces southeast. The Angles dug it to prevent the Romano-British using that road. Interestingly Saffron Walden was once 'Great (actually *Magna*') Walden' to differentiate it from the nearby Little Walden. ('Walden' is 'the valley where the Welsh live'.)

One Roman road (Route 6) crossed the Gipping at *Combretovium*. Of the two roads running north (Routes 4 and 5), the Romano-British built earthworks across one near Shimpling (where my mother once lived). Little trace of them (the War Banks) remain today. They may have been twelve feet high from the bottom of the ditch to the top of the bank. They shows obvious signs of being laid out by a trained engineer: they ran in straight lines with obvious and quite sharp angles. They faced north. Just west of Baylham, in Ditch Wood, an earthwork faces east. It would prevent Anglians crossing the Gipping near *Combretovium* from advancing further south west. The area is over-watched by two Tyes within a mile or so. More generally, however, the Roman roads in this area went almost entirely out of use. Very little of any of them is in use today. In only a few places are they even marked by field boundaries, or similar. It seems that the Essex-Suffolk border was a frontier for a long time.

At some stage one particular group of Anglians came to prominence in south-eastern Suffolk. The area around Ipswich was the homeland of the dynasty which came to rule East Anglia: the Wuffings. That may explain why the Sutton Hoo burial site overlooks the River Deben. The Wuffings may have won some territory from the East Saxons. It is not obvious whether the group of 10 '-ings' between the Stour and the Brett were Saxon or Anglian. If Anglian, were they early settlers? Did they arrive with the Wuffings? The border between Essex and Suffolk ran along the River Stour. However, we have no idea when that boundary was fixed.

Twenty-two of the 35 or so Tyes and Teys lie around Colchester or further north. The remainder are typically in west Essex and look north.

Essex is a low-lying coastal region, much of which was only drained in the late nineteenth century. Numerous rivers and creeks flowed out of the marshes to the sea. Just over a dozen are large enough to take a seagoing Dark Age ship. Fifteen have an '-ing' sited on a low ridge overlooking the water. In addition the name of the village of Canewdon, sited to look north over the River Crouch means 'the hill of Canna's people'. Harwich, on the tip of the Stour estuary, means 'army camp'. Earthworks, which seem to have been defensive fortifications, were visible at Harwich until the eighteenth century. The estuary of the River Colne leading to Colchester is over-looked by Fingringhoe, which probably means 'the hill of the people who live on the finger of land'. That finger lies in the 'island' between the Colne and the Roman River. Two Tyes overlook the marshes near Greys Thurrock on the Thames Estuary, and the last Tye is an '-ing tye', which overlooks a creek. So the 20 largest rivers and creeks in Essex all had a settlement (an '-ing' or similar) located to watch over them.

In addition, there are more than 46 '-wick's (not 'wich's) in Essex. That is far more than any other county. They are almost all very small today; typically a hamlet or just a farm (my uncle farmed one of them for over 50 years). The great majority lie near to the coast or within a mile of a tidal river. There is a group of eight just west of Clacton, of which six are coastal or estuarine. Many of them are near, or between, coastal '-ing' villages. They seem to have been smaller than those '-ings'. Perhaps they were originally just one settler and his household. The coastal '-ings', together with the '-wicks', would have formed a network for observation and perhaps protection against seagoing raids: a return to the original function of the Saxon Shore. We should probably also include Ipswich, which (as described above) is now in Suffolk. There are incredibly few '-wiches' in Essex. Were it not for the highly distinctive way in which '-wick's are distributed, we might simply think that '-wick' is an East Saxon variant of '-wich'. However, it is surely no coincidence that almost all of the 46 '-wicks' in Essex are sited on or near the coast. Just 9 are well inland. (The coastal '-wicks' are not shown on Figures 4-6 and 4-7 for clarity.)

Therefore practically every sizeable creek in Essex had an '-ing' (or similar) sited to overlook it. A chain of '-wicks' gave observation along the coast and the major inlets. Well over half the 'Tyes' or 'Teys' in Britain are sited along the Essex-Suffolk border. Others protect settlements in west Essex. In addition to the three 'ambros-' place names along the Suffolk border, there are four more along the roads from London; but only one more, in Kent, within fifty miles. The East Saxons appear to have been organised and settled to defend what is now Essex and the eastern approaches to London in a very deliberate and thorough way. They were, at least for a time, supported by a force of cavalry based in the Colchester 'Islands'. By comparison, for example, there are only two '-wicks' along the coast in Suffolk and none in Norfolk. That is scarcely a coincidence.

We know something of the dates of the arrival and revolt of the Jutes in Kent. In contrast, all we really know about dates for the Anglians in Norfolk and Suffolk, and the Saxons in Essex, is by association with 'Ambros-' place names; hence perhaps the 460s to the 490s AD. It was at about this time that Arthur appears. His name, and even, existence is shrouded in myth and legend.

5

Revolt on The Saxon Shore

There is no archaeological evidence for Arthur: none. The historical traces are few, much later, and clearly highly garbled. One historian put it that 'only a romantic novelist would seek to find the real Arthur'. That has not stopped many writers trying. More than 30 books about Arthur have been published in Britain over the last 30 years. Gildas did not mention Arthur at all, but the oldest copy of Gildas we have was made 300 years after Gildas' (and Arthur's) death. Mention of Arthur might have been removed. Welsh sources pre-date the Norman Conquest, but were not written down for centuries after the events they describe. Geoffrey of Monmouth wrote about Arthur at length, but only in 1136 AD. His account is garbled in many ways and is taken from several different sources. It does, however, have one or two intriguing aspects. The Archbishop of London, discussed below, is one. Thomas Malory's famous 'Morte D'Arthur' was written in the 15th century.

The first mention of Arthur as a king is from 1191 AD, when monks at Glastonbury Abbey miraculously found what appeared to be his tomb. The Plantagenets had ruled England from 1154. Finding evidence of Arthur would have been extremely convenient for the Plantagenets and therefore, presumably, also for the Abbot of Glastonbury. The first mention of Camelot is in the work of Chrétien of Troyes, also from the 12th century. The early historical and literary sources mention Arthur and his contemporaries visiting places known to have been Roman cities, such as London, York, Lincoln, Canterbury, Winchester, Chester and Gloucester. They are spelt either in the Latin or, more commonly, the language of the day. The principal exception is Camelot. Why would a Frenchman from east of Paris associate Arthur with a place called Camelot, which did not exist when he wrote it? The explanation is quite simple. Camelot is a corruption of *Camulodunum*, but Chrétien of Troyes would not know (and would have no way of knowing) that *Camulodunum* had become Colchester. The 'Camelod' or 'Camelot' that he had heard of, or seen written down, was actually Colchester. Maps would not become common until well after Chrétien of Troyes's time. Contemporary spellings of Camelot start with a 'k', which suggests that the name came to him from Breton sources.

Well-intentioned speculation them made a simple error worse. Where was Camelot? John Leland, who lived from 1503 to 1552 AD, wrote that Camelot was South Cadbury in Somerset. Leland's information was based on folklore, and the fact that two nearby villages are named for the River Camel. The rest is history; but poor history.

There does, however, seem to be some basis for the existence of Arthur as a war leader. The evidence points to him being a highly effective commander who dealt the Anglo-Saxons a major shock at the battle of Badon in perhaps 509 AD. The shock was so great so that they were largely peaceful for a couple of decades after he died at, or as a result of, the battle of Camlann in 519 or so. His death created a power vacuum. With no apparent successor to Arthur, some of the Anglo-Saxon kingdoms established themselves over the following decade.

Arthur was a major war leader. He is described as fighting 12 battles, but we cannot be sure where any of them took place. 12 battles would today place him in the same league as a major commander who fought in both World Wars: Patton, Rommel, Montgomery or Slim perhaps. The early battles might have been fought when Arthur was quite young, and only the later ones as a senior commander. There is little direct evidence that he had cavalry, but the early Welsh poems and what we know of the later Pennine kingdoms suggest that he did. So does the survival of a dragon as the national symbol of Wales. The early sources tend to describe Arthur as having a larger force than his enemies. That is unusual; epic sources usually stress how their hero wins despite being outnumbered. If Arthur generally did have more troops available on a given day of battle, that may represent better organisation and discipline (as well as bigger numbers overall). In today's terms, the roads may have been a force multiplier.

Arthur's wife merits some discussion. 'Guinevere' is a French name and probably reflects the French origin of many of the Arthurian sources. There was a Saint Genevieve. She was Frankish, and lived about half a century before Arthur. Chrétien of Troyes may have confused the two, accidentally or otherwise. Both St Genevieve and Lupus of Troyes were associated with Attila the Hun's invasion of 451 AD. Genevieve had met St Germanus in 429 AD. Lupus visited Britain with Germanus that year, and Genevieve escaped from Paris to Troyes at the time of Childeric's siege of 464. We can assume that Chretien (of Troyes) was fairly familiar with the history of St Genevieve. 'Genevieve' and 'Guinevere' are effectively the same name. Both are variants of the Celtic name 'Gwenhayfor' (or similar), meaning 'pure and yielding' or perhaps 'white wave', as in 'blond-haired'. So Arthur's wife had a British name which comes down to us today as 'Gwyneth', or similar. Another clue is tantalising. The legendary Lady of Shalott was reputedly Guinevere's sister. An early version of her name was 'Elaine of Astolat'. That leads us to Astol. 'Astol' is phonetically the closest place name in England today to 'Shalott', 'Astolat' or other versions such as 'Ascolat'. Astol is a farm in Shropshire. It is within half a mile of a Roman road that leads to *Viroconium Cornoviorum*, Wroxeter, the 4th-largest city in Roman Britain, about 15 miles away. We know of at least nine Roman villas in the area of Wroxeter. Perhaps Guinevere's family came from what is now Shropshire.

The Battle of Badon was highly significant. After Badon the early Anglo-Saxons stayed in their enclaves for 20 years or so. Much ink has been spilt over the location of Badon. Most writers assume it was Bath. That is simply a confusion of medieval mis-copying and poor toponymy. One version of the Welsh Chronicle describes the battle taking place at 'Badon, that is Bath'. Lo! A legend was born. The text 'that is Bath' was added centuries after the original, and does not appear in the oldest copies. The Romans called Bath *'Aquae Sulis'*, which is how Gildas would have described it. 'Bath' is a Germanic word which Gildas would not have known. It seems more likely that 'Badon' is the transliteration of a different Germanic word which Gildas would not have known or understood. The most likely contender is 'Barton'. In Old English it would sound something like 'Beerton' or 'Bearton.'

There are hundreds of modern Bartons, but they only exist in a few counties. The most likely contenders, given the date of the battle, are on the edges of Germanic enclaves. That narrows it down to two main contenders: Great Barton, east of Bury St Edmunds in Suffolk, or Barton just west of Cambridge. After a protracted fight, which may have continued for three days, Arthur slaughtered over 900 of the enemy: apparently single-handed. It probably wasn't single-handed and the number appears differently in different versions of the Welsh Annals. A figure described as 900 or so deaths implies a massacre on a catastrophic scale for, say, the East Anglians. It would left many villages almost completely without men folk. It seems reasonable to conclude that Arthur fought 'for a long time' and 'a lot of the enemy' died.

Of those two possible locations, Great Barton is well inside East Anglia proper and would have been reached up the Icknield Way. Badon is described as the siege of a hill or mountain in Gildas, but not the Welsh Chronicles. Great Barton is on a very slight rise and is within a mile or so of a Roman road. Intriguingly, however, the church in the only village in England which contains the name of Saint Genevieve lies about two miles west, at Fornham St Genevieve. The church is named for St Genevieve in the Dooomsday book. The connection is tenuous. The saint lived about a generation before Arthur. The Anglians seem to have memorialised the name of the wife of the man who defeated them so badly. However, St Genevieve's name was not associated with Arthur's wife in writing until the 12th century. Barton near Cambridge may be a much better contender for the site of the battlefield. Haslingfield, a *Saxon* village, lies just over a mile south. Comberton, 'the village of the British', is about a mile west. Barton lies in the bottom of a valley on a Roman road.

That road drops, from Fox Hill about three miles to the south west, down into a wide but fairly deep valley overlooked from both the north and the south. Did Arthur catch a large Anglian raiding party on the road with his cavalry? The valley would have been marshy. Although it is above the 10 metre contour, most of it is below the 20 metre line. It is very flat-bottomed and several streams cross it. The road would not reach reliably dry ground until Cambridge, almost three miles north east of Barton. Exploiting their superior mobility, cavalry could have trapped an Anglian warband either on the lower section of the road, or with their backs to it. The Anglians may have been trying to withdraw along the road with their booty but were cut off by a detachment of cavalry, who had perhaps used the Cambridge-Huntingdon road to get behind them. There are a couple of very slight hills in the area. The warband might have made for one of them, and become surrounded by the cavalry. Arthur could then have summoned reinforcements; perhaps from Colchester, Lincoln, London, or even York. Cavalry from any or all of those places could have arrived in three days. A massacre on such a scale may have been what motivated the Anglians to start, or continue, to build a massive series of earthworks on the line of the Icknield Way.

In some ways Arthur's last battle, at Camlann, is even more intriguing. It took place a decade or two after Badon. Camlann may mean 'the crooked river', or it may mean 'the meadows by the river Cam.' If the latter, then it may also have taken place near Cambridge. However, since 'Cam' simply means 'river', there are several rivers which might be identified as the site. Geoffrey of Monmouth describes Camlann as the place where Arthur fought Mordred, the traitor who had had an adulterous affair with Guinevere. We shall return to that idea later.

East Anglia's border with Essex was thoroughly defended. However, Anglians had expanded south west along the Icknield Way towards the Roman towns of *Duroliponte* (Cambridge) and Great Chesterford. There were Saxons at the Saxhams and Saxon Street, and at Haslingfield ('the open land of the Haeslingas') about five miles south west of Cambridge. See Figure 5.1.At some stage there were *Suevi* (Swabians) at Swaffham Prior and Swaffham Bulbeck. It was obviously an area of conflict, both locally and regionally. At one stage the Anglians defended the line of the River Lark. The Fens appear to have been impassable below the 10m contour or so, so Lackford (about five miles north west of Bury St Edmunds) may have been the lowest ford over the Lark on the Icknield Way. An earthwork ran north and south along a stream about a mile and a half west of Lackford. It is still visible in two sections called the Black Ditches. One is just south west of Icklingham, the other half a mile south east of Cavenham. It is still up to six feet high in total. It faced west and would have denied the use of the ford to the Romano-British.

The Anglians advanced southwest along the Icknield way, almost as far as Royston. As we have seen, the Icknield Way was not one single route. In summer, the shortest route around the edge of the fen would have been along the water's edge. There are short dykes at two of the three streams closest to the Lark, at Landwade and Badlington. Like the dyke at Icklingham, they are relatively close to their respective streams and face west. So it seems that the Anglians, in the first half of the fifth century, tried to deny the use of those crossings as they slowly expanded westwards from the Lark. We shall look at the dating in a little more detail later.

What happened next, over a period of at least 20 years, is possibly one of the most fascinating episodes of warfare (and particularly fortification) that has ever taken place in Britain. Something highly significant, such as a disaster on the scale of the Battle of Badon, made them dig in to prevent it ever happening again.

Just outside modern-day Royston the Anglians may have found a series of ancient earthworks dating from before the Romans. Those dykes cut the Icknield Way from marsh or swamp in the north to woodland in the south. There were three ditches

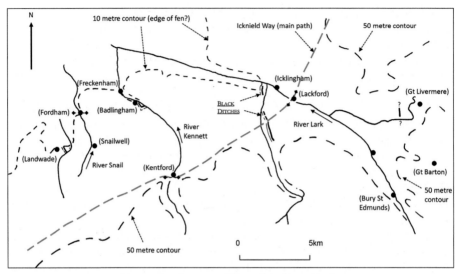

Figure 5.1 Crossings West of the River Lark.

about five to eight yards apart, up to about four feet deep. The banks would have been up to four feet high. They seem to have faced south west. The first two were fairly sinuous, but the third was fairly straight. A horse jawbone dating from about 2000 BC was found in one. They silted up very slowly, from the Roman to the late-medieval periods, so they were not in use as fortifications in the Dark Ages. They were called the Mile Ditches. Antiquarians wrote of them, but practically no trace of them is visible today. They have been excavated by archaeologists.

We don't know whether or not the Anglians knew of the Mile Ditches. However, they built a major earthwork of their own across the Icknield Way about five miles further east. It ran from woodland to the south northwards to the lake called the Fowlmere, which drains into the Fens. It was about two miles long. Today it is known as the Bran Ditch. Little trace of it remains.

The Bran Ditch was the first of an astonishing series of four major fortifications. They were built over a period of years. They got successively bigger. Each was built further east than its predecessor, so the furthest east is the newest. They are respectively the Bran Ditch, the Brent Ditch, the Fleam Dyke and the Devil's Ditch. They are astonishing not just for their massive scale (the Devil's Ditch was over forty feet high) but the fact that they represent huge amounts of labour over several years.

They were sited and planned by highly skilled engineers. Their profile, their alignment and their siting all show very sophisticated features. The sequence shows that their engineers clearly carried forward lessons from one dyke to another. They were planned and laid out by surveyors who measured in Roman feet. We don't know who those engineers were, but we know that the dykes probably date from the fifth and early sixth centuries. They face west-south-west. Their primary purpose was not tactical, but operational. They close the Icknield Way 'avenue' into East Anglia.

Figure 5.2 shows the general area. It assumes that land below the 10m contour was fenland. The fact that all four dykes end on the 10m contour, and that only land below the 10m contour is named 'fen' on Ordnance Survey maps, tend to support that. It also assumes that the land to the south east (which is generally higher than the chalkland) was heavily wooded. The roads shown are numbered according to Ivan Margary's classic 1957 survey of Roman roads. The M24 (Worsted Street) runs along a chalk ridge parallel with the River Granta. It runs south east to Haverhill and thence on towards Colchester. The M23a runs up to Cambridge from the south west. The M21b runs broadly parallel with it, but about 10 miles south. It passes through Great Chesterford and joins Worsted Street. A secondary road, the M300, runs in from the south east (generally parallel with Worsted Street) and meets the M21b at Great Chesterford. Importantly, no other Roman road ran north into East Anglia until the road past Shimpling, about 20 miles further east.

All four dykes had ditches with flat bottoms and sides that sloped at slightly more than 45 degrees. Bran Ditch was about six and a half feet deep. The bottom of the ditch was about seven and a half feet wide. The bank would have been about 10 feet

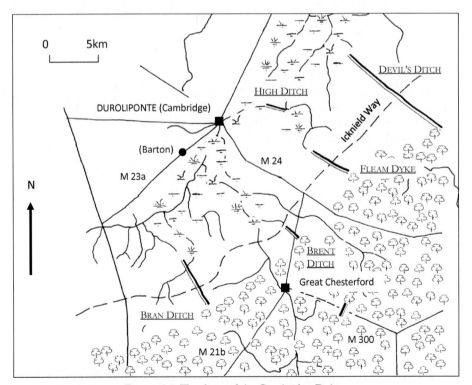

Figure 5.2 The Area of the Cambridge Dykes.

high. Brent Ditch was a foot and half deeper and the bottom of the ditch about a foot wider. Fleam Dyke was much deeper: six feet deeper, in fact. Its bank would have been about three feet higher as well. The Devil's Ditch was, by comparison, massive. It was only about two feet deeper, but it was much wider. The bottom of its bank was about 23 feet wide (thus more than twice as wide as the Fleam Dyke). Its bank would have been a staggering 27 feet high and the total height, from bottom of the ditch to the top of the bank, 45 feet. Even today it is up to 34 feet high in places. Figure 5.3 shows the profiles of the four dykes, superimposed for comparison and to scale.

The warrior figure is drawn to a scale height of five feet, seven inches. The dykes are all very carefully aligned to place them on subtle and gentle reverse slopes, about a quarter to half a mile back from a crest. Few of those crests are more than 15 metres (about 50 feet) higher than the ground at the site of the dykes. Such siting is quite an achievement, given the nature of the ground. Even at the height of the Cold War, when we went to great lengths to find reverse slopes for defensive positions on the rolling North German Plain, we would have been hard pressed to site as well as those Dark Age surveyors did. When I described their siting to a colleague (a former

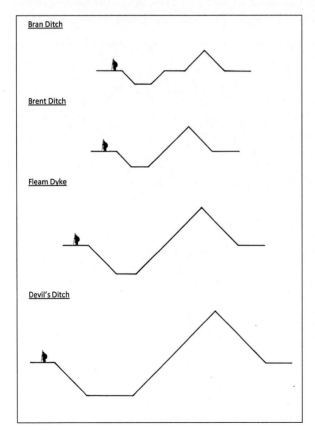

Bran Ditch

Brent Ditch

Fleam Dyke

Devil's Ditch

Figure 5.3 The Profiles of the Cambridge Dykes.

lieutenant colonel in the Royal Artillery, and for many years a 'Cold Warrior' like me), he suggested that nobody who wasn't a soldier would even have noticed. He kindly suggested that in fact only an infantry officer (such as I had been) would have noticed. His remarks were most kind, but prompted me to go and re-check in detail, both on the map and on the ground. I did.

The price of being sited on reverse slopes is that the dykes are not dead straight, nor as short as they could be. Bran Ditch and the Devil's Ditch could both be about a quarter of a mile shorter if aligned solely to minimise their length. Why they are on reverse slopes is not obvious. The reverse slopes are so gentle that there is no risk of anyone on the (home) bank being overlooked by anyone within bowshot on the enemy side. Similarly, all of their banks would have concealed soldiers on foot immediately behind them. In the case of the bigger ditches, they would have hidden soldiers some distance behind them. The dykes would, however, not be visible *at all* unless the enemy came within about a quarter or a half a mile. That may have concealed their construction from prying eyes: after all, each of them would have taken several months to build. Alternatively the reverse slope may have been intended for psychological effect: the enemy would march up to a crest and find an earthwork stretching right across their front, from fen to forest. I do not know why they were sited on reverse slopes. But they were.

So much for their profile and their alignment. Their locations tell us a lot about why they were built where they were, and what happened (see Figure 5.2).

Bran Ditch is not particularly big, although big enough to form a credible obstacle to anyone coming up the Icknield Way. That, however, is its weakness. It could be, and it probably was, outflanked by an advance up the M21b through Great Chesterford. It would be relatively simple for the Romano-British to make a demonstration up the Icknield Way in order to lure the Anglians to man the dyke. The attackers could then move rapidly up the M21b and outflank the defenders. They could then either attack them in the rear, or bypass them and raid and burn their villages. That would be particularly easy if the Romano-British had cavalry. The M21b could be blocked with a detachment of defenders, but ensuring that it was blocked would be difficult without radio communications.

In Chapter Five we saw that the road that we now identify as M300 was blocked with a dyke, at Grimsditch Wood. It is possible that M21b was also blocked with a dyke, which we cannot identify. The M21b largely went out use, unlike the M23a to its north. But the general truth remains: the Bran Ditch could be outflanked fairly easily.

The Anglians' response was to dig another ditch, the Brent Ditch, slightly bigger but further back. Siting it north east of Great Chesterford and tying its northern end on a tributary of the River Cam meant that it could be quite short. It was only about two miles long. That tributary is crossed by a branch of the Icknield way which was only usable in the summer, at a ford. There are two more fords lower down the Cam before Cambridge. *Duroliponte*, Roman Cambridge, was on the north side of the Cam and there was a Roman bridge there. Those crossings could also be defended by small numbers of men. Lying northeast of Great Chesterford, the Brent Ditch also prevented any attack by way of both the M21b and the M300.

However, the Romano-British do seem to have had cavalry. Not least, the berm on the Bran Ditch was deleted from the design of the Brent Ditch. The berm would have made it easier for cavalry to cross. The Brent Ditch position was defeated, probably by outflanking and probably by cavalry. We can be confident that it was outflanked because the next position, the Fleam Dyke, was built about four or five miles further back in a position where it could not be outflanked. We can be confident that the Bran Ditch was outflanked by cavalry because the profile of the Fleam dyke was very much taller. The Brent Ditch had a total height of just under 19 feet; the Fleam Dyke about 29 feet. 19 feet is more than enough to resist infantry. There is no credible reason why a skilled engineer would build a higher dyke if the problem was just infantry. 19 feet is more than three times the height of an average man.

Anybody can walk up a 45 degree slope, given time and with nobody at the top trying to kill him. That applies to a 45 degree slope of almost any length. Cavalry, however, would have great difficulty climbing a 45 degree slope, if mounted. The longer the slope, the harder that would be. It is, however, quite conceivable that a cavalry force could dismount and lead their horses up the 45 degree slope of a linear earthwork; if no-one at the top was trying to kill them. Not least, the great height of the Fleam Dyke may have been designed to deter Romano-British cavalry from even trying to cross it.

The Brent Ditch was probably outflanked by a combination of a demonstration (a 'show of force') and superior, mounted mobility. Once a few cavalry had broken through, the defenders would be in a desperate position. They were outflanked and could be attacked from behind. Remember the battle scene from 'Gladiator'. The Fleam Dyke could not be outflanked.

The Fleam Dyke did, however, have a weakness. It was in two sections. The shorter, northern section is known as High Ditch. It lies north east of the Fulbourn Fen, which the Little Wilbraham River and Caudle Ditch flow through. The longer, southern section is separated from it by almost two miles in a straight line, or three miles around the edge of the fen. Three miles takes about an hour on foot; certainly not less than forty minutes for a formed body of men. One group of Romano-British cavalry made a demonstration against the southern section whilst another group galloped up to the northern section, dismounted and led their horses over. Or it may have been the other way around. Either way, the Anglians would once again be in a very unpleasant position.

There is another suitable position about two and a half miles behind the Fleam Dyke, but detailed analysis suggests that the site actually chosen for the Devil's Ditch (about two miles behind that) is even better. It could not be outflanked. It was in one continuous section. The engineer decided that even more height was needed to make it even more difficult for cavalry to cross. He needed more height in total, but every foot dug down meant that more and more earth had to be carried higher and higher up. His solution was to dig the Devil's Ditch only slightly deeper, but considerably wider. We have no reason to believe that it didn't work.

The Cambridge Dykes are the source of considerable mystery. It is clear that the archaeologists, who have studied them in great and meticulous detail, have a very good picture of *how* they were dug, but not *why*. They have been variously dated to a broad period from the late fourth to the early seventh centuries. Even the highly technical processes used cannot, however, date them more closely than that. It requires analysis of tactical, operational and strategic context to suggest when they were built; by who; and against which enemies.

On only two occasions researching for this book a cold chill has run down my spine. One of them was late one evening after I had been analysing the dimensions of the dykes. I had been working with data in metres. I had checked with one of the archaeologists, and knew that the original measurements were taken in a mixture of feet and inches (until the year 1960 or so) and Metric units. The original Imperial measurements had subsequently been converted to Metric. However, I knew that Roman engineers used feet and inches. Roman feet and inches were not identical to Imperial ones, but the difference is small (a Roman foot was almost exactly 1% bigger than an Imperial foot, but engineers generally do not build earthworks to that sort of accuracy). I converted the metric data to Imperial. That is when the cold chill ran down my spine. *Several of the measurements were almost exact multiples of feet.* But then I calculated that the correlation is *even closer* in Roman feet.

The Bran Ditch was, on average, six feet six inches deep. Its floor was seven feet six inches wide. The Brent Ditch was eight feet deep. The Fleam Dyke was, on average, 14 feet deep: to within one third of an inch. When the engineers calculated the theoretical height of the bank of the Bran Ditch, it would have been nine feet, six inches high: to within about a half of an inch. That is what was so chilling. Even today engineers do not build earthworks that accurately. The dimensions were averages, but the more averages you take, the closer the average comes to the planned or intended figure (a phenomenon known as 'reversion to the mean'). We don't know high the banks actually were.

The dimensions of the dykes are in Metres in columns (b) and (c) of Figure 5.4. They are repeated in Roman Feet in columns (d) and (e) (see next page).

All feet used in the Figure are Roman, rather than (British) Imperial. It is surely not accidental that the figures in columns (d) and (e) were generally almost exactly multiples of whole feet and common fractions of feet (a half, a quarter or a third): to within about ⅓ of an inch (0.03 feet) in five out of the eight cases. (The 12 inches in a foot can easily be divided by two, three or four.)

The height of the bank in column (j) was calculated making some simple assumptions, using techniques which we know that Roman surveyors used. Those assumptions are:

a. That trained engineers, or surveyors, designed and oversaw the construction of the dykes.
b. That the designers used simple cut and fill calculation techniques: namely, that the area of cut equals the area of fill.

(a) Dyke	(b) Depth of Ditch (m)	(c) Width of Ditch floor (m)	(d) Depth of Ditch (Feet)	(e) Width of Ditch floor (Feet)	(f) Assumed Depth of Ditch (Feet)	(g) Assumed Width of Ditch floor (Feet)	(h) Calculated Area of Cut (Square Feet)	(i) Assumed Area of Cut (Square Feet)	(j) Calculated Height of Bank (Feet)	(k) Discrepancy: Depth of Ditch (Inches)	(l) Discrepancy: Width of Ditch floor (Inches)	(m) Discrepancy: Area of cut or fill (%)	(n) Discrepancy: Height of Bank (Inches)
Bran	2.00	2.32	6.49	7.53	6½	7½	91	90¼	9½	0.12	0.36	0.83	0.47
Brent	2.44	2.58	7.92	8.38	8	8⅓	130⅔	132¾	11½	0.96	0.56	1.20	0.83
Fleam	4.32	2.95	14.03	9.58	14	9½	329	324	18	0.36	0.96	1.54	0.76
Devil's	4.87	6.97	15.81	22.63	15½	22⅔	600⅝	600¼	24½	1.72	0.43	0.05	0.06

Figure 5.4 The Dimensions of the Cambridge Dykes.

c.   That the designers used simple geometric techniques.

d.   That the engineers measured and set out using Roman feet and inches.

e.   That they calculated to round numbers of feet and common fractions of feet (halves, thirds and quarters).

f.   That they could calculate square roots, possibly by successive approximation, to the same degree of accuracy.

Note that the calculated heights of the banks, in column (j), are all simple multiples of feet and half feet. Columns (f) to (i) show the figures which I assumed the surveyors worked to. We can then compare how close the assumptions above are.

a.   Column (k) shows the discrepancy between the assumed and the recorded depth of the ditch, in inches.

b.   Column (l) shows the discrepancy between the assumed and the recorded width of the floor of the ditch, in inches.

c.   Column (m) shows the discrepancy between the assumed and the calculated cross-section of cut or fill (that is, ditch or bank), as a percentage.

d.   Column (n) shows the discrepancy between the assumed and the calculated height of the bank, as a percentage.

The match is remarkable: normally well within an inch for assumed values (columns 'k' and 'l'), and between practically zero and two per cent, or an inch, for calculated values (columns 'm' and 'n'). To put it simply: if I had been a Roman surveyor and designed the dykes to the measurements in columns (f) to (i), and then the actual builders had built them to those figures,

a.   My calculations would have been accurate to within two per cent or so; but, astonishingly,

b.   The dykes are generally built to within an inch or so of those dimensions.

None of this proves that whoever built the dykes used Roman measurements 'beyond all reasonable doubt'. But it does seem 'more likely than unlikely'.

The deduction is clear. Roman-trained engineers built a series of major fortification, over a period of years. They learnt from experience and improved their designs as they progressed. The Ordnance Survey guide to Britain in the Dark Ages says that the 'most impressive monuments of the Dark Ages in Britain are the great linear earthworks'. The Survey's principal archaeologist, writing in the 1960s, was clearly very familiar with them. He mentions the Devils' Ditch in particular. It is astonishing that they have not received more attention. There is an elephant in the room. We shall probably never know why Roman or Roman-trained engineers were working for the Anglians.

This may all seem wildly improbable, but there is a most intriguing parallel. In the Prusso-Danish War of 1864 (also called the Second Schleswig War), the Danes

initially occupied their fortifications on the historic southern border of Denmark –
the Danevirke. The Danevirke is a series of earthworks about 30km long. It runs
from one river to another, cutting the Jutland peninsula off from the rest of mainland
Europe. The Danevirke was rebuilt several times over a period of several centuries. By
1864 it included bastions and even detached forts for artillery. Of more interest to us,
however, is that the *second* phase of work dates from about the year 500 AD.

As far as is known, the Romans never conquered Denmark. There had been a
Roman presence in Frisia (the modern Netherlands), but by 500 AD that would have
disappeared. So the *original* Danevirke may, or may not, have been built to defend
against the Romans. But by whom?

Angeln, the home of the Anglians, is just north of the Danevirke. Jutland is further
north again. That suggests that the Danevirke, an earthwork several kilometres long
and about two metres high, was built by Anglians. They may have had Jutish help. At
one stage they may have been defending against the Romans. Like several earthworks
in England, the Danevirke ran from river to river across a ridge. The parallel is clear.

Strategically, we know that the Cambridge Dykes worked, in the long run. Norfolk
and Suffolk remained Anglian, and in the 570s a Wuffing leader made himself king
of the East Angles. The Romano-British may have had a significant advantage in
cavalry, but that was of itself not a war-winner. The Devil's Ditch was. It negated the
use of cavalry. East Anglia survived, but it did not become a single, separate kingdom
until the 570s. The Dykes were critically important: at the strategic level, and in the
long run. The military engineering was exceptional. But, ironically, it seems that
whoever led the Anglians during this period were not good tacticians at anything
above the very lowest level. Their earlier dykes were either outflanked or defeated by
fairly simple manoeuvres. They concentrated enormous effort on getting the small
things right, but got some of the big things wrong. There is a lesson there even for
today's commanders.

There are traces of Anglian villages between the various dykes. From the fourth
century we see Germanic settlement only as far west as the River Lark. Then, in
the fifth century, there was a major expansion, for about 30km along the Icknield
Way, almost as far west as Cambridge. There was no further extension westwards
until the seventh century. That is hardly surprising. The Bran Ditch marked the limit
of Anglian expansion in this period. Naturally the Anglians would have settled on
the land behind it. The whole process of digging a dyke, being forced off it, digging
another and being forced off that until, finally, the Devil's Ditch held firm would have
taken years; probably decades. That section of the Icknield Way is high, dry chalkland
which would have been good for grazing. It has a number of streams to provide water
and support crops. Compared to the forest to the south and the fens to the north, it
would have been ideal. Just as we cannot date the dykes precisely, we cannot date the
creation of individual villages accurately either. Those villages may have been settled
before, during, or after the dykes were built. Conversely there is very little trace of
pagan Germanic settlement north and west of Cambridge. The Anglians seem to
have been bottled up in East Anglia for decades, and possibly for more than a century.

The story in Essex, however, was quite different. We have seen that most of modern Essex seems to have been settled quite deliberately with Saxons: some for coastal defence and some to protect the northern border. Very few cremations have been found in Essex. There was definitely some continuity of occupation. For example, a barn at Rivenhall (on the London-Colchester road) was built in the fourth century and stayed in use until the sixth. There is evidence of occupation within the Roman walls of Colchester in the fifth century and possibly the sixth. The remains of a *Grubenhaus* has been found within the walls. There are signs of violence: one of the gates seems to have been deliberately burnt down after the Roman period. We discussed the earthworks around Colchester in Chapter Four. They suggest that Colchester was used as a base for cavalry in the post-Imperial period. The Roman roads within Essex remain in use today, largely on their original alignment, as far north as Colchester and west to Ermine Street at Braughing. North and east of that, however, they went out of use. The Suffolk border was a frontier. There was no traffic on the roads and the trees grew back.

Nowadays we tend to think of Essex as being a well-defined region. Traditionally, its western boundary lay on the River Lea, which rises near Luton and flows south to London. West of there was the land of the Middle Saxons. Beyond that was Wessex, but that is how we see things today. However, there is little evidence that Essex and Middlesex were separate until the eighth century. With the exception of Kent, there were Saxons in the whole of the Thames basin at least as far as Reading. 'Surrey' means something like 'the southern region'. What we now call Surrey may simply have been the southern region of a Saxon area. We know practically nothing of how the area was governed, except that the part which became known as Essex emerged as a kingdom in the 520s AD. Even then, we don't know where its western boundary was. In particular, we know very little about London.

Geoffrey of Monmouth, writing in the early 12th century, mentions a Romano-British Archbishop of London. In the 12th century there were only two archbishops, in Canterbury and York. We don't really know anything about the structure of the late-Roman church in Britain. Was there one bishop per province (hence London, Lincoln, York and Cirencester), or one per city (so 28 or so in total)? It is, however, inconceivable that there would be an archbishop anywhere else other than in London. So, as in other instances, Geoffrey the unreliable historian hints tantalisingly towards a probable truth: that there had been a Romano-British archbishopric of London. However, we know nothing of it nor what happened to it. Bede wrote, in a number of places, that bishops were *subsequently* appointed to the East Saxons, and that their bishopric was in London. Parishes in Essex were under the Diocese of London until 1846.

According to legend, Aelle landed on the Sussex coast in 477 AD. He was probably not the first Germanic leader in the area. There was a Saxon Shore fort at Portchester, on an inlet north of Portsmouth, and another at Pevensey 60 miles further east. Pevensey was still occupied. Portchester may have been. We do not know whether Aelle actually did land in 477, and if he did, whether he was invited or not. History tells us that he fought one battle on arrival; a second in 485 or so; and burnt the fort at Pevensey, massacring all its inhabitants, in 490. Thereafter Sussex disappears from the history books for centuries. It reappears as an earldom many years later. The reason is that the Romano-British bottled them up into a small enclave, and in doing so defeated them so badly that they almost never caused trouble again.

The geography of Sussex is key to understanding the events. It is dominated by the South Downs, a chalk ridge that rises from the river Itchen near Winchester and stretches east for about 70 miles. It rises slowly from the Winchester area to Butser Hill just south of Petersfield. At 270m, Butser Hill is one of the highest points in the south of England. From there the Downs continue slightly south of east to the sea near Beachy Head. From Butser Hill eastwards they have a fairly steep escarpment on the north side. On the south side they fall gently to the coast. From the area of Chichester westwards, the coast is low-lying and contains many inlets and inland bays. East of Chichester, the Downs run straight down to the sea. In places they are cut by narrow, steep sided and (what were) wooded valleys. Hence places east of Brighton such as Rottingdean, Woodingdean and Roedean. Two rivers, the Arun and the Adur, cut straight through the escarpment from what would have been a low-lying marshy area north of the Downs. They flow into the sea at Littlehampton and Shoreham respectively. Further east, the River Ouse cuts through the end of the escarpment at Lewes and flows into the sea at Newhaven. Much of the area from the mouth of the Arun west to the Meon would have been low-lying and fairly marshy. Much of the area north and east of Pevensey was either swamp or at least tidal, as witnessed by the many '-ey' place names (that is, islands. See Figure 2.7). Further north again was the great Wealden Forest, which ran almost all the way from Kent to the Solent.

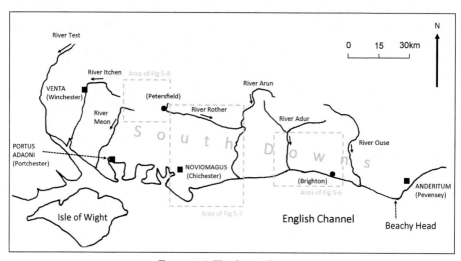

Figure 5.5 The South Downs.

The marshes and the forest effectively cut the Sussex coast off from the north. Two Roman roads ran down into the area from London. One ran to Lewes, the other to Brighton. It is possible that the Romans built them primarily to exploit iron ore workings in the Weald. A third road, Stane Street, ran down to *Noviomagus* (Chichester). Roads then ran west across to Portchester, and from there to Winchester and the Solent. Another Roman road ran down to Chichester from Silchester. The Romans also built a lateral road, north of the Downs. It connected the three north-south routes out of London and then ran east to Pevensey. Another road ran eastwards from Chichester to Brighton. When the Roman roads went out of use, the Sussex coast could easily not be reached from London during the winter until 1770 AD, when the turnpike to Brighton was built.

The South Saxon heartland lay between the valleys of the Arun and the Adur. There are many '-ings' in that area. Worthing, Angmering and Lancing are among the most well known. There are many early pagan burials and other archaeological traces in this area, and a few high on the Downs further west. The area east of the Adur (around Brighton) seems to have been more deliberately settled, with an Eastwick and Southwick. There is a Halewick (Farm) in Lancing, and several 'wick's, '-wickhams' or similar along the east-west road north of the Downs. Cemeteries have been found at Alfriston, Bishopstone and Selmeston. Saxons appear to have settled in the valleys, but grazed flocks on the high, relatively sparsely-wooded downland above them. Chichester was in use as late as the second quarter of the fifth century, but there is no sign of it being in used by Aelle's time.

Chichester lies on the west side of the shallow valley of the River Lavant. From a military perspective, the Downs would have presented a difficult problem. The Wealden forest lay to the north, and Pevensey Bay to the east. The roads down to the Weald from London ran through thick forest, and may have been abandoned when the Romans stopped extracting iron ore.

Trouble started in the time of Ambrosius Aurelianus. The (south) Saxons, possibly under Aelle, revolted. It may have been in 477 AD. The Romano-British could use the road north of the Downs to approach either from the west (Chichester) or the east (Pevensey), or both. The route due east from Chichester crossed several streams and was marshy. That made it easy for the Saxons to deny its use to cavalry, but relatively easy for them to raid across on foot or in small boats. More of that, shortly.

There are a few routes from the Rother valley up to the ridge of the Downs between the Arun and the Adur. From the Romano-British perspective, they shared two serious disadvantages: they were very steep and the Saxons might be at the top. In practice it seems easier for them to attack down the west bank of the Adur. It is not easy to understand why that would be so, but the Saxons fortified it with an extensive set of earthworks. See Figure 5-6.

There is a series of earthworks, hedges and possible steepened slopes which run west from near the back wall of Lancing College, for just under three miles. In one section the topography has now been altered by a landfill site. In some places the

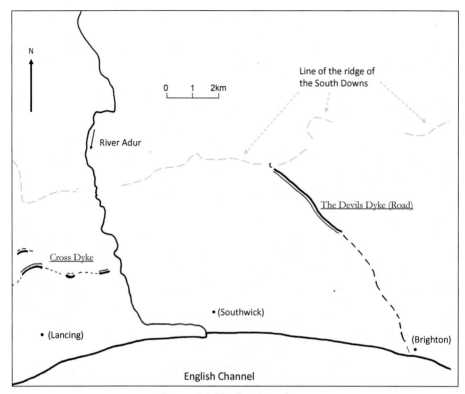

Figure 5.6 The Brighton Area.

defences seem to be up to ten feet high, but over much of their length the remains are considerably smaller than that. They face north. They are referred to in various places as 'Cross Dykes'.

That would stop the Romano-British getting in, but not the Saxons getting out. Romans could be thoroughly single-minded and determined, as the conduct of their sieges at Masada in Palestine in 73 AD and hill forts such as Hod Hill in Dorset in 43 tell us. Taking a leaf from their book, sometime during the late fifth century the Romano-British had had enough. They marched from the Portchester area and reoccupied Chichester. They then employed their fortifications not defensively but offensively. Experience had told them that the Saxons would use hit-and-run tactics out of the woods to the north. The Romano-British dug. The Lavant valley is very shallow, so they first dug a short earthwork along the west bank, northwards from the walls of Chichester for a mile or so. That would stop the Saxons attacking them directly, but could be relatively easily outflanked by crossing the Lavant further north. The Romano-British therefore dug westwards as far as the Bosham Stream. That is about three miles. Even then their flank could be turned, but three miles represents at least an hour on foot. A warband trying to outflank the whole position would leave its own flanks and rear badly exposed, as well as its villages near the Arun. These dykes are easy to find today. They are shown as '1' in Figure 5.7. They are seven or eight feet high in several places. They tend to run in straight sections, with sharp angles between them.

The Romano-Britons had not yet defeated the Saxons. Their next move was more of the same. They extended their earthworks north along the Lavant valley about a mile, to near the modern village of Mid Lavant, and then westwards again towards the headwaters of the Bosham Stream. In building these dykes they may have used their old tactic of keeping some of the men under arms whilst the others dug. That slows down the rate of progress, but is much more secure. These earthworks ('2') are also quite easy to find. They are up to 12 or 13 feet high in places today. They would originally have been about 18 feet high (from the bottom of the ditch to the top of the bank).

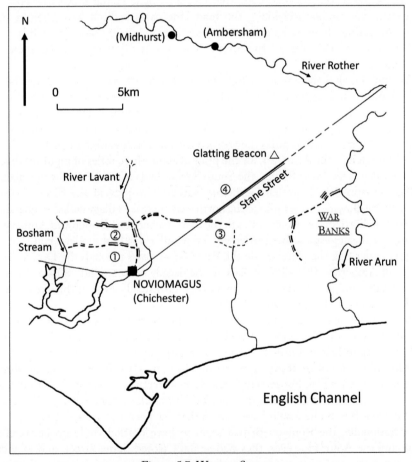

Figure 5.7 Western Sussex.

In one area, near Oldwick Farm, the line of earthworks looks as if it has been taken around existing field boundaries. The clue may be in the name. 'Oldwick' means 'old *vicus*'. Perhaps the military commander felt obliged to accommodate the wishes of a local landowner. Perhaps he was that landowner. Alternatively, that section may have been built earlier by local landowners for self defence, and incorporated into the overall line.

The third stage was to dig eastwards from Mid Lavant for about three miles ('3'), with the dyke facing north as before. The eastern end was anchored on a creek that runs into the marshes to the south, possibly the stream called the Aldingbourne Rife. By this stage the Romano-British had effectively reoccupied the coastal plain but, again, not yet won. The next stage was imaginative, bold and decisive. Stage '3' had brought them to Stane Street. Starting where their new earthworks crossed that road, they advanced along it, digging out the ditch on the east side and forming a bank on top of the old road bed. That created a dyke facing south east ('4'). The alignment was simple: dig along the road. The eastern ditch gave them a start. Communicating along its length would have been relatively easy. They didn't stop until they got to the crest of the South Downs near Glatting Beacon, about five miles away.

We don't know if there was any fighting, but the South Saxons would now be in a difficult position. They were effectively bottled up on the Sussex coast. Their response was to dig in. They dug from the Arun to the crestline immediately west, then along the south-west side of the re-entrant that runs down the front of Rewell Hill towards Fontwell. After about two miles they turned the line southwards and anchored it on a creek that ran into the Arun. So, for the price of about three miles of digging what are known today as the 'War Banks', the South Saxons had ensured their own protection.

The Romano-British settled Germanic warbands to prevent the Saxons moving north off the Downs. A few miles to the north west there is a village called Ambersham: 'Ambrosius' Settlement'. Many miles to the east, Amberstone Bridge and Amberstone Grange Farm suggest another settlement a few miles north of modern Hailsham. In between, guarding the place where the River Arun flows through the Downs, is the village of Amberley. This all took place in the decade or so around 480 AD. There are also a small number of 'Tyes' and a few moated farmsteads. One of the Tyes is near a 'wick' *and* a moat: shades of north Essex.

(In 1903 Thomas Codrington, a member of the Institute of Civil Engineers and a Fellow of the Royal Geographical Society, wrote what was the standard work on the Roman roads in Britain until the 1950s. He clearly wrote that Stane Street had been banked up, as described above. Yet, writing 34 years later, Myres wrote in 'Roman Britain and the English Settlements' that Stane Street remained open. It didn't, and if Myres had either read Codrington's book or visited the section between Chichester and Glatting Beacon he would have known that. Myres is not always reliable.)

Operationally, the Romano-British seem to have bottled Aelle up between the Arun and the Adur. However, they had actually closed Stane Street, and may have had to use the east-west road north of the Downs cautiously, for fear of ambush.

Ambrosius seems to have died at or around this time and there may have been some treachery (see Appendix 1). We are told that in 485 AD Aelle fought and won a battle at a place we cannot identify. The result seems to have been that he could now expand eastwards across the Adur.

The Romano-British in Pevensey responded by building a dyke which has hidden in plain sight for centuries. Today it is called the Devil's Dyke (or Dike) Road and leads north west from central Brighton to: nowhere (see Figure 5.6 above).

It seems that over the centuries people came to assume that it was 'the road to the Devil's Dike' and started to call the steep-sided, narrow valley at its northern end the Devil's 'Dyke'. So, the road *along* the Devil's Dyke became the road *to* the Devil's Dyke, and people forgot that the road was originally a track along an earthwork. The first large-scale Ordnance Survey maps did not show the Dyke at all, just the line of the road. The Dyke does not seem to have been investigated by archaeologists, probably because they accepted that it was the road *to* the geological feature.

The southern half of the Dyke is now entirely within the built-up area of Brighton and no trace remains. Further north, it is a continuous strip of hedged but unused land just east of the tarmac road. It is typically just under thirty yards wide and shows some undulation across its section. It falls about ten feet from east to west in several sections. It seems to have been a forward-slope defence about five miles long. It might have been about 20 feet high in total. It would have run from the crest of the Downs to the sea, and prevented any advance by the Saxons. Immediately north of the Downs was an area of sandy streams which flowed into the Adur. That would also have helped contain the Saxons.

However, despite the Dyke, Aelle burnt Pevensey in 490 AD and slew all its inhabitants. Historical statements like that tend to be exaggerated, but this one probably does mean that Pevensey was destroyed as a Romano-British fortress. That may explain why the Devils Dyke (road) is so eroded. Taking the dates literally means that it cannot have been built before 477 AD (and probably not before 485). It would have been abandoned after 490. Unlike several dikes discussed in this book, it had a relatively short useful life.

After the fall of Pevensey, the Saxons continued to push inland. The initial settlements on and south of the Downs were followed by more in the Rother valley to the north. Today one can count about 25 '-ing' place names in a belt up to about ten miles deep, north of the Downs. They become much rarer further north. Aelle may have led this second wave of migrants. This seems to be quite typical. The initial Germanic arrivals were invited, or came largely in peace. It was the next generation, migrating from homelands outside the Empire, who did not feel bound (or effectively were not bound) to keep what remained of the *Pax Romana*.

Operationally, the remaining Romano-British were in the west: at Portchester, Winchester or perhaps Chichester. Stane Street was closed. The easiest route into the Rother valley was the Roman road from Chichester north in the direction of Silchester. However, Saxons could now get to the ridge of the Downs and move along its length. A mile or so east of where the Silchester road crossed the ridge there is a 'Harepath Wood'. As we shall see elsewhere, 'harepath' (or 'herepath', or similar) means 'army road': a route used by soldiers, a warband, or similar. The location suggests a relatively easy route up to the ridge and an alternative to the rather steeper Roman road. A Romano-British force using the Roman road down into the Rother valley now risked being cut off on its way back. The road to Silchester went completely out of use.

Accordingly the British now attacked from the direction of Winchester. The Rother valley, around modern Petersfield, lies about 50-60 metres lower than the Meon valley to its west. The ground falls away rapidly off an escarpment running north-south known variously as Stoner Hill and Wheatham Hill. Those hills are almost 200m above the valley floor. The Rother Valley is connected to the headwaters of the Meon. The valley of the Meon, which flows west, is very close to the source of the Tillmore Brook, which flows east into the Rother. See Figure 5.8.

The escarpment is very hard to climb, up or down. There are few tarmac roads up it today. The easiest runs past a hamlet called The Slade to the village of High Cross. 'Slade' means 'valley': there is a very shallow re-entrant which runs up from the west and almost reaches the escarpment. That was the route the British used; probably several times. As we have seen, after some fighting (and probably some negotiation) the British had settled *foederati* north of the Downs as a paramilitary border force. There is a cluster of five '-hams' centred on Ambersham, about two miles east of Midhurst. There are a few just north of Amberley and some near Amberstone (including Hailsham). '-Ham's are quite rare on the Downs.

Settling *foederati* seems to have worked in Essex. It failed in Kent. We don't know what happened in the Rother Valley. We do know that today the five '-hams' are

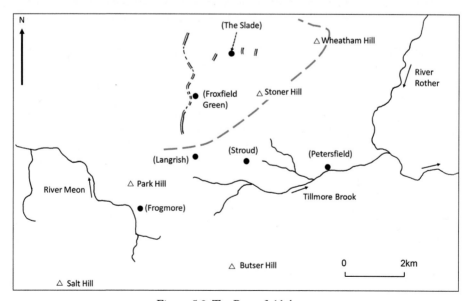

Figure 5.8 The Petersfield Area.

surrounded by a group of eight '-ings'. We can also be fairly sure that the Saxons (with or without the help of the former *foederati*) revolted again. The evidence lies near The Slade. It is shown on an 1:25,000 scale Ordnance Survey map, but not the 1:50,000 version.

The British had used the Slade to enter the Rother Valley. The Saxons walled it off, with a short dyke about 300 yards long, about a quarter of a mile from the escarpment. Today it is easy to find, and faces west. It seems to have been part of a concerted plan. It was followed by a further dyke, parallel with it and about 400 yards further west. That, in turn, was followed by a third about half a mile further west again. All three are more or less the same length and height. All three face west.

The top of the escarpment is several miles from the nearest '-ing'. Given some warning, the Saxons could man the first dyke and repel Britons attacking along the Slade. The first dyke would have given them both a firm base and the confidence to build the second, just five minutes' walk further west. Similarly for the third, about ten minutes' walk west again. This may sound very cautious, but we should not forget the devastating effect that a force of Romano-British cavalry could have if it caught the Saxons in the open. We can assume that the flanks of each dyke rested on woodland.

There was a purpose to all this, which shows that the Saxons were now thinking above the tactical level. The eventual purpose was to stop the Romano-British raiding into the Rother Valley. The Slade (valley) was the easiest, but not the only, route to the escarpment. Eventually the Saxons had to deny the use of the whole length of the escarpment. That is, from where it fell to the marshes to the south and for several miles to the north, beyond the Slade. That would require a dyke several miles long. The short dykes across the Slade were just the means of getting to the point where that could be dug.

The final dyke is about half a mile west again. Today it can be traced over two miles or so. It is typical of Roman engineering. It has very obvious, straight sections and definite angles. That suggests a thorough knowledge of survey and construction techniques. At its southern end it is up to about twelve feet high today. The ditch is about five or six feet deep, and the bank about the same height. It faces west. It appears to end on the line of the modern A272 Winchester to Petersfield Road, which may seem a little odd. However, the detail of the end of the dyke was clearly altered when building the road. The A272 today drops over 50 metres in half a mile to Langrish – 'the tall, or long, reed bed'. To the south west is Frogmore, 'the marshy place'. Just east of Langrish is Stroud: 'the marsh'. The defenders probably didn't mind if any attacker tried to outflank the dyke to the south. Good luck to them.

These earthworks run through the village of Froxfield Green, which has a curious resonance for me. On the village war memorial is the name of Major L P Storr, DSO, 7th Battalion, Duke of Cornwall's Light Infantry. He died in the First World War and is no relation of mine. The connection is even more unusual. He died during the retreat across the old Somme battlefield on 23 March 1918, almost exactly 42 years before I was born. His body was never found, so his name is recorded on the Memorial to the Missing at Pozières near Albert in France. When he died he was a

38 year old major, serving with the King's Regiment. I had known nothing about him until I visited the Pozières memorial myself. At the time I was a 39 year old major in the King's Regiment. It is at moments like that that one can feel a connection with those who went before. When I stumbled across the Froxfield Green memorial I was reminded of that, and of countless others who had gone before, since time immemorial.

By building this earthwork through Froxfield, the Saxons had seemingly stopped the Romano-British raiding into the Rother Valley. The timing is interesting and does not seem to have occurred to other academics or writers. Aelle, Cerdic and Arthur were all broadly contemporaries. Cerdic is only known to us from his actions in Hampshire and the Isle of Wight. Aelle is only known to us from his actions in Sussex. We don't know where Arthur operated with any certainty. Cerdic and Aelle were obviously important figures in the heritage of the West and South Saxons respectively. We can conjecture that some of their apparent greatness reflects the identity of their opponent or opponents, but there is no hard evidence on which to base that conjecture. For that reason, the idea is developed not here, but in Appendix 1.

Whoever the leaders were, with the building of the Froxfield earthworks the British couldn't get in to the Rother Valley. Conversely the South Saxons couldn't, or wouldn't, get out. The modern boundary of Sussex lies just east of Petersfield. The 12 '-ings' described above are all in Sussex. There is not a single '-ing' in that part of Hampshire. As we shall see, Hampshire became a part of Wessex, not Sussex.

Confusing the picture slightly more is the fact that there are also traces of Jutish settlement on the Isle of Wight and on the Hampshire coast opposite; that is, the New Forest and the Meon Valley. Those traces are Jutish, not Saxon. A Jutish cemetery was found north of King's Worthy, just north of Winchester. Since the *southern* and *eastern* gates of Winchester were blocked up at some stage in the Dark Ages, the story is clearly somewhat complex. Were those Jutes enlisted once the South Saxons revolted, or were they there before them, but remained loyal? We do not know. The Anglo-Saxon Chronicle gives a clearly garbled account of two nephews of Cerdic, Stuf and Whitgar, ruling the Isle of Wight; but we should not give too much credibility to that.

As an aside, we should remember that all the Romano-British rulers appear to have been Christians, whilst the first Anglo-Saxon to be baptised – Aethelbert of Kent – did not adopt Christianity until 597 AD. Most were not baptised until the middle of the seventh century. There are references to Arthur carrying the sign of the cross, and some late-Roman armies appear to have worn an early Christian badge on their shields (a combination of the Greek 'chi' and 'rho', which are the first two letters of the Greek word for 'Christ'). Arthur and his men may well have felt as if they were conducting a crusade against the pagans.

The Anglo-Saxons generally adopted Christianity in the seventh century, after their leaders were baptised. Adopting Christianity should be seen as a largely political issue. Saint Augustine baptised Aethelbert of Kent in 597 AD. It was not so much that he brought Christianity to Britain, as reading Bede might suggest. The critical issue was that Augustine brought Christianity to the *Anglo-Saxons*. It took perhaps a century for them all to convert from paganism. Pope Gregory, who dispatched Augustine, may have done so largely due to disaffection with the British Churches. They broadly rejected the rule of Rome until the Synod of Whitby in 664, more than sixty years later. Even at that point, Roman (Catholic) rule over British churches was not complete.

To return to Arthur, after Badon in 509 AD or so the Anglians were bottled up in East Anglia. The Jutes had been contained in Kent for perhaps fifty years. The South Saxons had been penned up on the South Downs and the Sussex coast a few years before. They slowly edged northwards into the Weald: there are dozens of '-inghams' and '-ingtons' just north of the South Downs; but the South Saxons never again emerged as a military force. There is no record of Mercians or Northumbrians causing trouble in this period, and their kingdoms only emerged about 20 years later. Essex seems to have been pacified by establishing the East Saxons as a sort of paramilitary border force. Little is known of the rest of the Thames basin (London, Hertfordshire, Middlesex and Surrey), except that they show very few Germanic remains. That suggests that any Germanic arrivals were settled and assimilated fairly peacefully.

In London, the area just outside the west gate (the modern Temple Bar) became known as the 'Old *Vicus*', hence 'Aldwych'. The rest of the city had shrunk to an area around the modern Tower of London at the eastern end, although the walls were more or less intact. Bishop Mellitus, a successor to St Augustine, built the first St Paul's Cathedral in 604 AD. He built it in what was probably derelict land, inside the walls but between those two settlements. London was clearly not particularly important. Mellitus became bishop of London, but did not move the Archbishopric there from Canterbury (he was archbishop of Canterbury as well as bishop of London). London developed a haphazard, typically medieval street pattern which indicates that the former Roman government had ceased to have any authority. London and the Thames basin are variously described as belonging to Mercia, Kent and Wessex at different times in Anglo-Saxon sources. The kings of Wessex (and thereafter England) were generally crowned in Winchester. London may have been relatively unimportant, other than for the (ironically) Viking trading base which later sprang up along the Thames and particularly the Strand. 'Strand' name means 'beach'. The Strand was, until Tudor times, a road running along the top of the bank of the river where the ships were beached, or 'stranded'.

Gildas, writing about 40 years after Badon, used alarmist language which has been taken literally. A more measured analysis of his work suggests that Britain was largely at peace, and there is no immediate reason to think otherwise. There are only two roads running west from London; one north west through *Verulamium* (near St Albans) and the other just south of west through Silchester. *Verulamium* was in use at least until the late fifth century, when its water supply was rebuilt. That suggests a working knowledge of engineering, and some form of urban administration to organise and supervise the water supply. A very worn Roman coin found in Silchester, and other evidence, suggest that it was in use in the late fifth and possibly early sixth centuries.

Its north and east gates were blocked, which indicates that in time a threat did emerge from the direction of London. Silchester is another example of an interesting anomaly in Geoffrey of Monmouth's work. He refers to both Arthur and another (probably mythical) king being crowned there. By Geoffrey's time Silchester was a tiny place: a village huddled inside one corner of the walls. The walls were (and are) impressive. They are the most complete circuit of Roman Walls in Britain. Silchester was named in Nennius, but without translation (the name used is 'Caer Segeint'). How would Geoffrey had known that Silchester had been an important city in post-Roman Britain? Surely it was more than just imagination.

Further afield, burial patterns in York, the London Basin, the Wash and Abingdon show Germanic elements, and differences from one area to another. However, those patterns show little change for about two hundred years, which would typically be until the advent of Christianity. So, in the early sixth century, it appears that Arthur had contained the major Anglo-Saxon threats (from East Anglia, Kent and the South Saxons). Things would fall apart sometime after his death, but that was not necessarily obvious. With the exception of Kent, no Anglo-Saxon ruler called himself the king of a territory, rather than of a people, until the eighth century: two centuries later. To Gildas, the main problem was not the Anglo-Saxons but tyrannical Romano-British rulers. One suspects that Arthur was not a ruler but a military commander, and that after his death the Romano-British rulers squabbled amongst themselves with tragic strategic consequences.

The major anomaly in this picture is that of the Abingdon Saxons. As Sir Frank Stenton wrote in his Oxford History of Anglo-Saxon England, their origin is still an open question. As we have seen, however, the prominence of the area may have more to do with its proximity to Oxford and Oxford-based archaeologists. No cremation-only burials have been found in the area. Some of the archaeology was carried out decades ago, and the dating is now suspect. Finally, even if we assume that there was a significant Saxon settlement in the area, that tells us nothing about what their allegiance was, nor who settled them there. The absence of cremation-only cemeteries suggests that they were assimilated fairly quickly.

The sources, from Gildas to Saint Germanus and Saint Patrick, refer to a functioning Roman civilization in Britain. It had educated and capable commanders such as Ambrosius and Arthur. This picture continued through the fifth century into the sixth. By the end of the sixth century, however, warfare had become heroic and epic rather than disciplined. Fear and hatred dominated the Romano-Britons' relations with the Anglo-Saxons. As the American historian Christopher Snyder put it: although divided politically, the Britons shared a common language and a common faith, and for those reasons saw themselves as superior to and separate from the pagan Saxons. For those reasons Bede could never forgive them. (Let us not, therefore, take Bede at face value.)

In many places where Germanic invaders or settlers took over the land, they kept the same field boundaries. They ignored other boundaries. The pattern of land use, rather than the pattern of the fields, changed. Whole areas went out of use, and areas which were once thought to be ancient forest (such as on the edges of the Wealden Forest) have been found to have been cultivated in Roman times. Britain was changing, and the rate of change would be fastest in the decades after Arthur's death. The time when Gildas wrote, in the 540s, may have been the long, slow autumn of post-Roman rule. The Plague of Justinian may have ravaged Britain in the late 540s AD. It was recorded in Egypt in 541-2, Constantinople in 543 and Gaul in 544-5. By reducing the population, and possibly the Romano-British more than the Anglo-Saxons, it may have dramatically altered life in Britain. It might have been the Plague, rather than any political or military factor, that brought about the dramatic collapse of post-Roman Britain. The Anglo-Saxon conquest picked up momentum in the 570s. It may have been the means, but not necessarily the cause, of that collapse.

6

Cerdic and His Following

The revolt of the South Saxons seems to be a fairly straightforward case of a rebellion by *foederati* or migrants. The story of the West Saxons, however, is quite different. The name 'Cerdic' is probably not Germanic. It seems to be a corruption of 'Ceretic': a Celtic and hence British name. That of his alleged son, Cynric, is if anything Irish, being derived from 'Cunorix'. Alternatively it may mean 'ruler of the kindred', or similar. The names of several rulers of what became the West Saxons appear to be British. That suggests that their mothers were British, over several generations. So, rather than an invasion or the rebellion of *foederati*, we seem to have something like a civil war. A British leader tried to carve his own domain out of the main Romano-British territory. Yet the story is more complex than that, for three reasons. Firstly, that group clearly became identified as Saxons. Secondly, there was a complete change of theatre of war, from the south coast to the upper Thames. Third, there is a break in the historic record of about two decades, linked to the change of location. Writers have had major problems rationalising those three issues. Strategy, geography and place-name evidence can, however, help us enormously. The results are surprising. The key issue is to disregard the legacy of some appallingly bad place-name attribution.

The story starts in the area on both sides of the Solent. In the east, the South Downs rise just east of Winchester. From there they rise steadily eastwards towards Butser Hill. South of Petersfield the main escarpment is about 100 metres higher than the Rother Valley to its north. The River Itchen rises about ten miles east of Winchester. Some of its tributaries actually flow northwards, off the northern (scarp) slope of the Downs, before the joining the main river flowing west. The Itchen then turns south, flows through Winchester and on to the Solent about 20 miles away. It is paralleled in some ways by the River Meon, which rises in what was an extensive bog near East Meon (about three miles east of Petersfield) and flows west. After a few miles it turns south, flowing through a gap in the Downs and on for about 15 miles to the coast below Fareham. Petersfield lies on a bend of the River Rother, which flows down from the north and turns east to run along the bottom of the escarpment of the Downs before joining the River Arun. On the south side of the Downs lie the creeks and inland bays that we now call Portsmouth, Langstone, and

Chichester Harbours. A Roman Saxon Shore fort, possibly called *Portus Ardaoni* (now Portchester Castle), lies on the north shore of Portsmouth Harbour. The Roman road from Chichester ran inland of Portchester and, after a couple of bends, ran more or less north to Winchester. A branch road ran west to the bank of the Itchen at Bitterne, where there was a Roman settlement. See Figure 6.1.

Much of the west side of Southampton Water was swampy marsh. The ground rises slowly westward; much of what is now the New Forest is less than 50 metres above sea level. The Beaulieu and Lymington Rivers drain that area, but the next big river is the (Hampshire) Avon, which rises well north of Salisbury. From there it flows almost due south for about 25 miles to meet the sea in Christchurch Harbour. The River Stour also flows into Christchurch Harbour, from the north west. The area between Southampton Water and the Avon only became known as the 'New' Forest in Norman times, but the large number of '-leighs' and '-leys' among its place names tells us that it was largely wooded in the Dark Ages. Modern Salisbury lies around the site of the Cathedral built in 1258 AD. The earlier city was at Old Sarum, above the river and about a mile and a half north. The Roman name for Sarum was *Sorviodunum*, and several Roman roads led to and from it. One ran south west towards Dorchester. We should be hesitant, however, in thinking that that area was open downland. There are several '-leys' and other woodland place names in that area. Several of the high ridges around there are covered by the remnants of much bigger forests.

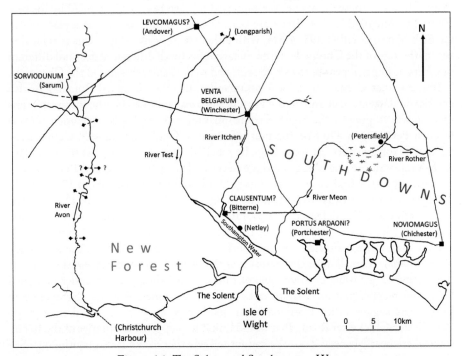

Figure 6.1 The Solent and Southampton Water.

Another Roman road ran west from Sarum towards Bath. The third ran north east to Silchester, and the fourth eastwards towards *Venta Belgarum,* Winchester. Sarum and Winchester are about 25 miles apart. That road crosses the River Test, which flows south out of the chalkland of Salisbury Plain to join the Itchen in Southampton Water. Once again, much of this area is open farmland today, but the names of areas such as the Harewood Forest tell us that it was much more heavily wooded in the Dark Ages. The valleys of the Test and the Avon show extensive signs of human drainage today. They were boggy. Places with names such as 'bridge' or 'ford' are rare, suggesting that crossings of these valleys (which are about a mile wide in places) were a long way apart. In fact there does not seem to have been any fords across the Test for most of its length. 'Leckford' means 'ford over a side-channel'. Other than at Leckford, there are no 'ford' place names on the lower Test. The lowest ford marked on the Ordnance Survey map is at Longparish, near Andover. That means that before the Romans came the Test could not easily be crossed for most of its length. There seem to have been only four crossings over the Avon below Sarum: at Blashford, Fordingbridge, Charford and Britford. There was possibly another at Barford.

The Anglo-Saxon Chronicle describes just a handful of events relating to Cerdic. In 508 AD he fought a British leader called Natanleod and killed him at Natanleigh. He took over as leader of the West Saxons, and fought the Britons at Cerdic's Ford, in 519. In 529 he fought the Britons at Cerdicsley. In 530 he conquered the Isle of Wight. In all of these events he was supposed to have been accompanied by his son, Cynric. Cerdic died in 534. There are tales of him 'coming ashore', at a place called Cerdic's Shore, in either 495 or 514; with either three or five ships. This is typical of the mythology of the Chronicle. Different accounts (with different dates, and different numbers of ships) appear both in different, and in the same, versions of the Chronicle.

It seems that Cerdic was a local commander, possibly of mixed Romano-British and Saxon descent, in charge of the Portchester area (and possibly the fort itself). His mission was to prevent the South Saxons breaking out. Aelle's last recorded act was to burn Pevensey in 490 AD. The first reference to Cerdic was in 495. Cerdic led a band of Saxon warriors. At some stage he rebelled, then dug in against the inevitable British reprisal. He dug along the ridge between the upper Meon and Itchen rivers. That line of earthworks faces north. It would originally have been about 12 feet high. The remains are fairly easy to find and up to six feet high in places today. He anchored the eastern end of his defences on Park Hill, which overlooks what were the marshes where the Meon rises. The hamlet at the bottom of the hill is called Frogmore: 'the marshy place'. The main ridge of the South Downs rises steeply from the south side of that marsh. A small dyke cuts across it at that point. The main east-west section of the earthwork is visible over a couple of miles, before disappearing under ploughed fields and reappearing for a short section about five miles west. Its alignment and siting there suggests that it originally ran south west down a ridge and crossed the Winchester-Chichester Road. That would link it to one of the tributaries of the Itchen somewhere near Marwell Zoo. We cannot tell whether or not it was continuous. See Figure 6.2.

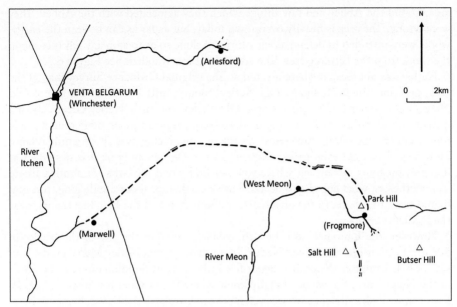

Figure 6.2 East Hampshire.

We don't know where 'Cerdic's Shore' was. We have some idea where Natanleigh, Cerdic's Ford and Cerdicsleigh are. The toponymy for the present Netley (on the east shore of Southampton Water between the Itchen and the Hamble), Charford (one of the fords on the Avon) and Setley (in the New Forest) seem about right, at first sight. All three are close to long linear earthworks.

Archaeologists noticed what appear to be parts of two broadly parallel earthworks near the shore, close to the site of the medieval Netley Abbey. They assumed that they were connected to the Abbey. They assumed that the earthworks were aqueducts to bring water from the headwaters of Tickleford Gully (which flows into Southampton Water about half a mile north). Curiously, they noticed that the reservoirs or sluices that would be needed upstream were never built. Curiously, they did not notice that the earthworks were huge: the ditches are up to about eight feet deep, even today. Compare that with a Roman aqueduct for a city the size of, say, Dorchester. That would perhaps be four feet wide and three deep.

Curiously, the earthworks seem to have a V-shaped profile, which is not good for carrying water. Aqueducts tend to have flat bottoms. Curiously, the archaeologists did not notice that in some places the alignment of the earthworks would make the water flow north east, away from the Abbey; not south west towards it. Curiously, they did not noticed that the Abbey had fishponds watered by their own stream. Curiously, the archaeologists did not associate the earthworks with the name of one of the earliest locations given for Anglo-Saxon activities in the Anglo-Saxon Chronicle. It is a good case of people not seeing what they were not looking for. They were investigating the area around the Abbey and saw things which they associated with the Abbey. They were wrong. The area is heavily overgrown today, but as far as can be seen the earth-works were intended to defend along a forward slope so as to stop any advance along the shore from the Bitterne area. The area inland was wooded. See Figure 6.3.

Netley was not located where it is today. The original Ordnance Survey map of the area, published in 1871, shows 'Old Netley' about a mile inland, at the site of Old Netley Farm. Confusingly, what is now 'Old Netley' was then 'Netley Green', about a quarter of mile from the Farm. The modern Netley was not much more than a single row of houses (including three pubs). So the original Netley was about a mile inland. However, it was not even called 'Netley'! In the Domesday book it is described as 'Latelie', meaning 'a clearing where you can find wood for laths', or similar. There is, nonetheless, what appears to be a defensive earthwork about a mile long, running inland from the shore, in the area between the Itchen and the Hamble: that is, near the mediaeval Abbey.

However, the Chronicle also says the whole area from the site of the battle (in 508 AD) to Charford was named Netley. That is why we find Netley Marsh on the *west* side of Southampton Water. It is about five miles west of Southampton, at the north of the New Forest. So, we don't really know where the original battle took place. If, however, we look at the map we see even more earthworks in the Forest. Some are parts of a park pale: a low ditch designed to keep wildlife inside a medieval hunting reserva-tion. Two other earthworks further south near Hatchet Gate and Sway face west. They would have initially been about ten feet high, but are little over three feet high today. They suggest that the area was fought over in our period. A local path near Fawley is called the Harepath, meaning 'army way' or similar. Even more interesting are the earthworks about fifteen miles north west, on the far side of the Avon above Charford.

There are many earthworks in this area. It takes a lot of careful study to analyse them. Some are prehistoric and associated with a cursus, a religious avenue (like the one which leads up to Stonehenge). The first earthwork to interest us can be traced over more than two miles from the area of the Castle Ditches at Whitsbury north to Clearbury Ring. Both are hill forts. The earthwork runs along the crestline west of the Avon. Today it (like many other earthworks in the area) is called Grim's Ditch. Unusually, it faces west. It would have been about ten feet high. Oddly, about five miles north east, near Pitton and east of the Avon, there is another section of what is called Grim's Ditch, which seems to face west as well. Even more oddly, it lies in a 'Great Netley Copse'.

The second earthwork to interest us is about six miles further west and is also called Grim's Ditch. It tends to be overlooked because it is close to (and in one point joins) the much better known Bokerley Ditch (which we will see in more detail in Chapter 12). It is quite small, perhaps only seven or eight feet high in total. It is perhaps two miles long. In the north it ran from the relatively steep-sided re-entrant of Chickengrove Bottom. In the south it ran up to Blagdon Hill, which is on a high ridge: the highest ground for miles around. Importantly, it crossed the Ackling Dyke, the Roman road from Dorchester to Sarum.

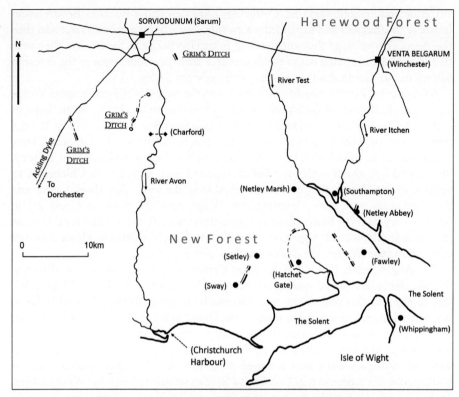

Figure 6.3 Southampton Water to the Wiltshire Avon.

Piecing all the evidence together, it seems that Cerdic rebelled. Fearing the inevitable reprisal, his initial response was to dig in east of Southampton Water, with earthworks along the high ground between the Itchen and the Meon valleys and in the area of Netley Abbey (as discussed above). In or about 508 AD, he fought another Romano-British commander called Natanleod (perhaps a version of the biblical Nathaniel) west of Southampton Water and expanded his territory west across the Avon. He expanded westwards, digging in at each stage: at Hatchet Gate; at Setley; then (perhaps after defeating Natanleod) west of the Avon. He dug to protect the crossing at Cerdic's Ford (Charford). He then pushed a few miles further west, not least to deny the British the use of the Dorchester–Sarum road.

The citizens of Winchester did not join Cerdic. They dug in. They closed off the main gate leading south, and dug not just one but two ditches across the road in front of it. Gates are normally weak points in a set of walls. One way to get in was to bring up a battering ram along the road to the gate, and batter it down. Digging a trench across the road made that much, much harder. Digging a trench close to the gate made it almost impossible (because the attacker would have to swing the ram uphill).

Cerdic and his followers (the 'Cerdicings') had defeated a Romano-British leader (possibly 'Nathaniel') and expanded westwards across Southampton Water and then the Avon. At one stage they cut the road from Dorchester to Sarum. Yet they were then defeated and chased out of the Solent area fairly unceremoniously. The defeat in 529 AD was at 'Cerdicsleah' or 'Cereticsleah': modern Setley.

Along the back of the marshes near Fawley on the west side of Southampton Water, an almost dead-straight earthwork runs for about five miles. It was about seven or eight feet high originally, and faced east. That is, it faces Southampton Water. We can envisage two hypotheses as to how and why it was built. The first is that, once Cerdic had rebelled, the British built it stop him crossing Southampton Water. If so, it failed. The second hypothesis is that the British repeated their tactics from Chichester. In order to defeat Cerdic, they counter-attacked from the west. They threw Cerdic and the Cerdicings back across Southampton Water, after the battle at Cerdicsley in 529 AD. They built the Fawley dyke as a temporary measure to keep him bottled up on the east side. The second stage was to then clear the east bank (that is, Hampshire east of Southampton Water). We don't know how that happened.

The Anglo-Saxon Chronicle describes Cerdic conquering the Isle of Wight in 530 AD, dying in 534 and passing the island to his nephews Stuff and Wihtgar. We should not give this part of the story too much credence. 'Wihtgar' seems to be an invention designed to justify the name of the Island as being Germanic ('Wight' from 'Wihtgar'). It is more likely that 'Wight' comes from its Latin name, *Vectis*, meaning 'the island in the fork (of the Solent)'. Furthermore, writers persist in translating the name of Wihtgar's settlement (ravaged by Cerdic, and Wihtgar's burial place) as Carisbrooke. Carisbrooke may have been a Roman settlement, but the 'Wihtgarabyrg' in the Chronicle is not like any known spelling of Carisbrooke. If anything, it is more likely to be the same root as the hamlet of Wippingham, near Cowes. That is another example of poor, and unquestioned, toponymy.

That was the end of Cerdic. It seems that he was kicked off the mainland, settled on the Isle of Wight and died there in relative obscurity. His followers would not return to the Winchester area until the year 652 AD or thereabouts; that is, about 120 years later. In any case, there is no real evidence that he had ever held Winchester. There is a vague legend about his burial place being near Hurstbourne Tarrant, north of Andover. Cerdic's actual burial place is not known. What may have given rise to the legend is a Neolithic chambered grave near the Chute Causeway, a few miles from Hurstbourne Tarrant. It was excavated in the eighteenth century. It was empty, and lies in the middle of a field very close to the Causeway, a Roman road. The Causeway is fascinating and very much part of our story. We shall look at it in Chapter 11. For now, though, the story continues with a bunch of landless Saxons, much further east and a decade or so later. Cerdic had been kicked out of his enclave, but had gained the one thing that warriors dreamed of: fame. The main thing which the Kingdom of Wessex later clinged to was that its leaders were descended from Cerdic. He had rebelled and succeeded, albeit briefly. The details of his later demise would be glossed over. A few years later his successors would try again.

The next stage of the story starts in the Thames basin, perhaps in the 540s AD. As for why, let us look at the strategic situation. The East Anglians had been bottled up behind the Cambridge dykes, the Fens, and the Essex border. The East Saxons were settled north east of London and showed no signs of rebelling. After some excitement in Kent, the Jutes were bottled up behind their defences south of the Thames. The South Saxons had been contained in the eastern section of the South Downs, behind the Weald. Cerdic's followers had been booted out of the Solent area. We don't really know what was happening in the Thames Basin area; that is, the area east of the Chilterns and, say, Reading.

Operationally there were only two routes west from the Thames Basin: the Silchester and St Albans roads. The reason was the Chilterns, a high ridge of land that reaches up to 260 metres above sea level. The crestline runs above 200 metres above sea level for about 30 miles, roughly south west from the area of Whipsnade Zoo near Dunstable. Eastwards from Dunstable the Chilterns run for several more miles to Royston or thereabouts, steadily losing height. Royston is a few miles down the Icknield Way from Cambridge. Dunstable is on a Roman Road north from London, known to us as Watling Street and just west of the source of the River Lea near Luton. See Figure 6.4.

Having run south west at or above 200 metres above sea level from the Whipsnade area, the Chilterns continue south west, losing a little height until reaching the Thames near Goring. Even here the Chilterns reach to about 160 metres, whilst the river is just 40 metres above sea level. The Thames flows east through a narrow defile known as the Goring Gap. From hilltop to hilltop the valley is not much more than a mile wide. The stretch of the Thames from Goring east to Reading was narrow. The bottom of the valley would have been marshy, but the main course of the river would have been fast-flowing. The Romans did not build a road along that stretch of the river. The Chilterns were high, dry and remote. Even at the time of the Doomsday book there were very few settlements in the Chilterns. The only road through the Chilterns (Akeman Street) branched off Watling Street at St Albans and ran northwest through the valley of the River Bulbourne (and what is now Berkhamsted) towards Bicester. On the north west (i.e. scarp) side of the main ridge of the Chilterns the land falls away fairly sharply. It loses 150 metres in a mile or so.

Operationally, if any Anglo-Saxons in the Thames Basin wanted to attack westwards they had either to make their way through miles and miles of forest (the Chilterns to the north of the Thames, or the Weald to the south), or use the roads via St Albans or Silchester. But both St Albans (strictly, *Verulamium*) and Silchester (*Calleva Atrebatum*) were held by the Romano-Britons. To understand what happened, we need to look at the ground in a little more detail. Five rivers drain the Chilterns south and east into the Thames Basin. The Gade and the Bulbourne meet (at Hemel Hempstead) and flow south into the Colne. The Chess and the Misbourne join the Colne further south. The Wye flows into the Thames further south again. Those five valleys (of the Gade, Bulbourne, Chess, Misbourne and Wye) form narrow, winding fingers that reach north westwards right up to the ridge of the Chilterns. All provide possible

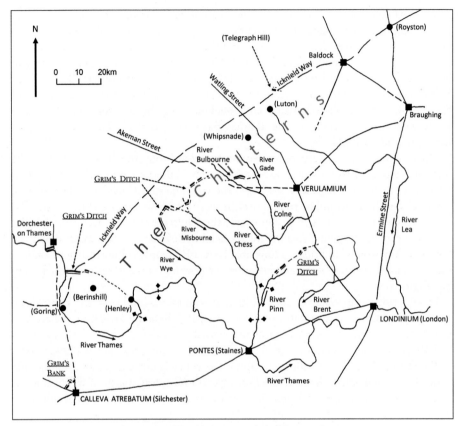

Figure 6.4 The Chilterns and the Thames Basin.

routes through the hills. The best route is the Bulbourne Valley, which explains why Roman engineers built Akeman Street from St Albans to Bicester through it. The next best route is the valley of the Wye, which does not quite penetrate the Chilterns, but is the route followed by the A40 and the M40 today.

The Colne drains much of the land east of the Chilterns. The River Ver, which flows past *Verulamium*, is one of its tributaries. The Gade, Chess and Misbourne join it further south east. The Colne then flows almost due south to the Thames, just south of Heathrow Airport. On the way it is joined by the River Pinn, which gives Pinner its name. The next river east, the Brent, drains a wide area and crosses Watling Street. It gives its name to both Brent Cross (about a mile east of Watling Street) and Brentford (where it flows in to the Thames, seven or eight miles west of Roman London). This topography became very important to the Romano-British.

At some stage, probably in the late 540s AD, the Cerdicings appeared on the north bank of the Thames, west of London. We don't know why or how, but we can be fairly sure that they caused trouble. The British responded, once again, by building a dyke. It connected the Pinn to the headwaters of the Brent, north of Edgware. Today it is more than eight feet high in several places, and over 12 feet in some. Once again, it is called Grim's Ditch. It can easily be followed on a map from the Ruislip area (where it connected with the Pinn) almost to the former RAF Fighter Command HQ at Bentley Priory. Archaeologists have found traces within a few hundred yards of Watling Street.

The Pinner Grim's Ditch seems to be in an odd place; until you look for fords. From where the ditch connected with the River Pinn down to its junction with the River Colne, there was just one ford. On the Colne between the Pinn and the Thames there was also only one, at Langford. Up the Thames from there, there were just two crossings as far as the Goring Gap. One was at Harleyford, near Hurley. The other was at Wargrave ('the grove by the weir', or similar). Given that the southern end of the Chilterns was a great wooded wilderness, Grim's Ditch closed off many of the routes west, from the Thames above Henley as far as Watling Street. Watling street runs across a saddle of high ground near Elstree, between the headwaters of the Rivers Colne and Brent. Watling street lead to *Verulamium*. So Grim's Ditch had considerable operational impact. At one point there was a Roman watchtower very close to the line of Grim's Ditch, about a mile south of Elstree. It has not been dated.

According to the Anglo-Saxon Chronicle, in 552 AD the Saxon leader Cynric fought the British at Searobyrg (or Searobyrh), and put them to flight. For centuries scholars have translated that as Sarum (the Roman *Sorviodunum)*, and fitted that in with the account of Cerdic on the Solent. In Old English 'Searobyrg' means 'the city with walls', 'the city with fortifications', or even 'the city with artillery'. That only means that it was one of the more than 40 walled towns in Roman Britain, and from that list it seems that it was *Verulamium*.

Saint Alban was the first British Christian martyr. He was executed on the hill outside *Verulamium* in 280 AD or thereabouts. An abbey was subsequently built there, and the town later grew up around the Abbey. The chronicler, and Bede, may not have known that Verulamium is near (but not actually at) St Albans. Even if they did, they may not have associated a battle at 'the fortified city', reported verbally for over two centuries, with *Verulamium*. They may even have believed, wrongly as it happened, that Searobyrg was *Sorviodunum*.

So somebody, named as Cynric and possibly the son of Cerdic, fought at Verulamium. Verulamium is north of the Pinner dyke, which suggests that the Saxons either marched around it or somehow crossed it.

It may have been at this stage that *Verulamium* was either conquered or abandoned. By then it had very little economic significance. Its fortifications may have been useful as part of a defensive system. It may have had prestige value, but the British may have been too practical to worry about that. They built another dyke. This one ran from the River Gade to the Wye. It is easy to trace on a map from east of Berkhamsted to west of High Wycombe. It is not easy to demonstrate that it actually connected the River Gade to the Wye, but Figure 6.4 suggests that it did. It was relatively big: possibly up to 25 feet high. Several sections are over eight feet high today. Its total length was over 12 miles. It is typical of Roman engineering. It is dead straight over hill and dale, but changes direction at deliberate angles to fit its overall alignment to the major valleys.

Archaeologists have described its course as wandering over the Chilterns without apparent reason, which is highly informative in itself. In the spring of 2010 I gave a seminar at Birmingham University. I put up a map of the Chilterns, and highlighted the line of the ridge and the river valleys. I then highlighted the alignment of the dyke (called, not surprisingly, Grim's Ditch). I asked my colleagues, many of who were from the Centre for First World War Studies, whether it was credible that the dyke was built to deny access through the Chilterns. Their response (there were about 30 of them) was almost unanimously 'yes'. First-War historians clearly understood it. Archaeologists didn't.

In the 1920s Sir Cyril Fox excavated the Chiltern dykes. He thought that they were intended to stop chariots. Logically, that is an assertion. It should have become an hypothesis, which was then tested. Was there evidence of, for example, the wreck of a chariot the bottom of the ditch somewhere?

No.

The Chiltern dyke seems to have fulfilled its purpose. The next Saxon attack, four years after Searobyrg, was at Beranbyrg. Once again, poor toponymy has let us down. 'Byrg', or 'berg' in modern German, means hill or mountain. With a large dose of wishful thinking and misled by the Solent hypothesis, scholars have picked places such as Barbury Castle, just south of Swindon. As a progression from Sarum, almost 30 miles south of Swindon, that has some logic. But in terms of place-name evidence, it has very little. A better fit is with 'Berins Hill' and 'Berins Hill (or Berinshill) Wood', three or four miles north east of Goring The Saxons found another narrow valley leading west from the lower Thames. It starts about a mile north of Wargrave. Today it doesn't have a stream, let alone a name. In places it is called Harpsden Bottom or Stony Bottom. In the east it opens out onto the Thames valley just south of Henley-on-Thames. If you follow it west and slightly north you eventually come to the ridge of the Chilterns, just south of the village of Nuffield and a mile or so from Berins Hill. That's not easy; in places there is not even a footpath, let alone a road, along it. Even today much of it is thickly wooded. Perhaps by coincidence, just where it reaches the ridge there is an 'English Farm' and 'English Lane'.

The Saxons worked their way through the Chilterns to Berins Hill and fought the British. There are clear signs of linear earthworks at Berins Hill, but it is not a hill-fort. A house nearby is called 'Bibury', or 'near the fortification'. The Anglo-Saxon Chronicle does not say who won. The Saxons may well have won the battle: a tactical success. But operationally it got them nowhere. The British responded once again by building dykes. The first simply cut off the east bank of the Thames, from the Chiltern ridge to the river just south of Wallingford (between Dorchester and Goring). Its main section is almost dead straight for about four miles. It was originally about 20 feet high. Today it is eight feet high in places. The ditch appears to have been ploughed in, in some places; but the bank is visible over most of its length. Once again, it is called Grim's Ditch. Seen from the south, it dominates the skyline over much of its length. It rises above what would have been a series of marshy valleys draining west-wards into the Thames. At its eastern end, near the village of Nuffield, it shows four major and two minor bends in a distance of perhaps a mile. It was clearly built around the top of the re-entrants near English Farm which lead eastwards all the way down towards Wargrave. Its alignment looks very rectilinear.

At one place, Morrell's Bottom (about a mile west of Nuffield), a rectilinear enclosure about 300m by 200m was built on the north side of Grim's Ditch. The Ditch forms its southern face. The enclosure is surrounded by a ditch and bank which would have been about six or seven feet high. It is tucked into a re-entrant to give it shelter from the weather. It looks as if it was designed as a camp for troops operating on, or from, Grim's Ditch.

Rectilinear camps are not found in pre-Roman Britain.

There are traces of earthwork stretching through the Chilterns all the way east, from that Grim's Ditch almost as far as Henley-on-Thames: perhaps another five miles. One section is called the Highmoor Trench. Further east, as it runs through Lambridge Woods, it is called Grim's Ditch again. This section is far more sinuous, which suggests it was built later. Overall, it seems that the British dug right across the great bend of the Thames from near Wallingford to near Henley in two phases. The Cerdicings had got across the Thames into the southern Chilterns (possibly at Wargrave), but the British were determined to stop them getting further north.

However, access to the south western end of the Chilterns also posed a threat to *Calleva*, Silchester. As Figure 6.4 shows, there were virtually no crossings of the Thames between London and Goring. The Romans had built a bridge at Staines, and there may have been a ford at Chertsey, about three miles downriver. So, whilst any Anglo-Saxons were kept east of the Colne, it was simple to stop them approaching Silchester. Once the Gewisse (or Gewissae) got into the Chilterns there were two more crossings to watch: not a big problem. However, after Beranbyrg the Gewisse could potentially cross the Thames to the west above Goring. They could then threaten Silchester from the north. So, considerably further south, the British responded by fortifying the northern approaches to Silchester. See Figure 6.5.

Two Roman roads ran northwards from Silchester. One ran north towards Dorchester on the Thames (and thence to Bicester). The other road just north of west and eventually arrived at *Cunetio*, near modern Marlborough. Until the Saxons had broken through the Chilterns, Silchester was protected against attacks from the north. If, however, the Saxons could penetrate the Chilterns they could come down the Thames to the Goring area and then simply follow the Roman road to Silchester. So the British fortified the high ground between the Clayhill Brook (which runs north east, and eventually flows into the Kennet near Reading) and a stream just south of the road to *Cunetio*. Once again, the dyke is typically Roman; very rectilinear. Today it is up to ten feet high in places. It is visible in many places but disappears under the modern Heath End in the west. Today it is called Grim's Bank.

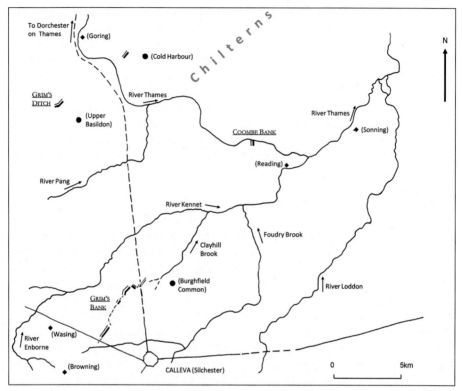

Figure 6.5 The Silchester Area.

There are not many '-ings' in that area, but the fact that there are instances at Reading (on the Kennet, near where it flows into the Thames), at Goring and at Wasing (just north of Heath End) may be significant. So may Sonning, Eling and Browning (Hill). The British may have located Germanic settlers there, to protect Silchester from the north east and to block movement along the banks of the Thames. That is not the whole story. The Coombe Bank, just west of Reading, is still about three or four feet high today and seems to face west. Near Cold Harbour, about two thirds of the way to Goring and above the north bank, another earthwork (up to about seven feet high in places) also seems to face west. These short sections of earthworks might indicate rebellious Saxons in the lower Thames protecting themselves against British raids eastwards along the Thames below the Goring Gap. There are other earthworks in the area which we shall refer to later, and one of direct interest here.

The Roman road from Silchester to Dorchester on Thames is assumed to have run north to the Thames at Pangbourne and then along the west bank of the river. There are, however, traces of an alternative route over the Downs through Upper Basildon a mile or two to the west. Another Grim's Ditch, about five or six feet high today, cuts that route about a mile north of the village. It is visible over about 600 yards today, and faces north. How it fits into the overall sequence of events is not obvious. What it does, however, is point out what may have been, in the long run, an even more important truth.

By breaking through the Chilterns to Berins Hill, the West Saxons achieved a tactical success. Operationally, it got them nowhere. The British fortified the east bank below Dorchester on Thames, and above Silchester. Much of the land on the other side of the Thames there was a marshy swamp which stretched on for miles. It is more or less flat almost as far as Swindon. A few island, such as Cholsey Hill or Blewburton Hill, stuck out of the swamp. The strip lynchets on Blewburton Hill tell us that it was an island in otherwise unusable land. The Saxons could have tried to settle on the north slopes of the Downs west of the Thames, but that would have put them in a narrow neck of land between British in Dorchester and those in Silchester. They could try to attack Dorchester from the west bank, but the British built not one but two massive parallel dykes on their side of the river there (see Figure 6.4 above). The banks are about 12 feet high in places today, and would have completely cut the neck of land between the Thame and the Thames.

The Roman road to Silchester crossed the Thames there. By building those banks, the British in Dorchester severed their connection with Silchester. The next Roman road west ran through Cirencester, about 40 miles away and requiring a detour of more than 60 miles. Tactically, Berins Hill may have been a success for the Saxons. Operationally, it got them nowhere. Strategically, and probably completely by chance, it had a major impact. It divided the British in Silchester from those in the upper Thames valley. Roughly 15 years later, around 571 AD, the northern group were decisively beaten. In 577 they were destroyed. Silchester, however, seems to have survived for several more decades. The Roman road from Dorchester to Silchester had been operationally significant, but it went out of use. Today there is almost no sign of it.

Cynric is supposed to have lead the West Saxons at Searobyrg. At Beranbyrg it was both Cynric and his successor Ceawlin. The genealogy of the Cerdicings appears to have been doctored, principally to give legitimacy to Ceawlin. Cynric is supposed to have died four years after Beranbyrg, in 560 AD or so. We know very little about the Cerdicings (who called themselves the 'Gewisse', namely 'the trusted ones' or similar), but what happened next is instructive. The next battle, in 568, was fought against the men of Kent under Aethelbert, who were chased back to Kent. That year they also fought at a place called Wibbandun. The best suggestion to date is that 'Wibbandun' was probably *not* 'Wimbledon'. We can, however, have some confidence as to where it was. Modern Whipsnade is derived from 'the detached piece of ground belonging to Wibba'. So Wibbandun may mean 'the hill belonging to Wibba'. If so, it would be near Whipsnade. That is, somewhere near Watling Street in the area of Dunstable (see Figure 6.4).

That tells us very little of itself, but think what it means on an operational scale. Before 552 AD the Cerdicings had been penned up south and east of the Colne. After Searobyrg they had gained ground to the north, but were then trapped by the Chiltern dykes between the Wye and the Gade. In 556 they tried to break out due west and got as far as Beranbyrg, but found that they were in a dead end. 12 years later, with a new leader in charge, they fought the men of Kent. Then, buoyed up with their success, they tried to the north up Watling Street. They fought near Whipsnade, but don't seem to have got through. The British did not fortify that route. They had a short dyke across the Icknield Way just east of Luton on Telegraph Hill. It faces north east, and is still about five or six feet high today. That may have been to protect against Anglians trying to break out of the Cambridge dykes, built at any time over the previous 50 years or so since Badon. Alternatively, the British may have thought that the Cerdicings were not likely to get through on the Watling Street axis. They could, conceivably, bypass it and then turn the Chiltern dykes by marching west along the Icknield Way. That was possible; another Roman road leads northeast from *Verulamium* and came out on the Icknield Way near Baldock, about 12 miles east of Dunstable. That meant a detour of about two day's march for a well-organised force. See Figure 6.6.

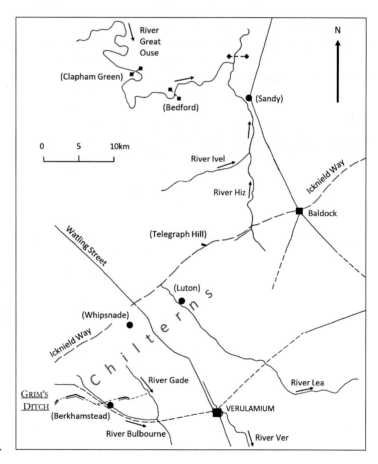

Figure 6.6
Turning the
Chiltern Dykes.

We don't know the details, but just three years after Wibbandun the Gewisse did try something like that, and they succeeded. Operationally, an attack via Baldock and the Icknield Way could be described as 'short right hook'. In practice the Cerdicings tried a 'long right hook'. It worked.

A turning movement exploits an open flank, typically to force a defending force out of a defensive position. The leader of the Cerdicings was Cuthulf, who seems to have been the same person as the Cutha, Ceawlin's brother, who fought with him at Wibbandun. Cuthulf may not have had the formal military knowledge to know about turning movements. What he did, however, was to march through the Chilterns, probably via Baldock, and then north. We can be confident that he did that because of the location of the next battle, in 571: 'Bedcan forda'. In the Anglo-Saxon Chronicle it is described as 'Bedanforda' for a different event, in 917 or 918. That is about 350 year after Ceawlin's time. It is Bedford, on a bend of the Great Ouse river. The road north from Baldock would put Cuthulf's force east of the River Hiz, then the Ivel. There are few fords until the Ivel meets the (Great) Ouse. We know that Cuthulf fought and won a major battle at Bedcanford and we can now see how. The Ouse has a series of major bends just west of modern Bedford. After some manoeuvring, Cuthulf marched for the ford at Clapham Green, about two miles north of the ford at Bedford. He did so slowly and obviously, drawing the British to follow him on the west bank. He feinted across the ford at Clapham and marched fast back to Bedford. It is about two miles, and even across country he could have done that in two hours. Unfortunately for the British, the distance around the outside of the loop of the Ouse is about three times as far. When they arrived, Cuthulf would have been waiting for them. It may have been the other way round: a feint at Bedford and then a crossing at Clapham Green. Or it may have been a complete surprise; or some other ford. We are conjecturing. To use modern military terminology, we are conjecturing that Cuthulf exploited interior lines to gain a tactical advantage, having previously employed a deep turning movement (the 'long right hook') at the operational level.

It had been about 19 years since the fight at Searobyrg (*Verulamium*) in 552 AD. There was probably no-one at Bedcanford who had fought in the battles around the Solent. Even the alleged seizure of the Isle of Wight had taken place over 40 years before. But the eventual outcome was very significant. As a result of Bedcanford the Cerdicings, or Gewisse, seized a vast tract of land. It included estates at Limbury near Luton, Aylesbury, Benson, and Eynsham west of Oxford. Limbury is where the Icknield Way crosses the River Lea. Eynsham is about 45 miles from Bedford as the crow flies. The fact that the Cerdicings could seize and retain so much land tells us that they inflicted a major defeat on the British. Cuthulf did not long enjoy the fruits of his triumph. He died later that year. Ceawlin led the Cerdicings thereafter. The land they had won lay south west of Bedford; south west along the Icknield Way, across into the vale of Aylesbury and them into the upper Thames Valley near Oxford. To the north lay the land of the Mercians, which had been ruled by the Icling dynasty for something like 50 years. We shall see what the Mercians had been doing in Chapter 10. But the immediate problem facing the Gewisse were other Britons, further west.

7

Beyond the Goring Gap

The area which the Gewisse occupied after Bedcanford was, initially, the upper Thames valley. It is, broadly, bounded to the south by the Berkshire and the Marlborough Downs. To the west is the valley of the Gloucestershire Avon. Northwest lie the Cotswolds. The Chilterns bound the area to the east. The area was huge: about a thousand square miles. That would be enough to give 100 acres to over 6,000 Cerdicings. 100 acres would be a large holding, and it is hard to believe that there were that many West Saxon warriors. It would have taken a long time to work out what land should be given to who; then divide it up, settle on it, plant crops and so on. Not least, the British population probably did not all leave. Many would have been subjugated; perhaps enslaved; probably reorganised; and so on. The next major battle that we hear of was just six years later, in 577 AD or thereabouts. In a sense it is surprising that it was so soon.

That battle was at a place called Deorham. Dyrham in Gloucestershire, just north of Bath, has been assumed to be the site of the battle ever since a Victorian antiquarian identified it. There is a hill fort nearby, but it was never called Deorham. In the 17th century it was called Burrill; more recently Barhill. To locate the real battlefield we must look at the geography. See Figure 7.1.

After Bedcanford the British dug in again. They dug in on the west bank of the River Glyme, barring any advance west along Akeman Street towards Cirencester. That earthwork was perhaps two miles long and runs into what is now Blenheim Great Park. Traces of it are up to eight feet high today. It can easily be confused with a later earthwork which we will look at later. Slightly further south, near North Leigh, they dug another earthwork which seems to have linked the River Evenlode to streams which run into the River Windrush. Very little of that can be seen today: not much more than a slight ridge and depression in a field. It lies about three or four miles north west of Eynsham, which was one of the settlements which the Cerdicings captured. Tactically, these earthworks stopped the Saxons moving west along Akeman Street. Operationally, in conjunction with very extensive swamps and marshes all along the upper Thames at least as far as Cricklade, those fortifications contained the Cerdicings in the land between the Thames and the Berkshire Downs. We shall look at the Downs shortly.

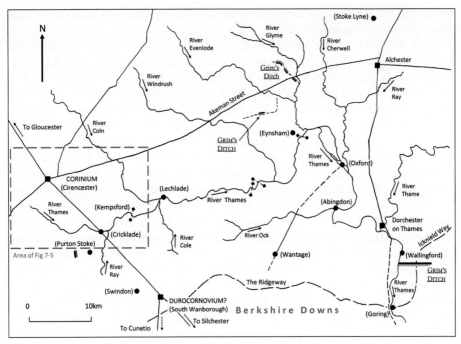

Figure 7.1 The Upper Thames Valley.

Cricklade lies near the Roman road from Silchester and *Cunetio* (near Marlborough) to Cirencester. The Roman road crossed the Thames there. The suffix '-lade' probably means 'a difficult crossing, particularly one liable to flooding'. There is another '-lade', Lechlade, about seven miles downstream. There is one ford (Kempsford) between the two, and very few other crossings downstream as far as Oxford: perhaps three fords in 20 miles or so. Upstream of Cricklade the ground was probably even more marshy. If the Cerdicings (who we shall call the West Saxons from now on) could reach Cricklade, they could cross and advance north towards *Corinium* and *Glevum* (Cirencester and Gloucester). There is good reason to think that the West Saxons could get to the Cricklade area. A Roman road left Oxford and ran south and west towards Wantage. It may have gone on to *Cunetio*. A ridge of relatively high land divides the upper Thames Valley from that of the River Ock, now called the Vale of the White Horse. That high ground is roughly the line of the modern A420 through Highworth. Moving westwards along the ridge and crossing the upper reaches of the River Cole would bring the West Saxons to the area of modern Swindon. The remains of an ancient trackway runs to the west, just north of there. It runs through Hayes Knoll and Purton Stoke, past a hill fort at Bury Hill, and then perhaps on to Minety. In places it is called Stoke Common Lane. It seems to have been a major east-west route until the B4040, originally a turnpike, was built west from Cricklade through Minety over a thousand years later.

There are no 'Deorhams' in modern England. There are two 'Dyrhams'. One is the site in Gloucestershire described above. Another is right on a major Dark Age dyke. Unfortunately that is the Grim's Ditch near Pinner referred to in Chapter Six. It is now the site of a golf course and, incidentally, where the musician W. S. Gilbert (of Gilbert and Sullivan) drowned in 1911. It is far too far east. There is also a 'Dereham', in Norfolk. That is also much too far east. So, if there is no good site called 'Deorham', we should look for things that sound like it, and for other evidence.

Travelling west along Stoke Common Lane from Purton Stoke, you come to an earthwork at right angles to the Lane. It is only a foot or two high now, but seems to be very wide. That is probably because it has been ploughed out, so it is hard to know how large it was. It can be traced for about half a mile nowadays, and may have run from a very low hill to the north down to a stream to the south. The land around there is very flat, so even a slight rise may have been significant. There is also a trace of another earthwork at right angles to it, just north of Stoke Common Lane, but the remains are so slight that there is no clear evidence that it was a linear fortification. The next stream to the west is the Derry Brook. There are very few 'Derrys' in England. The term is Celtic, as in 'Londonderry' in Northern Ireland and several places in Scotland. So, in this corner of Wiltshire we have: an earthwork; some theatre- (that is, campaign-) level reasons to believe that the battlefield could be in this area; a Roman road that leads to Gloucester and Cirencester, but a difficult crossing that could easily be blocked; and a very rare place name that could be related to Deorham. We also know little of the battle other than the fact that three British rulers were killed and that the cities of Bath, Gloucester and Cirencester were taken. The suggestion is that the three rulers (whose names appear in the Anglo-Saxon chronicle) were the rulers of those three cities. So 'Dyrham' could be a now-forgotten hamlet on or near the Derry Brook.

Gloucester is on the Severn. It is over 40 miles from Swindon. Bath is just under 40 miles away. If we take the Chronicle literally, the West Saxons had seized another thousand square miles or so just six years after Bedcanford. They may have done. We have no firm evidence that they did not. But if they did, they would probably have overextended themselves. Cheltenham calls itself the 'Capitol of the Cotswolds', but it is well east of the main Cotswold escarpment, which overlooks the Severn 12 or 13 miles further west. There is very little archaeological evidence, and no credible historical evidence, of the West Saxons penetrating west of the Cotswold escarpment for many years. There is some evidence that they did not even get that far. To reach Bath, the West Saxons would have to cross the Gloucestershire Avon. They may have done. However there is no real evidence that the West Saxons crossed south of the river, into what is now Somerset, for decades. We'll return to this issue later.

It is time to look south. We last looked at the inhabitants of the Silchester region responding to the Battle of Beranbyrg (or Beranburh) by digging an earthwork a few miles north of the town. The threat posed by the West Saxon breakthrough at

Bedcanford was far greater. All the land north of them was now in enemy hands. The British in the Silchester area had been safe for decades, because the only real threat (since the expulsion of Cerdic in the 530s AD) was from the east. If the Saxons could now get south of the area of the Thames and the Ock, they could roam British territory at will. The battle at Deorham then made things much worse. It implies that they could get to the Cirencester-Silchester road. At South Wanborough (whose Roman name was probably *Durocornovium*) a road branched off to the south, through *Cunetio*, giving access to Winchester, Sarum and Dorchester. From Cirencester the Fosse Way ran southwest to Bath, Exeter and the south west. The whole of southern Britain was open to the West Saxons.

The British response was, in one sense, predictable. In another sense it was breathtaking. Once again, they dug a dyke. This time, however, they did so on a strategic scale. They dug all the way from Goring on Thames to the Bristol Channel. In a straight line that is about 70 miles. Hadrian's Wall was 80 miles long. What the British built now was almost as long.

It wasn't continuous. It probably wasn't built in one piece. It was never anything more than an earthwork, and in places it didn't last for very long. Conversely, the British didn't have the resources of the Roman Empire. Strategically, however, it was, bold. As we shall see, it probably held back the West Saxons for over seventy years. Not over its whole length: the Silchester region seems to have fallen after about 30 years. However, it was an amazing achievement, given the relatively small number of people involved.

We know nothing in practice about who these British were. We know only that they now occupied the south of England, west of Surrey and south of the upper Thames valley. Geographically that meant a line across the Berkshire Downs, the Marlborough Downs, the Gloucestershire Avon and then to the Bristol Channel. The area it defended included several towns and cities, but we know very little about how those places were inhabited. There is some sign that some of them had been occupied in the fifth century, but this was now the mid to late sixth century. There are very few signs of anything, let alone evidence of settled habitation, in those places at that time. There is, however, evidence that several hill forts were reoccupied around this time.

One of the very few, but arguably very important, pieces of evidence is a stone inscription found inside *Calleva* (Silchester). It is inscribed in Ogham and is dated to the sixth century. Ogham is an early form of writing that seems to have originated in Irish Celtic areas. It is little known outside Ireland. On the British mainland it is rarely seen outside the far west, in places such as the Devon-Cornwall border, Pembrokeshire and the Isle of Man. A few Ogham inscriptions have been found near Poole Harbour, and two in Shropshire. Other than that, none have been for about a hundred miles to the west of Silchester. Its presence there is a most important anomaly. Anomalies tell us that we are looking at things in the wrong way. Up to now, there has been no credible explanation as to why a sixth-century Ogham inscription was found in *Calleva*. It makes perfect sense, however, if the Silchester region was still in British hands in the mid to late sixth century.

We have already considered the earthworks built to the north and northwest of *Calleva*, seemingly in response to the battle of Beranbyrg in 556 AD. They are sited to protect relatively short-ranged incursions along the west bank of the Thames and down the Roman Roads to *Calleva*. They are not well sited to cut southern England off against an enemy who could attack anywhere from the area of Dorchester on Thames to west of Bristol. The British now started further north, from about a mile north of Goring. In simple terms, the line ran initially along forward edge of the crest of the Berkshire Downs. As one would expect, however, its detailed siting was quite complex. See Figure 7.2.

Strategically, the object was to defend southern England. Therefore the line ran from Goring to Bristol. Its length makes it far too long to describe the tactical details of its siting here, although we will look at a few details in due course. Operationally, the first issue was that after 571 AD the West Saxons were present in strength in the upper Thames valley, possible as far west as the Roman roads south and south east from *Durocornovium*. Geologically the Berkshire Downs is made up of two separate features. The obvious one is the crestline, which for much of its length runs at well over 200 metres above sea level. At Wanborough, where the road from Cirencester starts to climb the Downs, the land is only 90 or so metres above sea level. The crestline of the Berkshire Downs is over 100 metres higher. The crestline falls slowly eastwards, so that near Goring it is generally not much over 150 metres above sea level.

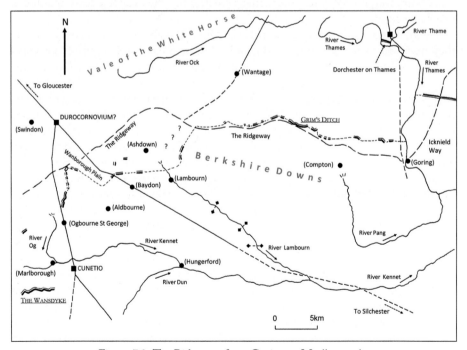

Figure 7.2 The Ridgeway from Goring to Marlborough.

However, there is also a second, lower terrace to its north. In places this is so close as to be indistinguishable from it: for example, just east of Wanborough. In other cases, however, the two are distinct. There is a plateau a few miles wide between them. In the east, Wantage sits on that plateau. A few hundred yards from Wantage, Chain Hill is at 143 metres above sea level. However the horizon to its south is dominated by the main ridge about two miles away, at well over 200 metres above sea level. So, driving south down the A338 through Wantage or the A34 past Abingdon, one climbs one ridge only to find a second, higher ridge a couple of miles further on. That second ridge is the route of the Ridgeway. The Ridgeway is the continuation of the Icknield Way westwards, after it crosses the Thames near Goring.

Linear earthworks can be traced on the ground for much of the distance from Moulsford Downs (on the west bank of the Thames just north of Goring); then along the Ridgeway, across the A338 and then on for about another three miles. They are visible in places on a 1:50,000 Ordnance Survey map. They can be seen in rather more places on a 1:25,000 map. Tellingly, they can be seen in even more places on older Ordnance Survey maps. That is, in some places all trace has disappeared in the two centuries since the Survey was first completed. The earthworks are generally on the northern (that is, forward) slope. They do, however, correspond to the topography. They change direction to get the best overall line, sometimes running north-south rather than east-west.

There had been a pagan Roman temple on Lowbury Hill about three miles west of Goring. The dyke ran almost to it from the east. It then ran north for a few hundred yards before running westward again across Aston Upthorpe Downs and then Blewbury Down. The alignment is reasonably obvious if you go and look at it on the ground. This area presented the surveyor with a particular topological problem. A north-south valley cuts the line of the Downs here. The village of Compton sits in it. North of Compton it is dry. Just south of Compton we find the headwaters of the River Pang, which flows south, east and then north to flow into the Thames at Pangbourne, about five miles west of Reading. We shall return to that area in Chapter 10.

The main ridge of the Downs, the Ridgeway and the earthworks (called Grim's Ditch here) run generally westwards south of Wantage. The advantage of occupying the forward slope here is that the dyke protected the Ridgeway, so that the British could move troops along it. About four miles west of the A338, the surveyors came to another challenge. A major valley cuts into the Downs from the south. In two places it nearly cuts the Ridgeway: there are two low spots (about 30 metres lower than the main ridge) within half a mile of each other. Some miles further west there are even bigger valleys, which were the routes of the Roman roads from Cirencester to *Cunetio* and Silchester. Looking at how to best defend the whole area, the decision was taken to turn the dyke south here. Traces of it can be seen on the hillside east of the Farringdon Road (the B4001), which may have been the route of the (now lost) Roman Road from the Oxford to *Cunetio*.

The earthworks can be traced near Lambourn. They run west again across Row Down and Bailey Hill and cut the Roman road just west of Baydon. I do not think that this Baydon is the site of the Battle of Badon. I think it is too far west. Myres, however, was wrong. The 1:25,000 scale map clearly shows earthworks near Baydon.

Baydon is on a narrow spur along which Roman engineers had chosen to run the Cirencester – Silchester road. It had climbed onto the lower terrace at Wanborough, three or four miles to the north west. The upper terrace is pierced here by a massive re-entrant, the Wanborough Plain. It is dry today. Where it narrows to the south there is a spring at the village of Aldbourne. Tellingly, there is almost no settlement in the Wanborough Plain and probably never has been. For centuries it was probably a boggy, forested swamp. Its west side is a long, narrow ridge called Sugar Hill which shields another valley, currently the route of the B4192 from Aldbourne to Swindon. The west side of that Valley rises to what is once again the main ridge of the Downs, at up to 277 metres; but, confusingly, running more or less north to south. It is easy today to find many sections of earthworks facing north of west, near the crestline, from Liddington Hill in the north to Ogbourne St George in the south. What is not obvious is how the earthworks crossed from the Baydon area to Sugar Hill and thence to Liddington Hill. There are one or two clues along the way.

The road south from Cirencester divides just north of Wanborough. The Silchester road ran through Baydon. The other road ran more or less south to *Cunetio*. In a sense, the ground there is like that of the Wanborough Plain three miles to the east. It is now a high, dry valley on the lower terrace. The upper terrace overlooks it to the east. As you drive south down the modern A346 (which is on the line of the Roman road, as far as Ogbourne St George) you can easily see the dykes on the hillside. In the west the ground rises again to the Marlborough Downs. The Og valley narrows towards the south. 'Ogbourne' means 'the source of the River Og', a short river that flows into the Kennet at modern Marlborough. This area, the northern approaches to *Cunetio*, was fought over at length. We shall look at that in Chapter 10. We should remember that we are only about ten miles from Derry Brook, northwest of Swindon. We have conjectured that that area was the site of the Battle of Deorham, with all its strategic significance. We can now see how important the roads leading south of Wanborough were, and why their use had to be denied to the West Saxons.

There is, in fact, almost no evidence of how that was done. There is a little evidence that the original line of these dykes had not run southwards past Lambourn then to Baydon, but on a more northerly course (across Russley Downs, about two miles further north). Similarly there is some evidence that the dykes crossed the middle of the Marlborough Downs, through the area of Rockley and Overton Down thence to the ancient site of Avesbury. In passing, we have just described a 'Russley' and a 'Rockley'. There is also a 'Rabley', and a Woodsend which is nowhere near a wood today. The Downs are downland today. When the Saxons arrived, they were not. See Figure 7.3.

The whole area was dominated by woodland for several miles. The Savernake Forest today is a small part of what it was. The core of the forest was in the Vale of Pewsey, a few miles south of Marlborough. That area is geographically highly significant. The River Dun flows east and joins the Kennet at Hungerford. Nowadays it is largely

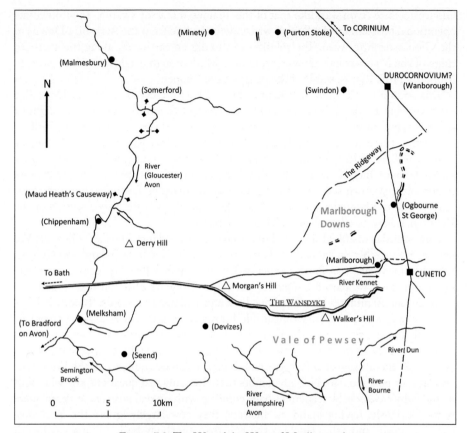

Figure 7.3 The Wansdyke West of Marlborough.

captured by the course of the Kennet and Avon Canal. Within a mile of the headwaters of the Dun are those of the River Bourne. Confusingly, there are two Bournes in this area. This one flows south through Salisbury Plain to join the Hampshire Avon. (The other is the Bourne Rivulet, which flows past Hurstbourne Tarrant to join the Test at Longparish.) Only a mile or two further west are the headwaters of the Hampshire Avon, which flow south across the Plain through a different valley towards Salisbury. The Hampshire Avon drains much of the Vale of Pewsey, as far west as Devizes. However, within a mile of some of its headwaters are the headwaters of the Semington Brook, which flows west to join the Gloucestershire Avon between Melksham and Trowbridge.

At the theatre or operational level, this topography is important. The Marlborough Downs form a kind of bastion. South of there, the Vale of Pewsey is one of the most important watersheds in England. Rivers flow east to the Thames, west to the Bristol Channel, and south to the English Channel. Much of the valley of the

Gloucestershire Avon was, like that of the Thames, a marshy swamp. The immediate operational problem for the British was to defend a line from the Berkshire Downs to the Gloucestershire Avon. The solution was to dig an earthwork along the southern ridge of the Marlborough Downs, from near Marlborough, slightly south of west, to Morgan's Hill. That is, south of the valley of the Kennet.

This section is stupendous. It is probably the best preserved section of Dark Age earthworks in England. It rivals the Devil's Dyke at Cambridge not for its height (it is smaller) but for its length and its breathtaking siting. If you climb Morgan's Hill, or the section between Milk and Tan Hills about five miles east, the views southwards across the Vale of Pewsey are breathtaking. More importantly, you are standing on an earthwork which is about 15 to 20 feet high and 40 to 50 feet across. Even more importantly, you can see it stretching off into the distance for miles, left and right. And you would be under no doubt that it faces north. It is the major section of the Wansdyke. Few people in Britain have even heard of it.

One Saturday in 2009 I was in Marlborough. I bumped into a former colleague. We had served together, in the same infantry company, in Northern Ireland and Cyprus. He asked me what I was doing. I explained, over a cup of coffee. He seemed genuinely interested, so as we parted I suggested he go to Morgan's Hill and take a look. He went. About 20 minutes later he phoned me and said just two words: 'Bloody hell!'

He, like I, was an infantry officer. He knows something about digging trenches. He could tell at a glance that the Wansdyke is immensely impressive. It was excavated very thoroughly in the nineteenth century by the famous archaeologist and anthropologist, General Augustus Pitt Rivers. His conclusion was quite clear: the Wansdyke was late- or post-Roman. Nobody doubts that. The only real questions are 'who built it' and 'why'? Curiously, academics have come up with no real answers to those questions. Curiously, having found no answers, they now largely ignore the questions. Massive, major anomalies (such as the fact that somebody built a major earthwork for dozens of miles in the late- or post-Roman period) simply go unanswered. That is curious.

At the west end of Morgan's Hill, the Wansdyke runs onto and captures the line of the Roman road from *Cunetio* to Bath. Like the Chichester to Silchester road, it seems that the British deepened one of the road's ditches (in this case, the northern one) and mounded the spoil onto the road bed. The picture is a bit confused in places, because the Ridgeway became hollowed out in later medieval times. In addition, the Roman road dropped further west to cross the bogs of the Avon.

Codrington's book on the Roman roads was first published in 1903. It makes it quite clear that the Wansdyke ran along that section of the Roman road, almost as far as the gorge of the Avon near Bath. Codrington describes quite clearly how the ditch on the north of the road had been dug out and the spoil built up on top of the roadway. That had been very obvious when the wealthy antiquarian Sir Richard Colt Hoare had surveyed the area a century earlier. As recently as the 1920s, the bank was over 12 feet high in places. It is now typically only about two feet high. There is almost no record of it having been excavated since Pitt River's times.

The siting and purpose of this section of the Wansdyke is easy to describe, as are its details at the western end at Morgan's Hill. It is less clear what happened at its eastern end. It seems to run out in the middle of a field south of Marlborough. We have seen that originally the British may have defended north of the Kennet, on the upper section of the Marlborough Downs. So we don't really know what happened between the area of Ogbourne St George and the area south of Marlborough. We don't know, and won't pretend that we do, but will find a bit more evidence in Chapter Ten.

At first sight the Wansdyke seems to wander across the Downs in a fairly meaningless manner. We heard the a similar remark about the Chiltern Dykes. The Wansdyke is less rectilinear. It is adapted more closely to the contours. It does, nonetheless, follow a fairly meandering course. If, however, one plots the course of two re-entrants which run south from the Kennet almost as far as the crest line on the north side of the Vale of Pewsey, the alignment becomes easier to understand. It is also obvious that the Wansdyke was not dug to a uniform profile. This eastern section is appreciably smaller than that further west. There is no apparent reason for that, except that place-name evidence might indicate that the eastern section was dug amongst woodland whilst the western section was largely open downland.

West of Morgan's Hill, the Roman road to Bath descended into, and crossed, the valley of the Gloucestershire Avon. That river drains a large area. Place name evidence tells us that much of it was a large swamp. South and west of Devizes several streams flow into the Semington Brook. Seend and Seend Cleeve stand on what would have been an island. South of that we find 'Marston' ('the settlement in the marsh') and 'Stoke's Marsh Farm'. Further north is an area where the valley of the Avon was fairly narrow. Dry ground could be found close to both banks. Not surprisingly, that is the area where the Romans built their road to Bath. Further north the valley widens again. East-west passage across these marshes was very difficult. There were few fords. From Malmesbury to Bradford on Avon, a distance of about 20 miles, there may only have been three or four fords. Some candidates (such as Christian Malford) appear to have been fords over tributaries. Somerford was probably only passable in the summer. There may have been a ford at Dodford Farm, but even in early Victorian times there was no path to it on the west bank. In 1474 AD a wealthy widow called Maud Heath endowed a huge amount of money for the construction and maintenance of a causeway across the marshes about two miles north of Chippenham. She left what was, at the time, the huge sum of eight pounds per year for maintenance. Chippenham and Melksham are obvious places for bridges, but we have no evidence of early crossings there. 'Chippenham' means 'Cippa's promontory'. The original settlement may well have been on the ridge above the river, but that does not tell us that there was a crossing there.

We should remember, however, that there are very few 'derry' place names in England. One of them, Derry Hill, is about three miles east of Chippenham. Much of the logic that placed the battle of Deorham at Derry Brook north west of Swindon could apply to Derry Hill. It is about two miles north of the Roman road from *Cunetio* to Bath. Derry Hill overlooks what was the main road to Bath, now the A4. It runs

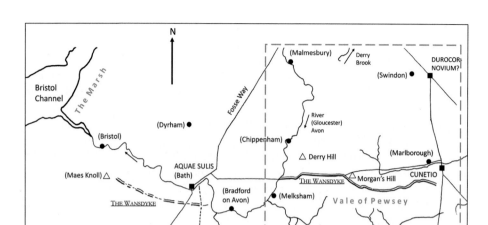

Figure 7.4 Marlborough to the Bristol Channel.

through Chippenham. In the Dark Ages it may have been an alternative to the Roman road. We cannot locate the site of the battle of Deorham for certain. See Figure 7.4.

If it was very difficult to cross the Avon from east to west, it would have been just as hard to attack southwards. Even if the Wansdyke had not extended west of Morgan's Hill, it would have been very difficult to attack southwards through the marshes of the Vale of Pewsey. Further west, however, the Avon flows through a narrow gorge. It ran from just west of Bradford on Avon past Bath. The Avon then flows through some fairly flat land in a series of bends and loops past Bristol to the marshes and then the sea. The gorge would have been very easy to defend. The area beyond was not only fairly low-lying, but the bends and loops would have enabled an attacker to repeat the trick of Bedcanford. That is, to draw the defender to one area then cut across a bend or loop which the defenders would have to march around.

The British resolved those problems by digging a further section of dyke, also known as the Wansdyke. It ran from just south east of Bath, across the high ground south of the Avon, for a little over 10 miles to the hill fort at Maes Knoll. Maes Knoll is at the east end of a high, steep sided ridge about three miles long which runs westwards to Dundry. There is plenty of speculation as to what happened to the earthwork from there, but little real trace of it. It might not have been necessary to do anything. The hill is high and steep (it rises over 140 metres in less than a mile) and a number of streams flow north out of it into the Avon. It is possible that in practice anchoring the Wansdyke on Maes Knoll effectively stopped it being outflanked. The area just north of Bristol was historically called 'The Marsh'. Bristol was historically the lowest crossing of the Avon. The name 'Bristol' refers to a bridge built there in medieval times. However it was done, by extending the Wansdyke to and beyond Bristol the British had protected themselves from the Thames to the Bristol Channel.

We need to review the strategic situation after the battle of Deorham. Just six years after the West Saxons had seized the Oxford region, the British rulers of Gloucester, Bath and Cirencester had been defeated. If Bedcanford had extended the West Saxons, Deorham would have extended them even further. It is hard to think of the West Saxons having enough people to settle all that area, and there is evidence that they did not. West of Oxford, they may not have been able to hold any territory north of the Thames at all; nor any west of the Gloucester Avon; or even much beyond Swindon.

History tells us a little about a people called the Hwicca. The name may reflect the name of a Roman cohort, the *Victores Iuniores Britanniaci*. Linguistically 'Victores' could easily become 'Hwictores', then 'Hwicca', or similar. The Hwicca gave their name to an area of modern Gloucestershire, Worcestershire and Oxfordshire. The Wychwood Forest in Oxfordshire and Wychbold in Worcestershire, many miles apart, may both have been within their lands. We know very little about them. We have, however, found earthworks which would stop the West Saxons using Akeman Street just west of the River Glyme. That was the eastern edge of the Wychwood. In about 584 AD, just seven years after the Battle of Deorham, Ceawlin and Cutha (or Cuthwine) fought a battle at a place called Fethanleag. Cutha was slain; Ceawlin 'took many towns, as well as immense booty. He then retreated to his own people'. That sounds as if Ceawlin won the battle, and raided many settlements, but couldn't hold them and withdrew. Fethanleag is assumed to be at or near Stoke Lyne, just north of Alchester and Bicester in Oxfordshire (see Figure 7.1). Tellingly, a lane near there is now called 'Featherbed Lane'. Featherbed was Fethanleag? Possibly.

The location is significant. At Bedcanford the West Saxons had crossed the Great Ouse. For decades – in practice centuries – they stayed south of that river. The reason is simple. In the 25 or so miles from Bedford to the area of Stoke Lyne there are only three fords. Stoke Lyne is about five miles south of the Great Ouse. The Roman road north east from Alchester (and Bicester) crossed the Ouse at Water Stratford, about six miles north east of Stoke Lyne. In practice this area is the headwaters of the Great Ouse. A West Saxon warband could try to cross the river above the higher fords, where it is so narrow that it is effectively no more than a stream. Alternatively they could simply skirt slightly farther west. The area north west of Stoke Lyne is the watershed between the headwaters of the Great Ouse and the valley of the River Cherwell. So it would have been possible to simply walk around the headwaters of the Great Ouse in order to get north. As with all these battlefield sites, a few miles is not significant. We don't know where the site of the battle actually was.

If Fethanleag was in the general area of Stoke Lyne, Ceawlin fought on the northern edge of his territory but could not keep hold of land further north. We shall see in Chapter 10 that the West Saxons repeatedly had problems on their northern border. We don't really know who the Hwicca were. They appear to have been Christian well before the king of Mercia was baptised, which suggests that they were Romano-British. They eventually became a part of the kingdom of Mercia, well after Fethanleag.

The account of Fethanleag does, nonetheless, say that Ceawlin 'took many towns, as well as great booty'. The battle may be significant in other ways. It may be that Fethanleag weakened the Hwicca, enabling Mercia to expand. We shall return to that in Chapter 10.

Even if the West Saxons did get across the upper Thames, it seems that they were at some stage turned back in the customary way. Somebody, perhaps the Hwicca, dug a ditch. Not surprisingly, this one crossed the Roman road north out of Cirencester, near Daglingworth. It is easy to trace just east of the road (the modern A417), but seems to seems to have been ploughed out on the west side. That stretch of the road runs along a high ridge between two valleys. The earthwork cuts it not at the highest point of the ridge, but at its narrowest. That is a very common feature of such earthworks. This section faces south, towards Cirencester. There are a number of other earthworks in this area. They are associated with Bagendon, the site of the capitol of the *Dobunni* before the Romans built Cirencester (*Corinium Dobunnorum*). Bagendon is about three miles north of Cirencester. Unlike those other earthworks, however, the dyke which cuts the Roman road would make no tactical sense unless the road was present. That is, it appears to have been built after, and as a consequence of, the road. It is post-Roman.

There are two further intriguing aspects of this area. The first is a road which ran from Fairford, on the river Coln, to the Roman road north of Cirencester and just above the dyke we have just discussed. It is called the Welsh Way. That is, it is a route which the Anglo-Saxons thought that the post-Roman Britons had used. See Figure 7.5.

Since Akeman Street was closed some distance to the east on the River Glyme and there was also a dyke at North Leigh, the Welsh Way looks to be a bypass. It seems to be a way of getting from the Gloucester area to the 'front line' at North Leigh or the Glyme without going through *Corinium*. So, perhaps the British did actually lose Cirencester, but not Gloucester, after the battle of Deorham. They could not regain Cirencester, but they could still deny the use of Akeman Street, which they had done since the battle of Bedcanford. It implies a very shrewd use of ground, because without Akeman Street it would be very difficult for the West Saxons to exploit westwards. It now seems that they did not, for some time.

The second interesting aspect of this area lies about five miles west. 'Wold', as in 'Cotswold', meant 'wood'. The area west of the A417 would have been a heavily wooded wilderness, made more so by very deep and narrow river valleys. An ancient trackway leads westwards across this area. It is now called the Daneway, but has nothing to do with Vikings. 'Dane' probably comes from 'denu', meaning 'valley'. If a traveller had left the Roman road north of Cirencester and turned off along the Daneway, he would cross two deep and narrow valleys. As he climbed the far side of the second valley he would be faced with a massive dyke, called The Trench today. The name is an understatement. It is only about 400 yards long. It cuts right across a spur. The bank is not particularly high; at most six feet today. The ditch is very deep. Even today it is about 20 feet deep. However, what makes it very impressive is that it was

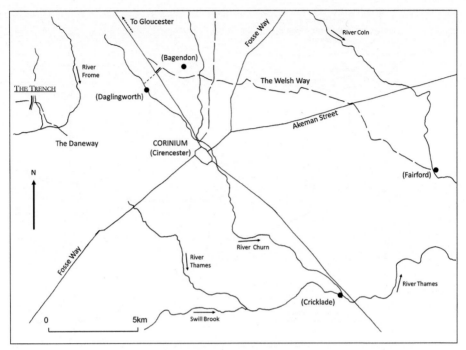

Figure 7.5 The Cirencester Area.

very clearly dug into Oolitic limestone. Just stop and think what it must have taken, even with iron tools, to dig a trench like that into bedrock.

It is perhaps meaningless to look for the capitals of post-Roman kingdoms. It is, however, well worth looking at the area five miles west of The Trench called Rodborough Common. The Nailsworth Stream flows into the River Frome just below Stroud. They form an isthmus just over a mile wide and two miles long. See Figure 7.6.

The Frome, the Nailsworth Stream and other watercourses form narrow, steep-sided valleys cut deeply into the plateau of the Cotswolds. The valleys are almost 200 metres deep and, in places, less than a mile wide. The isthmus is cut off by a dyke and related earthworks. The main dyke is called 'The Bulwarks', a much later name. It is up to 30 feet wide and 10 feet high overall today. It faces generally south and south east. It is sited on a very subtle reverse slope. That is best observed by standing on the dyke as it crosses Minchinhampton Common and looking across to that village.

The Bulwarks appear to have been extended, possibly twice, in the area shown as 'A' on Figure 7.6. That seems to have been intended to prevent access to, or along, the river, which would have allowed The Bulwarks to be outflanked. In practice the earthworks eventually ran right across the summit of the isthmus.

'Rodborough' means 'the fortified enclosure in the clearing'. It is not clear which part of the isthmus was originally called 'Rodborough'. The present hamlet lies off the

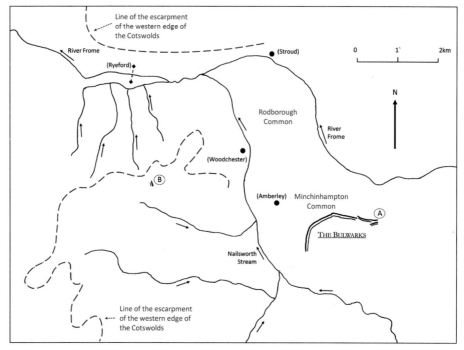

Figure 7.6 Rodborough, Woodchester and Amberley.

plateau, at the north of the isthmus. There is also an 'Amberley' and a 'Woodchester'. The remains of a Roman villa have been found at Woodchester. There are at least 16 other '-ley' and 'leigh' place names within five miles. The area was clearly wooded, and settled in Roman times.

At Amberley there is a much smaller enclosure, formed by earthworks to the north east and south east and the Nailsworth valley to the west. There is also what appears to be an intermediate set of earthworks. They also protect Amberley but (unlike the Bulwarks) do not cut off the isthmus. Some of these earthworks may be Iron Age, but none of them form a typical Iron Age hillfort.

Seven or eight miles east, the Roman road north west from Cirencester was blocked by a dyke at Daglingworth. Five miles east, the Daneway was blocked at great effort at The Trench. The valley of the Frome would have been very difficult to cross between there and Stroud, because is it almost suicidally steep-sided and the river is fast-flowing. The Bulwarks cut off any access through the isthmus. Another earthwork ('B') might have been intended to prevent the Bulwarks being outflanked to the west. There was only one ford over the Frome below Stroud, at Ryeford. That is well below the escarpment of the Cotswolds, and the Severn is only five miles away.

The Bulwark is typical of Dark Age fortifications. It may mean that the Rodborough area was, effectively, the capital of the Hwicca (whatever that implies). It may be part of a series of defences built by the Hwicca to keep the West Saxons south of the River Frome. It may have been a base from which the Hwicca could operate against the South Saxons. It may have been all three. As with almost any aspect of the Hwicca, there is very little evidence at all.

It seems that the West Saxons had seized Cirencester, but couldn't get to it along Akeman Street. They couldn't go north because of the dyke near Daglingworth. They couldn't go north west through the Wolds because of The Bulwarks, The Trench and related obstacles. There may have been more earthworks which we can't find today, or trees felled across paths through the woods. The British by-passed Cirencester using the Welsh Way. There are also signs of earthworks further north into the Cotswolds, near another ancient trackway called the White Way which leads north from Cirencester. It is hard to say which way they faced. There were several Roman villas in this area (around the village of Withington), which suggests that those earthworks could be related to post-Roman Britain.

We are almost at the end of our story, for the time being. After a long and circuitous journey Cerdic's Folk had established a kingdom in the upper Thames Valley. By 584 AD or so they had conquered a great amount of land but probably couldn't hold it all. They were somehow contained to the north and to the north west. They were contained to the south. They did try again. In 592 or thereabouts Ceawlin led an attack to the south and came up against the British at a place known as Woden's Barrow. There was, apparently, much slaughter of the British. But there is no evidence that Ceawlin won. He probably didn't. He was deposed and died a year or so later. That means that he probably lost.

There are two possible sites for Woden's Barrow. One is at Walker's Hill, where a re-entrant cuts into the southern Marlborough Downs and almost meets the ridge (see Figure 7.3). The Wansdyke is there today. It probably was there at the time. If not, it was soon afterwards. Woden's Barrow is now known as Adam's Grave and is a prehistoric burial mound high on Walker's Hill. There are dozens of earthworks around there. Some are probably prehistoric. The ridge overlooks the Vale of Pewsey to the south which, as we saw, was a vast wooded swamp. Ceawlin's army could have followed the re-entrant up from the Marlborough area and reached the ridge. They would then been stuck, because any to further progress would expose their flanks to any British force moving along the Wansdyke. Adam's Grave is within a mile of the Wansdyke; the battle was possibly an attempt to breach it that failed. One can speculate enormously, but without a definite site for the battlefield, it would be fruitless to do so.

Another possible site for Woden's Barrow ('Woddesbeorge') is Wanborough, about 10 miles to the north. All that the Anglo-Saxon Chronicle says that 'there was a great slaughter of Britons', and then that Ceawlin was driven from his kingdom. Wanborough is straight down the Roman road from Cirencester; about ten miles south of the crossing of the Thames at Cricklade. At Wanborough the road climbs the escarpment; it is the first significant hill south of the river. That may mean that the Hwicca invaded Wessex by crossing at Cricklade, and that Ceawlin met them on the first good defensive site. This version of events sees Ceawlin defeating the Hwicca, but possibly losing the trust of his warriors (perhaps by taking too many casualties?) and being deposed.

Ceawlin failed to break through to the south, across the Wansdyke. He was held up on the Thames in the Swindon area by the Hwicca. There would be no significant West Saxon expansion in this area for about fifty years. The Wansdyke held. Tellingly, many Roman villas north of the Wansdyke were burnt down. South of it, that is more rare. South of the Wansdyke, several hillforts were reoccupied in the Dark Ages. North of it, that is rare. The Wansdyke appears to be an example of a fossilised frontier.

So, by 600 AD, it was over 60 years since the Cerdicings had been forced out of the Solent area. It was about 40 years since the battle at Searobyrg. It was almost 30 years since the great breakthrough at Bedcanford. Something significant had kept the Cerdicings together through that period. Since the battle of Bedcanford in 571, that had probably been somewhat easier. Nothing succeeds like success. From that perspective, the true founder of the kingdom of the West Saxons was Ceawlin. He had led them since Beranbyrg. He was now dead. It would be more than a generation before the West Saxons moved forward again in this part of Britain.

In all of the time since they reappeared in the Thames basin, the Cerdicings do not appear to have built a single dyke of their own. They were strategically, and hence operationally, on the offensive. They had perhaps not yet realised that fortifications, although tactically defensive, can be used offensively. In due course they would. The fact that they did not build any dykes for decades also suggests that they were not concerned about enemy cavalry. The Hwicca may once have been the *Victores Iuniores,* but the *Victores Iuniores* were infantry. In the south, the last cavalry had disappeared.

This Chapter has dwelt on a small part of England (much of it entirely within modern Oxfordshire) and a period of just 30 years or so (from 571 AD or so to 600). It has done so for two reasons. Firstly, that period is a critical stage in our story, and hence English history. Secondly, it show how a detailed look at the geography, through the prism of toponymy and a detailed look at the siting of earthworks, allows us to reconstruct the events of the past to a reasonable degree of detail.

8

Bernicia

Northumberland is unique. It is the only part of modern England which was largely outside Roman Britain. Most of it is north of Hadrian's wall. However, the Anglo-Saxon kingdom of Northumbria originally stretched from the Humber more or less to the current Scottish border, and further north at times. As this book is about the origins of England, we will not look north of Northumbria in much detail.

The Romans advanced north of Hadrian's wall, and built the Antonine Wall, in the second century AD. They conducted some expeditions as far north as Aberdeen. The Antonine Wall ran across the narrowest part of Scotland, from the Clyde to the Forth. The Romans held it for over 20 years from 140. They then withdrew back to Hadrian's Wall and controlled the Scottish lowlands though a series of treaties backed up by armed force. They maintained forts in the lowlands for several years. The *Notitia* shows no Roman units north of the Wall, but when it was written the lowland tribes had been extensively Romanised. The tribes were the *Votadini* on the east coast, the *Selgovae* in the Cheviots and further north, and the *Trinovantes* in the west, including Galloway. Some tribes in Scotland spoke Goidelic (Q-Celtic). So it is unclear whether they migrated from Ireland or simply spoke the same language as the Irish.

The *Notitia* makes it clear that the Roman Army considered that there was still a major threat to northern England. Of the 56 units in Britain, 23 were on the Wall and a further 14 were available as reserves to the Duke of the Britons. That is well over half of the Roman Army in Britain. Of those reserves, two infantry cohorts were along the east coast (although garrisoned inland). The Sixth Legion and the Duke's cavalry escort were in York. Two other cavalry *alae* were in or near the Vale of York. They could get to the Wall by road in or about two days, via either the east or west coast routes. The remaining eight cohorts were all within two day's march of the Wall. The reason for this concentration of forces may have been a major Pictish incursion across the Wall in or about 296 AD. It is unlikely that the Romans would have kept 37 units on or near the Wall for over a century if there was no credible threat.

There is lots of evidence that the forts in Northern England, and particularly on the Wall, were not abandoned around 410 AD. Many show sign of occupation in the fifth century, and some in the sixth. The names of northern post-Roman British kingdoms may reflect the names of Roman Army units in the Notitia. Perhaps the best example is the kingdom of Elmet. The Duke of the Britain's cavalry escort was the *Equites Dalmatorum*, or the *Dalmatae* (from Dalmatia on the Yugoslavian coast) for short. From 'Dalmatae' to 'Elmet' is a short phonetic hop.

North Roman Britain was incredibly remote. On the west coast, the only city north of the Mersey was Carlisle, practically on the Wall. On the east coast there were only two cities north of York, Catterick and *Isurium Brigantium* (Aldborough, near Boroughbridge on the A1). The geography is important. The Pennines run right down to Derbyshire and divide the country in two. The Vale of York on the east side is very good farmland today. As usual, the question of how much of it was wooded, and when, is important. The north coast of Northumberland is also quite good farmland. Today much of it is arable up to about 200m above sea level, hence a long way inland. The valleys of the Tweed and its tributaries (particularly the Teviot) run far inland and are relatively low-lying for many miles. They separate the Cheviots (to the south) from the Southern Uplands. See Figure 8.1.

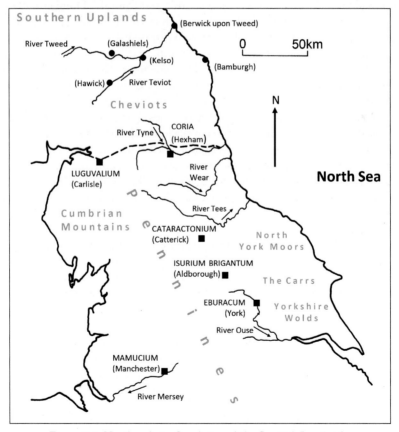

Figure 8.1 Northumbria, Cumbria and the Scottish Lowlands.

Plate 1 The Roman Walls of *Calleva Atrebatum* (Silchester). The best preserved set of Roman town walls in Britain. They are well over ten feet high in a number of places.

Plate 2 Wildlife near Netley in Hampshire.

Plate 3 Strip lynchets in the Vale of Pewsey. The fields below the lynchets now support sheep and crops. That land was clearly not available for use when the lynchets were built.

Plate 4 The Devil's Ditch near Newmarket. Even today it is up to 34 feet high in places.

Plate 5 The Wansdyke near Morgan's Hill. This section is about 20 feet high in total.

Plate 6 The Wansdyke stretching off towards the horizon, over three miles away.

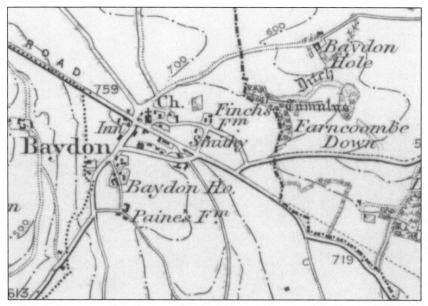

Plate 7 The area around Baydon in Wiltshire: one inch to the mile Ordnance Survey map of 1895.

Plate 8 Baydon: one inch to the mile Ordnance Survey map of 1947.

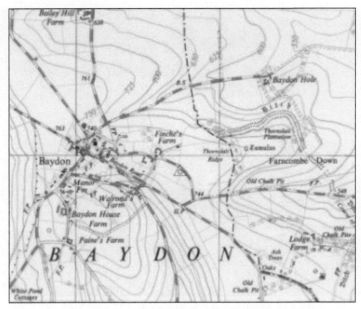

Plate 9 Baydon: 1:25,000 scale Ordnance Survey map; drawn 1921-2, revised 1961.

Plate 10 A narrow valley in the Yorkshire Wolds. An earthwork runs down
the slope in the middle distance on the right, and onto the bottom of the valley.
It faces downhill (towards to camera).

Plate 11 Wildlife near the Hobditch in Warwickshire.

Plate 12 Hippenscombe Bottom and Fosbury (a hill fort) in Wiltshire.
The Chute Causeway runs along the skyline on the left of the picture.

Plate 13 The Trench, northwest of Cirencester in Gloucestershire.
The rock is Oolitic limestone.

Plate 14 Stane Street near Glatting Beacon in Sussex.
In 1913 the bank on top of the Roman road surface was five feet high.

Plate 15 Grim's Ditch on the Berkshire Downs.

Plate 16 Grims' Bank, near Silchester, in Berkshire.

Further south, a number of rivers such as the Aln (at Alnwick), the Coquet, the Blyth, the Tyne and the Wear flow fairly directly from the Pennines and Cheviots to the sea. They often have deep but narrow valleys. The Romans avoided that area and routed their main road north to Hexham, about 25 miles from the sea. One road then ran almost due north, arriving at the mouth of the Tweed near Berwick. As a result, the road to Berwick ran inland, not along the coast. The other road ran further inland, close to modern Galashiels and then towards Edinburgh. See also Figure 9.7.

South of Hadrian's wall lay more difficult, moderately high and wooded country (which would become County Durham) as far as the River Tees. Inland, around modern Catterick (which is near a bridge over the river Swale) was the northern end of the Vale of York. East of there, and south of the Tees, is the great massif of the North York Moors. The Moors have been remote and virtually uninhabited since the last Ice Age. South again lie the Yorkshire Wolds. They are rolling upland farm-land today, but were high woodland in the Dark Ages. The Moors and the Wolds separate the Vale of York, which is broadly the valley of the River Ouse, from the sea. The Ouse joins other rivers such as the Wharfe at the south end of the Vale of York to form the Humber. Rivers such as the Wharfe give their names to their valleys, hence 'Wharfedale'. 'Dale' means valley; the modern German word is 'tal', as in 'Neanderthal' or 'Emmental'. Collectively the area of the eastern slopes of the Pennines is known as the Dales.

The land to the west was almost deserted. The Cumbrian Mountains, just west of the Pennines, are known today as the Lake District. Before the railways they were practically unvisited. South of there, much of present-day Lancashire was either moor-land or coastal swamp. The Domesday Book shows very little population north of Cheshire. The exception was the Eden Valley, sheltered from the worst of the Atlantic storms behind the Cumbrian Mountains, and a narrow oasis of good farmland. The Eden Valley is, in simple terms, the historical reason for the existence of Westmorland (see Figure 2.2). It made little sense in a modern context, so it disappeared in 1974. Before the railways and the motorway it made very good sense.

There were, in simple terms, three roads north: one in the west, and two up the Vale of York and on to Hadrian's Wall. We have seen how two roads ran north from the Wall. The west coast road continued from Carlisle more or less to Glasgow. There were few east-west roads. One ran west from Catterick (to Penrith), one ran along the Wall, and one ran diagonally from the west coast into the area of the Teviot and Tweed to join the Edinburgh road. The Roman road north from Chester through Penrith to Carlisle entered the Eden valley near Shap Fells. Driving that route on the M6 today, between huge fells on either side, you get some idea of how remote the area was. From Chester to Carlisle is about 110 miles, or more than five days' march on Roman roads. There were virtually no settlements in between.

Ironically the climate may have been milder, simply because there was far more tree cover. The effects of wind and frost would have been less severe. Today we see open hillsides grazed by a few sheep. In the Dark Ages there would have been much more woodland. Rather than today's monotonous pine plantations, there would have been hardwood trees with fairly varied flora and fauna underneath. Many of the valleys in the Borders contain large numbers of mature hardwood trees today. That is a good indicator of what there would have been, right over the tops of the hills. The best land was lower down, so the valleys were probably cleared first. That may have been in pre-Roman, Roman, or later periods. But we should not imagine the wide, open moorland over much of the landscape as today. Much of it could be, and would have been, covered with hardwoods unless cleared by man and then grazed continuously.

History tells us almost nothing in this region until the beginning of the seventh century. That is, almost two hundred years after the end of Imperial rule and at least sixty years after Arthur's time. That would almost be like saying that we know nothing of British history between the Battle of Waterloo and today. It is a huge gap: up to eight generations. Perhaps surprisingly, Welsh sources tell us a little. Welsh tradition is important because the Romano-British were in some fashion pushed westward. To that extent, Welsh tradition is the tradition of the Romano-British from what is now England. A large part of that tradition is from the *Hen Ogled,* the Old North. So it is relevant here. Perhaps the most significant is the tradition of Cole Hen: 'Old King Cole' to us. He is semi-mythical, seems to have been the ruler of much post-Roman north, and may have been a Duke of the Britons. In subsequent generations many British rulers claimed descent (that is, sought legitimacy) from him.

York was occupied throughout this period, although possibly not to any great extent. A basilica was in continuous use until the ninth century, when it was deliberately pulled down and rebuilt. The Roman *Principia*, or legionary headquarters, was used in some manner until the seventh century. The current York Minster was built over the foundations of the *Principia*. Carlisle was in use in the fifth and possibly sixth centuries. When St Cuthbert visited in the mid to late seventh century, Carlisle still had a circuit of walls and a working water supply.

The broad outline of the origins of Northumbria can be told quite quickly. Two Anglian enclaves formed along the coast: Bernicia (based on Bamburgh) in the north; and Deira (based in the Yorkshire Wolds) in the south. Ida, the first king of Bernicia, is said to have fortified Bamburgh in 547 AD. There are then almost no details of what happened until the next century, and the lineage of the kings of Bernicia in that period is confused. Deira was in conflict against the British in the Vale of York, resulting in almost trench warfare in the Wolds for several years. In one battle in 580 or so, two British leaders were killed, but it is not clear whether Deirans or Bernicians were responsible.

Bernicia spread slowly inland, but was almost destroyed in 590 AD or thereabouts (see below). Ten years later, in a critical battle somewhere in the valleys of the Tweed and the Teviot, the men of Bernicia fought a major battle and destroyed the *Votadini*, together with what may have been the last cavalry unit in Britain. The Scots, including perhaps the Goidelic-speaking Dal Riada, were beaten a few years later in 603 or so in a battle at Dagestane. The crucial victory, however, was in about 607 when the Northumbrians destroyed the last remnants of an organised, post-Roman army and conquered the Vale of York. About that time Deira and Bernicia were united, initially under a Bernician king, for the first time. They became the Kingdom of Northumbria. A decade or so later, in 620, they overran the kingdom of Elmet, the last surviving British kingdom in the east.

Apart from mentions of Cole Hen, we know practically nothing of the British in the region. South of the Wall the British splintered into a number of groups, of which only two were significant. Elmet seems to have been centred on the Vale of York, whilst the kingdom of Rheged lay across the Pennines, perhaps centred on Carlisle. Goods from the Aegean, the Mediterranean and Anatolia (including wine and pottery) were imported by the British and Scottish peoples in these areas during this period. The few poetic and literary sources we have tell us that the British (and the Scots) fought each other as much, or more, than they fought the Anglo-Saxons.

Arthur is said to have fought his first battle on the River Glein. 'Glein', possibly 'Glenn' or 'Glen' today, is probably Celtic for 'clean-flowing river'. There were probably several River Gleins in England. Most were renamed by the Anglo-Saxons, but two survive. One is in Northumbria, the other in Lincolnshire. Both are places where the Romano-British and Anglo-Saxons fought in the late fifth and early sixth centuries. It may be significant that the first recorded rulers of Bernicia are known to us from some time after Arthur's death. The first reasonably firm date we have is 547 AD, when Ida can to the throne.

Although Bernicia shows signs of settlement as far south as the Tyne, its heartland was around Bamburgh. Bamburgh Castle sits on a crag overlooking the sea. The Farne Islands lie offshore to the east, whilst Holy Island or 'Lindis Farne' is a few miles to the north. The name suggests that the original colonists came from Lindsey, and the archaeological record is of Anglian artefacts. Between the River Coquet and the Tyne to the south are traces of a different group. All that really tells us is that there were Germanic settlements for 30 miles along the coast. Bernicia may originally have been a British grouping called the Bryneich, which Germanic warriors took over. The archaeological evidence points to a small number of Anglo-Saxon warriors taking over a British population. It suggests that they imposed their language and law, but otherwise had relatively little impact on the population. Relatively few Anglo-Saxon artefacts have been found.

About three miles inland from Bamburgh there is a linear feature called the Bradford Kaims. It is perhaps a mile long and appears to face west on a forward slope. It is big. Even today it is at least fifteen feet high in places. The modern topography of Northumberland is confused by large number of disused quarries. The Bradford Kaims earthworks seem to be man-made, and do not appear to be related to quarries. Nor do they appear to have been excavated by archaeologists. They do, however, appear to have been part of a system which cut off about ten square miles of land around Bamburgh. It is fairly sinuous and does not look as if Roman engineers built it. We cannot tell whether it was built before or after the siege of Bamburgh in 590 AD. There is a considerable amount of Neolithic archaeology around the dried up lake below it. The earthwork may be Neolithic, but even if so it would have been there when the Bernicians occupied Bamburgh. It may have been the western limit of the Bernician enclave at some early stage.

The main British group in this area were the *Votadini*, who had been Romanised to some extent for centuries. Their capital, at Yeavering, shows many signs of a semi-Roman culture. It seems that the Bernicians around Bamburgh and the *Votadini* around Yeavering lived alongside each other for some time, possibly with Bernician enclaves amongst what was largely *Votadini* territory. Over the years the name of the *Votadini* evolved into 'The Gododdin'. That gives us the name of one of the greatest epic poems of the Dark Ages.

Rocks marked with 'cup and ring' insignia are generally thought to be prehistoric and occur over much of Europe. Of 18 recorded sites in Britain, there are one each in Wales, Derbyshire and Lancashire. There are two each in Northumberland and Yorkshire. The rest are in Scotland. Or so it appears until you look at the map. You then find 19 sites just in (English) Northumberland. If you plot them on a map, they appear to lay out a border which could be that between the Gododdin and Bernicia at some stage. It is odd that nobody counted those. See Figure 8.2.

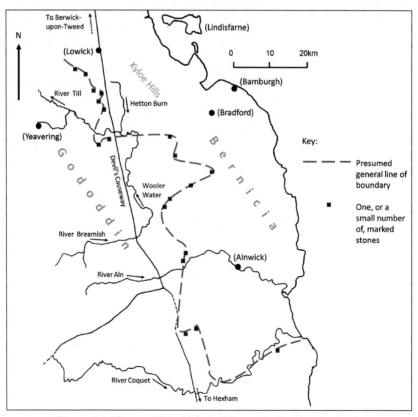

Figure 8.2 'Cup and Ring' Marked Stones in Northumberland.

The fact that they all lie along a discernible line is remarkable. There were at least 12 '-wicks' in the area (including Berwick and Alnwick). All bar one are east of the stones. The sole exception is just half a mile west of, and 120m down a hill from, a group of four marked stones. If the stones did mark the boundary, then the Gododdin retained control of the Roman road to Berwick to within a few miles of Yeavering. What looks like a dangerous salient on the River Till becomes less so when you inspect the topography in detail. The Till flows through a narrow gorge just west of where the Hetton Burn joins it. In broad terms, when you plot the cup and ring marked rocks on a map and then look at the topography, the line looks very much like a boundary.

We don't know how far, how fast, or how much the Bernicians enlarged their territory. The first we know is that in about 590 AD a coalition of the British (including men from Rheged under their king Urien, some Gododdin, some from Elmet, and some others) besieged Hussa, the king of Bernicia, in Lindisfarne for three days. Hussa, and Bernicia, survived. Urien was possibly a descendent of Cole Hen.

At some point the Bernicians started to settle in the valley of the Tweed, further north. For the first 25 miles or so inland, the valley is fairly broad and low lying. As the Bernicians advanced south west up the Tweed, they could encircle the Votadini (in the valley of the Till) from the north. See Figure 8.3.

High above the village of Yeavering is Yeavering Bell. It dominates the valley of the River Glen, which flows into the Till, which then flows north into the Tweed. Yeavering Bell is a hillfort which shows signs of occupation in the Dark Ages, although it had been a Neolithic hill fort centuries earlier. More relevant to our discussion here, however, is 'Ad Gefryn'. It is a Dark Age site in the valley, near modern Yeavering, to which it gave its name. It has been extensively excavated, and shows some fascinating Romano-British or early Anglo-Saxon features. They include what appears to be a parliament building, built on Roman principles but a highly individual design. It was built of wood.

The heartland of the *Votadini*, or Gododdin, was the valley of the Till, which is largely surrounded by fairly high ranges of hills. The valley floor is at about 35 metres above sea level. Only a mile or two to the east it is separated from the coast by high ground, such as the Kyloe Hills. They reach more than 200 metres above sea level. Most of those hills have hardwood trees growing right up over their peaks today. In the Dark Ages the Till and Glen valleys had been cleared in several places, but the hills to east and west were still wooded. However, the Bernicians now hemmed the *Votadini* in to the north and east. As they advanced further up the Tweed and its tributaries, the Bernicians could threaten the *Votadini* from the west as well. A stream called the Kale Water flows north from the Cheviots into the Teviot and then the Tweed. At the seemingly aptly-named hamlet of Morebattle its valley connects with the valley of Bowmont Water. Since 'battle' is a Norman French word, we should not read anything into the meaning of the name. Bowmont Water is a tributary of the Glenn. It is a fairly easy walk from the Tweed near Kelso, up the Teviot past Roxburgh, up Kale Water to Morebattle, down Bowmont Water and then to Yeavering.

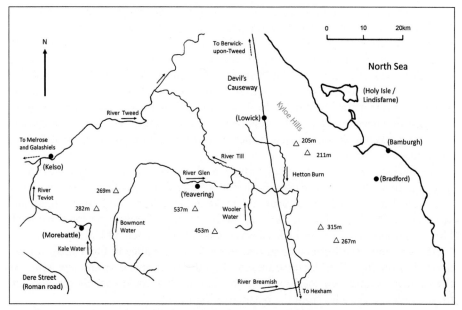

Figure 8.3 The Tweed, Till and Glen Rivers.

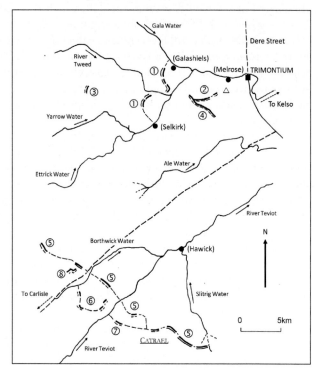

Figure 8.4 Dykes in the
Tweed and Teviot Valleys.

From Kelso it is about ten miles up the Tweed to the area of Melrose and Galashiels. The Bernicians got that far and then faced a dilemma, as shown on Figure 8.4. The Gododdin (or *Votadini*) were just one Romano-British group. They had a small territory in the Northumbrian valleys. But they could find allies from Rheged, Elmet, and perhaps other (Scottish) kingdoms. The Roman road from Hexham to Edinburgh (Dere Street) crossed the Tweed just east of present-day Melrose. The Romans built a major fort called *Trimontium* there, and a signal station on top of the nearby Eildon Hills. A road from Carlisle met the Edinburgh road just south of *Trimontium*. Scots from the Edinburgh region could easily march down Dere Street. Forces from Rheged could come up from the south west. Other Scots could come over a drover's road from the west (see below). Forces from Elmet could come up Dere Street from the south, and could join the Gododdin on the way. The Melrose – Galashiels – Selkirk area presented a major challenge to the Bernicians. Armies were small. The Bernicians could possibly hold their own against any one of its potential enemies. A coalition, however, not only provided numbers. It would also have geography on its side. The middle reaches of the Tweed around Melrose gave them an easy meeting place.

In 590 AD, Urien of Rheged would have approached Bamburgh by the road over the hills from Carlisle. If Urien and his allies had destroyed Bernicia, then what we call Northumbria today might be part of Scotland. However, that was not to be. The Bernicians' response was to fortify the Tweed and Teviot Valleys on a large scale.

The first Bernician defences in the area seem to have been built across the line of the Tweed. They ran south from Gala Water to just west of the junction with the Tweed, then south again to Ettrick Water near Selkirk. That suggests that at least one threat came from the west: probably Scots. The alignment did not take the shortest line, nor run from crest to crest. It took a practical line, typically on a reverse slope about two thirds of the way from the river to the crest. That suggests a sensible balance of accessibility, length and defensive strength. It is shown as line '1' on Figure 8.4. As we saw with the Cambridge Dykes, reverse slopes can be advantageous. The position was augmented by a short section facing south, south of the Tweed (2), anchored at one end on a stream and at the other on the Eildon Hills. The Hills were quite steep and had older fortifications on their summits. This section of earthworks would have faced any Gododdin coming from the south east. The total length of all these sections was about five to ten miles. They may have been about ten feet high initially. An old drovers' road leads west between the Tweed and Yarrow Water. It is cut about four miles further west by another short section of dyke (3).

We can't tell whether those earthworks were in place before the siege of Lindisfarne. They might have been, or they may have been built as a result of it. At some stage, however, the Bernicians seem to have swept the Gododdin out of the Till valley and consolidated in the Tweed. Initially, the section of dykes running to the Eildon Hills was extended in a straight line to the south east, incorporating much of what is now good agricultural land south of Melrose (4). Soon, however, the Bernicians were much more adventurous. They advanced up the Teviot to the area west of present-day Hawick and then fortified their newly-occupied lands. The scope was vast. The earthworks in this area ran across the headwaters of Ale Water, cut the Roman road alongside Borthwick Water, crossed the Teviot, ran south east again below the major peaks in the area (which reach over 500 metres above sea level), and end on the headwaters of Slitrig Water. It is Line 5 on Figure 8.4. In all, it is about 20 miles long. Parts of it are called the Catrael. It is so remote that few people have heard of it. It is generally about four or five feet high today. It can easily be followed for more than a mile at a time.

It was improved several times. An approach from the southwest, down the line of the Teviot, would expose a weakness. It would be relatively easy to breach the Catrael with a surprise crossing on the high ground between the Teviot and Borthwick Water. Those hills are over 100 metres high, so defenders in the valleys would need a lot of warning to forestall such an attack. A further section of dyke along the high ground, about a mile further forward, cut off that approach. In one place it now looks like three separate sections. However, each runs from one burn (stream) to another, or closes off an easy climb up. That, however, produced a major salient (6). Moving an adjoining section forward by about half a mile and linking it to the salient shortened the whole line considerably (7). Another extension (8) blocked any attempt to climb the north slopes of the valley of Borthwick Water. It might have been possible to outflank that from the west, but without knowing where any woodland lay, and so on, we can only conjecture. The configuration of these dykes is much easier to understand with three-dimensional mapping. Figure 8.4 can only give a general impression.

The Catrael (sections 5 to 8) blocked the road from Carlisle. Its siting indicates that it was built later than the more northerly sections (1 to 4). Its alignment was improved three times. That suggests that it was in use against an active enemy for some time. There is reason to believe that it was built, or in use, soon after the siege of Lindisfarne in 590 AD. The reason is quite simple: the next battle, in about 600, was at Catraeth. Linguistically 'catraeth' and 'catrael' are very close. They are closer than either *Cataractonium* (the Roman name for Catterick), or 'Catterick' itself. Writers have clung to Catraeth as being Catterick. They have overlooked other possibilities and ignored military geography.

The poem 'The Gododdin' suggests that a post-Roman cavalry unit, stabled and garrisoned in permanent accommodation and provided with regular rations, fought at Catraeth. There were, according to differing sources, either 300 or 363 of them (363 being a remarkably precise, poetic, and therefore unlikely number). They fought for three days (poetic language for 'a long time': Arthur is reputed to have fought for three days at Badon), and almost none survived. The poet, Taliesin, recounted the tale and may have been the only, or almost the only, survivor. The poem does not necessarily imply that the cavalry were *Votadini* (that is, men of the Gododdin). Nor does it mean that the Gododdin could still occupy Yeavering Bell; the campaign may have been fought to regain it for them. The poem should be taken to mean no more than that, perhaps 200 years after the alleged end of Imperial rule, a force of 'Roman' cavalry finally met its end. It may have been one of the five *alae* stationed along the Wall. It may have been the last mounted force that the *Dalmatae*, who became the men of Elmet, could muster.

It fought as part of a force led by the Gododdin. If it did manage to fill 300 (or more) saddles by the time of the battle of Catraeth, it had not done too badly.

Milan, the capital of the Piedmont, didn't cease to exist when Rome became the capital of the united Italy in 1870. Richmond, Virginia didn't cease to exist when the Confederacy lost the American Civil War in 1865. Similarly, *Ad Gefryn* (Yeavering) didn't cease to exist when the Gododdin were defeated at Catraeth. There is reasonable evidence that the Bernician kings took it over as their capital. St Paulinus preached there in about 632 AD, less than a generation after the Gododdin were defeated. Both Yeavering and Bamburgh existed side by side for some time, although Yeavering was abandoned at some later stage. Bamburgh may have fewer inhabitants it today than it did in 600.

Strategically, the Bernicians had neutralised Rheged and beaten the Gododdin. The men of Rheged never again appeared east of the Pennines. Three years later the Bernicians defeated another force of Scots, including the Dal Riada, at a place called Dagestane. There is no good clue as to where that is, but the valley of the Liddel Water has been suggested. That is possible. To get there, a Bernician army would have to climb the valley of Slitrig Water, cross the peaks and descend the far side, heading south west towards Carlisle. It would only be a day or two's march from the Catrael. That would be much easier than some of the other suggestions which have been made.

Defeating the Gododdin, and destroying the last cavalry, would have put Bernicia in a very strong position. The ruler of Bernicia from a year or so after the siege of Lindisfarne was Athelfrith. He was probably the first Northumbrian to merit the term 'king'. He held the throne for about 23 years and was the first to unite Deira and Bernicia. He commanded the Bernicians at Catraeth and Dagestane. Until the Gododdin were destroyed, Britons from Elmet could march north up the Roman road from Hexham into the Till valley. Conversely the Bernicians could not easily move down the coast. Once the Gododdin had been destroyed, however, Athelfrith had a good route to the south. That led to Hadrian's' Wall and on towards York.

It was probably Athelfrith who built a further, highly significant dyke on what became his southern border with Elmet. It was about nine miles long and ran from the River Swale to the Tees. It is called the Scots Dyke. The Roman road north from Hexham crossed the Tees at a bridge (at modern Piercebridge). If that were destroyed then the lowest crossing of the Tees was at Gainford, about three miles further west. The Scots Dyke seems to have denied the use of that ford to attackers from the south. Nowadays the largest section of the Scots Dyke is just west of Scotch Corner. Today that is the junction of the A1 and the A66. The A1 here is Dere Street, the Roman road from York to Edinburgh. The A66 is the Roman road which branched off it and ran west to Penrith. The bank of the Scots Dyke is up to eight feet high. In places the ditch is almost 20 feet deep, although in most places it is significantly less than 10 feet deep. When first built, the Scots Dyke would have been about 40 feet high in total. See Figure 8.5.

The Scots Dyke had a weakness. It could be outflanked. The Swale Valley is quite steep-sided near Richmond, but a determined army could keep heading west until

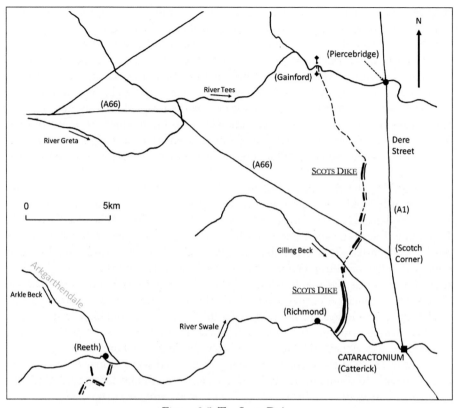

Figure 8.5 The Scots Dyke.

they found somewhere to cross. Unless, of course, the Swale Valley were blocked. Therefore it is not surprising that there is are five sections of earthwork near the village of Reeth, about 12 miles upstream of Richmond. The two main sections are similar in profile to the Scots Dyke, and face east. The other sections seem to be sited to prevent those being outflanked. Just west of there a modern road runs north west up the side of Arkengarthdale, from which another road leads north over the moors towards the A66. We cannot say whether it existed in the Dark Ages. Today it is one of the very few roads that do lead north over that section of moors. If there was a path or track there, it could have been used to man and therefore guard the dykes near Reeth in Swaledale.

Earthworks on the scale of the Scots Dyke don't just happen. They have to be built, at great effort, and they are built where they are for good purpose. The location of the Scots Dyke and the fortifications in Swaledale would stop the army of Elmet getting north. It also stopped them using the Roman road west from Scotch Corner to rein-force Rheged across the Pennines. This suggests that the Scots Dyke was built after the Battle of Catraeth (in 600 AD or so) and before the next big battle, in about 607, for reasons we shall come to.

Catterick, just south of the Scots Dyke, is about 80 miles from Bamburgh; a huge distance on foot. Conversely York is about 40 miles from Catterick. There were Germanic settlers along the coast from Bamburgh as far south as the Tyne (yet still north of the Tees). We do not know whether they were subject to Athelfrith when he came to the throne. It is reasonable to suspect that, after the Gododdin were destroyed, they soon would be. Destroying the Gododdin would have created a power vacuum. As we saw with the West Saxons, however, it takes time to assimilate large gains in territory. We shall leave the story of Bernicia here for a moment.

9

Deira, and Northumbria

Archaeological evidence suggests that Germanic *laeti* were settled in the Yorkshire Wolds in the fourth century. Some of the artefacts found in the area were from Angeln, rather than Lindsey. Some were Saxon, some were Allemani, and some were Frankish. Remains have been found in two main areas: around Driffield; and around Market Weighton. South east of Driffield there is a small collection of '-ing' place names: Billings Hill, Nunkeeling, Toffling, Fitling, Skeffling and Rowlings. The north east of England is overlain with many later, Viking, place names; so a list of just six '-ings' should not surprise us. South of Market Weighton, outside the village of Sancton, is a massive Anglo-Saxon cemetery. It is one of the biggest ever found. It was in use for several centuries. As before, we should be careful about over-identifying burial habit with ethnicity and then political allegiance. It is fair to say that the area around Market Weighton was significant to the Germanic settlers in the region. When the pagan King Edwin of Northumbria was baptised in 627 AD, one of his first acts was to destroy the main shrine of the Deirans, which was at Goodmanham. Goodmanham is just two miles from Sancton. There also seems to have been settlement at Driffield and south east of there. The Wolds were the heartland of Deira. See Figure 9.1.

The Wolds are a ridge of chalk in a great crescent, running north from the Humber near Brough (Roman *Petuaria*) almost to Malton (*Derventio*), then east across to the sea near Scarborough. The ridge rises to over 200 metres above sea level. It is over 45 miles long. The Vale of York lies to the west. Its southern end was a huge swamp. In the north west the Wolds almost connect with the Howardian Hills. They were separated only by the River Derwent at Malton. To the north of the Wolds lie the Carrs, which at the time was a vast marsh which the Derwent meandered through. In this sense the word 'carr' means wet woodland, typically dominated by alder or willow (which thrive in wet ground). The Carrs are now good farmland. They are about 20 miles long and about four miles wide, north to south. To their north are the foothills of the North York Moors. Importantly, strips of dry land (now housing villages about a mile or so apart) runs along both the north and south sides of the Carrs. The ridge of the Wolds shields another low-lying, marshy area to its south east. Today that area is drained by the River Hull and a comprehensive system of man-made ditches and

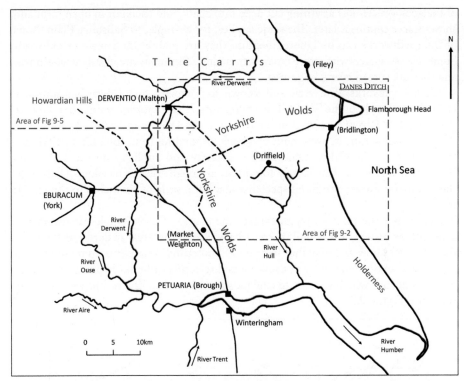

Figure 9.1 East Yorkshire.

canals. Further east of that is a low-lying strip of land called Holderness. It is rarely as much as 20 metres above the sea. Unsurprisingly, all the '-ings' lie on that strip.

The River Derwent gave its name to *Derventio* and may have been the origin of the name 'Deira'. It seems that a group of Anglo-Saxons of that name came into conflict with the British who lived in the Vale of York sometime before 600 AD, and probably before 580. It may have happened decades before that. It may have lasted for several decades, if not generations. But, as we shall see, the Anglo-Saxons do not seem to have taken Malton until quite late in this period.

Imagine a Deiran chieftain standing in a clearing near the summit of the Wolds, a few miles east of Market Weighton, in perhaps 580 AD. He is looking to the south and west. He can see for miles. To the south is the vast expanse of south Yorkshire and north Lincolnshire. There is no high land in that direction for at least 60 miles. To the west, he can see the long ridge of the Pennines, about 40 miles away. In between is the lush farmland of the Vale of York. Nowhere in or behind the Wolds behind him to the east can he see anything like that far. A man has to dream.

The 1:25,000 Ordnance Survey maps of the Wolds are criss-crossed with earthworks. There are dozens, and perhaps over a hundred, of them. In part this is a product of the geology. Almost anything cut deep into chalk, and then left in open farmland, shows traces centuries later. The same applies, for example, to Salisbury Plain. Some of the earthworks can be ignored because they are plainly the course of old roads. Some are associated with pre-Roman settlements. But many are clearly post-Roman, and they are spread over a huge area.

These earthworks were very well known to Victorian and Edwardian antiquarians. The called them the 'Wolds Entrenchments'. The Victorian antiquarian General Augustus Pitt Rivers excavated in the region in the 1860s and 1870s. He considered that the Entrenchments were built by people expanding from the east, fortifying as they went forward. Others continued to excavate and publish into the 1900s. The Entrenchments were then largely forgotten, although the Archaeology Division of the Ordnance Survey produced specialist maps at a scale of six inches to the mile in the 1960s.

Here is not the place to try to explain the course of every single earthwork, nor explain how or why it was built there. I have visited the great majority of them and thought about how and why they were built. Sometimes I have proven myself wrong, and started again. After a lot of thinking and rejecting different hypotheses, I developed a sequence which appears to explain what happened. The results are quite startling. See Figure 9.2.

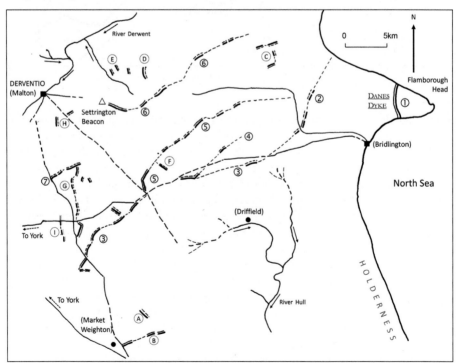

Figure 9.2 Earthworks in the Yorkshire Wolds.

Consider the situation in the mid fifth century. Germanic settlers in and around Holderness rebelled. They don't appear, at least initially, to have anything to do with those near Market Weighton. Romano-British forces from York, Malton and the rest of the Vale of York attacked them time after time. The countryside, however, was very difficult. Place-name evidence tells us that much of it was wooded. In one place what is now called a 'wold' is about five miles from the village which gave it its name. That strongly suggests that, in that area, the woodland receded five miles before disappearing entirely. For several miles around the River Hull, much of the land was marshy. There are several '-ey' place names, 'meres' and so on, as well as a lot of straight blue lines on a modern map (which indicate deliberate drainage in more recent times). There were few Roman roads. One ran from York to a harbour at Bridlington, and one from Malton south to Brough.

The Germanic settlers, who we shall now call 'Deirans', pushed northwards to drier and better land. They built a dyke to defend themselves against the Romano-British. It ran from the sea to the sea, but only across the neck of Flamborough Head, a distance of about two and a half miles. It was big, and still is. In places it is fifteen feet high today. Near the southern end there is a double dyke which defends a narrow gulley, the easiest way in. The earthworks there are about 22 feet high from top to bottom, even today. It is called the Danes Dyke, but is almost certainly not Danish. It is shown as '1'on Figure 9.2.

It encloses about six square miles. That would be enough to house thousands of people; but, more importantly, enough to graze a lot of livestock. A sizeable population could, if necessary, live inside it for months. It seems to have worked: Deira was not exterminated. Indeed it expanded. The next fortification was six or seven miles further west, running from the sea towards the south west. It seems to have been anchored at the southern end on one of the streams that ran into the River Hull ('2'). Although some miles longer than Danes Dyke, it now defended the whole of Holderness as well.

Many miles to the south west, the British around Brough had been raided by Deirans coming across the marshes. They built a short dyke ('A') across one of the dry spurs than ran up out of the marshes onto the main ridge of the Wolds, about five miles north east of Market Weighton. Perhaps emboldened by the success of their new earthwork (2), the Deirans expanded again, infiltrating along the northern end of the marshes and then digging an earthwork right across the Wolds ('3') . If it was linked to the previous section ('2') then it ran for about 25 miles. By gaining the ridge north of Brough, they outflanked the short dyke north east of Market Weighton (A) and cut the road to Malton. The Romano-British response was another dyke ('B'), running east-west and facing north, right across the ridge, about four miles long. They were still in contact with York via the direct road which ran across the marshes to north west.

In an interesting display of tribal politics, these two dykes were in practice defending one group of Germanic settlers from another. Both earthworks are north of the massive early Germanic graveyard at Sancton. The geography, however, suggests that (at least at this stage) the Sancton Germans remained loyal to the Romano-British. The latter were now, effectively, on the defensive. The Deirans appear to have mastered the technique of using fortifications offensively. That is, they would infiltrate forward and dig in, then settle the land they had just gained. Digging each section of dyke would take weeks or months; perhaps over a winter. The British might have been unaware of what was happening, or quite unable to do anything about it. The Deirans might have repeated the process year after year, or not for a few years.

At some stage they broke through to the north. Near Filey a fairly gentle slope runs down to the low-lying strip of land (less than 50 metres above sea level) that separates the Carrs from the sea. This presented two dangers to the British. The first was that the Deirans would infiltrate westwards along the *south* edge of the Carrs. They defended against that by building a dyke of their own on the escarpment, on Flotmanby Wold ('C'). However, they could not prevent the Deirans advancing north and then infiltrating westwards along the *north* side of the Carrs. We shall look at that shortly.

Meanwhile, back in the Wolds the Deirans expanded northwards again three times, consolidating with a dyke each time ('4', '5' and '6'). The British did not give in entirely, however. The escarpment is not continuous. A fairly major re-entrant breaks it about five miles west of Malton. It doesn't have a name, but the village of Wintringham sits in it. The third Deiran dyke (6) ran along its southern edge, looking north. From the north, the line of that dyke now dominates the horizon to the south. It runs along a strip of wood about a mile north of the two Luttons and Helperthorpe, near the 174 metre triangulation point. For the Deirans it was an obvious line to pause on and defend. The Deirans then encroached along the main escarpment from the east. The British built a short section to defend against that, on the east side of the valley ('D'). The Deirans seem to have persisted: the British had to dig three more earthworks, successively losing ground down the escarpment ('E'). Alternatively they may have been using 'bite and hold' tactics of their own, working their way up to the top. (A series of four earthworks facing up a hill can be interpreted in two ways. Without any other context, we cannot discriminate between them.) Finally, the Deirans consolidated their hold on the Wolds with a further earthwork ('7').

The expression 'bite and hold' was used in later stages of the First World War to describe sequential, deliberate, set-piece attacks. They were less costly than the all-out attempts at breakthrough that had been attempted in 1915 and 1916. The pattern of earthworks visible on the escarpment, south of Malton and southwest of Wintringham, suggest very strongly that that is what took place here. Having reached across from the sea to the escarpment, the Deirans 'bit and held' repeatedly. Each time, they protected what they had seized with a new dyke. The British response was to retrench: to dig a further earthwork facing the new dyke, or sited to counter its effect. Sometimes that meant abandoning a position and falling back to an entirely new line. They seem to have built about three successive positions ('F', 'G' and 'H').

The earthworks in this area show a particular feature which is not common elsewhere. It is partly a result of the geology. Much of the escarpment of the Wolds dips very gently to the south and east, but their eastern-facing slopes are cut into by long, narrow but not particularly deep valleys. They are typically about 50 metres deep but perhaps half a mile wide. In places there are several of them, more-or-less parallel and less than a mile apart. What we see today is a series of short sections of earthworks that seem to cut the valley sides, and perhaps the bottoms; but not the ridges above them. They almost invariably face east. There are two possible explanations. See Figure 9.3.

The first possible explanation is that the British fortified right across the whole area, but only the valley sections remain visible today, due to ploughing. The second possible explanation is that the valleys were good infiltration routes for the Deirans. The British fortified them to stop infiltration and force Deiran raiders to attack onto the higher ground, which might have been open (or, at least, less closely wooded). There is little sign of ploughing there today: much of the area supports sheep. We can't easily tell what has, or has not, been ploughed in the past. It would be difficult, however, to plough the steepest slopes before the age of tractors.

In the end, the British seem to have been forced out of the Wolds entirely. The evidence is that one position, on Langton Wold about two miles south of Malton ('H'), is three miles west of the escarpment. It seems to have cut the Roman road south east from Malton (which went out of use), and is a triple dyke. In general multiple

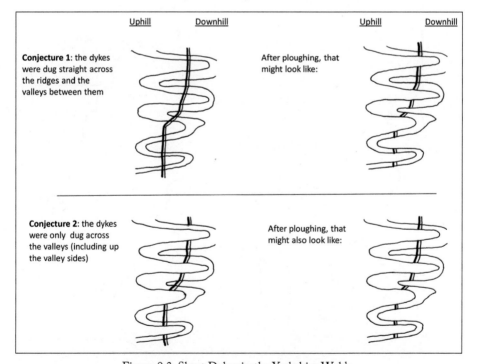

Figure 9.3 Short Dykes in the Yorkshire Wolds.

earthworks seem to be pre-Roman. Another triple dyke a few miles away does seem to be pre-Roman. The siting and alignment of this section (H), however, suggests that it is Romano-British. Another section at Garrowby Street (or Cot Nab) on the A166 ('I') cut the direct Roman road from York to Bridlington. It would prevent the Deirans exploiting down off the Wolds.

At some stage the Deirans broke out of the Wolds and advanced northwards past Filey. At Scarborough they occupied a massive flat-topped crag which sticks out into the sea. For centuries it has been the site of Scarborough Castle. It is easily defended. There is only one good approach. The British couldn't ignore the Deirans, but it would take a massive effort to evict them from Scarborough. Instead, the British responded with what would now be described as a distant blockade. They built large entrenched camps about five to ten miles away at Ebberston Common (shown as Ebberston Low Moor on some maps), Sheepwalk Plantation north of Hutton Buscel, and the Thieves Dykes north west of Scalby. They occupied them during the fighting season. See Figure 9.4.

Most of modern Scarborough lies about 25 metres above sea level. The castle is at about 75 metres. About a mile and a half inland, a ridge runs parallel with the coast. It rises to about 170 metres above the sea, and cuts Scarborough off from the area

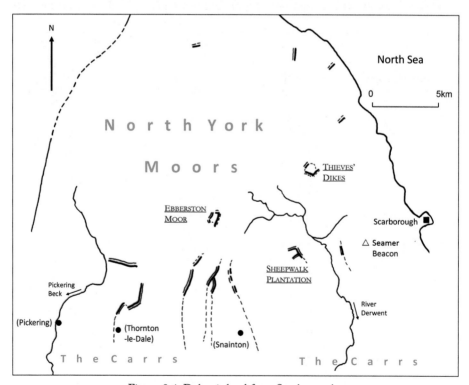

Figure 9.4 Dykes inland from Scarborough.

inland. The Romans had put one of their lookout stations on Scarborough Head, but it was not visible from inland because of the ridge. A man-made mound on top of the ridge, now called Seamer Beacon, was in plain view of the signal station. The station was about three miles away and 100 metres lower down. To the south west, there is another man-made mound 15 miles away on the Wolds: Settrington Beacon (shown on Figure 9.2). It is in line of sight from Seamer Beacon. It is also in plain view of the Roman fort at *Derventio*, Malton, which is about four and a half miles further west and about 170 metres below it.

(In 2014 HRH the Prince of Wales visited a government listening post close to the Seamer Beacon. It was built on the outbreak of war in 1914 to monitor the radio traffic of the German High Seas Fleet in the North Sea. It is the oldest continuously manned electronic warfare station in the world. It was built there precisely because it was on high ground overlooking the sea.)

In the *Notitia*, only three cohorts under the Duke of the Britons' command were more than two days' march from Hadrian's Wall. The Sixth Legion, the Duke's personal reserve, was in York. The *Numerus Nerviorum Dictensium* was at Old Winteringham, on the south bank of the Humber. It guarded the mouth of the largest river in the north of England. Winteringham was also at the south end of the ferry where Ermine Street, the direct route from London to York, crossed the Humber. The *Numerus Superventium Petueriensium* was at Malton. Roads ran south from there to the ferry at Brough (and therefore Winteringham); east to the coast and port at Bridlington; and north over the moors in the direction of Whitby. With just two intervening signal posts (Seamer and Settrington Beacons), the Romans could signal from the coast at Scarborough to Malton.

Malton is about a day's march from Scarborough. York is half a day further west. Brough is two days' march to the south (45 miles), and the *Nervii* were stationed on the south bank. An *ala* of cavalry, the *Dalmatae*, were also at York. Smoke signals would be used by day, and bonfires by night. Light travels at the speed of light. Once lit, a signal at Seamer above Scarborough would be visible at Settrington (above Malton) immediately. An answering signal lit at Settrington would also be visible at Malton. Now, in practice, visible signals don't work immediately. Sometimes they don't work at all (how many foggy days are there in a year in Yorkshire?) However, if the signals worked, the Romans could get one cohort and one cavalry *ala* to Scarborough in just over a day. A second cohort could be there the next day, and a third on the next. Scarborough is just one place on the Yorkshire coast. However, we can now see how the Roman Army could have responded to a sea-borne incursion down the coast from Scotland quite effectively. Three cohorts and an *ala* was nominally about 2,000 men. It is unlikely that the Roman Army had to deploy that size of force against a seaborne descent onto the north coast of Britain once the system was in place.

By 600 AD that, of course, was almost two hundred years in the past. We can see, however, that Malton would have been an important place as long as some semblance of Roman military practice held. By the late sixth century that might have almost completely disappeared, but *Derventio* (Malton) was important for a different reason.

The British (or possibly the Romans before them) had built large, entrenched camps inland from Scarborough (described above). We can identify three today, but we have no idea which was occupied at any one time. They are big: anything up to a square kilometre each. That suggests that they were designed as protected grazing for cavalry. So the *Dalmatae*, who became the men of Elmet, deployed up towards Scarborough for a few months at a time. Whenever the Deirans in Scarborough got a bit brave and ventured away from their fortress, the cavalry would hunt them down. It helped enormously that the fortress of Scarborough was in full view of Seamer Beacon. Not surprisingly, the Beacon attracted attack. Not surprisingly, it was protected by earthworks. Three sections of earthworks are visible today along the top of the ridge near the Beacon, protecting it from attack from three different directions. It is also probably no coincidence at all that the three camp sites (at Ebberston Common, Sheepwalk Plantation and the Thieves Dykes) are in line of sight from Seamer Beacon. Detailed computer analysis of the terrain tells us that an observer in or near each of those camps could see Seamer Beacon, assuming that a few trees were chopped down at each site as required. Trees didn't have preservation orders in those days.

So, for a while (perhaps several years) the men of Elmet kept the Deirans in Scarborough bottled up. It didn't last for ever. It would have been much harder without cavalry, and the British were operating a long way from their homes. About a mile west of the Beacon the Skell Dyke faces west. That implies that at some stage the Deirans managed to seize the Beacon and start to expand westwards. Eventually they established a footing about five miles further west, on Sawdon Heights north of Snainton, and dug in to consolidate their gains. That would have given them several square miles of good farmland, between the moors to the north and the Carrs to the south. Their initial defences ran north to south on the forward slope of a gentle re-entrant called the Wy Dale. We will probably never know how they did it. It might have been simply by digging the dyke through the winter when the men of Elmet were many miles away. See Figure 9.4.

A dyke, however, is a *fait accompli*. The day it is finished, it is finished. The men of Elmet responded by digging a dyke of their own along a forward edge overlooking a narrow valley about four miles west, above Ellerburn north of Thornton-le-Dale. In fact the position uses two streams, and incorporates cross dykes to the north to prevent being outflanked. These earthworks are up to about seven or eight feet high in total today, and fairly easy to find. It is notable that several of the earthworks in the east are rectilinear, which suggests Roman-style engineering. Further west they, and most of those which face west, are more sinuous.

The British kept up the offensive. They continued to raid, and kept the Deirans under pressure. The Deirans responded with 'bite and hold' tactics. There are as many as six separate dykes north of Snainton. They include the Scambridge Dykes, the Givendale Dike and the Oxmoor Dykes. Some seem to be double. Most seem to face west. Some are almost impossible to find now, due to recent forestry work. They clearly interact with each other, suggesting that early sections were used as a basis for later ones. The main deduction is that there was conflict in this little piece of Yorkshire for several seasons.

Over ten miles to the north east there were at least three more dykes. They face north and north east. They defend the Scarborough area from the north. It seems that the British used the Roman road to cross the moors to the coast, then raid southwards. It is a long way, but it could be done on horseback in a day. That forced the Deirans to dig dykes to block the way south along the coast. If, or when, the British lost any cavalry they had, those earthworks would become redundant.

We don't know how the Roman road which ran north from Malton crossed the Carrs. A look at the map suggests that it ran south from Sinnington, following spurs which are anything up to 50 metres above the Carrs. It possibly reached the south side of the Carrs in the area of Amotherby (see Figure 9.5). There is reasonably good evidence of it running just east of north from the Sinnington area, and then over the moors towards Whitby.

At some stage the Elmet position at Ellerburn was defeated. Another dyke, today called the Double Dyke ('A' on Figure 9.5), seems to have cut the Roman road just east of Sinnington. It seems to face east. It is easy to envisage its purpose. It prevented the Deirans from using the road south across the Carrs; denied access westwards along the good land on the southern edge of the moors; and held open a crossing of the River Seven. It would make a good, short defensive line once the Ellerburn dykes had been lost.

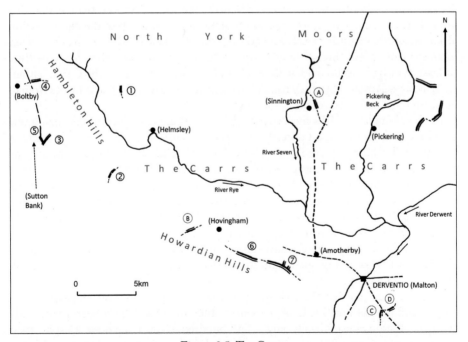

Figure 9.5 The Carrs.

This all seems to have taken place towards the end of the sixth or the beginning of the seventh centuries. That is, in the decades around the year 600 AD. The Battle of Catraeth, sometime around that year, may have spelt the end of British cavalry. That may have been what allowed the Deirans to break out from the Scarborough area. But we cannot be sure that Catraeth was actually the end of British cavalry.

At some stage the Deirans broke through, or past, the Double Dyke (A). They advanced westwards towards the Hambleton Hills. They fortified a series of intermediate positions as they went, shown as '1' to '5' on Figure 9.5 (and see also below). They then turned south onto the Howardian Hills (which are named for the area around Castle Howard). In Hovingham High Wood an earthwork runs along the crest, apparently facing north ('B'). The British response to losing the Double Dyke had therefore been to deny the road across the marshes of the Carrs (the direct route south), and fortify the first ridge which the Deirans would come to when they advanced from the north west. At some stage that (B) failed. A long stretch of dykes runs along the crest of the Howardian Hills for about three miles ('6'). It is just on the forward slope. It faces south. In places it has an effective height of about 18 feet. That is due to careful steepening of the existing slope. The Deirans had broken through (or around) the dyke in Hovingham High Wood (B), and then consolidated their hold on that section of the south side of the Carrs with section 6.

A glance at the map suggests that the Deirans might have captured Malton at or about this time. It could be assumed that the section of dykes on the Howardian Hills (6) ran towards Malton to the east. A detailed inspection, however, suggest that this is not entirely true. Two short sections of earthwork running up to the main position from the north, towards its eastern end ('7'), suggest that the Deirans had to defend against a subsequent threat from the area of Malton. So it seems that, for some time at least, they had captured a few miles of land on the south side of the Carrs, but not even as far as Amotherby. They hadn't been able to get across the Carrs by the Roman road, and had had to go round to the west.

In the Hambleton Hills five separate dykes (1-5), none of them more than a few hundred yards long, suggest a steady process of expansion by the Deirans to the west and north. The best preserved section is the Hesketh Dike (4). It is high on the escarpment, faces north, and is seven or eight feet high in total. It is a mile or two east of the village of Boltby. The road, path and track that runs north along the top of the Hills here seems to have been a pre-Roman route. Just east of Hesketh Dyke, running down to Boltby, is one of the few routes up onto the escarpment. The next route to the south is Sutton Bank. It is so steep that today it is very difficult for large lorries, and prohibited to caravans. The Deirans consolidated their hold on this area by building the Hesketh Dyke facing north, and the Cleave Dyke (5) at the top of Sutton Bank denying the route up.

Overall, it seems that the British were slowly losing a lengthy campaign in the Wolds and on the north side of the Carrs. They might not have been particularly worried. There were probably only a few hundred Deiran warriors. Despite their successes, they were still bottled in, up on the Wolds and on the edge of the Moors.

If and when they eventually came down into the Vale of York they would be out in the open and much easier to beat. Elmet could possibly put more warriors into the field, but whilst the Deirans were up in the hills it would be hard to make numbers count. Not least, earthworks were intended to allow a few to defend against many. Similarly, Bernicia was a long way away. Why should the men of Elmet worry about the Bernicians?

Given a good leader, however, and a certain vision, that could change dramatically. In 607 AD or thereabouts, it did. One version of the Anglo-Saxon Chronicle says 607; one version of the Welsh Annals says 613. The key breakthrough in the north, reminiscent of Bedcanford in the south 60 or so years earlier, took place at *Urbs Legionis*, the City of the Legion: York. Athelfrith of Bernicia was the winner. The British were badly defeated. The kingdom of Elmet had to abandon York and flee westwards. We shall look at that soon, but first we should look at one particular aspect of the battle of *Urbs Legionis*.

The sources are garbled. Bede wrote that about 1200 men of God, monks who had come to pray for the British, were killed. The Anglo-Saxon Chronicle says that all but 50 of 200 monks were killed. The sources tell us that they came from the abbey of Bangor, a religious house so big that it was divided into seven parts. Each had a (father) Superior in charge, and not less than 300 monks. That would mean a religious house of at least 2,100 souls. That would make it probably the largest monastery Britain has ever seen, and the largest single human institution in Britain for a couple of centuries before or since. Clearly the tale is mythical, but most myths have some basis in fact. The fact and the myth are sometimes completely different.

Here the basis in fact may be quite simple. The last vestiges of the Roman Army in Britain fought and were defeated at the Battle of *Urbs Legionis*. Some late-Roman units carried large, oval shields decorated with the Greek letters 'Chi' and 'Rho', which are the first two letters of the word 'Christ' in Greek. So: men of God? There probably weren't 2,100 of them. There probably weren't even 1,000 of them. There might have been 200. But, significantly, they stood apart from the main body of the army of Elmet and they came from an organisation which, historically, had had seven cohorts; each with a minimum strength of 300 men. We might be looking back to Cole Hen. The Duke of the Britons had originally commanded 37 units: 29 infantry cohorts and eight *alae* of cavalry. Might his successors have managed to create a reduced force of seven cohorts and hold it together for some time, perhaps decades or even generations? Possibly.

'Bangor' is a common Celtic place name. It means something like 'a fenced enclosure'. There were probably many 'Bangors' in late Roman Britain. Wherever the original 'Bangor' with its mythical abbey was, it was probably renamed by the Anglo-Saxons.

When York fell, the strategic picture in the north of post-Roman Britain changed dramatically and decisively. The last of the four provincial centres (London, Lincoln, Cirencester and York) had gone. The two Anglian enclaves of Deira and Bernicia were now physically connected. Athelfrith of Bernicia soon united them as the kingdom of Northumbria. So, instead of two Germanic kingdoms there was now one large one, more powerful than any other kingdom in the north. Elmet had been defeated and withdrew westward. That had a knock-on effect on Mercia to its south. Britain was now a very different place.

Ejected from York, the men of Elmet tried to defend the western part of their territory. They used the terrain to their advantage. Ermine Street, the road north from London, had crossed the Humber at Brough. An alternative route, avoiding the ferry, ran via Doncaster and Tadcaster. The River Wharfe flows down from the Pennines to join the Humber just below Tadcaster, where the Doncaster road crossed it. One of the roads north from the Vale of York originated not at York, but west of Tadcaster. It crosses the Wharfe about two miles upstream. At some stage the Romans had built a fort there. The men of Elmet used that road as the basis of a dyke from the Wharfe to the Cock Beck (or a stream running into it) about a mile and a half west of Tadcaster. The road is called the Rudgate today. The dyke was excavated by archaeologists in 1962. It faced east. It was rock-cut, 10 feet wide and four and a half to five feet deep. Using a Roman road as the basis for a dyke is reminiscent of the use of the road from London to Chichester on the south side of the Downs, perhaps a century before. See Figure 9.6.

It didn't last. The British had to fall back. They moved their capital to the area of Leeds or Halifax. Their next move was to defend the line of the Cock Beck. The Roman road crossed it at Aberford. The name seems, at first sight, to be a rare mixture of a British word for 'river' and the Anglo-Saxon word 'ford'. From the village, several stretches of what is now called the South Dyke run eastward, on the south side of the river. It runs along the top of the ridge overlooking the Cock Beck. It can be traced for almost two miles and faces north. To the west is the village of Arthursdale. This area really is a trap for the unwary. Aber Ford? Arthur's Dale? Is this clear evidence for Romano-British activity in this area? Of itself, no. 'Aberford' actually means 'Eadburg's Ford', and Arthursdale isn't even shown on the first Ordnance Survey maps. There are more, and more important, dykes in the Aberford area. We shall look at them in the next chapter.

The Cock Beck flows north east into the River Wharfe. However, just a few miles east of Aberford the land falls away to what was a very large swamp. It was almost 25 miles across and almost impassable. The Wharfe flows into the River Ouse about five miles south east of Tadcaster. It is joined by the Derwent (from the Carrs and Malton) and the Aire (from the west) above Goole. The Trent, the largest river in the east Midlands, joins it from the south about eight miles further east (see Figure 9.1). The Romans routed the London the York road via Aberford and Tadcaster, about thirty miles west of Ermine Street, because they couldn't find a better, shorter route. It was a huge diversion. In practice the South Dyke didn't have to run very far east of the Cock Beck to secure its eastern end on the swamp.

The area immediately east of Aberford may not have been entirely impassable. It was a spur and may have been wooded. Two things make this strip of land interesting. The village on top of it is called Saxton, which may mean that Saxons (Saxons, not Anglians) were settled here. The second is that, eight centuries later, the Yorkist forces moving north towards York in 1461 met the Lancastrian army about a mile north of here. They defeated it at the Battle of Towton. A minor road, roughly parallel with the modern A162 from Tadcaster to Sherburn in Elmet, is called 'the old London road'. That implies that at some stage the Roman route through Aberford was abandoned for one just west of the Cock Beck. That is probably the route which the Yorkists were taking in 1461. They had crossed the Aire at Pontefract a few miles to the south. In passing, note that the Lancastrians had held York, and the Yorkists were advancing from the south. Any notion of a modern, trans-Pennine version of the Wars of the Roses is simply wrong.

Eventually, however, the South Dyke fell. Elmet's subsequent defence was on a north-south line about six miles long. It ran from the River Aire to marshes on the

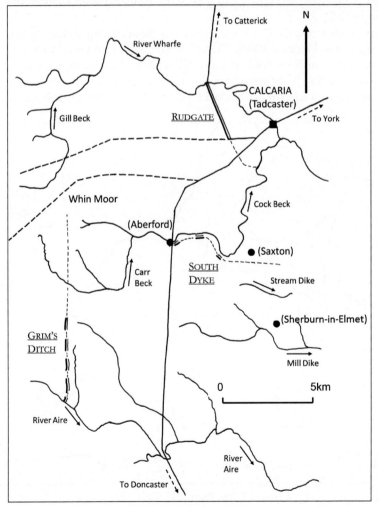

Figure 9.6
West of York.

Whin Moor, which drain into the Wharfe. Today it is called Grim's Ditch. The most southerly two miles of Grim's Ditch are visible today, or have been traced by geophysical survey. It has a bank up to five feet high and a ditch up to seven feet deep. It faces east. In places it was cut into the rock.

Several local place names, such as Barwick in Elmet and Sherburn in Elmet, reflect the name of the British kingdom. Today Sherburn in Elmet is a sprawling, low-lying small town. However, its old church is on top of what was the last piece of dry ground for miles towards the east. We know from historical sources that Elmet was conquered by Northumbria in about 620 AD. We don't know how it happened. It survived for over a decade after the fall of York. When it fell, the last traces of Roman rule east of the Pennines were extinguished. There wasn't much at all west of the Pennines. There were virtually no Roman settlements between Chester and Carlisle. See Figure 9.7.

There were few roads across the Pennines. Even today there are only about a dozen. One ran along the line of Hadrian's Wall. There may have been a road from Catterick to Lancaster. The next ran from Aldborough to Ribchester, near modern Preston. The next ran from York and Tadcaster across through the Leeds area to *Mamucium*, Manchester. Lateral routes seem to have linked Ilkley on the Aldborough-Ribchester

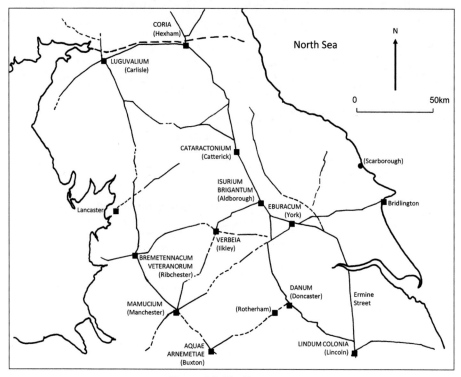

Figure 9.7 The Pennines.

road with both Tadcaster and Manchester. Not surprisingly, Ilkley is mentioned as the garrison of a cavalry unit (the *Equites Catafractarorium*) in the *Notitia*. There may have been a road from Doncaster to Rotherham (which we will consider in the next chapter). There was a road from there to Buxton, where it met one of the main routes north to Manchester and up the west coast. There is little, if any, sign of these routes being closed by earthworks. The main exception is the road from Doncaster to Buxton. It is closed by a dyke, the Grey Ditch (which faced east) at Bradwell. We will look at that later.

Indeed there is little sign of the Northumbrians crossing the Pennines. In 638 AD King Oswiu of Northumbria married a princess from Rheged. That implies a peace treaty. One story has St Cuthbert being given land in Cartmel (the north side of Morecambe Bay) by another king of Northumbria in 685. The story *appears* to come from a land charter, which actually relates to land in Yorkshire. Like many early land charters, it is probably a forgery. What is now Cumbria and Lancashire (that is, where we believe that Rheged once lay) later came under the control of Stratchclyde British. From the tenth century it was settled by Vikings from Norway. Place names in Cumberland, Westmorland and northern Lancashire are a real hotch-potch of Celtic (Crummock Water, Penrith, Helvellyn), Old Norse (Threlkeld Bridge, Grayrigg, and a lot of '-bys') and Old English. The name 'Westmorland' tells us that the Eden Valley was settled from the east. That is, from east of the Pennines. So there was settlement, but there may not have been conquest. There is evidence that the last king of Cumbria, Dunmail, died in 945 when the area was harried by King Edmund (a grandson of Alfred the Great). Edmund was effectively the second king of a united England. England may nominally have been united in the Tenth Century, but Edmund's authority clearly did not cover the whole country. Dunmail may actually have been a Strathclyde Briton.

The pattern of land usage (so-called 'medieval open fields') in Yorkshire and southern parts of County Durham is similar to that of central and southern England. The pattern in Lancashire, Westmorland, Cumberland and Northumberland is not. That suggests, firstly, that Northumberland was taken over by a group of Germanic warriors, but relatively few Germanic settlers. Secondly, if there was migration into the land west of the Pennines, it was relatively limited and may not have been associated with conquest.

It is far from clear whether the Anglo-Saxons really conquered Cumbria. The existence of a strong regional accent, and the use of Celtic-based numbers for highly traditional purposes such as counting sheep, point to the continued existence of a largely independent territory right up to the Domesday Book. If little is known of Cumbria, even less is known of the early history of Lancashire. There are only a few entries in the Domesday Book. The area became a county in 1082, but almost nothing is known of anything in Lancashire before that. In the next chapter we shall see some evidence of defending its southern boundaries. Here we will close with the thought that today England stretches as far north as the Tweed largely due to a few warriors, the Bernicians.

10

Mercia

In 571 AD the Gewisse broke through at Bedcanford and expanded rapidly into the upper Thames valley. In doing so they unleashed a series of other significant events. In order to understand those events, we need to look at the map and then go back 50 years or so.

The geography of the Midlands is dominated by three river systems: the Thames, the Severn and the Trent. The Thames drains the south Midlands through the Goring Gap and out past London. Most of the rivers in the west run into the Severn, which flows south into the Bristol Channel. For example, the Gloucester Avon flows into the mouth of the Severn near Bristol. The Warwickshire Avon rises a long way north east (east of Rugby). It flows past Stratford on Avon to join the Severn at Tewkesbury. Some of the Severn's tributaries rise almost as far north as Chester or Manchester. The eastern Midlands are dominated by the Trent. It rises on the west of the Pennines, flows around the southern end of them, then flows north east, and finally north, to the Humber. See Figure 10.1.

Some rivers flow in quite confusing directions. The River Witham flows roughly south east from Lincoln to the Wash. However, it rises well south of Lincoln (in fact south of Grantham) and flows generally north, almost meeting the Trent. At one stage it flows *west* for almost five miles. It turns east before reaching Lincoln, and then turns south east. Some scholars have clearly not checked the map. Lindsey was historically described as being bounded in the west by the Witham. It probably was, but the resulting maps don't include Grantham. They clearly should.

Ermine Street, the Roman road from London to York, ran through Lincoln. The Newport Gate there is the only Roman archway in Britain still used by traffic. Just north of Lincoln the road splits. The land route via Tadcaster swung off to the north west. The direct route ran almost due north, to the ferry over the Humber. There was a Roman garrison at Winteringham on the south bank, and *Petuaria* (Brough) lay on the north bank. There were several other Roman roads in the area. The most important was the Fosse Way, from Lincoln to Exeter. It ran via *Ratae Corieltaviorim* (Leicester), *Corinium* (Cirencester) and *Aquae Sulis* (Bath). Another important road, Watling Street, ran from London through St Albans to Wroxeter.

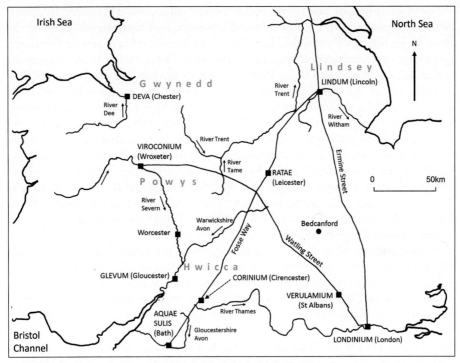

Figure 10.1 Rivers in the Midlands.

Wroxeter (*Viroconium Cornoviorum*) had been a legionary fortress for a short time. However, it is more important to us as one of the last Roman towns to be inhabited in Britain. It had been the fourth largest city in Roman Britain. A carved stone (the 'Cunorix' stone) found at Wroxeter has been dated to 460-470 AD. There is evidence of extensive rebuilding of Roman buildings with wood in the period 530-570. Those buildings were used (by Romano-Britons) for about 70 years. That is, well into the seventh century.

As far as we can tell, there were four post-Roman British kingdoms in the Midlands. Gwynedd was originally centred in the Cheshire plain, and may originally have been based on Chester (*Deva*). Its territory may have stretched east to, or beyond, the Pennines. Gwynedd seems to have been founded by Cunedda in the fifth century. Cunedda was a late or post-Roman noble who may have belonged to a family appointed by the Romans to rule the Votadini (see Chapter Eight). His grandfather, whose name translates as 'Paternus of the Red Cloak', may have been the first of those rulers. Cunedda was tasked to defend the Cheshire plain against Goidelic- (Irish Celtic-) speaking tribes further west. He may have taken some of the units from Hadrian's Wall with him. As discussed below, Cunedda may have built Wat's Dyke. Cunedda gave his name to Gwynedd.

Powys was originally based in the middle Severn valley, around Wroxeter. Its eastern boundary, probably with Lindsey in the fifth century, may have originally lain on the River Tame. South of Powys, the Hwicca may have been based in or around Worcester, Gloucester or Cirencester. Cirencester is the most likely, having been a provincial capital, but may have fallen to the West Saxons after the Battle of Deorham in 577.

Right over in the east, Lindsey probably held sway over a large area of what we now know as Lincolnshire, Nottinghamshire and perhaps Leicestershire. However, Lindsey does not appear to have controlled the area west of the Trent. That area shows no evidence of pagan Germanic burials. That helps us reconstruct events to some extent, but does not tell us who controlled the area west of the Trent. As we shall see, Lindsey seems to have fallen under Anglian control quite early. There is some rather intriguing evidence about Lindsey (and specifically Lincoln) that we shall look at later. Lincoln had been a provincial capital. That province (*Flavia Caesariensis*) would have included Leicester. Leicester is on the Fosse Way, in the direction of the other former provincial capital at Cirencester.

There is evidence of very early Anglian settlement in Lindsey. There is what might originally have been a small cluster of '-ing' place names on the coast: Immingham, Killingholme, Stallingborough and Healing. The situation is, once again, confused by a later overlay of Viking place names and suffixes. There are also some '-ings' north-east of Lincoln: Beckering, Barlings, Minting and The Hardings. There is archaeological evidence of very early Anglian cemeteries around Lincoln and at places such as Sleaford and Ancaster further south. Further south again, at Kempsford near Bedford, there is evidence of Anglians as early as the fifth century. There is also evidence of Saxons in the late sixth century; but nothing in between. This reinforces the idea that somebody – perhaps Arthur – wiped out early Anglian settlement in the area. Of one of his battles was at the River Glen. That could refer to one of the two small rivers which flow east into the Fens just north of Stamford. The *end* of the gap in the archaeological record reinforces the idea that the West Saxon victory at Bedcanford in 571 AD allowed Germanic peoples start moving westwards once more.

Arthur seems to have died in the 520s or 530s AD. Several Anglo-Saxon kingdoms seem to have been founded soon afterwards. An Anglian called Icel founded what would become the kingdom of Mercia in 527 or so in a somewhat unexpected place. Watling Street crosses the River Tame just south of modern Tamworth ('the enclosure by the River Tame'). The Tame flows north to join the Trent about six miles away. The east bank of the Tame is the heartland of Mercia (see Figure 10.1 above). Why is that?

'Mercia' is sometimes taken to be 'the Marches': the western borders of Germanic settlement. That settlement was presumably centred further east and therefore in Lindsey. But it may have had nothing to do with Lindsey. 'Old' Mercia may have been the most westerly Anglian settlement in this area, but if we backtrack about 20 miles down Watling Street, we reach the Fosse Way. We then find fifth-century Germanic settlements down the Fosse to Stratford on Avon and even further. The earliest Anglian settlements in Mercia were small, poor, and sixth (rather than fifth) century.

The settlement pattern is quite clear. There was early Anglian settlement along the Fosse Way for a long way south, but almost nothing north of the Trent. The Trent was the southern border of something Romano-British for a long time. We don't know quite what. It may have been part of the kingdom of Gwynedd, Powys or even perhaps Elmet. Mercia may have been able to develop in the sixth century because it was a long way from what remained of any of the post-Arthurian kingdoms. It was almost equidistance between Lincoln, Wroxeter, and Cirencester. It may be significant that there is some trace of an earthwork about six miles east of Tamworth, near the south bank of the Trent and very close to the border of Staffordshire. It is called the Mansditch and appears to face east. Perhaps Mercia's early enemies were to its east.

Lindsey may not have been an Anglo-Saxon kingdom. There is some doubt that it was a kingdom at all. As we shall see, there is some evidence that it survived as a broadly British, and Christian, enclave until swallowed up in the disputes between Mercia and Northumbria.

The picture for much of the sixth century, after Arthur had perhaps hammered Anglian settlers in the east Midlands, was of gradual Anglian expansion along the general line of the Fosse Way. That settlement did not cross the Trent but did include the east bank of the Tame. This expansion was greatly eased after the Battle of Bedcanford in 571 AD. The Gewisse concentrated their efforts on expanding into the upper Thames Valley, but that left behind a power vacuum. Not surprisingly it was the most powerful kingdom that took advantage of that. That kingdom was East Anglia. Ermine Street leads north, between Cambridge and Bedford. A British defeat at Bedford would open the way for expansion from East Anglia into the south and east Midlands. Soon after, the battle of Fethenleag in 584 (discussed in Chapter Seven) may have halted West Saxon expansion northwards. By distracting the Hwicca southwards, it may also have given the fledgling kingdom of Mercia time to consolidate.

It was another twenty years before the next major event. In Chapter Nine we saw that that in about 607 AD Athelfrith of Bernicia had defeated the British at *Urbs Legionis*. He then united Bernicia with Deira to form Northumbria. The men of Elmet were forced to defend first at Tadcaster, then at the Cock Beck, and finally at Grim's Ditch east of Leeds. Critically, defeat on the Cock Beck opened the Roman road south for the Northumbrians; towards Lincoln and London.

It may have been at about this time that somebody (perhaps the men of Gwynedd) built a short dike just south of Brough. It cuts the Roman road from Rotherham to Buxton over the Pennines. Today it is called the Grey Ditch. It is about six feet high and about half a mile long. It faces north east to defend against the Northumbrians. There are traces of two other earthworks about five miles east and south east of Buxton, called The Ditch (near Farditch Farm) and Priestcliffe Ditch. Taken together, they may represent Romano-British measures to protect Buxton and hence keep the road from Manchester to Derby open. See Figure 10.2.

The key to understanding this area is the topology of the Dales, which are shown as grey dotted lines on Figure 10.2. In this area they cut deeply down into an otherwise undulating plateau. They are often over 50 metres deep but narrow (perhaps just 100

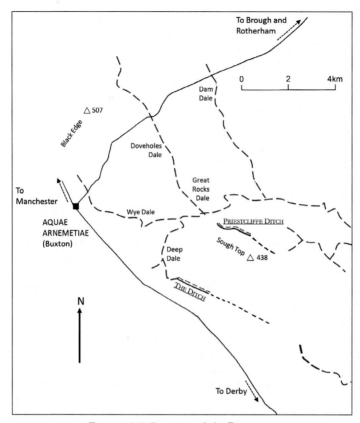

Figure 10.2 Buxton and the Pennines.

to 200 metres wide) and very steep-sided. They would be far more effective as a military obstacle than any man-made dyke. The Ditch and the Priestcliffe Ditch should be seen as part of a system, largely based on the use of the Dales, for defence against an enemy to the north east.

Given the circumstances of Bedcanford and the defeat of Elmet, it is perhaps not too surprising that the next key event took place where the army of East Anglia (expanding north) might meet the army of Northumbria (expanding south). The battle took place in about 617 AD and is known to us as the battle of the River Idle. See Figure 10.3.

Somebody, probably the Anglians, had built a dyke. That suggests that the Anglians were prepared to defend Lindsey, since the Idle flows into the Trent. The dike is not actually on the Idle. It is about a mile or so south of where the Roman road crosses the Idle at Bawtry. It is on the south bank of the River Ryton. Today it is called the Roman Bank and is up to about ten feet high. It faces west and north west. The Roman road from Lincoln runs along a spur which the Idle bends around. The area to the north

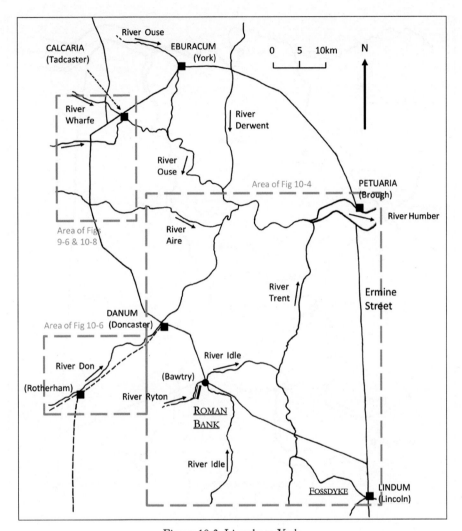

Figure 10.3 Lincoln to York.

was part of the great area of marsh which linked up to the Ouse and the Humber. Bawtry is over 25 miles from the Humber. However, even at Bawtry the flood plain is about half a mile wide, but is only three or so metres above sea level. It would have been marshy and tidal. There were no fords across the Idle or the Trent below Bawtry. The Roman crossing at Bawtry would have been over a narrow causeway which was easy to defend. The area a mile or south would have been dry land, and it is there that the Roman Bank was built. See Figure 10.4.

At some stage the Roman road was abandoned as the main route to York. The alternative route, which later became a coaching road, was the Great North Road.

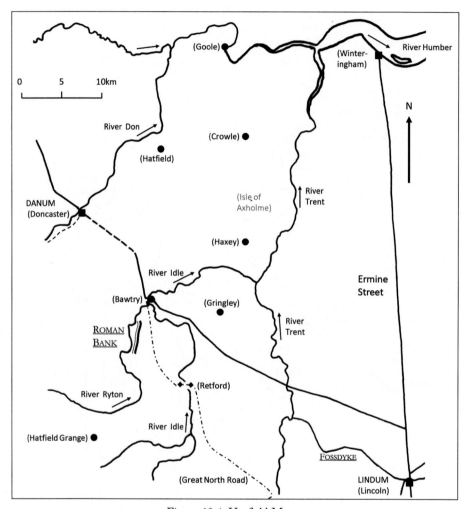

Figure 10.4 Hatfield Moor.

It branched off Ermine Street just south of Grantham, then ran up the west side of the Witham, the Trent and the Idle. Why it did that, or when, is not obvious. If the Witham was the western border of Lindsey at some stage, the new route took the road out of Lindsey. Importantly, however, the Great North Road joined the road from Lincoln to Doncaster, Tadcaster and then York at Bawtry. It came in from the south (crossing the Ryton at Scrooby, about a mile south of Bawtry). The Roman Bank would protect the Great North Road as well.

The Battle on the Idle in 617 AD had a devastating effect. Athelred of Bernicia had evicted Edwin of Deira when he took over as king of Northumbria. Edwin took shelter at the court of Raedwald of East Anglia. Athelred was killed at the Battle of the Idle, and Edwin returned to take the throne of Northumbria. It was Edwin who destroyed Elmet a few years later.

Northumbria was defeated and had a new king. Within a few years it destroyed Elmet. It then extended its power south, and west across the Pennines. That brought it into conflict with Gwynedd. Edwin crossed the Pennines. He built, or got, boats and raided as far as the Isle of Man and Anglesey. It was at about this time that the Northumbrians fortified the southern border of the territory they had seized in modern Lancashire.

The Mersey starts at Stockport, where the Rivers Goyt and Tame meet. They rise high in the Pennines. In the area just east of Stockport, however, they are slow-flowing and meander considerably. They would have been fairly easy to cross. Below Stockport the Mersey was broad and marshy. It could only be crossed at two fords. One was at Crossford, south of Stretford (which does not lie on the Mersey). The other was much further west, at Latchford near Warrington. See Figure 10.5.

Roman roads used both fords. It was surprisingly easy to defend southern Lancashire. All that was needed was to bar the two fords and build a dyke for about six miles in the east. Today the dyke is called the Nico Ditch. It ran from a stream that ran into the Mersey (possibly the Platt Brook) in the west. In the east it was probably anchored on Ashton Moss. There was a lot of marsh and swamp in this area, as place names with 'moss' (such as Moss Side) suggest. The Nico Ditch is hard to trace today. It appears as a ditch and a bank in various places, rarely more than two feet high. It was more obvious on the early Ordnance Survey maps, but the area is now the southern suburbs of Manchester. We don't know how long Northumbria held control of southern Lancashire, nor who they lost it to (if they did). We know very little about Lancashire in the Dark Ages.

What is now Cheshire remained in the hands of Gwynedd. The king of Gwynedd was Cadwallon, who was one of the greatest British kings of the seventh century.

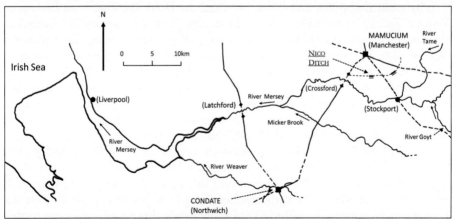

Figure 10.5 Crossings of the Mersey.

Cadwallon was descended from Cunedda, the founder of Gwynedd. In or about 629 AD Edwin of Northumbria may have managed to trap Cadwallon on a small island just east of Anglesey for a while. In or about 633 Cadwallon took his army east against Northumbria. Penda of Mercia was with him. Their route was east to Derby, then north to Chesterfield and Rotherham. There is no known Roman road from Rotherham to Doncaster, but it seems highly likely that there was one. From there the route ran north to Tadcaster, via Aberford. That route was barred, however, so they tried to find a route across the marshes east of there.

That area is called Hatfield Moor (see Figure 10.4). Hatfield village is up to ten metres above sea level, but most of the surrounding land is at five metres or even lower. The route to Hatfield from Doncaster is at about seven metres. Just east of Hatfield is a place called 'Slay Pits', which could refer to a mass burial. It is possible that Cadwallon and Penda's route was slightly further east, along what is now the A161 running through the Isle of Axholme. There is a series of what would have been islands in the marsh (starting near Gringley and passing through Haxey, then Axholme to Crowle) that lead more or less to Goole. If it was passable that far, it offered an invading army the opportunity to approach York from the east and outflank a defending army waiting at Aberford. Cadwallon and Penda fought Edwin and killed him. Northumbria fell apart. Athelfrith's sons Eanfrith took over Bernicia, and Edwin's cousin Osric took over Deira. A year or two later Eanfrith died and his brother Oswald succeeded in Bernicia.

Another possible site for the Battle of Hatfield is Hatfield Grange near Cuckney, just north of Mansfield and about 20 miles south of Hatfield Moor. The skeletons of at least 200 warriors were found in a mass burial under the church in Cuckney in 1951. A battle north of Mansfield would suggest that Cadwallon and Penda marched up the Fosse Way from Leicester. They were north of the Trent and were trying to get round the headwaters of the Idle. That may have been because the crossing at Bawtry was blocked.

Why could Cadwallon and Penda not cross the Don? The road from Lincoln to York via Tadcaster crossed the Don at Doncaster. That is as far east (downriver) as the Roman surveyors could find a manageable, all-weather crossing. The valley was wide, shallow and marshy there. The crossing would be easy to defend. A mile or so upriver (between Sprotbrough and Conisbrough) the river passes though a narrow, steep-sided valley for about two miles. That would also have been easy to defend. The next five or six miles near Sheffield and Rotherham would have provided several good crossing sites. The valley is broad, but was only marshy in a few places. That is why the Northumbrians built a dyke on the home bank. See Figure 10.6.

It is called the Roman Ridge. It is obviously a defensive fortification. Today it can be seen in Wincobank (about a mile south of the M1 Motorway). It then ran along high ground for about ten miles to Swinton. The northern section was re-aligned. It originally ran into what are now the southern suburbs of Swinton, along the crest of a ridge which overlooked the valley of the Collier Brook. The newer section ran further north, meeting the River Dearne about two miles away (see below).

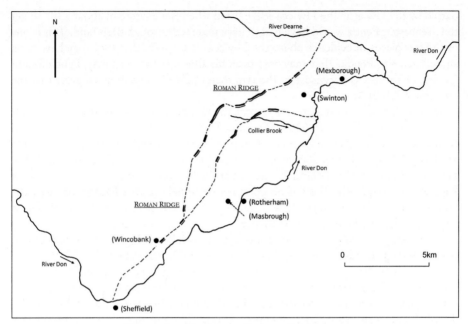

Figure 10.6 The Roman Ridge at Rotherham.

Cadwallon and Penda defeated and killed Edwin at Hatfield Moor. Cadwallon then campaigned in Northumbria. Bede wrote that Osric besieged Cadwallon in a walled town, but Cadwallon sallied out on a sudden foray with all his forces, defeated Osric's army and killed him. We don't know whether that is true, but we do know that soon after that Oswald of Bernicia successfully reunited Northumbria. The city may have been York.

Soon afterwards, perhaps in 634 AD, Cadwallon fought Oswald. Cadwallon lost. He died. The battle was at a place called Heavenfield. No place of that name exists. The Anglo–Saxon chronicle says 'at Deniseburn near Hefenfelth'. The Welsh Annals say 'Cantscaul', which would be 'the estate of a young noblemen', or perhaps 'of a ghost'. The Roman road from York to Manchester crosses the Pennines and has an old fort (ironically, called *Camulodunum*) near its summit at Slack. Some place-name evidence suggests that the battlefield could be near there; in, or near, the valley called Dean Head. Alternatively it could have been much further west, where that road crosses the River Dean at Northwich (see Figure 10.5). Either location would make sense. An alternative site is the Rowley Burn just south of Hexham. All of these options see Cadwallon crossing the Pennines from the west on Roman roads. But the consequence was stark: Cadwallon was dead and Gwynedd went into decline.

Penda had been king of Mercia since about 626 AD. In 628 he had marched south west down the Fosse Way to Cirencester. In Chapter Seven we saw how the West Saxons may have seized Cirencester after Deorham in 577, but their way north was barred by the Hwicca. The Hwicca still existed when Bede wrote in about 730. To get to Cirencester, Penda would have had to have marched through their land. This is one of the few pieces of evidence about the Hwicca. It suggests that they may have been subordinated to Penda. They may have been his allies. Be that as it may, Penda fought Ceolric of Wessex at Cirencester. The two then made a treaty. That suggests that the outcome was a draw.

The events at Cirencester are, effectively, the first evidence we have about Mercia. It does not amount to much. In 626 AD Penda of Mercia fought Wessex at Cirencester and then made a treaty. About six years later, in 632, Penda fought alongside Cadwallon at Hatfield Moor. Neither statement says that Mercia was particularly powerful. We tend to think that Mercia (and Penda in particular) were powerful because of what happened subsequently. There is no good reason to believe that Mercia was particularly significant at this stage. It was only on the death of his ally Cadwallon that Mercia, under Penda, rose to prominence.

In the later 630s AD, the situation was broadly as follows. Northumbria was united under Oswald. Lindsey seems to have been part of Northumbria. In 627 Paulinus, Bishop of York, had preached in Lincoln, and consecrated Honorius of Rochester as Archbishop of Canterbury there. But why would you consecrate an archbishop in a substantially deserted city? Bede states that Paulinus built a stone church in Lincoln. That is highly significant. There was very little building in stone in the early seventh century. If it was true, the church might have been the only stone building erected in England for several years. That would imply that Lincoln was an extremely important place. Lincoln had been a Roman provincial capital and would have had a bishop. Bede wrote of the Middle Angles being converted to Christianity. That would broadly correspond to the modern counties of Leicestershire, Rutland, Northamptonshire and Huntingdonshire (see Figure 2.2). It many have included Nottinghamshire. He does not mention the conversion of the people of Lindsey. He does discuss the appointment of a bishop for the Mercians, Middle Angles and Lindsey; each by name. Put together, that implies that Lindsey was already Christian. It seems more likely that Paulinus found surviving Romano-British Christians, and perhaps even a church building. Lindsey may have changed hands, and temporarily become Northumbrian, after the Battle of Hatfield Moor.

There is evidence that steps were taken to defend Lindsey against attack from the south and the south west. Just south of Grantham, Ermine Street appears to have been cut by an earthwork (suggested by the name of Washdike Lane) near Great Parton. A few miles west, a prehistoric route now known as the Viking Way is cut by King Lud's Entrenchments. A few miles west again, the Roman road from the Fosse Way to Ermine Street appears to have been cut by an earthwork, suggested by the name of Landyke Lane and Farm (and possibly by Cranyke Farm). King Lud's entrenchments are multiple, may be prehistoric, and appear to face south. Little if any trace of the other two dykes survives. See Figure 10.7.

The Fosse Way does not seem to have been cut. However, the Vale of Belvoir (the area north of Landyke) would have been marshy almost as far as the Fosse Way. In

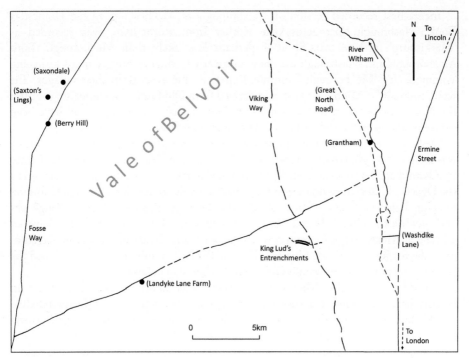

Figure 10.7 Southern Defences of Lindsey.

that area the Fosse Way runs down a Berry Hill (the name possibly means 'the site of a fortification') to cross a valley. Nearby there is both a 'Saxondale' and 'Saxton's Lings'. The area is a long way from the traditional sites of Saxon settlements.

Penda was a successful warrior and the first really effective ruler of Mercia. In 641 AD he invaded East Anglia. It is not clear what that means, because the East Anglians may have controlled the east Midlands at that point. In 642 Penda marched against Oswald of Northumbria again. They met at Maesfeld. Oswald, a Christian recognized today as St Oswald, was killed. The traditional site of the battle is at Oswestry. However, there is no good reason to think that a battle fought between Mercia and Northumbria was fought *west* of Mercia. At the time, that area probably belonged to Powys. A much better suggestion is at, or near, Mexborough near Rotherham. There are several reasons for thinking that. The first is that Rotherham is on a Roman road from Derby. It probably ran on from Rotherham to Doncaster and York. The second is that that places the battle in the area between the Trent, Gwynedd and Northumbria. We know little about that area, but it may have been contested after the death of Cadwallon. The third is that 'Mexborough' could be derived from 'Maesbeorg' ('the walled town near the marsh') and could be near a Maesfeld ('the field by the marsh'). The last, and perhaps the most powerful reason, comes from looking at the valley of the River Don.

The earliest recorded version of 'Mexborough' is 'Mechesburg' in the Domesday Book. Masbrough, just across the Rother from Rotherham, was recorded as 'Markisburg' in 1202 AD. So it is perhaps less likely than Mexborough. Both Mexborough and Masbrough are shown on early Ordnance Survey maps as having 'commons' (eg 'Mexborough Common') up to a mile away from their villages. The word 'common' is Middle English and derived from Old French. It came into use after the Norman Conquest. It is reasonable to believe that both areas would have been called 'fields' (as in 'Maesfeld') before they were referred to as commons.

We looked at the Roman Ridge above Rotherham earlier (Figure 10.6). If Lindsey was in (East) Anglian hands in 642 AD, the line of the Don would be a natural place for Oswald of Mercia to defend. Mexborough is north of the River Rother but west of the Dearne. Victorian Ordnance Survey maps show the area of Mexborough Common as being 'liable to flooding'. That may be why the original, shorter Roman Ridge was anchored on the Collier Brook. Anything further north east was marshy. However, a battle at Mexborough Common would suggest that Penda of Mercia managed to cross the Rother and the marshes in that area. The Northumbrians later re-aligned the Ridge to cover the Mexborough Common (but see also below).

Oswald died at the Maesfeld and there was another succession crisis in Northumbria. Oswald was succeeded by his brother Oswiu, but Deira rebelled and kicked Oswiu out. Eventually Oswiu managed to reunite Deira with Bernicia in 654 AD and then ruled Northumbria for 16 years. In the long run this series of short reigns in Northumbria were a bad thing. Conversely Mercia benefitted from a succession of long reigns. For much of the seventh century (from 606 to 704) Mercia had just four kings. In the century or so that followed (704-96) it had six, but two of them (Athelbald and Offa) ruled for 90 years between them. Dynastic stability was a major factor in Mercia's rise.

During Penda's reign (from about 626 to 655 AD) Mercia developed a strategic problem that it never entirely overcame. It was sandwiched between Wessex and Northumbria. Penda died on yet another foray against Northumbria in 655. The place was called 'Winwaed'. The best translation for that is Whinny Moor or Whinmoor, just outside Leeds. Penda was accompanied by Ethelhere, the brother of King Anna of East Anglia. Anna had died the previous year, possibly killed by a Mercian army. Whinmoor is effectively the same place as Aberford. It is shown on a modern map as being about four miles to the west, but the whole area has 'carr', '-mire' and '-ley' place names all over it. It would have been a tangle of thicket, woodland and swamp. The South Bank still stood overlooking the Cock Beck, and Grim's Ditch to the west, facing east.

In 655 AD, Penda and Ethelhere had managed to cross the Don and met Oswiu of Northumbria in the area of the Cock Beck. This was the Oswiu who had lost the throne of Deira in 644. It was possibly his reunification of Northumbria in 654 which prompted the alliance of Mercians and East Anglians. Penda and Ethelhere reached the Cock Beck but could get no further. They failed, and both died in the attempt. Why did they fail?

Somebody had built a dyke. It is in three parts and has three names: the Ridge, the Becca Banks and the Rein. See Figure 10.8. (The South Bank is not shown on Figure 10.8 for clarity.)

It is not obvious whether it was built in one, two, or three stages. They are all very impressive. The Ridge is a fairly conventional earthwork, about 20 feet high and half a mile long today, just north of the Cock Beck. It is on the northern edge of the flat valley floor. The Becca Banks is a single (or possibly, in some places, multiple)

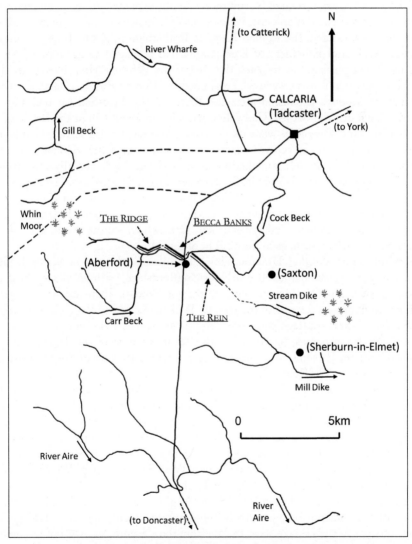

Figure 10.8 South-facing Defences on the Cock Beck.

earthwork immediately above the river bank. Today it is about a mile long and about 20 feet from top to bottom. East of the Roman road, the Rein is a single, more-or-less straight ditch and bank running for about a mile south east. It runs from the south bank of the Beck to the summit of a low hill. It is about 12 feet high today. As we saw in Chapter Nine, we cannot know exactly what that area was like at the time. On the south east side of the hill, the line of the Rein continues as a road to meet a small brook (and thence on to Sherburn in Elmet). It is possible that the Rein continued as far as the brook and cut off the Saxton ridge completely.

When Penda died, Oswiu of Northumbria rapidly exploited his death and took over the throne of Mercia. It didn't last. Penda's son Wulfhere gained the throne of Mercia about three years later. The Roman Ridge at Rotherham might have been realigned because Penda and Ethelhere of East Anglia had managed to get past it, despite Northumbrian precautions, to reach the area of the Whinny Moor in 655 AD. That would suggest that it was Oswiu who realigned the Roman Ridge, after that battle.

Much of Mercia's expansion after the Battle of the Maesfeld (in 642 AD) was westward, against the British. Cadwallon had died in about 634 at the Battle of the Heavenfield, and Gwynedd went into decline. Another British leader, Cynddylan, rose to prominence about ten years later, and fought against the Mercians. In about 655 or so he raided Lichfield, and died a year or two later. We don't really know who he was. He might have been a minor leader of either Gwynedd or Powys. His importance to us is that he is remembered in the Welsh epic poem, the 'Elegy for Cynddylan'. It is hard to decipher, and was not written down until centuries later. However it makes frequent mention of a place and a river called 'Tarn', which is unknown to us but seems to relate to the River Tern, as in Ternhill in Shropshire.

Ternhill is near Market Drayton, about 15 miles north west of Stafford. There are a few pagan place-names in south-east Staffordshire, such as Wednesfield and Wednesbury. Both of those names refer to the god Wodan. There are no other places with pagan names in the rest of the county. Wulfhere came to the throne of Mercia in 658 AD, and was baptized soon after. So we can be reasonably sure that those few places with pagan names, just south of the Trent but west of the Tame, had been founded by then. It seems that Mercia only conquered the rest of Staffordshire and into Shropshire in Wulfhere's time.

Wulfhere was perhaps the most successful of all Mercian kings. In about 661 AD he turned his attention south. Wulfhere managed to separate the Isle of Wight from Wessex and hand it to the South Saxons, and probably forced the West Saxons to pay tribute to him. He had Ethelwald, King of the South Saxons, baptised. He also appointed a bishop over the people of the Isle of Wight. At or about this time Dorchester on Thames had a Mercian, not a West Saxon, bishop. We shall look at some details of that campaign in Chapter Twelve.

These events are described briefly in the Anglo-Saxon Chronicle. They seem to agree with the contents of an extremely important document, the Tribal Hidage. The extant versions of the Hidage seem to date from the eleventh century, but its contents are earlier. It seems to be a register of all the lands which paid Wulfhere tribute. After

661 AD he would have been able to demand tribute from the West and South Saxons as well as those areas of Mercia which he ruled directly. His father Penda had had some form of relationship with East Anglia, possibly through having killed Anna and taking it over. It is therefore quite possible that most of England less Northumbria (but including Kent and Essex) was under Wulfhere's control, directly or indirectly.

The lands listed in the Tribal Hidage cannot all be identified directly, but there are some obvious omissions. Northumbria is the biggest one. Rheged, or indeed anything west of the Pennines, is another. The Cheshire Plain is also missing. That is consistent with Gwynedd surviving in the area of Cheshire until after Cynddylan's death (soon after 655 AD). The Hidage mentions what appears to be the Hwicca, and a people in the Wroxeter area. The latter are described as the 'wreoconsaete', which might mean 'the people who live around Wroxeter', 'the people who live under the Wrekin (hill)', or both. Wroxeter was occupied by the British into the early seventh century. Separately, a Mercian bishopric was created for the Hwicca in about 680 AD by Archbishop Theodore. This all suggests that Wulfhere both seized the Wroxeter area and annexed the Hwicca in the 660s or 670s. The British who fled Wroxeter seem to have been the founders of what became Powys. 'Powys' is a Welsh name. It may relate to the Latin term which the inhabitants used to describe themselves. It meant something like 'the country-dwellers'. That would make it similar to 'Cymru' for 'cumbroges' or 'companions'.

In about 675 AD Wessex rejected the terms which Wulfhere had imposed in 661. Wulfhere invaded again and got as far as Bedwyn, on the River Kennet. We don't know the outcome, but Wulfhere died later that year. We also know that it was the last Mercian invasion of Wessex for 40 years. We can therefore be confident that the Mercians came off worst at Bedwyn. Wulfhere was succeeded by his brother Aethelred, Penda's fourth son. He ruled for the next 24 years, apparently largely at peace. The peace was broken once during his reign, in 680, by Aelfwine of Northumbria, who was killed by Mercians somewhere on the Trent. We don't know quite where the border lay at that time, so we can't be sure that it wasn't a Mercian incursion into Northumbria. It looks like a Northumbria incursion into Mercia. Aelfwine died, and Mercia's northern and southern borders were both at peace for a generation.

Aethelred of Mercia was succeeded by his son Ceolred in about 709 AD. In 715 he invaded Wessex and fought Ina at Wanborough (the same Wanborough where Ceawlin had attempted to breach the Wansdyke in 592). It seems that, like Ceawlin, Ceolred failed. He died the following year, possibly poisoned, and his successor was not a close relation. It was Aethelbald, who was not descended from Penda, but Penda's brother Eowa. Aethelbald ruled for about 40 years: the dates we have are 716-757. He was responsible for the last great expansion of Mercian territory. It was under Aethelbald that people started to call themselves 'Gens Anglorum' or 'Aenglisc': English. Not Saxon.

It was in that period that Gwynedd and Powys were definitively chased out of what we now call England. The frontier at the end of Athelbald's reign is broadly the borders of Wales today. Chester was seized. We have no dates, but place-name and similar evidence can help us. Much of Shropshire has place-names which suggest a single, sudden conquest. There are a large number of 'Newtons', and many 'north-', 'south-', 'east-' and 'west-' place names (such as Norton, Sutton, Aston and Weston). That reflects an obvious and fairly deliberate pattern of settlement.

The British didn't give up. The men of Gwynedd moved their capital along the Welsh coast to Deganwy, near Conway and Great Orme's Head. They had been pushed off all the good agricultural land, but resorted to raiding the rich farmland they had once owned. Aethelbald seems to have responded by digging a major earth-work, now known as Wat's Dyke, to protect most of what we now know as Cheshire. Wat's Dyke stretched for about 40 miles and was originally over 20 feet high. See Figure 10.9.

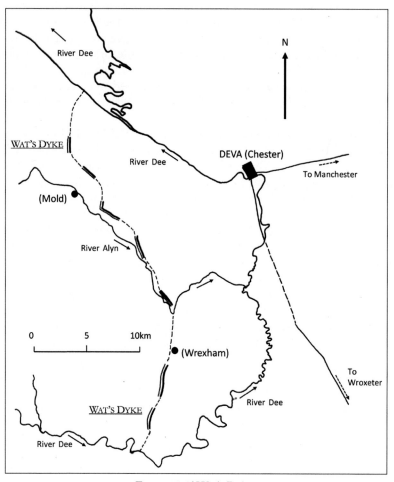

Figure 10.9 Wat's Dyke.

Wat's Dyke is about eight feet high in several places today. If you find a vantage point in or near Chester and look west and south with a map, it is clear that Wat's Dyke was dug on the last defensive line before the Welsh hills. (Archaeological evidence may indicate that it had been dug in the mid-fifth century, as discussed above.) The northern section, as far south as the point where it crossed the River Alyn, clearly protected the good farmland south and west of Chester.

The Cheshire Plain is fairly flat and low-lying. The land to the south, west of the Severn, is not. The upper reaches of the Severn flow more or less east to Shrewsbury (and Wroxeter, a few miles away). It rises in the Cambrian Mountains which cover much of Wales. Further south, the land west of the Severn is hilly for several miles westwards before meeting the mountains. This area is a tangle of valleys and what is obviously the remains of old woodland. It shows many signs of glacial activity. In several places there are wide, deep valleys. The streams and rivers which they contain might flow northwards at one end, but southwards at the other; or east and west. Some of the valleys, and particularly the wider ones, had been cleared long before the Dark Ages. Some of the narrower valleys appear to have been wet, dark and wooded. The best routes through those areas were not the valleys but the ridgeways. Most of the rivers eventually flow east into the Severn, but in the very south the Wye flows south directly into the Bristol Channel.

Territory like that is not easy to conquer in one swift campaign. It is more likely to have been a matter of raiding, ravaging and sudden seizures; one valley at a time. By analogy, when the Ottoman Turks arrived in the northern Balkans in the fourteenth and fifteenth centuries, it took decades to subdue the valleys of what are now Bosnia, Croatia and Slovenia. They were then the scene of fighting, on and off, for several centuries. The situation on the Welsh borders was fairly similar.

What we would expect to find it a 'fossilized frontier', and indeed we do. The Welsh borders abound with early Norman motte and bailey castles. The whole of Wales is ringed with King Edward the First's stone castles. They are all irrelevant here. What is of interest is a series of seemingly unrelated Dark Age dykes. In practice they *are* generally unrelated. They have a common function, but most of them were build in response to a local tactical or perhaps operational problem. Since there is no real way of working out the sequence in which they were built, we shall look at them from south to north.

The River Arrow flows into the Lugg just below Leominster. Above the town, the valleys of both rivers are broad and shallow, but are divided by a line of hills which rise over 200 meters above the valley floors. The valley of the Arrow, and probably that of the Lugg, had been farmed since pre-Roman times. Archaeologists have detected an extensive pattern of field boundaries. In places the Arrow Valley is over two miles wide. The river rises several miles further west, and a number of streams flow into it or allow access from the tributaries of the Lugg. That is, raiding the Arrow Valley from the west would have been relatively easy and profitable. The Mercians responded by building a dyke right across it, just west of modern Pembridge. It is called the Rowe Ditch today. It cut right through existing field boundaries, which implies that it was planned at high level, without particular heed to the wishes of the people farming the land. It faces west. It is up to ten feet high and cuts the valley at almost its widest place. By doing so it avoids the need for multiple short sections. It also avoids crossing high ridges, which would be needed if it were further west. See Figure 10.10.

Just north west of Leominster the Lugg Valley is wide and shallow. Upstream of there it passes through a narrow defile. Upstream again, it lies in a broad valley just east of Presteigne. The name of the hamlet of Broad Heath is indicative. Further west one finds a similar pattern. The valley of a tributary, the Summergill Brook, is over two miles wide at one point, but flows through a defile before joining the Lugg. The valley once contained a Roman fort. Further west again, a short dike across the valley floor above New Radnor cuts it off from the West. Today there is a bank about twenty feet wide but only two or three feet high. The ditch seems to have been ploughed in.

There are 23 recorded short ditches along the Welsh border. The dike west of New Radnor may be related to a medieval siege. Without far more accurate date evidence we are generally making conjectures about the purpose of any particular earthwork. We will return to that subject in Chapter 14. Another of those dikes is about five miles north of the Rowe Ditch near the village of Birtley. It is quite short.

The headwaters of the Lugg, however, are in a series of narrow valleys. An aptly named 'Short Ditch' cuts the ridge between the Lugg and the headwaters of the River

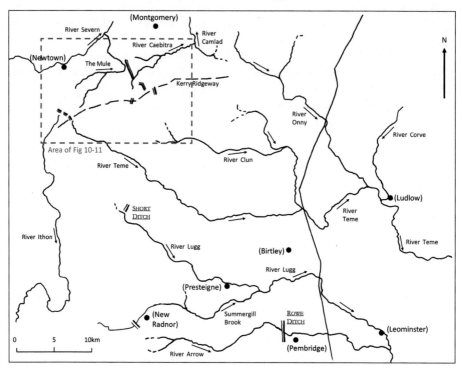

Figure 10.10 The Rivers of the Middle Marches.

Teme to the north. The hills here all reach well above 400 meters, and one (Pool Hill) 516 meters. Nevertheless it is easy to see that the only good east-west route was along that ridgeway. It is also easy to see why the Mercians cut it with a dyke. It is well-preserved section on Crown land open to the public. It is only six feet high, but easy to follow over about half a mile. It faces west.

We will break our north-south sequence here for clarity. About ten miles further north, a river called The Mule flows east for three or four miles before turning north west and flowing through hills into the Severn. That is not remarkable nor, of itself, important. What is more significant is that its upper reaches are easily reached from the valley the Caebitra and the Camlad rivers. In turn, they can easily be reached from the valley of the Onny.

If Mercian warriors advanced up the Teme from near Worcester they would reach the Onny just above Ludlow. Advancing up the Onny they would find the Camlad and the Caebitra. From there, near the hamlet of Sarn, they would find the Mule and a route to the upper Severn. This was the heartland of Powys after it was ejected from the lowlands. They had established their capital at Mathrafal, a few miles north on the River Vyrnwy, which is another tributary of the Severn. The men of Powys do not seem to have built many dykes, but they felt the need to build one here. It is called Wantin's Dike or the Wantyn Dyke. Two sections are marked on the map, but they seem to have originally formed one defensive line about two miles long. Part of that line seems to have been captured by a road. In one place it may have used a stream. It was not necessarily continuous.

Its siting, however, was very subtle. In the north it is anchored on a hill on the *east* side of the Mule. That denied access along the gorge north to the Severn. Its southern end lies on the slopes of a high ridge that runs east-west for miles. In that area the Wantyn Dyke denies access both to the main section of the valley of The Mule (which at one point is over a mile wide) and the valley of the Caebitra. Today the Wantyn Dyke is only two or three feet high. It faces east.

However, it had a weakness. The ridge to the south is an ancient cross-country route known today as the Kerry Ridgeway. The men of Powys may have used the Ridgeway to raid into Mercian territory to the east. The Mercians responded by cutting it with a short dyke, now known as the Lower Short Ditch, about a mile to the east. It is about seven feet high today, about half a mile long, and faces west. It is shown as '1' on Figure 10.11. (The two sections of the Wantyn Dyke are 'A' and 'B'.)

Mercian warriors didn't attend courses at a Royal (Mercian) School of Military Engineering, but they knew a few things about dikes. It was at about this time that the West Saxons learnt to use dikes offensively. The Deirans seem to have done so in the Yorkshire Wolds decades before. We will never know whether the Mercians got the idea from somewhere else or thought of it themselves. The next step, however, was both inspired and decisive.

They marched up the Ridgeway, outflanked the south end of the Wantyn Dike, and dug two sections of dykes. The first, now called the Upper Short Ditch ('2'), guarded against a British (or Welsh, as we can now call them) counterattack along the

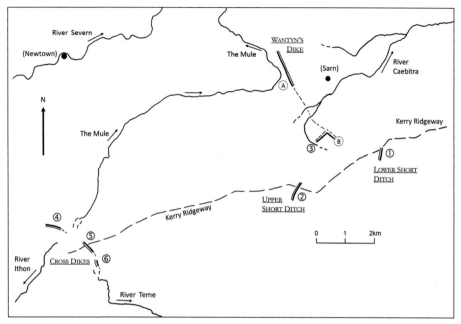

Figure 10.11 The Wantyn and Short Dikes.

Ridgeway from the West. It is about six feet high now, and about half a mile long. It runs from a re-entrant on the north side to another on the south, and faces west. The second section ('3'), which has no name, abuts the upper stretch of the Wantyn Dyke. If the Welsh tried to attack along the length of the Dyke from the valley of the Mule, they would now be faced with an earthwork across their path.

The two Mercian sections ('2' and '3') were probably never connected. The hillsides in that area are very steep. The gap between them lies across two very steep re-entrants.

The Mercians pushed further west, but not far and not for long. About five miles further west along the Ridgeway they found the source of the river Mule. The source of the Teme is only a mile or so south. The Mercians dug three short sections of dyke called the Cross Dykes. None of them is more than half a mile long. They span three re-entrants and link streams to form a continuous defensive line ('4', '5' and '6'). It would stop the Welsh entering the valley of The Mule, and possibly that of the Teme, from the valley of the River Ithon. The Ithon flows south and joins the Wye. The name of practically every place in the Ithon Valley is Welsh. Significantly, just where the Mule joins the Severn a few miles north is the town of Newtown. It was not Mercian. It was founded by Edward the First, centuries later, as part of his strategy of encircling and subduing Wales. It is surrounded by villages with Welsh names. The nearest English place names are a few miles east. We shall look at that area shortly.

So far we have looked at what happened along the Mercian frontier with Gwynedd and Powys. Further south the situation was different. Firstly, Mercia proper did not adjoin what we now call Wales. The land of the Hwicca was mostly east of the Severn. A small kingdom or tribe called the Ergyng lay west of the Severn. The lowest crossing of the Severn was the Roman bridge at Gloucester. The next was the ford at Worcester. Between those places the river is wide and tidal. There were no fords, and even today there are few bridges. It may have been possible to cross at Upton on Severn, the site one of the few bridges today. There seems to have been a bridge at Upton by the fifteenth century. Places such as Tewkesbury and Upton are still affected by floods, despite decades if not centuries of river improvement schemes. It was not at all easy to cross the Severn below Worcester. To that extent (and, to some degree, due to the presence of the Hwicca) Ergyng was protected from the Mercians. See Figure 10.12.

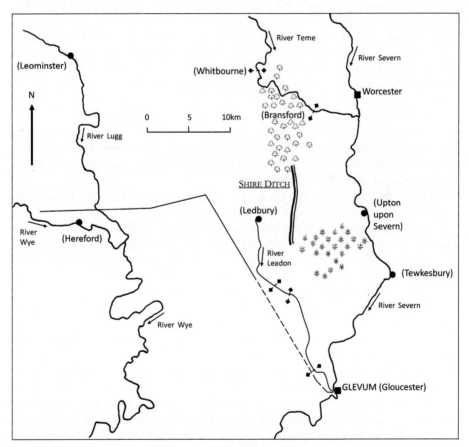

Figure 10.12 The Malvern Area.

That changed once the Mercians were established west of the Severn further north. Crossing at Worcester places you north of the Teme. There are fords across the Teme, but not many. There was one at Bransford, about three miles from the Severn. The next was at Whitbourne, about five miles upriver but, significantly, behind the wooded hills that extend north from the Malverns. It was difficult, but not impossible, to get across the Severn. The easiest way to get across the lower Severn was to cross in the north at Worcester, then cross the Teme at Bransford and go south. Eventually the Mercians had enough authority over the Hwicca to enable them to attack Ergyng. Either in anticipation of that, or in response to it, the men of Ergyng built an earthwork. It runs along the top of the Malvern Hills. The Malverns are up to two hundred meters above the plain and about seven miles long. They are extremely steep.

The earthwork didn't run all the way to Gloucester. It didn't need to. Although the Severn is about five miles from the Malverns, there are several streams. Towards the southern end of the Malverns they reach right up to the bottom of the ridge. Frogsmarsh, Marsh End and Longdon Marsh all lie in that area. To the north of the Malvern ridge, the hills are a tangle of close, dense woods even today. If Mercian warriors navigated the marshes they would come to the River Leadon, which joins the Severn near Gloucester. The valley of the Leadon would have been flat and marshy. The first ford across the Leadon, at Rudford, is about three miles from Gloucester. It is in the middle of a flat-bottomed valley over a half a mile wide. That was probably also marshy. There were only two other fords, at Ketford and Pyford Bridge. They are tucked behind the southern end of the Malverns. There were no other fords as far as Ledbury. Even if the Mercians found the fords, they would not have been good places to cross. They would have been overlooked from the Malverns and their line of retreat was across miles of marsh. No, thank you.

It may be no coincidence that the Roman road west of the Malvern hills stayed in use, whilst the southern section to Gloucester disappeared

Today the dike at the top of the Malvern Hills is called the Shire Ditch. Its remains are not very impressive. They possibly never were. They sit at the top of the Malverns, just to the east of the crest and facing east. To get to them an attacker would have to climb almost 200 meters in under half a mile. I've climbed the Malverns a few times. Whenever I did, no-one was trying to kill me. Rather you than me.

Towards its southern end the Shire Ditch runs up to, and then beyond, a hill fort called the British Camp. It is probably Iron Age. However, the name tells us that the Anglo-Saxons considered that the British had used it, presumably for shelter when manning the Shire Ditch.

The next ford on the Teme above Whitbourne is at Stanford (Bridge), about five miles further north. There is then another at Puddleford, about two miles away. The Mercians got across the Teme in this area. We know that because the western boundary of the Hwicca ran along the River Leadon, north along the Shire Ditch, up to the Teme, along it to Stanford and then east to the Severn. The Mercians went around their territory, to the north.

Once across the Teme the Mercians could outflank the men of Ergyng. They seem to have fallen back, or been pushed, to the line of the Wye. They held there for some time. The land that the Mercians now occupied became known as the land of the Magonsaete.

In a sense, Aethelbald of Mercia faced the worst of all strategic situations. Like Prussia in the eighteenth century, Mercia had enemies in three directions. Northumbria was to the north east, the Welsh to the west and Wessex to the south. There are strategies for dealing with that. The best is to be strong enough to beat all of them, and Mercia was a powerful kingdom. Another strategy is to defeat them one at a time, whilst ensuring that they cannot ally together. A third is to ally yourself to at least one of the others. Aethelbald seems to have used all those options at various times.

In about 733 AD he attacked Wessex. He didn't get far. He seized Somerton a few miles north of Oxford, attacking down the west bank of the Cherwell, but got no further. We shall look at that in Chapter 12. In 737 or so he ravaged 'the land of the Northumbrians'. We don't know where, nor for how long. It was a good tactic. Raiding and burning villages allowed you to carry off livestock and crops. It denied taxes to the enemy. Killing his men folk denied him manpower, and slaves (of both sexes) were always useful. Ravaging border lands also made it difficult for the enemy to approach your territory, because they couldn't live off the land which they would have to march through. It would typically take a generation for a thoroughly-ravaged area to recover. There were no Non-Governmental Organizations or international development funds in those days.

Whilst this was going on, the conquest of the western border lands continued. The king did not necessarily play much part in it. Typically, border vassals would fight campaigns every year, unless ordered not to. They did so in the anticipation of reduced taxes, exemption from fighting elsewhere, or a share in land conquered. The pattern continued right up to Plantagenet times. On the Scottish border it went on until the seventeenth century. Not many years after Aethelbald, Charlemagne would formally establish a series of 'Marches'. He created one against the Moors in the Pyrenees, one against the Slavs in Bohemia and, ironically, one against the Saxons in northern Germany.

In about 740 AD Cuthred came to the throne of Wessex. The Anglo-Saxon Chronicle says that he 'fought many hard battles' alongside Aethelbald of Mercia. In the Chronicle, 'fought with' means 'fought against'. If somebody fought *together* with someone against someone else, the Chronicle says 'and'. Aethelbald knew the value of having allies. In 743 he 'and' Cuthred fought 'with' the Welsh.

What does this imply? Apart from an alliance, it means that Cuthred of Wessex took his army north, and then west across the Severn. That is, unless the Welsh raided a long way eastwards, which doesn't seem likely. Assuming the Welsh had been pushed back from the Severn, Cuthred could have crossed at Gloucester. If not, it was probably Worcester. He would have to assemble his army, presumably somewhere near his north-western border. There is an interesting parallel. In 1461 AD, during the Wars of the Roses, a Lancastrian force under Queen Margaret was trying to get to Wales. On the 30th of April she left Bath. She went via Bristol to collect artillery from the royal armoury there. Even hauling the guns, her army was at Tewkesbury on the night of the Third to the Fourth of May. That is five days. She would have reached the bridge at Upton the following day, were it not for the fact that King Edward the Fourth had caught up with the Lancastrians. He gave battle and defeated them on the Fourth of May. So, in 743 Cuthred could have crossed the Severn about five days after leaving his own territory. In passing, from Bath to Tewkesbury via Bristol is about 51 miles. The days of marching 20 miles a day, day in, day out, were long gone by 1461.

Aethelbald of Mercia died in about 755 AD. Interestingly, despite his long reign, he seems to have been murdered by his bodyguards. His successor was no known relation. He didn't last long, however. A relation of Aethelbald seized power within a year. He was Offa, probably the greatest and most famous of Mercian kings. He ruled from 757 to 796. He, like Aethelbald, was descended from Eowa and thus Pybba (but not Penda). To be blunt, he had some legitimacy (as the great-grandson of a former king) and he seized power. That was enough, by the standards of the day. Offa's greatness stemmed in part from the legacy of Wulfhere, Aethelred and Aethelbald. That legacy consisted of a large and powerful kingdom which had achieved a physical and moral ascendancy over Northumbria, Wessex and the Welsh.

Offa did not conquer very much. It could be said that his greatest feat was to *appear* to be a great king. That would be unfair. He exercised power over much of England, including Kent, Sussex, Essex and East Anglia, for over 40 years. In terms of fighting the Welsh, he had two significant achievements. The first was the battle of Hereford in about 760 AD. Hereford is one of the few fords across the Wye. 'Hereford' means 'the army ford'. Offa got his army across the Wye, fought the men of Ergyng and beat them. As a result the area immediately south and west of Hereford, roughly as far as the River Dore, has English place names. There was a cathedral at Hereford in 803. See Figure 10.13.

Offa's second great achievement was his dyke, which has been the source of considerable controversy. It was believed to have run 'from sea to sea'; that is, for the whole length of the Welsh border. Sir Cyril Fox excavated it in three sections between 1926 and 1928. His conclusion was that it was *almost* continuous, except where it ran along a river or similar. Subsequently archaeologists have said that it *was* continuous, or that it was built in several separate sections. It might not have run literally from sea to sea. The present state of archaeology does not allow us to be certain. As I wrote in Chapter One, there is no proof.

We are confident that, in the north, it runs roughly parallel with and in front of Wat's Dyke. In some areas it is dead straight. In some areas it is well-adapted to the topography. In many areas the place names to its west are Welsh; to the east, English. We can be quite confident that Offa ordered that a dyke be dug to keep the Welsh out of Mercia, possibly from sea to sea. From a strategic or operational point of view, the details do not matter. From a tactical perspective, the details should, and do, vary at every point along its length. They may be unknown to us (not least, in Herefordshire

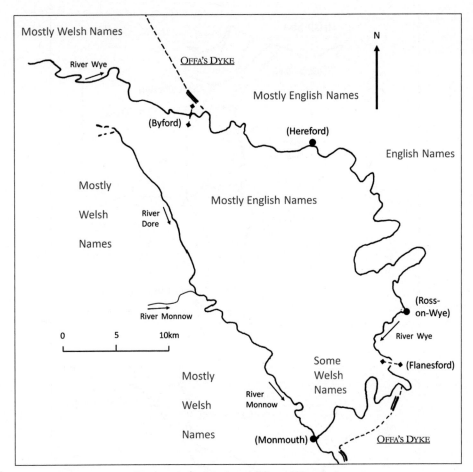

Figure 10.13 South and West of Hereford.

a lot of it seems to have been ploughed out), but do not particularly change the price of fish. From a historical point of view, Offa reigned for 41 years. His dyke seems to have been completed in his lifetime, so we can date its construction to within a few decades. That is probably good enough. See Figure 10.14.

It was a massive undertaking. In places it is huge: up to 30 yards across and 25 feet high. It had a wooden palisade. It does not seem to have been that big all along its length. In places the palisade was rebuilt in stone, and the west side (scarp) was faced with turf to create an almost sheer face. Let us assume, in the first instance, that: the ditch had been only about six feet deep and the bank six feet high; that a thousand men dug it; and that they worked for eight hours a day and six days a week. The figures in the Royal Engineer Pocket Book suggest that it would have taken about seven to eight months to build, assuming single handling.

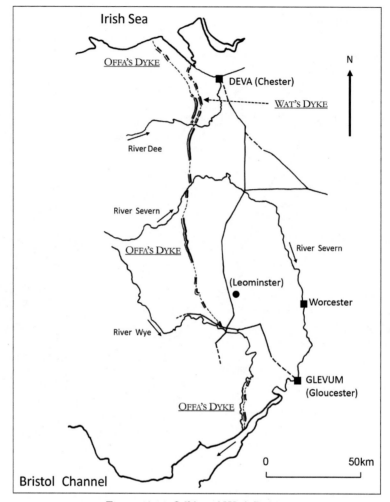

Figure 10.14 Offa's and Wat's Dykes.

No-one should believe that that was precisely what happened, but it is a useful way to look at it. At six feet deep it is actually too big to avoid double handling. That would either require more people or take longer. It may have been several hundred people, or it may have been over a thousand. If it was in the summer, they could probably do more than eight hours digging in a day. Did they work seven days a week? Was it all built in one go, or did they dig for a month in every year (which seems more likely)? The point of calculations like that is to establish an order of magnitude. Offa may have been able to direct the labour of much of the population of England. The figures suggest that it is reasonable to believe that he built it in a period of a few years; perhaps over a decade; given the resources at his disposal.

The story of *Mercian* wars against the Welsh is far from over. The Mercians killed Caradog of Gwent in 798 AD. In 822 they destroyed the stronghold of Gwynedd at Deganwy, and overran Powys. But, overall, they advanced no further. The story of *English* wars against Wales went on until the times of Edward the First. But the border, in simple terms, did not move again. With a few exceptions, Welsh place-names start immediately west of the line of Offa's Dyke. For a good example, look at Welshpool in a road atlas. Welshpool is on the upper reaches of the Severn. It lies on the west side of the valley. Offa's Dyke may not be marked on a road atlas. It is on the east side of the valley, a few hundred yards east of the B4388. There are a few Welsh names east of there, and a few English names west of there. But not many.

The Dyke crosses the valley of the Caebitra in an almost straight line about five miles east of Wantyn's Dyke, and therefore about ten miles east of the Cross Dykes overlooking the Ithon Valley (see Figure 10.10). There are very few English place names between Offa's and Wantyn's Dykes. There are none further west. The Cross Dykes overlooking the Ithon are the high water mark of Mercian penetration. They were of some passing military use, but there was no settlement east of there.

The line of Offa's Dyke did cut off some English settlements, and included some Welsh settlements; in some cases by a matter of miles. In the Domesday Book there are several accounts of Welsh people living just within the borders of England. The Book was written about three centuries after the Dyke was built. In a sense that attests to its success. The immediate area of the frontier was so peaceful that Welsh people could live to its east, and English to its west, for centuries. Genocide and ethnic cleansing did not take place. Offa's Dyke was never re-cut nor cleaned out. It wasn't necessary.

No Mercian coinage has ever been found west of Offa's Dyke.

Consider an urban, literate society on the far edges of the Roman empire. Town life decays. The few literate people in the towns either leave, their families die out, or they cease teaching their children to write. Few, if any, people in the villages could write. With the general decline of society, none learn. Invaders come. Many of the inhabitants are taken over by the invaders and learn their language. Some are pushed westwards; often into previously unsettled areas. Their history becomes folk memory. It becomes distorted by subsequent events and the people who tell it, or for whom it is retold. Centuries later, it is written down; perhaps in the form of epic poetry. Centuries later again, scholars try to interpret it.

That is, broadly, what happened to the western British. That is what is reflected in the Hen Ogled, in the Welsh Annals, and in poems such as the Elegy for Cynddylan. That was what happened to kingdoms such as Gwynedd and Powys, pushed out of the Cheshire Plain and the middle Severn Valley. It is not surprising that we know very little of the history of the western Midlands. The people forgot. The lowland British had become the upland Welsh. They never quite forgot their Christianity. The lives of several saints describe a long struggle to keep Christianity alive in the Valleys through the Dark Ages. The most famous was Saint David, the only indigenous patron saint in Britain. The people never forgot their hero Arthur, immortalized in many epic poems.

Ironically, although he was almost without doubt a British hero, and is without doubt a Welsh hero, there is little real evidence that he ever visited Wales.

The story is not quite true of Gwent, which was never really conquered by the Anglo-Saxons. The Normans never quite settled the issue either. It was only in 1535 AD (under Henry the Eighth) that the border area was divided into counties. Even then, the status of Monmouthshire (in the area of the former kingdom of Gwent) was ambiguous until 1974. It became part of Wales. My old school atlas, printed in 1971 (and a useful guide to county boundaries before the border revision of 1974) shows the Welsh border running down to the northern edge of Monmouthshire, and then stopping. The issue of whether Monmouthshire was Welsh or English was not clear.

Southern Wales retained a degree of civilization throughout the Dark Ages. The diocese of Llandaff (nowadays a suburb of Cardiff) can trace a line of bishops back with some confidence to the mid-sixth century, although not necessarily in Llandaff. It is not surprising that they resisted the guidance of 'catholic' bishops over issues such as the calculation of the date of Easter, since those Catholics were Anglo-Saxons. Much of Bede's work is taken up with ecclesiastical issues such as these. That's fine in itself, and no doubt served its purpose; but does not tell us much of use here.

Arthur died and left behind a collection of weak, fragmented kingdoms in the Midlands. Little happened for almost a century. A united Northumbria aroused hostility. It was checked at the Battle of the Idle in 617 AD. It was then defeated at the hands of Cadwallon of Gwynedd and Penda of Mercia in 633 at Hatfield Moor. But, in the process, Northumbria had grown stronger. Those strategic circumstances led Cadwallon to try again. He died, at the Heavenfield in 634. His death, and the resulting power vacuum, led to the emergence of Mercia and its conquest of the Midlands.

It did not happen overnight. By the year 650 or so, Mercia had consolidated its hold on the east Midlands and developed its ties with the Hwicca. It had not expanded significantly west of the Tame. Staffordshire, parts of Shropshire and northern Worcestershire were annexed under Wulfhere in the decades after 650. Wroxeter was seized soon after 650 and a Mercian diocese was created at Worcester by about 680. There was then a period of peace and consolidation for a generation under Aethelred.

It was well into the eighth century that expansion started again. The rest of Shropshire and Cheshire fell as Gwynedd and Powys were pushed out of the Severn Valley and the Cheshire Plain, perhaps in the 720s or 730s AD. Wat's Dyke stabilized the frontier in the north, but warfare continued for decades in the hills and valleys west of the Severn. The battle of Hereford in 760 or so was the last significant event. Offa built his Dyke soon afterwards, and the Welsh border has remained in place ever since.

The Anglo-Saxon conquest of the Midlands started on the Idle in 617 AD and lasted about 150 years. To that we should add the century or so from Arthur's death. If Arthur had hammered the Anglians in the east Midlands, it took them two and a half centuries for them to recover and win.

11

Breaching the Wansdyke

We left the West Saxons on the south side of the upper Thames Valley sometime after 584 AD. The British had dug dykes from Goring to the Bristol Channel, so the West Saxons couldn't advance south. They could not cross the Gloucestershire Avon to the west, nor the Thames to the northwest, due to the Hwicca. The Mercians were also to the north. The Mercians were increasingly a problem. See Figure 11.1.

By 652 AD, or perhaps 658, the West Saxons would conquer the southern half of modern Berkshire, almost all of Wiltshire and most of Hampshire. It took them about 70 years and in places the process resembled the siege warfare of the First World War.

Fords were hugely important. You can cross a stream almost anywhere. Rivers, however, must be forded. Fords were given names, just as streets and roads are today. Importantly, where a ford has no modern name it probably didn't exist in the Dark Ages. Not least, the rivers were sometimes deeper or marshier. There were no fords on the River Test below Longparish (see Chapter Six) and only three across the Hampshire Avon. It was much easier to cross their headwaters, such as the Bourne Rivulet, the Anton and the Wylye. That fact drove the later stages of the conquest of Wiltshire.

From the Romano-British perspective, the map reveals an obvious problem and suggests a solution hiding in plain sight. Silchester might be used as a base for forces defending the eastern section; but what about the west? *Cunetio*, near Marlborough, was tiny and possibly not far enough west. *Aquae Sulis*, Bath, was north of the Wansdyke; and there was no other Roman town in that area. The solution was to build such a base. It is at Devizes in Wiltshire and it has an area of about two thirds of a square mile. By comparison, Silchester's walls enclosed an area of about a sixth of a square mile. At Devizes the earthworks are up to 20 feet high in places today. They can be traced over just less than six kilometres. They run westwards from the area of the castle, away from the town centre. See Figure 11.2.

The earthworks are described on Ordnance Survey maps as a park pale. They are not a park pale: they face the wrong way. There was probably some form of a redoubt, or keep, on the site of the modern castle. As with Colchester and the cavalry camps on the North York Moors, it is far too big for conventional defensive purposes, unless

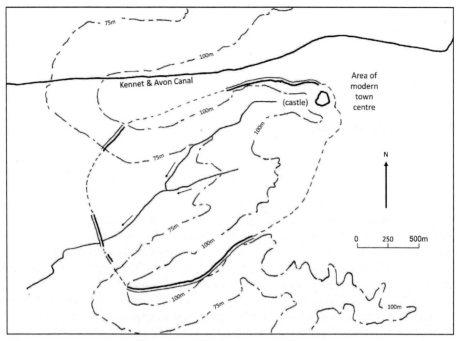

Figure 11.1 The Defences of Devizes.

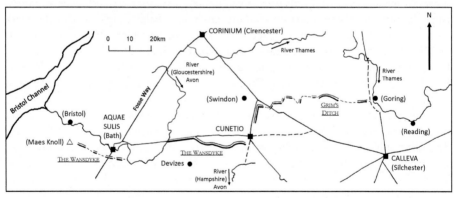

Figure 11.2 The Thames to the Severn.

it was planned to protect a force of cavalry. 'Devizes' is derived from '*(apud) Divisas*', 'the boundaries'. Apparently it had no pre-Norman name and the town is named for a Norman castle sited on the boundary between two Hundreds. But perhaps it was named in the seventh century to denote the fact that it was at the boundary between the eastern and western sections of the Wansdyke defences. That would imply that there was some form of unified command, at least initially. It seems to have been long-since abandoned by the time that Bishop Roger of Salisbury built the castle there in 1242.

We know very little about who the British in this region were. There seem to have been one grouping based around Silchester. There was probably a separate group, who emerged as the *Dumnonii*, to their west. In pre-Roman times the *Dumnonii* were the tribe of the far south west: modern Devon and Cornwall. By the later Anglo-Saxon period the name described all the British in south-western England. Eventually there was only one British king in southern England, the king of the *Dumnonii*. The name was the origin of 'Devon'. The first record of what we can discern as 'Devon shire' is in the Anglo-Saxon Chronicle for 851 AD.

In Roman times there were about five tribal *civitates* in the south and west of England. The provincial capitals were at London and Cirencester. The last remnants of whatever government had survived in the Cirencester area were probably swept away after the battle of Deorham in 577 AD. They may have become the Hwicca. South of the Wansdyke, we know even less. We can say that there was some element of unity across the area from Silchester to Bath and southwards at the time of the battle of Deorham. The evidence is the building of the Wansdyke from Goring to the Bristol Channel.

The fortunes of Mercia in the seventh and eighth centuries benefitted greatly from the long reigns of just a few kings. Wessex was not so fortunate. It suffered from a series of relatively short reigns, punctuated by a few long ones. Among them was Cynegils, who reigned from 611 to 643 AD; Cenwalh (643-72, with a short inter-regnum between 645 and 648); and Ine (688 to 726). In the ninth century Wessex benefitted from the reigns of Egbert (802-39) and Aelfraed (known to us as Alfred the Great), from 871 to 899. Between these were many others. They generally claimed descent from Cerdic, but rarely succeeded their own fathers directly. We won't dwell on the individuals much.

The first area of interest is around Grim's Ditch, which could be described as the eastern Wansdyke from the Marlborough area to Goring. It is shown as Section 1 on Figure 11.3. It didn't last long. The easiest direction for the West Saxons to attack Grim's Ditch from was the north west. We have seen that they could get to the Roman road running southeast from Cirencester and then advance along it. The road split at Wanborough, near Swindon. The main road ran south of east through modern Newbury towards Silchester. The other branch ran more or less south into the Savernake Forest. It crossed the River Kennet at *Cunetio*, just east of modern Marlborough. The Newbury route also ran into woodland, but it was higher and drier. Grim's Ditch turned south around there, which enabled the West Saxons to get a toehold on the high ground south of the Ridgeway. Somehow they managed to breach Grim's Ditch. That wasn't a major problem: the British retrenched from the River Lambourn northwards, from the area of East Garston (just east of the town of Lambourn), a mile or two east of the original line. It is Section '2' on Figure 11.2.

(In Figures 11.3 to 11.7, Romano-British defences are shown numbered '1' to '10' in order of construction. West Saxon earthworks are lettered 'A' to 'G'.)

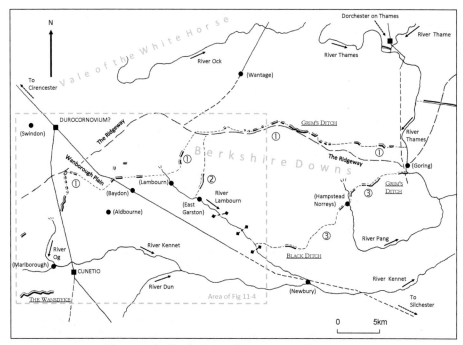

Figure 11.3 The Berkshire Downs, circa 570-610 AD.

In passing, some 40 years later (in about 648 AD) Cenwalh of Wessex granted 3,000 hides at Ashdown to his nephew Cuthred. 3,000 hides is a vast area: at least 180 square miles. Ashdown is about two miles north of Baydon. The 3,000 hides might be *all* the land from Grim's Ditch down to the river Lambourn and from Ashdown across to Goring. That would suggest that from the time it was seized by Ceolwulf it had been in the king's royal domain (ie, personal estates). By the time of Cenwalh, the king would have much more land further south in Hampshire. He could afford to grant large areas of downland to his relatives.

In general, we can sometimes see where a further section of earthwork was dug. That tends to suggest a retrenchment, or a realignment. Sometimes it suggests that a defended position was abandoned and a new one dug to its rear, as we saw in the Cambridge area. Sometimes it suggests 'bite and hold', as we saw in the Yorkshire Wolds. However, what we cannot detect is a counterattack. Of itself, that leaves no sign. So, in this case, the West Saxons may have managed to force a crossing of a section of dyke, or seize it by surprise. The British may have recaptured it at some stage in a counterattack. We would not be able to see that (without some incredibly detailed archaeology, which we would not undertake unless we had some idea where to look). So the earthworks tend to show us the long-term trend. The location and alignment of a given section can tells us something of its intended function. By looking at a number of earthworks, and considering the likely function of each one, we can deduce something about the sequence in which they were built. Of itself, it gives us almost no idea of timescale.

This process does, however, tend to underestimate the defender's success. A dyke might be defended successfully several times, or be regained through counterattack. We would not see that. We might see a realignment, which tends to suggest that the original line was not as good as it might have been: the defenders subsequently thought that its alignment could be improved. The only real indicator of the success of a set of earthworks is if they were defended over a long period, which we have to infer from other evidence (which we shall, shortly).

Counterattacks raise another issue. If the attackers had successfully seized a section of dyke (either by main force or surprise) but then been repulsed, it might occur to them that the next time they should dig in as soon as they had got across. That's not always possible. A credible earthwork can be thrown up in a day, or perhaps overnight (most of the trenches of the First World War were dug in the dark, at night). You wouldn't dig in as soon as you had crossed if you thought you had decisively beaten the enemy, and were intent on pursuing them. But, if you repeatedly managed to seize a section of earthwork and were repeatedly thrown back through counterattack, it might occur to you to 'bite and hold'. In very simple terms, that often happened in the First World War. We begin to see that in the area north east of Marlborough. See Figure 11.4.

The Figure shows what seems to be the sequence. The line shown as '2 ?' may have been dug at the same time as Section 2 to the east. It is not easy to demonstrate why that is so in a simple line drawing. It is much more obvious in three dimensions, which is why cheap three-dimensional mapping on a computer is so useful. It is quite easy to demonstrate on the ground, not least because army officers are trained to do that sort of thing. Seen from a distance, the precise details don't matter. That is one way of saying that the minor tactical details are only important in so far as they allow us to see the overall, campaign or theatre-level picture.

Two things happened as a result of events around Lambourn. The first was relatively sudden and dramatic, but left little trace. The second was in many ways far more interesting, and left more evidence, but in the long run had less impact. The first thing was the events which led to the fall of Silchester and most of what we now call Berkshire and Hampshire. We shall look at that first. We will then return to the sequence of events around and south of Marlborough. As we shall see, it almost looks like the Battle of the Somme in places.

Grim's Ditch on the Ridgeway (Section 1) is not generally as well-preserved as the Wansdyke proper. That is largely because it fell quite quickly. We can put some dates to the process, and will do so shortly. Grim's Ditch was breached again. We don't know quite where, but it was east of Lambourn. The British responded by withdrawing up to six miles in places, and preparing another defensive position. In the west, it seems to have used the River Lambourn. In the east, it ran from the Thames to the River Pang. A section of about six miles of earthwork connected the Lambourn to the Pang. It is shown as Line '3' on Figure 11.3. Its overall alignment allowed the British to retain the use of the Silchester-Cirencester road as far as Baydon, which would have been a significant advantage.

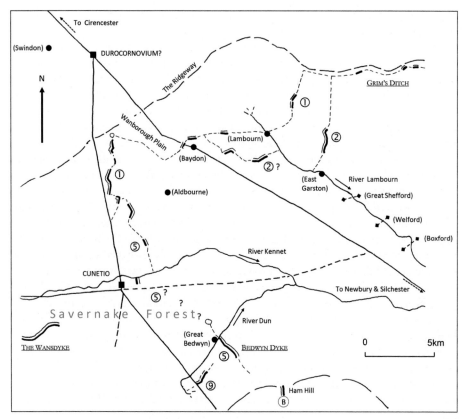

Figure 11.4 The Marlborough Downs.

The western end of the line connected to the existing earthworks in the area of Lambourn and Baydon (Section '2 ?'). There is no trace of earthworks along the River Lambourn, but there are three fords in that section: at Shefford, Welford and Boxford. The British may have simply defended the fords. From the River Lambourn, near Boxford, the line ran east across close, wooded and hilly country to the Pang. It is visible, as the Black Ditch, over a length of about half a mile roughly three miles north of Newbury. It may have swung north east and met the Pang immediately south of Hampstead Norreys. Alternatively it may have met the river at Marlstone Farm, east of Hermitage. From Hampstead Norreys it is much easier to trace. It runs north, above the east bank, for a mile or so before swinging east and eventually meeting the Thames about a mile south of Streatley, just south of Goring. Confusingly, that section is also known as Grim's Ditch.

The siting of that section is superb. It is one of the first areas that I surveyed systematically. At first it made little sense, but as I built up a mental picture of where it ran, why it was built there and what the defenders were trying to do, I was immensely impressed. In one area the tactical problems are significant and the engineering solution (particularly, the detailed alignment) is breathtaking. For reasons which will become apparent, we will call that area the 'Streatley Anomaly', and discuss it in Chapter 13. The earthworks from Streatley to Hampstead Norreys can be followed on a 1:25,000 scale map quite easily. They are marked in six places. On the ground they are up to seven or eight feet high. In one area they seem to have been realigned. They are sited to resist attack from the north and northwest, although in places they face slightly east of north.

Much of Hampshire is arable farmland. It has been for centuries, if not millennia. Much of this line may have been ploughed out. Apart from the section from Streatley to Hampstead Norreys, little trace of it is visible today and it is possible that it was never completed. That may have enabled the West Saxons to get past it, or it may have been breached. The British and West Saxons then fought for a number of years in the close, broken country along the River Kennet. In the east the British built at least three successive earthworks (Area 4 on Figure 11.5) across Greenham Common, a finger of high ground between the Kennet to the north and the River Enbourne to the south. One of the dykes is now lost under the former USAF airbase. In the west, the

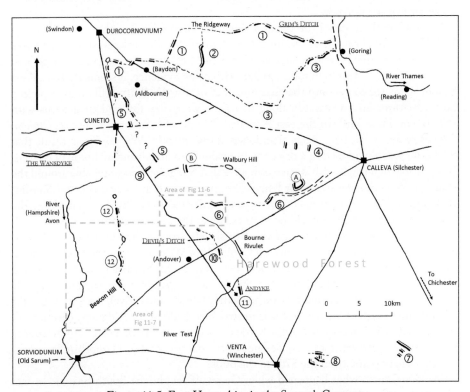

Figure 11.5 East Hampshire in the Seventh Century.

British dug at least one line of dykes facing west to protect the road from Winchester to *Cunetio* (Line '5').

After some time, the West Saxons penetrated as far south as Kingsclere and dug in there (Area A). At that stage the British started digging a third major line. It is shown as '6'. It abandoned the valley of the river Kennet and the Roman road from Silchester to Baydon. For about 20 miles it runs on top of the high ground south of the Kennet, known variously as Ham Hill, Inkpen Hill and Watership Down. In the east it connected to the old earthworks which the British had built just north and east of Silchester in response to the battle of Berins Hill, shown in Figure 6.5. In the west it was up to three miles south of the escarpment, so as to be anchored on the Chute Causeway. It was then extended westwards to the River Avon. We shall look at that shortly.

There is very little trace of that line today. There are sections along the escarpment. In the east the escarpment runs out somewhere south of Kingsclere. The country east of there is a tangle of small, irregular mixed woodland typical of decayed old forest. In this area the line ran a mile or two north of, and hence protected, the road from Silchester to Sarum. The British had lost the use of the road from Silchester towards Baydon. They could still use the Sarum road, then turn north west near Andover and make for *Cunetio* that way.

Not only is there very little trace of this third line today, but there is evidence of West Saxon fortifications in the area. On Ham Hill, well to the west and just three miles east of Bedwyn, a fairly massive earthwork ('B') cuts the escarpment and faces west. It is up to 12 feet high today. Taken with other evidence, it seems that the West Saxons managed to get onto the escarpment at or near Walbury Hill. They exploited both eastwards and westwards along it. In the west they fortified their gains with the dike on Ham Hill. In the east it spelled the end of Silchester. Like *Verulamium*, Silchester seems to have been abandoned fairly quickly. We need not think that Silchester was abandoned in a day or so in response to an advancing horde of Saxons. It is possible that the British started to realise that Silchester was untenable around the time the West Saxons arrived at Kingsclere. It may be that individuals and families thought that the situation was hopeless and just drifted away. But leave, they did. The Ogham stone found there could be from as late as the seventh century.

We can be fairly confident that the British left around then because the Anglo-Saxon chronicle tells us that in 607 AD Ceolwulf of Wessex fought the South Saxons. He could only do that if he could reach them. He could only reach them if he could get through, or past, Silchester. The South Saxons might have expanded slightly north beyond the Downs and the Rother Valley (see Chapter Five), but they were still several miles south of Silchester. So, if the earthwork along the Ridgeway (Section '1') was started in 577 in response to the battle of Deorham (or perhaps in 571 in response to the battle of Bedcanford), the defence of the eastern part of Hampshire lasted for perhaps thirty years, from the 570s to the 600s.

We don't know what happened when Ceolwulf fought the South Saxons. In fact almost the only thing we know about Ceolwulf is that he did fight the South Saxons.

The date, however, is useful because it tells us that eastern Hampshire, the area east of the River Test, was conquered in the early seventh century. It probably didn't all fall in one go. That would be unlikely, given the size of the area involved. In addition, there are earthworks south of Four Marks, about 20 miles south of Silchester, that face north east (Area '7'). There is another series of earthworks between Winchester and Alresford, just south of the River Itchen, that defend against an attack from the north and east (Area '8'). Both sets seem to be intended to defend the Winchester area from attack from the general direction of Silchester and perhaps London.

There are several sections of earthwork in both areas. That suggests that this area was defended for some time. That is, long enough for an initial defensive line to be improved. We cannot say more than that. We cannot say, for example, that they were part of a single defensive system; nor that they were physically connected. When Ceolwulf fought the South Saxons he may have advanced south from Silchester down the road to Chichester, bypassing those earthworks. So Winchester may not have fallen until sometime after 607 AD. There is, however, archaeological evidence of Saxon settlement in eastern Hampshire in the seventh century, after something of a gap.

Before leaving this part of England we should make two remarks about the geography, based on place name evidence. The first relates to the area immediately north of Winchester. That is, between there and the Test. It is open downland today. Almost all of it is arable farmland with a few woods and several long, narrow plantations. They were clearly planted in modern times as windbreaks. Curiously, however, there are very few place names. That is in stark comparison with, say, the Lambourn Downs or the Yorkshire Wolds. Near Lambourn almost every hillside has a name. In the Yorkshire Wolds almost every area is part of a named 'Wold'. Yet north of Winchester there are almost no area names shown on the map. The few names that exist often have woodland origins, such as Brockley, Bazeley, Dodsley, Embley and Crawley. There are another dozen or so '-leys' within ten miles. It seems that when the West Saxons took over the area in the early seventh century it was extensive woodland, and that it has virtually never been settled. The villages are a long way apart. Not least, most of the villages are near streams, and there are very few streams. It seems that the Harewood Forest once stretched much of the way from Andover to Winchester.

The second place name issue relates to the counties. We have looked at the origins of the county names in south-east England (such as Norfolk, Suffolk, Essex and Kent) previously. In the rest of England, county (and particularly shire) names are generally linked to the original county town, although that may not be obvious. In the case of Gloucestershire and Lancashire, they are. In the case of Somerset we have to know that the original county town was Somerton. For Hampshire it was (south) Hampton. Southampton and Northampton were probably only given their 'south' and 'north' prefixes after Mercia and Wessex were united in the late ninth or the tenth century. Wiltshire's county town was Wilton. Berkshire, however, is a mystery for two reasons. Firstly, there is no obvious county town name that would explain the prefix 'Berk-'. Secondly, its shape makes little or no sense. County boundaries are often sensible

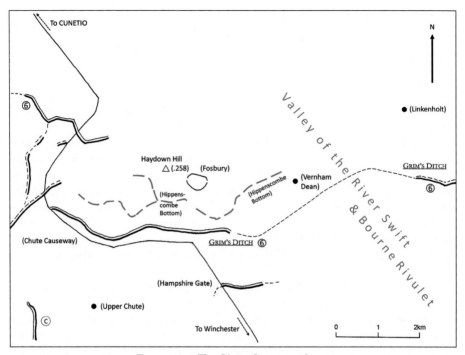

Figure 11.6 The Chute Causeway Area.

in terms of rivers, escarpments or crest lines. The counties were often planned quite deliberately in later Anglo-Saxon times.

Berkshire is an anomaly. We will look at it in more detail in Chapter 12. However, its southern boundary runs along the escarpment south of the River Kennet, and then east along a stream parallel with the river. It then obviously bends northwards around Silchester so as to include it in Hampshire. Why do that, for an abandoned town? It suggests that the land to the north, down to the Kennet Valley, was considered to belong to an older part of Wessex, whilst the land south of it (but particularly the town of Silchester) was acquired later.

We now need to look again at the area around Marlborough. We saw earlier how the West Saxons had got onto the Downs and forced the British to retrench repeatedly, as in Figure 11.4. The Roman town of *Cunetio* lay in the valley of the River Kennet, just south of the river. It was walled. At one time there had been a Roman fort on the escarpment to the south. The whole area is riddled with earthworks, facing in different directions and wandering off into the Savernake Forest (much of which is now Forestry Commission land and open to the public). In several places, such as near Stitchcombe (close to *Cunetio*), the earthworks clearly face east. The Saxons had got onto the Downs to the north east, and were trying to get onto the road in order to go south. At some stage they succeeded. They bypassed *Cunetio* to the east and got onto the road further south. South of the present Savernake Forest, the River Dun rises in the Vale of Pewsey. It flows east and joins the Kennet at Hungerford. Today we don't notice it because the Kennet and Avon Canal runs parallel with it (and uses its water). The valley of the Dun is crossed by a dike at Bedwyn, which faces east ('5'). It seems to have connected to the prehistoric earthwork at Chisbury on the north side of the valley.

West of Bedwyn, however, another earthwork cuts the line of the Roman road about half a mile south of the Canal ('9'). It faces north. The West Saxons had got onto the Roman road south of *Cunetio*, forcing the British to abandon it and block the road with an earthwork just south of the Dun. Soon afterwards the West Saxons reached Ham Hill ('B') from the east. That forced the British to withdraw again, two or three miles up the escarpment to the Chute Causeway. It was probably at about this point that the line from the Silchester area ('6') was continued west to the Avon. If anything resembles a map of the Battle of the Somme, it is the area around the Causeway. Figure 11. is relatively large scale: the whole area covers just a few square miles.

I worked for several years at Trenchard Lines, Upavon, about ten miles away. The local 1:25,000 scale map was the first sheet of the modern Explorer series which I ever bought. Digital technology had made 1:25,000 mapping much cheaper. The Explorer series is drawn in a clear style similar to the popular 1:50,000 Landranger series. I also had a copy of the Ordnance Survey Map of Roman Britain. Looking at the latter, I was struck by an obvious kink in the Roman road from Portchester (near Portsmouth) to Cirencester. In the whole of southern England it is the only major kink in a Roman road. I got out the 1:25,000 map, but couldn't make sense of the contours. I didn't understand why Roman surveyors would build such an obvious kink in the road. Everyone knows that Roman roads are straight! One summer evening I went to find out. There is lovely pub nearby (The Hatchet) which I used to frequent some years earlier when I served at Tidworth. I drove up onto the Chute Causeway and very quickly saw why there is a kink there.

The landscape is, at first sight, fairly flat. The horizon is fairly level. Until, that is, you look down into Hippenscombe Bottom. It is a glacial, U-shaped valley which winds its way around the south of Haydown Hill and Fosbury, another Iron Age hill fort. It is little over half a mile wide, but over 100 metres deep. If the Roman surveyors had taken the road down it and up the other side in a straight line, a legionary would have thought it was a bit steep. A cart would have had huge problems going down. It would have had even bigger problems going up the other side. The Causeway, however, loses just 35 metres of height in almost exactly four miles. It is, broadly, flat. The price of that is that it is about a mile and a half longer than the direct route. Over the years a lot of people with carts would have been very grateful, if they understood what the Roman surveyors had done. Archaeologists have confirmed that the Causeway is not a curve, but a series of short straights. That made it much easier for a surveyor to set out, and for legionaries to build.

In Chapter Four I wrote that in researching for this book a cold chill ran down my spine twice. The second time was when my calculations indicated that some of the

Cambridge Dykes were designed in Roman feet (see Chapter Five). The first was when I visited the area of Chute Causeway. A public footpath runs up the side of Haydown Hill. At the top it crosses another footpath. The map tells you that you are within feet of the precise spot where a Roman surveyor must have stood. The line of the road southwards, to Portchester, would pass within about 50 yards of you on one side. The line of the road northwards, to Cirencester, would pass within about 50 yards on the other side. The two roads diverge from one another by about seven degrees. That is to say, a Roman surveyor stood somewhere near where the track junction is now. He decided that he would bring his road up here from Portchester, turn west slightly, and then go on to Cirencester. Bends of a few degrees are not unusual. The precise spot at which the two alignments would meet is some distance to the north and on a reverse slope. From the track junction on Haydown Hill, however, the surveyor could see the course of both sections of the road, north and south. Unfortunately Hippenscombe Bottom gets in the way. But if you stand at the track junction, the horizon is almost flat. That is probably what gave the Roman surveyor the idea to bypass Hippenscombe Bottom and take the road around what we now call the Causeway. (It isn't a causeway in the accepted sense of a road or track across low or wet ground.)

It is strange to know that someone must have stood almost exactly where you are, almost two thousand years ago, and known almost precisely why. It is strange, but not directly relevant to our story. At a higher level, the West Saxons were trying to advance south east down the Roman road from *Cunetio* into Hampshire, in the direction of Winchester and then Portchester. The Causeway sits on an area of high ground which falls in every direction. The line of earthworks westwards from Silchester ('6') seems to have been anchored on the Chute Causeway above Hippenscombe Bottom. Figure 11.6 shows a gap of about a mile. The western section lies well north of the section running in from the east. That gap could be exploited. It looks easy on a map, particularly one (such as Figure 11.6) that has been designed to emphasize the earthworks. In reality the hillsides are steep and the topography is extremely complex. The Ordnance Survey map is a confusing jumble of contours. In practice it seems that the West Saxons went round to the *west* of the Causeway. That explains the short sections immediately west of the road. The British seem to have dug four or even five separate dykes in order to retain possession of at least some of the high ground. Eventually they were forced to fall back from the line of Grim's Ditch and build a position at what is now the Hampshire Gate. The fact that it is on the Hampshire county boundary is probably no coincidence. One or two sections of dyke in the area (such as 'C') face west. That suggests that the West Saxons eventually managed to break through in this area. They then dug in to protect their gains

In passing, in all the time I spent out in the countryside researching for this book, I got lost only once (briefly). That was in the woods in this area. I had a map and a compass. I pity the people who had to fight through the area all those years ago, without benefit of either.

About three miles to the south east is another section of earthwork called the Devil's Ditch. Old maps show it extending for about a mile and a half south eastwards.

About two miles further south another section of Devil's Ditch appears to have cut the Portway. Old maps, contextual evidence and inspection suggest that both sections faced north and east. However, both sections are very decayed today, and it is hard to be certain. They are shown as Section '10' on Figure 11.5. They seem to form a continuous line, about a mile west of the valley of the Bourne Rivulet.

The Andyke, south of Andover and about a mile east of the junction of the Test and the Dever, is shown as Section '11'. It seems to be sited to protect the Roman road, which crosses the two rivers just west of that junction. The Andyke faces east. On old maps it is shown as the 'Ansdyke' or 'Van Dyke'. It may have been called the Wansdyke. Taken together, it seems that the British were trying to keep the use of the road north-west from Winchester as far as the Hampshire Gap. The British seem to have defended lateral roads in this area as part of their defensive scheme. Lateral roads allow the rapid movement of forces to and between threatened sectors. They also support surprise raids and counterattacks elsewhere. All this digging seems to have taken place in the period after Silchester had fallen, but Winchester was still in British hands.

It is not obvious how the British were forced off this position. The siting of one of the west-facing sections of dyke west of Upper Chute ('C' on Figure 11.6) suggests that it happened near the Chute Causeway.

The next major step was for the British to close off modern Wiltshire. To do that they constructed a defensive line from the Vale of Pewsey, west of the Chute Causeway, almost due south ('12'). In the north, the line may have started at Ram Alley in the depths of the swamps of the Vale of Pewsey. There are signs of earthworks which face east there. It seems to have passed south over Easton Hill, then almost due south to the old hill fort at Sidbury Hill. From there it ran more or less south along Dunch Hill (where it is called the Devils Ditch) to the crest of Beacon Hill. It ends about a mile to the south east, near the junction of the modern A303 and A338. See Figure 11.7.

Detailed inspection suggests that it ran into and stopped at the River Bourne. Confusingly this is another river Bourne, as in the name of the village of Winterbourne Gunner. The Bourne has few of fords today. One, called 'Ford', lies on the Roman road from Winchester to Sarum. None of the others are named. That suggests that they didn't exist in the Dark Ages. The Bourne runs into the Avon east of Sarum (and Salisbury), and there are only three fords south of there: at Britford, Charford and Fordingbridge. At this stage the West Saxons dug in to protect their gains with an even longer earthwork. It faces the British line on the eastern side of the upper Bourne valley. It is line 'D' on Figure 11.7. The Figure begs the question of why the West Saxons did not try to outflank the British dyke on Dunch Hill (12) to its south. That is, go south of Beacon Hill. In simple terms they could, but it would do them no good. They could not in practice get across the Bourne, nor the Avon south of Sarum. They needed to cross higher up, in the north.

Up to this point it has been rare to find opposing earthworks facing each other. It has been just as rare to find the West Saxons building earthworks at all. From here onwards we shall see that more often. We shall also see the West Saxons using 'bite and hold' tactics.

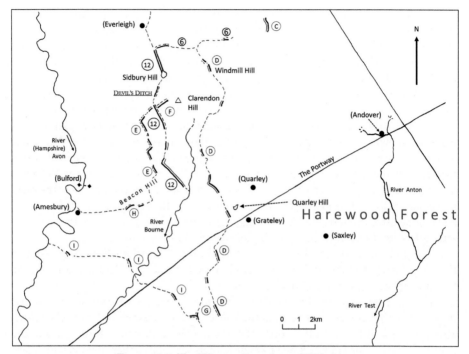

Figure 11.7 The Western Boundary of Wiltshire.

The West Saxons broke through the Devil's Ditch on Dunch Hill and dug in a few hundred yards west. They probably did so in two separate stages. The first is shown as 'E' on Figure 11.7. Section 'F' (between Clarendon Hill and the Devil's Ditch) seems to be linked to that phase. Section 'G' relates to a realignment in the south. Earthworks in the region of Bulford ('H') and south of the A303 ('I') then suggest a narrow salient pointing straight at Amesbury. The reason is now obvious. Having managed to get a toehold north of the Bourne, the West Saxons then attempted to cross the Avon at Amesbury, and possibly also at Bulford, about two miles north.

We can't date this process particularly closely. The West Saxons could get onto the Downs north east of Marlborough sometime after Bedcanford (in 571 AD), or perhaps Deorham (in 577). They probably broke through into Hampshire across the Kennet before 607. As we shall see, they probably didn't get significantly beyond Amesbury until 652. It was the grandsons, or perhaps the great-grandsons, of those who fought at Deorham who would get to Amesbury.

In the meantime, there had been trouble on Wessex's northern border. In 614 AD King Cynegils fought a battle at Bampton on the Thames. The village of Bampton is about a mile north of the river, on the north bank. It is between Lechlade and Witney. That stretch of the Thames has very few named fords and meandered about through an extensive marsh. Just south west of Bampton a very low-lying spur runs relatively close to the current course of the river. We don't know the precise course of the river in 614. It does seem that it was possible to get across. The location may have been near the site of the delightfully named Tadpole Bridge. The Anglo-Saxon Chronicle tells us that Cynegils, who may have been accompanied by his successor Cwichelm (who may have been his son) slew 2,046 Welsh. They would have been Hwicca. The figure is not credible. It does not seem to have been Wessex which benefitted. In the long run, the Hwicca fell under the control of Mercia.

14 years later Mercia tried to invade Wessex. Penda of Mercia came to the throne in 626 AD. In 628 he marched down the Fosse Way through the land of the Hwicca and fought the West Saxons at Cirencester. The outcome was a treaty, which suggests that the outcome of the battle was a draw. Strategically, for Wessex the way north was now closed. They made no significant progress northwards for the next two hundred years. For two centuries any expansion was to the south and south west.

South of the Wansdyke, much of the south west had enjoyed more than two hundred years of something like peace. In the fifth century there had been some Saxon incursion and settlement in Wiltshire, particularly in the south. However, apart from Cerdic's revolt, the south had not necessarily been the scene of any fighting. The British exported tin from Cornwall as far as Constantinople. One estimate suggests as many as 100 ship voyages a year between Cornwall and the Mediterranean. Excavations in places such as Tintagel and South Cadbury hill fort reveal extensive imports of luxury goods, such as olives and wine in amphorae, in the sixth century. South Cadbury had been extensively rebuilt, using a vast amount of mature timber (including baulks big enough to build eighteenth-century warships with). The Britons used Roman engineering techniques, a century after the Romans had supposedly left. The trade and prosperity extended across the Bristol Channel. It included Gwent (around Caerwent) and Glamorgan (around Dinas Powis and Llandaff).

We should be cautious about the evidence for what follows. The work of the English Place Name Society is less reliable from here on. The volumes for Somerset, Devon, Cornwall, Dorset and Wiltshire are either incomplete, have not been produced, or are not considered to be reliable. Those counties are almost exactly the area covered by the rest of this chapter and the next.

For clarity we will start a new numbering sequence here. The British line west from Silchester, previously Line '6', will now be Line '1'. The West Saxon dyke just west of upper Chute is now Line 'A'. The detail from Figures 11.6 and 11.7 has been removed for clarity on Figure 11.8.

The West Saxons had seized much of eastern Hampshire by 607 AD. They fought in the Marlborough – Chute – Andover – Amesbury area for decades. In the area immediately west of Sidbury Hill, on Salisbury Plain, there is a complex series of earthworks which are hard to explain. As one travels further west what emerges seems to be two parallel earthworks running more or less west towards Market Lavington. One runs just north of the ridge of Slay Down and therefore seems to face north. The other is on the south-facing slopes above Water Dean Bottom. It appears to face south. So, even before the West Saxons had broken through in the Chute Causeway

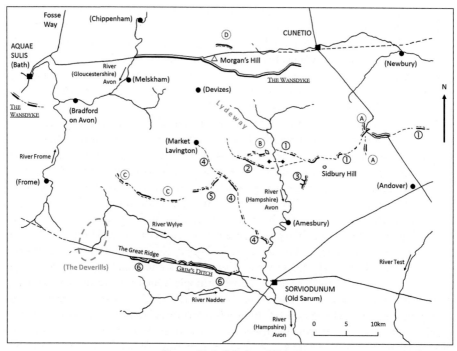

Figure 11.8 Salisbury Plain.

area they had managed to infiltrate around the north and seize a ford over the River Avon at Enford. The British retrenched by digging in along Slay Down ('2'). The West Saxons consolidated their positions on Water Dean Bottom with Line 'B'.

Figure '3' may be a defended camp built by the British at or about the time that the Sidbury Hill area fell. At some stage Amesbury fell, and with it the ford at Bulford. The British line on Slay Down ('2') was outflanked. The British fell back to a new line across the high ground of the Plain from the area of Market Lavington south east to the River Avon (Section '4'). Much of Salisbury Plain is an artillery impact area today. I went there many times whilst serving in the Army. I would normally be delighted if readers of this book went out and looked for Dark Age dykes. However I urge readers not to go onto any Ministry of Defence land without permission. It is dangerous and you could die.

For perhaps four decades, up to about 650 AD, the British had defended a series of defensive earthwork lines. They had been thrown out of Hampshire. The West Saxons were making progress, slowly, in Wiltshire, especially in the area of Salisbury Plain. What happened next was an operational, theatre-level break-through. It was the Battle of the Broad Ford in 652. In modern English that is Bradford-on-Avon. To understand how it happened, we need to go back to the Wansdyke and Morgan's Hill.

A glance at Figures 7-1 and 7-3 in Chapter Seven shows the problem quite clearly. It was difficult to march westwards via Cirencester. We don't know precisely who held what, but battles at Bampton in 614 AD and Cirencester in 628 suggest that the West Saxons could not get north across the Thames. The Roman road west from Morgan's Hill had been turned into a section of the Wansdyke. The area immediately north of that was a series of marshy valleys around modern Calne. The solution to crossing the Avon lay further north, at Great Somerford or perhaps even by marching north to Cirencester and then south west along the Fosse Way. But the land west of the Avon belonged to the Hwicca.

Another problem for the West Saxons was that the area around Morgan's Hill provided excellent views and a good base from which to raid into the upper Thames Valley. Who would want to march off towards Bath if the British were 20 miles closer to the attackers' villages?

The geography of the area of Morgan's Hill had theatre-wide implications, in much the same way that Messines Ridge did on the Western Front in the First World War. In 1917 British Royal Engineers more or less blew the top off Messines Ridge. The West Saxons didn't have that option. To protect their lateral movements they dug an earthwork of their own along the top of Cherhill Down (Section 'D' on Figure 11.8). Today it is about a mile long, but only about three feet high. It is on a gentle forward slope and faces south. The Anglo-Saxons called a military route or road a 'herepath'. The old route leading to Cherhill Down from the Marlborough area is shown on Ordnance Survey maps as either the 'Herepath' or 'Green Street'. The track westwards along Cherhill Down, just a few yards north of the earthworks, is now a section of the Wessex Ridgeway. It is also called the Old Bath Road. It was only in 1743 that the main road from London to Bath (and then Bristol) was re-routed off the Down. (It became the modern A4 and runs parallel with the Old Road, about 400 yards north.) In the Dark Ages, if you wanted to go west you had to use Cherhill Down. That route was protected by earthwork 'D', facing south.

That may have been enough to give the West Saxons the confidence to advance westwards. It is also possible that the critical events took place on Salisbury Plain, about seven or eight miles south. When the British were forced to dig a new line based on the Market Lavington area ('4'), it became difficult to maintain their presence on the Wansdyke. The easiest way across the Vale of Pewsey would have been the Lydeway. It started near where the Hampshire Avon enters the valley which takes it south through the Plain. The Lydeway ran north west to the area of Devizes. It used the watershed between the Hampshire and Gloucestershire Avons. It is now part of the A342. Once the West Saxons had dug Line B it would have been impossible for the British to reach the Lydeway. In order to reach Morgan's Hill they would have to reach Potterne, then Devizes, from the south west. That was across about two miles of marsh. It was obviously difficult. They may have abandoned Morgan's Hill, or not have been able to man it in enough strength to deter the West Saxons from heading west. Not least, a British force making for Morgan's Hill from Salisbury Plain via Devizes would expose its own flank and rear to West Saxons on the north side of the

Plain. 'Morgan' is a British name. Many Morgans are known to us from Welsh poetry. The name may be related to 'Morcant'. A Morcant was present with Urien of Rheged at the siege of Lindisfarne (and had him assassinated). We don't know why a hill in Wiltshire was named after a British king, but it may be significant.

Earthworks on the western end of Salisbury Plain seem to show a transitional phase. The more easterly section ('5') seems to face north, implying that it was a short-lived British position. The western section ('C') seems to face south, meaning that the West Saxons built it. It may be related to what happened next, in 652 AD.

Somehow, Cenwalh managed to get his West Saxons south of the Avon near Bradford-on-Avon in force. It is possible that they didn't cross the river, but advanced along the south bank. Alternatively Cenwalh may have been able to move through the land of the Hwicca as a consequence of the treaty at Cirencester back in 628. We don't know if, or how, he crossed the Wansdyke. Bradford lies in a gap between the two main sections of the Wansdyke: the section in the east between Marlborough and the Avon north of Melksham; and the western section from the River Frome to Bristol. The obvious suggestion is that Cenwalh got across the Avon using the ford at Bradford. Perhaps he gained surprise. History doesn't tell us.

Getting across the Avon at Bradford would force the British to fight without a dyke to defend. Effectively it turned (outflanked) the line which ran southeast from Market Lavington (Line 4). The British lost, and lost badly. They withdrew southwards, right across Salisbury Plain and the Wylye Valley. The Roman road west from Sarum ran along the high ground between the Rivers Wylye and Nadder, now known to us as the Great Ridge. Few people go up there today. There are earthworks running for about ten miles along the ridge and the Roman road (Line '6'). Yet again, they are called Grim's Ditch. They come to an end at the highest point of the ridge. In places they are two to three feet high, and face slightly east of north. The threat was not from the north west, but the north east.

The Battle of the Broad Ford was the high point of a highly successful theatre-level manoeuvre. It finally completed the conquest of Berkshire, Hampshire and Wiltshire, 70 years after Fethanleag.

12

The Conquest of the South West

In about 650 AD the frontier between the West Saxons and the British ran across Salisbury Plain, south east across the Harewood Forest, and then eastwards into the Weald. Silchester had probably fallen to the West Saxons, but Winchester had not. In modern terms that meant that northern Wiltshire and north east Hampshire belonged to the West Saxons. Southern Wiltshire and the rest of Hampshire did not. Somerset, Dorset, Devon and Cornwall still belonged to the British.

The Battle of the Broad Ford, or Bradford-on-Avon, in 652 AD turned the British out of their positions on Salisbury Plain. Unfortunately it didn't lead anywhere directly. If you move south from Bradford on Avon, as the West Saxons would have wanted to do, you find yourself in the valley of the River Frome (see Figure 11.7). At its northern end, near Bradford, it is obviously decayed old woodland. Further south, west of the Great Ridge around the Deverills, it appears to be open downland. Today, it is. A look at the place names, however, shows names like Berkely Down, the Bradleys, Dertley Plain, Keysley Down and Bockerly Hill. The underlying geology is different here, so this area would have been easier to clear. What we see today is, nonetheless, cleared woodland. When the West Saxons arrived it hadn't been cleared. That is probably why Grim's Ditch stopped at the top of the Great Ridge. The area west of there was probably difficult, but not impossible, to traverse.

The main effect of the Battle of the Broad Ford was, therefore, to outmanoeuvre the British off the Wansdyke (if they still held it) and their positions on Salisbury Plain. If Amesbury had held any significance, it was now gone. The British seem to have held on to Grim's Ditch along the Great Ridge; east to the Avon; then south to the sea. All of west Hampshire (and particularly Winchester) fell to the West Saxons. Winchester means 'a walled town called *Venta*' (from *Venta Belgarum*). It may have had a special meaning for the West Saxons. They may have had an emotional attachment to it since the days of Cerdic. The Cerdic legend was powerful. The West Saxons had last been in the Winchester area in the days of their great grandfathers.

The West Saxon ruler Cynegils had adopted Christianity in the 630s AD and established a bishopric at Dorchester on Thames. With the possible exception of Cirencester, Dorchester was probably the largest town that the West Saxons held at that time. It was at about this time that Cenwalh is reputed to have split the bishopric. The Anglo-Saxon Chronicle records that happening in 660. A new (ie, second) bishop was consecrated in Winchester. That suggests that Dorchester remained as the original bishopric. The situation is highly confused, as Wessex was reputedly divided into two again in 705.

Be that as it may, Winchester had become part of Wessex. Two British bishops went to Winchester that year, which clearly required them to travel into Wessex.

Cenwalh's conquests did not finish with the Battle of the Broad Ford. Six years later, in about 658 AD, he turned the British out of their defensive position again. The next major battle was at a place called *'ad Peornum'*, which is probably the area of Penselwood near the Dorset border. Cenwalh seems to have moved his army down the line of the Frome and arrived at the headwaters of the River Stour. See Figure 12.1.

He may have got as far as Cold Kitchen Hill, about four or five miles north east of Penselwood, dug in, and forced the British to give battle. There are perhaps a mile of earthworks on the southern slope of Cold Kitchen Hill. They face south. By reaching this area Cenwalh avoided the headwaters of the Nadder, which lay south of Grim's Ditch. He had effectively outflanked the British earthwork on the Great Ridge. After the battle Cenwalh is reported to have chased the British to the River Parrett, about 25 miles to the west. Well, he may have done. That does not mean that he could

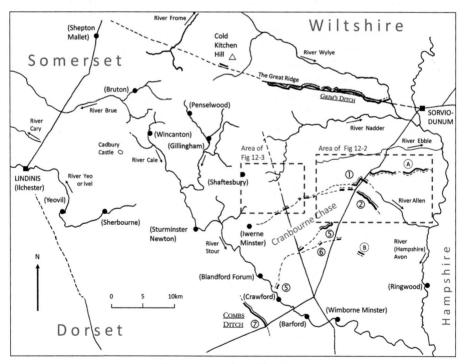

Figure 12.1 South Wiltshire.

occupy the land which he had chased them over. It was an operational withdrawal. The British, sensing defeat on the battlefield, broke off and withdrew. They kept withdrawing until the West Saxons were forced to give up the pursuit. That can be a devastating tactic, if you can keep your own army together and you have the space to withdraw into. The further the attacker advances, the more he lays himself open to counterattack, a long way from home. It was a painful lesson, but one which served Cenwalh very well a few years later. Two centuries later King Alfred employed it against the Vikings.

Once Cenwalh had given up the pursuit, he withdrew and consolidated what he had just won. It was, basically, the Nadder Valley, but that enabled him to advance down the west bank of the (Hampshire) Avon. There was a limit to what he could hold, since he had been unable to destroy the British army. His gains were not big. He could hold the Nadder and Ebble Valleys and some of the west bank of the Avon.

The British initially responded to their defeat at Penselwood by fortifying the high ground south east of Shaftesbury (see Figure 12.1). In the east, that is just south of the Ebble Valley. The earthworks run west from there through Cranborne Chase. Several sections can be seen in and around the woods in that area. Most face north. Some face east, perhaps to prevent West Saxon infiltration along the escarpment. Some are probably prehistoric. Some are very easily accessible today, and their profile is very obvious. Further east, in the area of Vernditch Chase, the line is more easy to follow today. It is line '1' on Figure 12.2. It seems to have been anchored on the River Allen.

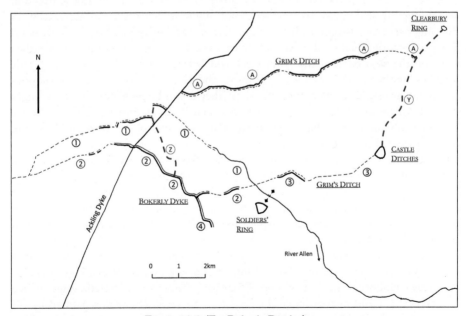

Figure 12.2 The Bokerly Ditch Area.

One section appears to incorporate a length of the dyke which the Cerdicings had built to cut the road from Sarum to Dorchester, more than a century before (line 'Z').

However, the West Saxons had learnt to dig dykes to protect their gains. They started digging on the escarpment south of the Ebble, further east. The dyke straddles the A354 today and then runs eastwards. It is line 'A' and faces south. At its west end it is about half a mile north east of the British ditch. The British then realigned their fortifications to the south east. The resulting set of fortifications is one of the best researched in Britain. They are easy to visit. There is both a car park and a lay-by on the A354. The dyke is impressive. It is at least 12 feet high today and is shown as line '2'. It is known as the Bokerley (or Bokerly) Ditch.

Pitt Rivers excavated the Bokerly Ditch in detail. Subsequent research has broadly confirmed his findings. The original ditch was about eight feet deep and had a relatively narrow flat bottom. The sides sloped at about 45 degrees. Unusually, the far side was widened and had a vertical step about four feet down from the original ground level. The ditch was later re-cut to about ten feet deep. Surprisingly, this was done on the home side. That meant removing much of the existing bank before digging down. It left a 'W' shape, with the middle only about four feet high (and well below the original ground level). Post holes tell us that there was a palisade, or perhaps just a row of sharpened stakes. It would have been a fearsome obstacle, and completely broken up any attempt to charge across it. The bank, or rampart, was about ten feet high.

It faced north east. It ran run from the escarpment above the Ebble in the north to Blagdon Hill. At some stage it was realigned and extended southwards along a ridge into what is now Martin Wood (line '4'). South from there are many small, irregular woods typical of decayed ancient woodland. There is, however, another earthwork running east from Blagdon Hill towards Castle Ditches (a hill fort at Whitsbury) (line '3'). Castle Ditches also seems to have been the southern terminus of Cerdic's dyke on the west bank of the Avon ('Y'), which faced west. However, from Castle Ditches another earthwork runs southwards and faces east. We have to be cautious about earthworks associated with hill forts. They might be prehistoric, or they might show us where Dark Age warriors anchored their dykes against the hill fort. So we cannot really know what happened at the south east end of the Bokerly Dyke, nor what the sequence of construction was.

Line 'A' defended the newly-captured West Saxon territory in the Nadder and Ebble Valleys. It is therefore probably no coincidence that it is broadly the southern border of Wiltshire today. Additionally, the Bokerly dike was the Britons' eastern boundary. It is therefore probably no coincidence that it is the eastern boundary of Dorset today. The area between, which is broadly the shallow valley of the River Allen, is part of Hampshire.

Further west, a series of earthworks near Shaftesbury tell us that the headwaters of the Nadder Valley was the western limit of Cenwalh's territory. See Figure 12.3.

Today Cranborne Chase lies on top of the more southerly of two chalk ridges which rise more than 100 metres above the land to their west. They are separated by the valley of the River Ebble. The Nadder Valley is north of the northern ridge. That

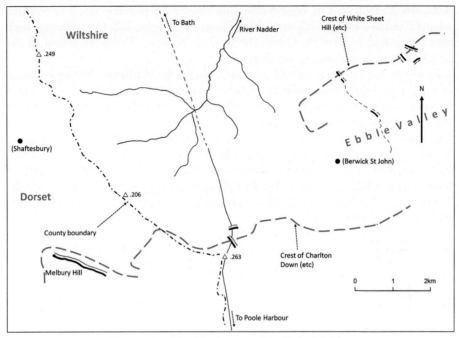

Figure 12.3 The Headwaters of the River Nadder.

feature is variously called White Sheet Hill, Swallowcliffe Down and several other names. Earthworks on White Sheet Hill, north east of Berwick St James, face north east. They suggest that the British tried to stop the West Saxons advancing westwards along the ridge, or west up the Ebble valley. Other earthworks face east, and may be West Saxon.

Some of the earthworks on the southern ridge, Charlton Down, seem to have been designed to stop the West Saxons both moving west along that ridge and south down the Roman road towards to coast. They may have been linked to the earthworks around the Bokerly Ditch. From this area, the modern Wiltshire border runs north east along the watershed of the Nadder to Penselwood.

After Penselwood, Cenwalh's aim was to attack south along the line of the Roman road which ran from Bath, east of south, to Poole Harbour. The Bokerly Dyke and associated fortifications thwarted that plan. Cenwalh also had other problems. In 661 AD Wulfhere of Mercia invaded. 16 years earlier his father Penda had managed to depose Cenwalh, who was in exile for about three years before regaining the throne. When Wulfhere invaded he advanced down the Icknield Way along the edge of the Chilterns. The Roman road from Alchester (near Bicester) south towards Dorchester on Thames had long since disappeared. Wulfhere met Cenwalh's army south of Thame (probably close to Postcombe, near the M40). Cenwalh was defeated, but withdrew westwards onto the Lambourn Downs. Wulfhere pursued him to Ashdown.

Ashdown is mentioned in West Saxon land charters; it probably refers to the area around Ashdown Park, north west of Lambourn (see Figure 7.2). Cenwalh may have been able to find a part of the Grim's Ditch on the Berkshire Downs to defend, deterring Wulfhere from pursuing any further.

However, the campaign of 661 AD was a success for Wulfhere. He seized much of Buckinghamshire and Oxfordshire, which we shall come to later. He managed to impose unfavourable terms on Cenwalh. They included the transfer of the Isle of Wight to the South Saxons, who were subordinate to Wulfhere at the time. In due course the West Saxons closed the Icknield Way to prevent Wulfhere using it again. They built an earthwork along Swyncombe Down, a spur of the Chilterns which sticks out about a mile towards the Thames near Wallingford. The dyke faces north. It is up to six feet high in places today. By linking it to boggy streams that ran into the Thames, the West Saxons could effectually block any subsequent advance south from Alchester. See Figure 12.4.

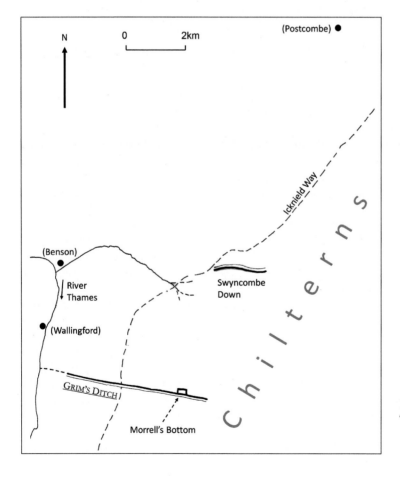

Figure 12.4
The Eastern
Borders of
Wessex.

Back on the Dorset border, the Bokerly Ditch is impressive. It is well-engineered and well-built. The fact that it was significantly re-cut on the same alignment suggests the work of highly capable engineers. It also suggests that it was defended for some time: years at least, and possibly several decades. The Battle of the Broad Ford (in 652 AD) had got Cenwalh south of the Gloucestershire Avon. Six years later, the battle of Penselwood had got him down to the Ebble Valley, and part of the valley of the Wiltshire Avon. His original aim seems to have been to expand southwards, but he was blocked by fortifications such as the Bokerly Ditch. He could not, however, get further west. The River Frome, and the dense woodland which it flowed through, had stopped him. When he got as far south as Penselwood he was blocked by the River Stour (see Figure 12.1).

The Stour is about 35 miles long from where it rises above Gillingham. There were five fords in the seven miles between Sturminster Newton and Blandford (Forum). There were three crossings in the three miles between Crawford and Barford. There was no ford in the eight miles from Gillingham to Sturminster Newton, and none between Blandford and Crawford. There were only two more in the 14 miles to Christchurch Harbour.

The area around Penselwood and Wincanton is one of those areas where the topography is critical. The Frome flows north into the Gloucestershire Avon. The headwaters of the Ebble, Nadder and Wylye all flow broadly eastwards. Slightly further west are the headwaters of the Stour. It flows southwards to Christchurch harbour and then, like the Wiltshire Avon, flows into Poole Bay (*not* Poole Harbour). The headwaters of the Stour are almost interspersed with those of the Yeo and the Brue, which flow west and north to the Bristol Channel. The valley of the River Cale, a tributary of the Stour, may have been even more of an obstacle. So, in practice, after Penselwood Cenwalh could not advance south, because of the Bokerly Ditch. Nor could he advance west. The headwaters of the Stour, the Yeo, the Brue and the Frome all stopped him. Initially he could not cross the Frome further north either.

Not only do all those rivers almost cross each other, but there were significant areas of marsh. Only a few miles west, the Fosse Way crosses the Yeo at Ilchester, the Roman *Lindinis*. The marshland in that area was probably several miles long and up to three miles across. In 665 AD Cenwalh did manage to break through to the west, at the second battle of Badon. The geography of Dorset may have deterred him from attacking on the Stour. It did not deter him from any offensive action, however. Seven years after the battle of Penselwood Cenwalh succeeded in a completely different area.

The second battle of Badon may actually have taken place at Bath, but the reservations we mentioned in Chapter Three still apply. In all of the few references we have to Bath before Domesday, none of them call it Badon. The Welsh Annals say that there was a second battle at Badon in 665 AD, and people have assumed that that was at Bath. Note, once again, that a *British* source refers to it as Badon, not an Anglo-Saxon one. It might be a 'Barton'. It is possible that in the seventh century a Briton might have known that the Anglo-Saxons sometimes called Bath 'Aet Bathan' or similar. There are many, many Bartons in England, but they tend to be grouped in just a few counties.

There is a small number in Gloucestershire, and all of them are on or near the Avon or the Frome. One (Barton Hill) is right in the middle of Bristol, but that is north of the Wansdyke. There are problems with all of the places in this area which might be 'Badon'. But it does seem that Cenwalh managed to force a crossing. He either got south across the Gloucestershire Avon west of the Frome, or west across the Frome itself. Either way, his success allowed the West Saxons to expand into what is, broadly, Somerset. They could then exploit down the Fosse Way from Bath. Significantly, the first (Anglo-Saxon) abbot of Glastonbury was appointed in about 667.

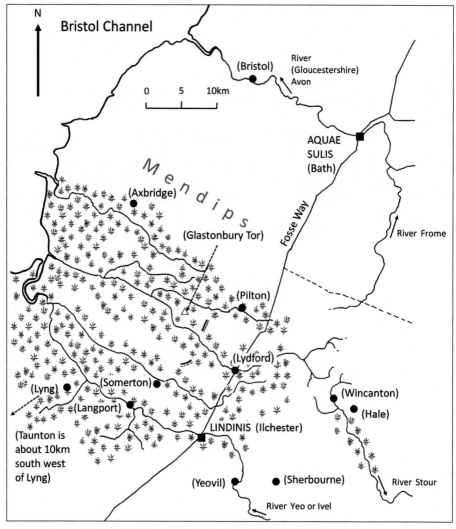

Figure 12.5 Somerset in the Seventh and Eighth Centuries.

Cenwalh's success got the West Saxons into Somerset, but they couldn't get out for almost two centuries. Figure 12.5 shows why.

Somerset was not just a great swamp. Much of it was, but a number of fingers of dry land pointed westwards between the valleys of the Rivers Axe, Brue, Cary and Yeo. That meant that travelling south was very difficult. Only the Fosse Way provided a good route, and that was barred at Ilchester by the Yeo. The fingers of dry land provided good refuges. For example, Glastonbury Tor was surrounded by marsh on three sides, and somebody built a dike (Ponter's Ball) facing east across the fourth side to defend it. Many years later, King Alfred would take refuge from the Vikings on the Isle of Athelney further west. The area is now called the Athelney Hills, because the swamps have been drained. In simple terms, the Second Battle of Badon gave Cenwalh and the West Saxons a way *in* to Somerset from the north and east. They could not, however, get *out* (to the south).

This situation persisted for many years. From the West Saxon perspective, it meant occasional war against Mercia and the Hwicca to the north and north west, but stalemate in the south and south east. Cenwalh died in about 672 AD. There was then a series of short reigns. The longest was that of Centwine, from about 676 to 686. The Anglo-Saxon Chronicle says that he drove the Britons to the sea. That suggests that he broke through as far as the Somerset coast. Bishop Aldhelm, writing about a generation later, suggested that Centwine won three great battles. We don't know where they were. That suggests that much of Somerset was conquered during his reign.

Ine came to the throne of Wessex in 686 AD or so. Ine is famous as a lawgiver. He created the first written set of laws of the West Saxons. He also fought several battles, which we will look at shortly, but he does not seem to have enlarged his kingdom very much. Given the expansion under Cenwalh and Centwine (which was, broadly, Wiltshire and Somerset), that was perhaps not surprising.

Ine was probably only the second king of the West Saxons whose name did not begin with 'C'. His ancestry is not clear. His law code specifically mentions various classes of *British* subjects. They were clearly important enough to be included under the law, yet also clearly separate. British noblemen are given status, but considerably less than that of Saxon noblemen. The 'blood money' payable to the kinfolk of a murdered British subject was about half that paid for an Anglo-Saxon of the same rank. By this stage, many of those considered to be British were not slaves, but clearly they were not English either. It is appropriate to use the term 'English' here. Ine's law code is perhaps the first document to use the word.

In 710 AD Ine killed a British ruler. In 715 the Mercians invaded, and Ine fought them at Wanborough. As before, we don't know whether that meant the Wanborough (implying that the Mercians came down the Roman road from Cirencester) or Woden's Barrow (implying that Ine defended on the line of the Wansdyke). It was badly advised. The Mercian king was Ceolred, who had reigned since about 709. He was defeated and died the next year: he was probably poisoned. Ceolred had been forced to cede Oxfordshire, and possibly Buckinghamshire, to Ine of Wessex. That extended the boundary of Wessex as far as the area of Banbury.

Three curious things happened in 722 AD. The first is that Ine's wife Aethelburgh burnt Taunton, which Ine had apparently built ten years earlier. The story is one of those tales that don't quite ring true. Apparently she was pursuing a renegade nobleman. Why would a queen do that? Women's Lib wasn't strong in those days. Secondly, Ine fought the South Saxons. Thirdly, there as a battle against the British at Hehil. There is no such place today. There is, however, a 'Hale', about three miles east of Wincanton (see Figure 12.1).

Hale is near the River Cale, the tributary of the Stour which flows through Wincanton. A few years ago a local farmer noticed that one of his fields had a very slight ridge across it. It isn't shown on any known map; not even a seventeenth century agricultural map. The ridge can just be detected with the naked eye. It is a bit more obvious, apparently, if you plough it. The tractor tends to slow as you cross it, then speed up briefly, which suggests a bank and a filled-in ditch. I've wandered all over that field with a metal detector and found nothing but a few medieval nails. The ridge, or dyke if that is what it is, is parallel with the river but about two miles east. The pattern of the hedgerows tends to suggest that an old drover's road (or similar) ran through the area, and a seasonal ford across the Cale parallel with the modern A303.

It is perhaps the best site for the Battle of Hehil. Taunton is about 30 miles west. Taunton lies on the west side of what was the Somerset marshes. It is hemmed in to the south by the Blackdown Hills and to the west by Exmoor. One guess as to what happened in 722 AD is that, whilst Ine was fighting the South Saxons, the British tried to get across the headwaters of the Stour and the Cale at Hale. It doesn't seem to have worked, and the frontier stayed put.

The Stour flows from the Wincanton area roughly south east to Christchurch Harbour. The Yeo and other rivers flow north west into the Parrett and then into the Bristol Channel. So, south and west of the Wincanton area, all the rivers flow either south into the English Channel or north into the Bristol channel. The south west of England is a classic peninsula. In simple terms the land to the south now lies in Dorset. The land to the north is Somerset, as far as Exmoor and the Blackdown Hills. West of that is Devon as far as the River Tamar. The Tamar rises near to the north coast and flows south to the sea near Plymouth, hence almost cutting right across the peninsula. As we shall see, the Tamar became (and largely remains) the eastern boundary of Cornwall.

Settlement patterns support this sequence of events. The pattern of Germanic burials in Wiltshire remained fairly constant through the fifth to seventh centuries. In the seventh and eighth centuries new settlements, as indicated by burials, sprang up. They were located in the Ebble Valley, in the area north east of Wincanton, and in the Vale of Pewsey. That is consistent with Cenwalh's victories at the Broad Ford and Penselwood. A large number of British river names have survived in Gloucestershire, Wiltshire and into the south west (the area is bounded by the Gloucestershire and Hampshire Avons). That suggests that the area was conquered, or settled, by the West Saxons later than the lands further east. There is some evidence of the survival of parish boundaries in the south west from pre-Saxon times. That implies that the area was taken over after 636 AD (the date of the conversion of the West Saxons to Christianity). Alternatively it may imply that the existing church organisation was allowed to continue intact; or both. There are no pagan burials in Dorset, which tells us that it was settled after the mid-seventh century. Many place names in Dorset are compounds of British river names with English suffixes. As in the case of Shropshire, that suggests fairly deliberate colonisation.

Cadbury Castle, near South Cadbury, was extensively refortified sometime after the end of Roman imperial rule. It was clearly an important place, as the evidence of high-value imports such as wine and olives found there tells us. It had a large post-Roman feasting hall. It is about six miles west of the Cale. It probably went out of use as a 'palace' or major residence in the seventh century, which is consistent with a battle a few miles away at Penselwood in 658 AD.

We looked at the Tribal Hidage in our discussion of Mercia. Another Hidage is useful to us here. The Burghal Hidage lists the fortified towns ('burhs', hence 'boroughs' today) in Wessex. The list we have has been dated to about 914 AD, just after Alfred's reign. We will look at it slightly more later, but here we should note that the pattern of burhs in Somerset suggests a fossilised frontier. Most of the burhs in Wessex were deliberately sited so that no part of the kingdom was more than 20 miles from a burh. So most of them were up to 40 miles apart. In Somerset, however, there are three (and possibly four) all within a 20 mile radius. They are Ling, Langport, Pilton and possibly Lydford (see Figure 12.5). As we shall see, the 'Lydford' referred to might be in Devon. There is then another burh, Axbridge, within 15 miles of Pilton. Taken together, it appears that the West Saxons had got into Somerset from the north and east, but could not advance much farther south west than the River Parrett. They built burhs in the late seventh or early eighth centuries on what was then the southern border. Interestingly, Taunton is not listed as a burh, despite apparently having been founded by Ine. It is about six miles south west of the Parrett.

Thus by the 720s AD the south west frontier of Wessex lay on the Bokerly Ditch and related defences as far west as the Stour or Cale; then the Yeo and the Parrett. Mercia invaded Wessex again in about 733. The Anglo-Saxon chronicle tells us that 'Aethelbald [of Mercia] took Somerton'. Somerton became the county town of Somerset, but only several years later. Are we really to believe that the Mercians penetrated all the way down the Fosse Way past Bath, into Somerset, and took a town which was so unimportant that it wasn't even listed as a burh? That is probably not what happened. A leader called Aethelheard had succeeded Ine as ruler of the West Saxons about five years earlier. Now if the Chronicle is slightly wrong and Aethel*heard* (of Wessex) had seized Somerton, from the British, and the place eventually became the county town, the picture would be more credible. However, it seems that the Chronicle is right but modern historians are wrong. It seems that Aethel*bald* of Mercia did seize Somerton. However, historians have identified the wrong Somerton.

The other Somerton is in Oxfordshire, and close to the border with Buckinghamshire. We saw earlier that the West Saxons had closed the Icknield Way and the east bank of the Thames south of Tame with a dyke on Swyncombe Down (see Figure 12.4).

The next best approach was down the west bank of the Cherwell. Somerton is on the east bank. The two Heyfords (Upper and Lower) are a mile or two to the south. 'Somerton' means 'summer settlement'. In this context that means a hamlet in an area where the meadow was dry enough to be grazed in the summer, but not through the year. 'Heyford' means 'hay ford', meaning a ford which was low enough to be used in the late summer when the hay is cut and brought in.

The place name evidence suggests that the Mercians had attacked in the summer when the river was low. If so, the West Saxons had a problem that would repeat itself every year. The Mercians would be able to get across every summer. The West Saxons built a dyke in order to defend without using the line of the river. The line starts in the south where Akeman Street crossed the Cherwell. There was probably a bridge there in Roman times. From there the fortifications run north east for about three miles, then swing north through what is now RAF Upper Heyford to Fritwell. There is little sign of it north of there today. It seems to have run north west to Souldern and then ended on the stream below the village. That stream is now the Buckinghamshire border. The earliest Ordnance Survey maps show a continuous line of earthworks from Akeman Street to Souldern, variously known as Ave's Ditch or the Wattlebank. It is up to four of five feet high in places today, and seems to face west. See Figure 12.6.

Today Bicester is in Oxfordshire. Buckingham, less than ten miles to the north east, was the county town of Buckinghamshire. Buckinghamshire stretches all the

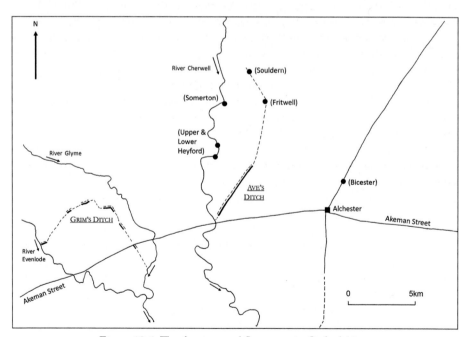

Figure 12.6 The Area around Somerton in Oxfordshire.

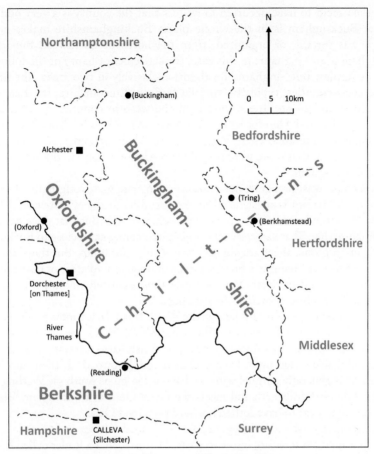

Figure 12.7 Counties in North-East Wessex.

way south to the Thames east of Reading. The geography of the county borders is rather odd around here, but we can perhaps now see why. See Figure 12.7.

It seems that, before (and perhaps just after) the establishment of the bishopric at Dorchester on the Thames, Wessex had been centred on Berkhamsted. It was conveniently sited on a Roman road through the Chilterns (Akeman Street). So the whole area was originally referred to in some way as something like 'Berkshire'. Oxfordshire north of Oxford was originally part of the land of the Hwicca (much of the Wychwood was in that area). When Wulfhere of Mercia invaded Wessex in 661 AD, he took over all of the Chilterns. He divided it into two parts: the land astride the Cherwell and adjoining the Thames as Oxfordshire; and the lands further east as Buckinghamshire. When Ine of Wessex defeated Ceolred of Mercia in 715, he took much of Oxfordshire (and possibly Buckinghamshire) back.

It doesn't seem to have occurred to writers that the county is a very odd shape, and that Buckingham is in the wrong place. Buckinghamshire makes no sense unless it was settled, or organised, from the north or northwest. Superficially, Buckingham is an '-ingham': in this case, the settlement ('ham') of the followers of Bucca, or similar. But '-inghams' lie almost exclusively in two areas. The first is in the east-coast counties: typically Norfolk, Suffolk, Lincolnshire, the East Riding of Yorkshire, and so on. The second is in the western counties of Mercia: typically Shropshire and Herefordshire. The nearest is 75 miles from Buckingham: Birmingham (in the area where Warwickshire, Worcestershire and Staffordshire meet). Other than that there were probably no Anglo-Saxon '-inghams' within 100 miles of Buckingham.

Buckingham was probably not, however, an '-ingham' originally. It was an '-inghamm'. A '-hamm' is an island-like feature, similar to an '-ey'. However, '-hamm's typically lie in the bend of a river (as Buckingham does). But that does not explain the anomaly, either. There are very few '-ing-' place names at all close to Buckingham. Apart from '-ingtons', there are almost none within 100 miles. But there are several '-hamms' (or former '-hamms'). So it is not uncommon to find areas of raised dry land, in marshes, in bends in rivers. However it is almost entirely unknown to call them after someone's followers, such as the Buccings.

There is one other piece to this jigsaw: the Welsh Road. In Chapter Seven we looked at the Welsh Way near Cirencester. The name 'Welsh Road' means 'a road used by the British' (as opposed to a Roman road). The Welsh Road starts up in Staffordshire at Brownhills: five or ten miles from Lichfield and Tamworth. It then runs roughly southeast. It is generally parallel with, and about ten miles south of, Watling Street. It passes through Kenilworth and meets the Great Ouse at Buckingham. The West Saxons do not appear to have settled north of the Great Ouse.

So, it seems that when Wulfhere of Mercia invaded Wessex in 661 AD he divided his newly-conquered territory into two parts. He instructed a leader called Bucca (or similar) to settle the eastern section. Bucca took his folk down the Welsh Road to what had been the edge of Mercian territory: the Great Ouse. He created a settlement on some dry ground in the bend of the river (which became Buckingham). He then explored, took over, and reorganised the land south eastwards for forty miles. That took him right through the Chilterns and down to the Colne. South east of Aylesbury and Wendover little of the land would have been of much value. The Chilterns were almost uninhabited for at least the next four hundred years.

Similarly, Oxfordshire ran through the Cotswolds to the Thames at Reading. It almost reached Surrey. Buckinghamshire ran alongside it, so that the county town (Buckingham) was left right up in the north end of the county. As a result, Buckinghamshire adjoined Middlesex along the River Colne *east* of the Chilterns. In addition, Berkshire no longer contains Berkhamsted, for which it had been named. The pre-1972 boundaries of Berkshire were about 45 miles from Berkhamsted. The map of Berkshire clearly suggests that it had had something bitten out of it. That 'bite' included much of modern Oxfordshire and Buckinghamshire.

Even odder, a salient was appended to Hertfordshire. It sticks out about five miles into Buckinghamshire, north west from the Chilterns near Tring. It makes absolutely no sense geographically, until you realise that it is at the head of the Bulbourne Valley. That is, its possession by whoever ruled the Thames Basin would allow free traffic through the Chilterns, without fear of being attacked (nor extorted for tolls) in the hills. That suggests that it was given to whoever controlled the Thames Basin in a treaty.

With the building of the dykes near Somerton, the east bank of the Cherwell was closed to the Mercians. The geography begs the question as to why Mercians would not then attempt to attack southwards down the west bank of the Cherwell. They may have done, or perhaps the West Saxons thought of it first. In either case, the West Saxons dug a linked set of earthworks from the River Glyme to the Evenlode near Charlbury (see Figure 12.6). Once again, they are called 'Grim's Ditch'. They are distinct from those which the British had built in the 570s AD in response to the battle of Bedcanford. In some places, however, they run into them. Most of the newer line runs on a forward slope above two streams. It starts in the area of (not surprisingly) Grimsdyke Farm and runs through (not too surprisingly) Ditchley Park, then west above Clarke's Bottom. It is visible in several places, up to four feet high today, and faces north. There is a gap between this section and Ave's Ditch of a couple of miles, between the Cherwell and the Glyme. It is now arable farmland, but was wood-land then. It has place names such as 'Wootton' and 'Tackley'. We cannot tell know whether the West Saxons did not dig a dyke through the woods; or that they did, and it has now been ploughed out.

In 752 AD or thereabouts, Cuthred of Wessex fought Aethelbald of Mercia at Burford and put him to flight. Fifty years later, in about 802, there was another battle in the region, at Kempsford. It was fought between Ealdorman Aethelmund of the Hwicca and Woxton, Ealdorman of Wiltshire. The men of Wiltshire won, but both leaders died. These two details from the Anglo-Saxon Chronicle tells us a lot about the northern border of Wessex, as Figure 12.8 shows.

We can now say something about Mercian operational thinking, if that is not too grand a term. In 661 AD or thereabouts Wulfhere of Mercia marched southeast, either down the Roman Watling Street or the Welsh Road to the Icknield Way. Continuing south west along the the Icknield Way, he fought the West Saxons near Postcombe and chased them to Ashdown. In 715 Ceolred of Mercia fought Ine of Wessex, either at Wanborough or Woden's Barrow. To do so Ceolred used the Roman road south through Alcester (not Alchester, near Bicester) to Cirencester then Wanborough. In 733 Aethelbald marched to Alcester, turned south east towards Banbury and attacked Somerton. In 752 Aethelbald marched south again. This time he was met at Burford by Cuthred of Wessex, who defeated him. Burford is near where Akeman Street crosses the River Windrush. In 775 Offa of Mercia used Watling Street or the Welsh Road again and fought Cynewulf of Wessex at Benson. Unsurprisingly, the existing roads affected the way that Mercian (and other) kings planned their campaigns.

The locations of the battles, and the location of earthworks, suggest that the frontier between Wessex and the Hwicca (and subsequently Mercia) did not move much from

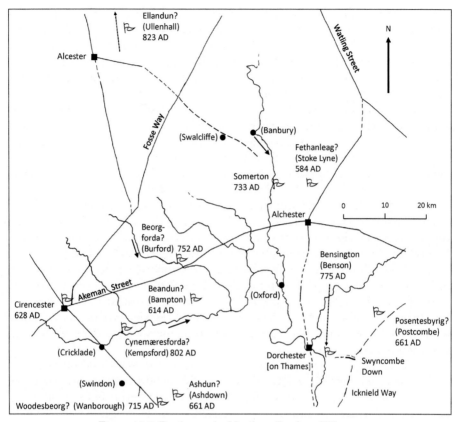

Figure 12.8 Battles on the Northern Border of Wessex.

571 AD. The northeast border of Oxfordshire ran for several miles along a series of ridges which include a feature called 'Ditchedge Lane'. Just west of there are an Upper and Lower Brailes. 'Brailes' is a rare surviving Primitive Welsh place-name, meaning 'manor house'. Slightly south of that is Whichford, 'the ford of the Hwicca'. The two place names suggest that Ditchedge Lane formed the border between part of Wessex and the land of the Hwicca. It is now part of the border between Oxfordshire and Warwickshire.

The Lane may have been a defensive earthwork. In some places there is a bank up to three feet high, but it is not clear which way the earthwork (if that is what it is) faces. The Roman road southeast from Alcester would cross Ditchedge Lane about six miles west of Banbury, heading east of south east. Halfway between the Lane and the Cherwell (which flows south through Banbury in the direction of Somerton and on to Oxford), the Roman road is cut by an earthwork. It can be seen in two sections near Swalcliffe. At Swalcliffe Mill the bank of the stream appears to have been steepened to create an obstacle over ten feet high. The earthwork can be traced over about a mile and a half and probably faced north east to defend against the Hwicca.

Oxfordshire changed hands several times. South and west of there, however, the border stayed on the general line of the upper Thames for centuries and is still there today. Cirencester is in Gloucester (and was presumably in the land of the Hwicca). In that area the Wiltshire boundary generally runs along the Thames. Interestingly, however, there are three enclaves north of the river: near the Derry Brook, at Cricklade, and at Kempsford. All three were significant to the West Saxons.

Down in the south, the British position on the Bokerly Dike did eventually fall. The British built another position to the south and west. Very little of that line remains. None is shown on a 1:50,000 scale map. It can be found on the 1:25,000 map. A meandering series of hedgerows appears to show its course over several miles. In this area most of the hedgerows are much, much later and are straight. However, parish boundaries follow the line of the earthworks. It is line '5' on Figure 12.1. The line runs more-or-less along the modern A354. It can be traced from the area of Pimperne to Gussage Hill, where it is quite easily visible. In that area it is a double ditch and bank, up to six feet high, and faces north.

The section over Gussage Hill clearly cuts a very gentle ridge running south from the escarpment of Cranborne Chase. Standing on the earthwork, you can see the woods of the Chase a mile or two to the north, but there are also clear views for several miles to the east and west. At the south end of Gussage Hill lies Harley Down. About two miles away is Handley Down. Next to that is Oakley Down. So there are at least three 'leys'. From Gussage Hill the village of Cranborne is about four miles away across open downland, but there is a lot old woodland east of there. We do not have to believe that the whole area was woodland in the eighth century. But much of it was.

Traces of another line of earthworks ('6'), diverging from the one along the A345, can be followed to the south of Gussage All Saints and St Giles Park, which suggests that the 'Gussage line' was turned, or breached, in the east. Line '6' is very difficult to trace, but some sections are quite prominent. Right over in the east a section faces south ('B'). That suggests that the West Saxons dug some of these dykes. Eventually the British abandoned (or were thrown out of) the area east of the Stour. They dug in above the west bank, south of Blandford.

The dyke they built is called Combs Ditch ('7'). It can be traced along a ridge for about three miles, from north of the A354 almost to the Roman road from Salisbury to Dorchester. It apparently did not cut the road, which is not too surprising. If the Sarum area had fallen to the West Saxons after the battle of Penselwood, there might have been little traffic on the road for well over a century by the time Combs Ditch was built. The siting of the ditch is obvious. To the south west, you can look down over most of central and western Dorset. Looking to the north east, the dyke covers the cluster of fords across the Stour from Crawford to Barford. It would not stop the West Saxons crossing. It would stop them advancing into what we now know as central Dorset.

The Anglo-Saxon Chronicle reports another battle on the Thames, in about 775 AD, at Benson. Benson is on the stream to which the earthwork on Swyncombe Down seems to connect (see Figure 12.4). The old part of the village is on the north bank.

If we take the Chronicle literally ('Cynewulf and Offa fought at Benson, and Offa took possession of the town'), then this wasn't Offa's greatest victory: he didn't necessarily even manage to cross the stream. However, Benson is well south of Oxford. So what it implies, however, is that Offa took most of Oxfordshire (and possibly all of Buckinghamshire) back from Wessex.

Dorchester (on Thames) is in Oxfordshire. The seat of the bishopric repeatedly changed hands between Wessex and Mercia. For much of the time from King Alfred to the Norman conquest Dorchester seems to have controlled a diocese which included a great swathe of Mercia. It ran right up through the east Midlands, into Lindsey, and reached the Humber. (The diocese of Lincoln was created by the Normans.)

A few years after the battle of Benson, in about 787 AD, the first Viking raid in England took place. Perhaps unsurprisingly, there were three ships. The Norsemen fought and killed a local official. The early versions of the Anglo Saxon Chronicle don't tell us where. In 793 Vikings raided Lindisfarne. Slowly, but surely, the strategic picture changed. There were increasing numbers of raids over the next 50 years or so. Then, in 850, a Viking party spent the winter in England for the first time (on the Isle of Sheppey in Kent). Raiding became conquest and, to some extent, settlement. For the Anglo-Saxons, after the 790s there was another enemy to think about. That enemy became increasingly significant. In simple terms, the Vikings overran Northumbria and fatally weakened Mercia. Wessex survived, despite some major reverses. It grew strong enough to conquer Mercia and unify England. In 1066 the English, under West Saxon kings, decisively defeated the Vikings at the Battle of Stamford Bridge. Tragically for them, the Normans landed at Hastings a few days later.

In the late eighth century, however, that was well in the future. In about 823 AD King Egbert lead the West Saxons' first ever invasion of Mercia. It reversed the strategic situation that had applied since 571. Egbert led his army through Cirencester and up the Fosse Way. He then turned onto the Roman road which ran through Alcester (south of Redditch in Warwickshire) to Watling Street at Wall. That road, Ryknild Street, pointed straight at the heart of Mercia. Wall is within a few miles of Tamworth (the capital) and Lichfield (the bishopric).

The two armies fought at a place reported as 'Ellandun'. It seems to be near Oldberrow, Ullenhall and Hallend, two or three miles north west of Henley-in-Arden. A man-made feature called the Hobditch cuts across the valley of the River Alne about a mile north of Hallend. It is quite unusual. It seems too wide to be a defensive earthwork. It is about half a mile long, and does not appear to be a Roman road. It may be a pre-Roman causeway across the Alne valley, but its orientation and route make little sense for that purpose. From the south, however, it seems to be very carefully tucked onto reverse slopes. That is quite difficult to achieve across a valley. The Hobditch is an enigma and its dating is uncertain.

Ryknild Street is about four miles to the west, but its original course had been lost by the time the original Ordnance Survey maps were made. That area of the Arrow Valley was probably a wooded swamp (on which much of modern Redditch was built). The name of Redditch probably does mean 'red ditch', and there are several intriguing

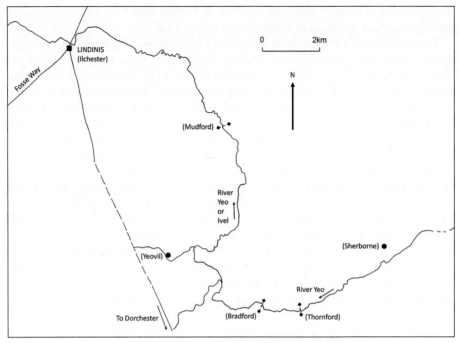

Figure 12.9 The Crossings of the River Yeo.

aspects to the geography and toponymy of the area. There may have been a dyke (hence 'red ditch') blocking the Roman road. Extensive research (both on old maps and on the ground) has revealed no evidence of it. Be that as it may, Egbert's army seems to have advanced slightly further east, up the valley of the River Alne. They met the Mercians in the Ullenhall area near, or on, the Hobditch. The Mercians were decisively beaten. They soon lost control of Kent, Surrey, Sussex, Essex and East Anglia to Wessex. The battle decisively shifted the strategic balance of power in England.

One day in the spring of 2011 I was investigating the Hobditch when I spotted a vixen playing with three cubs in the sunshine in some long grass. I approached quietly. They were quite aware of my presence. At one stage I was within ten feet of one of the cubs. It blinked at me, then trotted off into the bushes to join its mother. Things like that makes this work truly magical.

Back in Dorset in 823 AD, the British attacked whilst Egbert was invading Mercia. They tried to take advantage of Egbert's absence with an attack near Ilchester. The Anglo-Saxon Chronicle names the site as 'Gafulford'. 'Gaful-' probably refers to the River Yeo. The Yeo is also called the Ivel. In Anglo-Saxon times it was called the Gifle. So the battle at Gafulford took place at a ford over the Yeo. There are very few. There were none below Ilchester. Above Ilchester there is Mudford. There was possibly also a crossing at Yeovil. Higher up the river are Bradford Abbas and Thornford. None is more than ten miles upstream from Ilchester. A Roman road from Dorchester passes near Yeovil before going on to Ilchester. See Figure 12.9.

The outcome is uncertain. There appears to have been no long-term consequences. About fifteen years later, in about 838 AD, Egbert inflicted a major defeat on the British on the coast near Christchurch. Ironically, some Vikings may have been actors in the defeat of the British. A Viking force fought alongside the British. Given the site, at the mouth of the Stour and the Avon, the plan may have involved using Viking ships to carry British warriors across into West Saxon territory. Both the Stour and the Avon run into Christchurch Harbour, an almost completely enclosed bay, which then opens out into the English Channel. The name of the battle is recorded as Hengestdun, 'Hengest's hill' or possibly Hengest's (sand)dune.

Unfortunately the chronicler seems to have the place name wrong. He seems to have meant 'Hedena's dun' or similar, and not 'Hengest's dun'. The site would have to be close to the sea. We cannot envisage a Viking force fighting a long way from their ships in the early ninth century. Even as late as 1066 AD the protection of his ships was a major consideration for the Viking King Harald Hadrada in the Stamford Bridge campaign. In 838 the Vikings were a long way from home. Their ships were valuable. They gave the Vikings considerable military advantages. They were also, effectively, their insurance policy. If things went badly they could jump aboard and sail away. They often did.

There are very few coastal locations in the south west that could fit the bill. The best is the promontory which protects Christchurch Harbour, known to us as Hengistbury

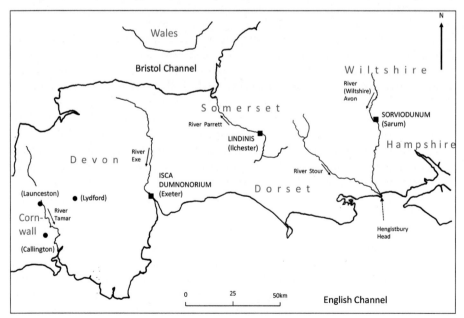

Figure 12.10 Western Wessex.

Head. It is easy to get over-excited by the name. Unfortunately the origin of the name seems to be 'Hedena's fort'. There are earthworks which cut off the headland. That appears to be an iron-age coastal fort. It was almost definitely occupied in Roman times. The location suits the strategic picture (of Wessex unable to advance west across the Stour for decades). The location explains how Vikings could cooperate with the British. It is the best contender for the site. It is known to us as a 'burh' (Hengistbury) today, due to the earthworks. Despite being a low-lying promontory only about a mile long, it rises to a respectable 28 metres above the sea. It is quite reasonable to believe that, in the ninth century, people thought that it was in some way connected to the fifth-century Hengest.

The outcome was decisive. Egbert won. We don't know what happened to the Vikings, but the British lost. They lost badly. Their army was effectively destroyed, possibly after being caught with the sea at its back. That is not a particularly bad position to be in if you are a Viking. It would be catastrophic if you didn't have ships (perhaps the Vikings deserted the British?) Within a decade or so the West Saxons overran all of Dorset and Devon, rolling up the rest of Somerset in the process. In 850 AD or thereabouts Egbert's son Aethelwulf evicted the last few British from Exeter. It was another massive seizure of territory. It explains why the place names in Devon (and west Dorset) gives it the impression of being colonised from about 840 onwards. See Figure 12.10.

60% of the place names around Exeter (in Devon) known to us from the ninth century are British. In the Domesday Book only 25% are. That suggests very strongly that the area was seized by the West Saxons in or after the ninth century. King Aethelwulf awarded charters in Devon from 844 AD onwards. Prior to that, virtually no charters had been awarded in Devon nor Dorset. Of those, a number seem to be spurious. It is possible that all of them are spurious in their present form. A good example is that of Sherborne Abbey. The Charter we know of is dated from 671. Sherborne is in Dorset, five or six miles west of the Stour. Sherborne later became a bishopric. Bede wrote that the West Saxons divided their kingdom into two bishoprics in 705 or so. Writers have hung a lot of assumptions around the date. If Sherborne became a bishopric in 705, then the frontier with the British was already west of the Stour: presumably quite a long way west. But Sherborne cannot be conclusively described as a bishopric until much later. There is a better case for the bishopric which Bede referred to being Dorchester or even Ramsbury, in Wiltshire.

St Aldhelm was a bishop around the year 700 AD. He wrote a letter to the then king of Dumnonia regarding church practices amongst the British. When he was appointed bishop he was allowed to keep the abbacy of Malmesbury in Wiltshire. Malmesbury is about 20 miles from Ramsbury and 30 from Dorchester, but over 75 miles from Sherborne. And notice that Aldhelm wrote to the king of Dumnonia. Although we cannot be certain, that suggests that the British still held much of Dorset and Devon at the time. In later years Anglo-Saxon writers would increasingly use the word 'Cornwall', or similar. They almost invariably did so after the British had been pushed back across the Tamar. It seems that the second bishopric created in 705 was not Sherborne. The bishoprics were reorganised again in 909, to create five. Sherborne *was* one of them. The others were Winchester, Wells, Ramsbury and Crediton. That list reflects quite closely what we now understand as Dorset, Hampshire, Somerset, Wiltshire and Devon. Interestingly, none of them was a county town (which were probably Dorchester, Southampton, Somerton, Wilton and Exeter). Interestingly, there was no bishopric in Cornwall.

No-one would suggest that the land at Sherborne didn't belong to the Church, nor that it hasn't for centuries. It is just that the present charter, dating back to 671 AD, had probably been falsified; possibly centuries later. It is possible that by then no-one actually knew when the Abbey was founded. It is also possible that the Abbey was originally British.

Bede did not mention Sherborne at all (he died in 735 AD). There are only two references in original Anglo-Saxon documents to Sherborne before the battle of Hengestdun in 838. Both are in charters in the Sherborne Abbey collection. Immediately *after* the battle, four charters awarded land to Sherborne within a period of 25 years. The first is dated to 844. It seems that Sherborne became a West Saxon church very soon after the battle. That in turn points to Dorset west of the Stour, and Devon, falling to the West Saxons immediately after the battle in 838.

King Aethelwulf was Egbert's son. Aethelwulf awarded land charters in Dorset after 844 AD. Alfred the Great was one of Aethelwulf's sons. Alfred awarded no land charters in Devon, but redistributed land (which had presumably become vacant, or was confiscated) in the rest of his kingdom. An area which had been newly colonised (in this case, by Alfred's father or grandfather) would need relatively little redistribution, because it typically takes at least three generations for a family to die out without heirs. Alfred organised the Burghal system. The Burghal Hidage shows three or possibly four burhs in Devon. The document lists burhs in a more-or-less clockwise loop around Wessex, so we can be moderately confident that the Lydford it identifies is now a village in Devon, not the one in Somerset. That would place it on the west side of Dartmoor, looking west to the Tamar. The Burghal Hidage is dated from the early tenth century. It lists no places in Cornwall.

A King Dungarth of Cornwall died in 875 AD. The West Saxons fixed the eastern boundary of Cornwall on the Tamar in the 920s or 930s. It seems that that was part of a treaty with the Cornish. There is evidence of Anglo-Saxon settlement in Cornwall, but not much. There is one small pocket in the far north, near the headwaters of the Tamar. There is another just across the river around Callington, about five miles west of Gunnislake. For centuries the lowest bridge on the Tamar was at Gunnislake. There were very, very few fords across the Tamar. The river would have formed a good natural frontier for the British.

Cornwall is different. In Cornish, the prefix 'tre-' in a place name means 'farmstead' or 'estate'. There are about 1,200 'tre-' place names in England. Examples include Trebartha, Trebithick and Trebiffin. A group of 'tre-'s separate the two Anglo-Saxon enclaves west of the Tamar. They include Tremollet, Trevistow and Tresallack. Almost all 'tre-'s in England are in Cornwall. There are just three in Devon. The prefix 'bod-' means a dwelling, as in Bodmin, Bodelva and Bodellick. The pattern of 'Bod-'s in England is similar to that of the 'tre-'s, but there are fewer of them. There are many Anglo-Saxon '-tons' in Devon, but very few in Cornwall. Several of them are compound names with British prefixes.

In Chapter Nine we discussed mediaeval fields, which tend to indicate Anglo-Saxon land usage. They are common across most of central and southern England. There are none in western Somerset and Dorset, nor in Devon and Cornwall. This is further evidence that we are right on the fringes of Anglo-Saxon conquest, reorganisation and settlement.

History tells us something else along the same lines. The places which the later Anglo-Saxon kings visited have been assembled in 'itineraries'. The two earliest proper itineraries (from Edward the Elder and Athelstan) tell us that those two kings visited Devon twice each, and Cornwall not at all. (Edward the Elder was Alfred's son.) The next eight kings visited Devon once between them. None visited Cornwall. Devon and Cornwall were not part of Wessex in the way that more easterly counties were.

The West Saxons did not conquer Cornwall. That is not surprising. Alfred's great problem was the Vikings, not the Cornish. The Vikings would be the biggest problem to face all subsequent Anglo-Saxon kings. We should remember that the Normans were originally Norsemen. They were Vikings who had been awarded land in France by treaty in 911 AD. The Norsemen won in the end. However, they did not change the language, nor the laws, as the Anglo-Saxons had done.

Cornwall wasn't, necessarily, pacified. When the Normans arrived, William the Conqueror sent his half-brother Robert, Count of Mortain, to govern Cornwall. Robert crossed the Tamar and built a castle at Launceston. It was on the first available site, within sight of the river. He slowly expanded his authority down the peninsula from there. 150 years later King Edward the Third appointed his eldest son, known to us as 'the Black Prince', to be the Duke of Cornwall. It was the first duchy created in England, and the title is still awarded to the eldest son of the Sovereign. Cornwall was clearly strategically important and not necessarily pacified. At or about the same time the kings of England started to appoint their eldest sons 'Prince of Wales'. They gave their eldest sons the toughest, and most important, jobs. (Much of the Prince of Wales' income today still comes from the Duchy of Cornwall).

It had been a long journey. In about 600 AD, the West Saxons had been a small kingdom sandwiched between Mercia and the Berkshire Downs. After the 660s they had control of Hampshire, Wiltshire and much of Somerset. But then they were held up on the Parrett and the Stour. Almost two hundred years later, in the 830s or 40s, they broke through to the Tamar. They didn't really get any farther. By then the Vikings were invading. Subsequent generations of Anglo-Saxon kings fought the Norse, rather than the British. Offa of Mercia had walled his British opponents in to Wales. His successors lost a series of campaigns against the Vikings. In practice, it was the Viking invasions which helped Wessex unify England as a single country with a single identity. From the time of Alfred onwards, Anglo-Saxon laws made no distinction between people of Germanic and British origin. By then, they were all English.

13

The Elephant in the Room

The general thesis of this book depends on two broad assumptions. The first is that most of these earthworks are defensive fortifications. The second is that they are from the Dark Ages. If they are Dark Age fortifications, how did they work, and what should we see today?

People tend to see only what they're looking for. It is surprisingly difficult to see things that you aren't looking for, even when they are in plain sight. The earthworks at Netley near Southampton are an example. They were assumed to be aqueducts to bring water to the medieval abbey. But there are ponds and a stream at the abbey site. An archaeological investigation pointed out that the cisterns and dams required to bring water from a second stream was never built. This is, seemingly, a minor unexplained anomaly.

The ruins of the abbey give context to the earthworks. The archaeologists thought that the earthworks were associated with it. It is the obvious solution. Netley, however, is the supposed site of one of the earliest battles of the Dark Ages, in perhaps 508 AD. Might it not have occurred to the archaeologists that the earthworks were related to the battle of Netley, and were defensive fortifications? Archaeologists are not stupid. But, as with any intellectual discipline, they tend to look at things in certain ways. In particular, they do not tend to associate long linear earthworks with Dark Age warfare.

There is an unsuspected elephant in the room. There are thousands of sections of linear earthworks across much of England and parts of what are now Scotland and Wales. In total they are hundreds of miles long. They took millions of man-hours to build, yet their existence is generally unsuspected. They are almost totally unexplained and largely ignored.

I spent over three months in the countryside investigating dykes, from Kent to Kelso and from York to Yeovil. I have spent many days studying maps, satellite imagery and three-dimensional computer imagery. I spent many more days drawing and revising maps. At every stage patterns emerged: between similarities of siting or construction; between sections in Yorkshire and Somerset; or between sections in Kent and Lancashire. That does not necessarily mean that my conclusions are correct. But I have seen an awful lot of them and thought about them a great deal. I have thought about them in ways which other people seem not to have.

The middle period of the War of the Spanish Succession (1704-1714) was dominated by fighting in the Low Countries (modern Belgium and the Netherlands). The leading Allied commander was the Duke of Marlborough. Campaigning was dominated by the Lines of Brabant, a continuous series of earthworks stretching across much of modern Belgium. Marlborough's campaign planning was dominated by the need to break through them and bring the French to battle. He wished to avoid time-consuming sieges of fortified towns. He fought three major battles (at Ramillies, Oudenaarde and Malplaquet) which, along with the slightly earlier Blenheim, were the first battle honours to be awarded to the units of the British Army (including my own regiment). There are several good books about the war, and Marlborough and his battles. They scarcely mention the Lines of Brabant at all. Furthermore, planning for the Blenheim campaign was materially affected by a major series of earthworks called the Lines of Stollhofen in Baden, the province between the Black Forest and the Rhine. Yet, again, they are almost ignored.

We are, actually, quite prepared to accept that there were extensive, theatre-wide earthworks such as the Lines of Brabant and Stollhofen in the 18th century. But people do not consider that the same may have applied in the fifth or sixth centuries. Yet much the same technologies were used: foot or horseback for scouting; voice (or perhaps written) messages for communications; and iron-bladed tools for digging. If an 18th-century general could organise the construction of major earthworks, why could a Roman general not? Or one trained by him, albeit at second or third hand?

In warfare, major earthworks are more common than people think. They have been used extensively in several epochs, and are often overlooked. The patterns which they leave on the landscape are sometimes not obvious, not least due to mapping issues. Ordnance Survey 1:50,000 scale maps often only show about a half of the earthworks visible on a 1:25,000 map. Each sheet of the latter shows only about a quarter of the area of the former. That has two consequences. Coverage of a given area is considerably more expensive, and a given area is more likely to be on the edge of a map. One area in Sussex is on the edges of four 1:25,000 maps *and* three 1:50,000 maps! Working out the configuration of the dykes on the ground takes a lot of maps, a reasonably well-developed sense of geometry and geography, and hours at the drawing board.

Why would anyone want to dig a ditch and build a bank, at least six feet high from top to bottom, for several miles? There are several possible reasons. The simplest that fits all of the known facts, with fewest anomalies, is that they were fortifications. Occam's Razor cleaves swift and clean. Furthermore, Anglo-Saxon freemen had three public obligations: to fight; to build or repair bridges; and to build fortifications. Add up all of the Anglo-Saxon freemen over several centuries and that could produce an awful lot of digging. We should expect some sign of it today.

The dykes were not waterways. Their siting was simply not appropriate, and their profile wrong. Only very few (such as the Car Dyke) could even possibly be waterways. The Car Dyke was not.

It has been suggested that some dykes were too shallow to be of any military use. But what would be 'of use'? Consider a V-cut ditch, just three feet deep and about six feet wide. The great majority of those earthworks had sides which slope at about 45 degrees. The bank will be about three feet high. Now, assume that the attacker is a fit young man. Can he take a running jump and clear a six-foot ditch? Possibly. Can he clear a three-foot high bank on the other side of a six-foot ditch? No. Try it, if you wish. Can he jump the ditch and reliably land on his feet on the (sloping) bank? I don't think so. Can he do so with a spear in one hand and a shield in the other? The shield is about three feet in diameter (quite awkward). It weighs 10-15 pounds. The spear is about seven feet long (quite clumsy). Finally, can he do that safely when the chap standing on the top is trying to kill him? I really don't think so.

So, charging at a dyke is not a good idea, even if the ditch is only three feet deep. Let us try the alternative: walk up to the ditch, walk or run down it and then scramble up the far side without losing your balance. If you try it, you will find that you almost always need one hand to balance or help you scramble up. That is either your spear hand or your shield hand: there is no other alternative. So you have to drop your guard. That makes it easy for the other chap to stab you. So even a three-foot deep ditch makes a credible obstacle.

Some writers have commented that the dykes cannot be fortifications, because they have open flanks. They seem stop in the middle of nowhere. You can walk round them. Even Bill Bryson said that, about the Cambridge Dykes. Well, you can walk around them *today*. We often don't know where the ends were, because they have been ploughed in (or similar). But if we do, we often find that there was forest or swamp there. Many of the dykes on the south side of the North York Moors run into the Great Carr. We can be fairly sure that that was a vast swamp. If you check the map, and walk the ground, you can almost always find a convincing explanation. In the Dark Ages you could *not* just walk round a dyke.

Several writers have suggested that the dykes were built primarily to impress. The idea is connected to anthropological ideas about ostentatious displays of material wealth or military strength. In fact they are rarely impressive. A few appear to have been faced with a white material, such as powdered chalk, to make them more obvious. That, however, is the exception. In practice their ability to impress was probably secondary, but nonetheless important. Standing on the Devil's Dyke at Cambridge, however, one *is* given a significant impression. It is very simple: 'you are not going to get across here'. That impression is formed by the sheer difficulty of getting across, even if faced with just a few defenders. The primary purpose of a dyke was to stop attackers getting across. If, by their size and perhaps their appearance, some dykes deterred would-be attackers from even trying, so much the better.

If the dykes were primarily intended to be symbolic, or a visible deterrent, they would typically be sited on crest lines. But a great many, probably the great majority, are not. Some are on the forward slope. Some are on the reverse slope. Many are across the narrow point of a ridge and are therefore overlooked. The Cambridge dykes are almost entirely on reverse slopes. Symbolism or deterrence is not the primary reason behind their siting. They are where they are for tactical, that is military, reasons.

One writer has suggested that they were, in practice, work-creation schemes. He thought that they were Neolithic. That is, he suggested they are from a period so luxurious that local leaders could afford to have their people build ostentatious displays of wealth and strength in order to keep underemployed hands from getting bored. Dream on! Pre-Roman Britain was a pre-urban society of subsistence farming. It was possible to direct labour for large monumental projects (witness Stonehenge). To suggest, however, that thousands of dykes were built across Britain purely for social benefit seems just a little far-fetched.

The dykes have also been described as boundary markers. Well, there are many much easier ways of delineating boundaries, such as thorn hedges. The dykes probably did serve as boundary markers, but in a simple and secondary way: if you cross this line we will kill you. We probably won't try to kill you unless you *do* come up to this line.

A further suggestion is that of Neolithic ranch boundaries. The idea is that Neolithic tribal leaders had ramparts built around their domains, both as boundary markers and to control livestock. Unfortunately they face the wrong way to control livestock (they would generally stop animals getting in, rather than out). Secondly, they never seem to enclose anything. Unlike hill forts, they are never continuous around an area. There are many examples of later, medieval, 'park pales' which do just that. Many are shown on modern Ordnance Survey maps. They are clearly different from the dykes which we are discussing (although some have been confused in the past).

The dykes have also been thought to have been designed to control movement and trade. What movement, and what trade? There was very little. Pre-Roman Britain was largely pre-urban. There were no real towns. There was a number of important centres, but the evidence for considerable regional trade is minimal. Bulk and volume was small. There certainly weren't daily convoys of pack animals traversing well-defined routes (let alone carts, on the largely non-existent roads). Of course there was some travel and some trade. But the idea of an extensive network of earthworks to control it seems far fetched. In addition, I have not found any evidence of gates or gateways in any of them. They do not seem to have been intended to control traffic. There are simpler ways of doing that. They include thorn fences and wooden palisades, which would probably require less maintenance. They would also be hard to identify today.

Some writers who accept a military purpose then say that they were intended primarily to provide a firm base for offensive operations. That would be analogous to the purpose of Hadrian's Wall. What that suggests is that they had an immediate defensive function (to protect) as part of a wider operational or strategic design. Well, that is entirely possible and entirely consistent with what we have discussed. Another theory is that some of the earthworks (such as the Cambridge dykes) were deliberately dug facing the wrong way to trap invaders from returning to their own lands with plunder. That would potentially place the defenders between enemies on both sides. That is not a good idea. It is more credible to believe that they were dug facing one way in order to defend that way.

In practice, there are several theories which cloud the simplest explanation: the dykes were defensive fortifications. They may also have served to impress. They may also have served as boundary markers, or as bases for offensive operations. All those functions, however, are secondary to the simple, clear purpose of denying access to an attacking force. Apply Occam's Razor.

There have been several alternative explanations for the Car Dyke. One is that it was a waterway for navigation: a transport canal. Well, the Romans do not seem to have dug any long-distance navigations anywhere in the Empire. They built a couple of very impressive coastal dock and harbour schemes, such as the port at Ostia near Rome. The Romans built one or two coastal navigations to improve access to major ports or perhaps for maritime safety. A canal from Narbonne to the River Aude in Gaul, and the *Fossa Druisiana* and *Fossa Corbulanis* in the Netherlands, are examples. The Romans cut off a few stretches of major rivers inland, such as at the Iron Gates on the Danube. But they did not build long inland navigations. Besides, why would they build a navigation from Peterborough to Lincoln, when Ermine Street runs past Peterborough to Lincoln?

Modern survey has demonstrated that the Car Dyke was never completed as a continuous section. If it had been, the water would all drain out. Ah, but that means that the Roman engineers got their levels wrong! Again, that scarcely seems likely. There are no known examples of major Roman projects being abandoned due to faulty surveying. There is a little, but high-quality, evidence of preliminary works being re-aligned due to minor local error. But in every case the project was completed. Given the topography, it would have been relatively easy to realign sections of the Car Dyke to make it continuous. Finally, the Car Dyke has little or no berm. A berm would be needed along an inland navigation as a towpath. How can you tow barges inland without a towpath? You can't. Why haven't archaeologists noticed that?

It has also been suggested that the Car Dyke was a drainage ditch, or part of a drainage scheme. Unfortunately, water flows down hill. For much of its length the Dyke hugs the bottom of the high ground on the Lindsey side. That means that it drains that high ground. It does not drain the fen. Why would the Romans build a long interceptor drain to drain the short uphill slope, which is generally well drained already? If they had meant to drain the fens they would have dug it somewhere in the middle of the low ground , as in Figure 13.1.

To get round that simple fact, people have come up with clever explanations about tidal action and double-drain systems. Such systems need sophisticated sluices. There is no evidence of sluices. Let's stick to a simpler explanation. It was not a drainage ditch. Besides, if it was not continuous, where did it drain *to*? The Car Dyke was not a drain, not a canal, not an aqueduct, nor was it a boundary. It was part of a defensive system. That is the simplest explanation that fits the known facts.

In several long linear earthworks we find what are described as 'ankle breakers'. They run along the bottom of the ditch and are typically about a foot deep and a foot wide. The theory is that they would typically have been hidden amongst debris such

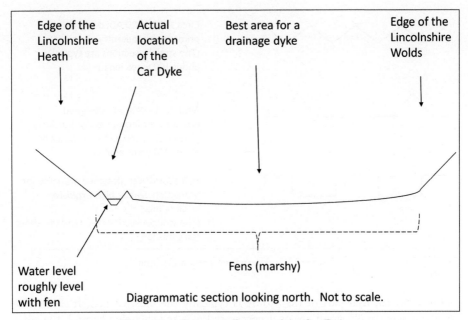

Edge of the Lincolnshire Heath

Actual location of the Car Dyke

Best area for a drainage dyke

Edge of the Lincolnshire Wolds

Water level roughly level with fen

Fens (marshy)

Diagrammatic section looking north. Not to scale.

Figure 13.1 Schematic Section of the Car Dyke.

as leaves. Attackers, in their haste to cross the ditch, would not notice them and break their ankles as they tripped on them. At the very least they might trip up.

It is hard to believe anything so fanciful. Attackers might break the odd ankle, occasionally. But the theory tells us that the people who dreamed up the idea had an odd idea of warfare. Why bother? Why not just plant stakes (which they did), or build a palisade (which they did)? Both would have been more effective. It seems more likely that 'ankle breakers' were actually drainage channels. Most of Britain enjoys between one and five yards of rain a year. All that water has to go somewhere. Having water pooling in a dyke is possibly a good thing. But if water flows rapidly and erodes the profile, it could be a bad thing. Several archaeologists have commented that, in places, the dykes were clearly consciously designed and show advanced engineering features. Occam's Razor suggests that so-called 'ankle breakers' were drainage features.

The dykes show several features in common. Conversely it is worth remarking on features which they do *not* show. They were clearly not designed for missile fire. In the gunpowder era earthworks were either zig-zagged (for enfilade fire from muskets) or straight but interrupted by redoubts (for enfilade fire from cannon). In the age of high explosive (such as the First World War) they typically had a crenellated plan, so that the blast from any one shell would be localised. See Figure 13.2.

Many of the dykes show evidence of some sort of palisade, although it would often have been in the upper section of the bank and the evidence has been eroded. Their banks do not typically show much evidence of a walkway along the top. Once

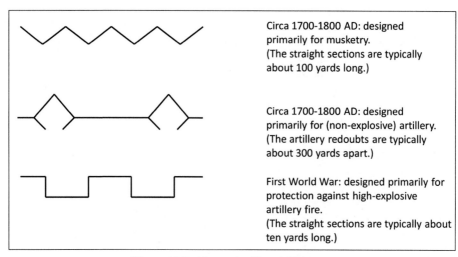

Circa 1700-1800 AD: designed primarily for musketry. (The straight sections are typically about 100 yards long.)

Circa 1700-1800 AD: designed primarily for (non-explosive) artillery. (The artillery redoubts are typically about 300 yards apart.)

First World War: designed primarily for protection against high-explosive artillery fire. (The straight sections are typically about ten yards long.)

Figure 13.2 Alternative Trench Designs.

again, however, that part of the profile is typically the most eroded. It seems that the defenders simply stood on, or if necessary knelt and sheltered behind, the crest. Archaeology from the Chiltern dykes suggests that the crests in that region were not finished to a sharp profile, but left rough or perhaps flattened.

So, since they appear to have been fortifications, were they from the fifth to the eighth centuries? A report from an emergency archaeological dig stated that 'where they have been dated, they have been shown to be Neolithic'. Is that true?

Excavations at Offa's Dyke, the Wansdyke, the Cambridge Dykes and the Bokerly Dyke have shown convincingly that those examples were either late-Roman or post-Roman. The archaeologists used a variety of dating techniques. Some were highly scientific; others were more traditional. There is no reason to doubt those findings. In the case of Offa's Dyke we have, uniquely, documentary evidence suggesting that King Offa dug a dyke or a series of dykes to separate the Welsh from Mercia.

Many of the dykes were laid out in straight lines with deliberate angles. As we have seen, almost nothing pre-Roman was laid out in straight lines. Virtually nothing which was (such as various 'cursuses') was more than a mile or so long. Yet we have many dykes which are straight, with deliberate angles, for several miles. My former military surveyor friend took one look at one of my maps. It showed a number of sections of earthworks in the Yorkshire Wolds. He said, without prompting, that they were laid out by trained surveyors. He should know: in a very varied and interesting career he laid out (among other things) a section of international border. Roman engineers, and possibly people who they trained, had such skills. There is absolutely no evidence that pre-Roman Britons did.

We have seen that Anglo-Saxon freemen were under a legal obligation that included building fortifications. The original texts are ambiguous. They might mean 'ramparts' rather than, say, 'fortifications' or 'walls'. We should not, however, expect eighth and ninth century clerics to have an advanced military technical vocabulary. They did not have the equivalent of the Royal Engineers' Pocket Book to refer to. In addition there is some ambiguity in German even today about the words used. The modern German word 'bauen' can mean either 'to dig' or 'to build'. To a primitive Germanic warrior, to dig *was* to build.

What is staggering, however, is the apparent 'coincidence' of the sheer numbers of dykes which are related to Roman roads. The Jutes are thought to have landed and formed an enclave in East Kent. Only two routes known to have been used by the Romans left Kent. They were the Canterbury-London road and the prehistoric ridge way along the foot of the North Downs. Both appear to have been cut by dykes.

Anglians formed an enclave in what is now Suffolk and Norfolk. Six routes known to have been used by the Romans enter that area. Five were Roman roads. The first road enters near Ipswich, where it crossed a tidal river. The next two roads run north from the Colchester area through what was thick forest. One appears to have been cut by a dyke. Both join at Ixworth; the road north east from there appears to have been cut by a dyke. The next route is the Icknield Way near Cambridge, which appears to have been cut by four dykes in succession. The last two roads into East Anglia are causeways through the Fens. They join where they meet dry land in Norfolk. The road is cut by a dyke just east of there.

The South Saxons landed on the Sussex coast. No known Roman roads led from the coast inland. Chichester is a few miles to the west. The roads north and northeast of Chichester both appear to have been cut by dykes.

The West Saxons are thought to have formed an enclave in Hampshire east of the Solent. There is no credible sign of the Roman road east to Chichester being cut, but the area is heavily built up nowadays (at Havant). There is no sign of the Roman road north to Winchester being cut, but see below. The Roman road west to the Solent at Bitterne appears to have been cut by a dyke at Netley.

The process by which the Thames basin became Anglo-Saxon is not clear. Only three Roman roads lead westwards from London. The road south west to Chichester was cut by a dyke, described above. The road to the west ran through woods to Silchester, from where five further roads radiate. Of those, the road south to Chichester appears to have been cut by a dyke, also described above. The road south west to Winchester may have been cut by a dyke (there are dykes north and east of Winchester), but see also below. The road west from Silchester to Old Sarum appears to have been cut by dykes in two places. The road north west from Silchester to Cirencester appears to have been cut by a dyke. The road north from Silchester to Dorchester-on-Thames appears to have been cut by dykes in four places. The third road from London runs north west to St Albans. It appears to have been cut by a dyke. The road west from St Albans through the Chilterns appears to have been cut by a dyke.

Ermine Street runs north from London to Lincoln. The road from Lincoln south west to Leicester appears to have been cut by a dyke. The road north west from Lincoln reaches the River Don at Doncaster, where it is tidal. The area immediately west of there is crossed by two dykes in succession, each about five miles long. The road north from Lincoln leads towards York across the Humber, which was neither bridged nor forded (a ferry was used, hence the alternative road via Doncaster).

Another Anglian enclave was formed north of the Humber. It became part of the kingdom of Northumbria. Place-name and other evidence suggest that the original enclave was in the Yorkshire Wolds. Three Roman roads lead west to York from that area. All three appear to have been cut by dykes. York is thought to have fallen to the Northumbrians just after 600 AD. All of the three roads leading west and northwest from York appear to have been cut by dykes. Another Roman road ran north from the York area. It passed through a thick forest (which may be why it did not run directly north from York). There is no sign of it being cut by a dyke. However, the parallel prehistoric route which runs along the crest of the Hambleton Hills (the west end of the North York Moors) appears to have been cut by dykes in two places.

The West Saxons do not appear to have expanded westwards from the Solent area, but rather from the Thames valley and Dorchester on Thames. The road west from that area to Cirencester appears to have been cut by a dyke. Their conquest of what became Wessex eventually included Wiltshire, Somerset, Dorset, Devon and Cornwall. Three Roman roads run into that area: one west from Silchester; one southeast from Cirencester; and one southwest from Cirencester through Bath (the Fosse Way). The Silchester road runs to Winchester, as described above. The road westwards from Winchester to Sarum appears to have been cut by a dyke, and both Roman roads southwest and west of Sarum appear to have been cut by dykes. Both Roman roads south from Cirencester appear to have been cut by dykes. Another Roman road runs northwest from Cirencester; it also appears to have been cut by a dyke.

The Anglo-Saxon conquest continued: westward to the sea, and northwards beyond Hadrian's Wall. There is evidence of more dykes impeding their progress. For example, the route across the Pennines into south Lancashire appears to have been cut by a dyke. Overall, of the 36 routes described above, all but seven appear to have been cut by dykes. Of those seven, three cross tidal rivers. The other four ran through thick forest or are now heavily built over. That means that out of 33 cases which did not cross tidal rivers, 29 probably were cut by dykes and all 33 may have been. This summary seems highly repetitive. It is: deliberately so. Time and time again when following a Roman road one finds a dyke crossing it. It seems greatly 'more likely that unlikely' that there is a connection between the dykes and the Roman road system. It seems quite convincing. We know that, in the cases that have been investigated, the dykes cut existing Roman roads and not vice versa. Those dykes are therefore definitely either late-Roman or post-Roman.

In practice, the more one looks the more one finds. That seems to be because there is an established pattern, which is related to the tactical and operational siting of the dykes. Once you have established the pattern, it is easy to find more. It is relatively easy to predict where you will find them. Sometimes they are not shown on a 1:50,000 scale map, but other evidence (such as minor place name evidence: 'White

Ditch Farm' is an example) suggests that there is something there. In such cases the 1:25,000 map usually shows an earthwork, and there is almost always something visible on the ground.

Stone-Age had tools would be simply not robust enough for prolonged digging on this scale. Bronze-Age (ie bronze) tools would be little better. Bronze is very soft. Practicality suggests that iron tools would be needed, and hundreds of them. The Iron Age only came to Britain from about 800 BC. By no coincidence, the great majority of hill forts in Britain were built in the Iron Age. Thus the dykes might have been dug in the Iron Age, given the kind of tools available, but not earlier.

However, pre-Roman Britain was pre-urban. Does it seem likely that a civilisation that did not even live in towns had a strategic and operational view of the world that sought to defend major areas of land on the scale of, say, a modern county? Even today, writers who accept that the dykes may have had a military purpose seem to think that they were dug to defend a particular village or perhaps a cluster of villages. The evidence, however, suggests that many were planned on a regional, if not a national, scale. That does not suggest the mindset of pre-Roman tribal chiefs. They thought in terms of defending hilltops, in order to protect their livestock, their grain and their people from raiders. We are asked to believe that, in pre-Roman Britain, tribal chiefs used *both* hill forts *and* operational or strategic earthworks. Conversely, centuries later and with a legacy of Roman military thinking, their successors used neither. That seems unlikely.

We know that some pre-Roman leaders used fortifications in Britain. Caesar relates that they did during his 'invasions' (strategic raids) of 55 and 54 BC. He describes localities defended with ramparts and palisades in low-lying areas. Colchester was probably one. In such cases we often see multiple ramparts, one immediately behind the other. We see the same in late Iron Age hill-forts. (Early hill forts tend to have only one ring of ramparts. Archaeologists call them 'univallate', as opposed to 'multivallate'.) We know that Arminius used reinforced ramparts when he ambushed Varus in the Teutoburger Wald in 9 AD. But we have no documentary (and little archaeological) evidence of earthworks used for operational or strategic purposes before Roman times.

The sheer number of dykes which cut Roman roads suggests that many are Roman or post-Roman. The number that are straight with definite angles suggest Roman or post-Roman surveying skills. Evidence from excavations, and documentary evidence, suggests that many are late or post-Roman. We have no credible literary evidence that *any* were built in Roman times. The dating of several of them places them in the Dark Ages. No-one seriously doubts that Offa's Dyke is post-Roman. We have found a series of fossilised frontiers from much the same age. So we seem to have found a very large elephant in the room. Several people have identified various parts of the elephant, but no-one has recognised the whole beast: until now.

Since they seem to be Dark Age defensive fortifications, what can we say about their strategic, operational and tactical purposes? Strategically the question reduces to 'why build a dyke in this part of Britain?' We know that Roman commanders had a clear idea of strategy and strategic purpose. They built Hadrian's Wall. They built the Antonine Wall, and abandoned it when it no longer met their strategic methods. They built the *Limes Germanicus* between the Rhine and the Danube. They pushed it forward (with astonishing accuracy) when they felt it appropriate. They fortified other imperial frontiers elsewhere, to other designs. Literary evidence indicates an explicit awareness of strategy unknown even in classical Greek times.

We also know that Offa built his dyke, and it seems quite reasonable to believe that he did it to keep the Welsh out of Mercia. We can believe that the Roman-British rulers of southern England built a dyke from the Thames near Goring to the Severn near Bath. Some time later the area around the Bokerly Dykes, together with the topography of Somerset, would have served as a part of a British national defensive border system. Later still, the British appear to have lost either the ability or the will to build strategic defences.

Being potentially a component of a national strategy brings us to operational, campaign or theatre-level considerations. The relevant question is 'why dig a dyke along this hillside, or blocking this valley?', or similar. Defensive earthworks at Cambridge would have formed a critical part of a system to stop someone (presumably Romano-British armies) invading East Anglia. The Chiltern Dykes would have formed part of a system to keep someone (presumably the *Gewisse*, soon to be the West Saxons) in the Thames Basin and out of the upper Thames Valley. The Meon Valley defences kept the Romano-British out of the earlier, 'Cerdicing' area of south Hampshire. The Roman Rig served to keep Mercians from the southern area of Deira (and hence Northumbria). And so on. This 'theatre (of war)' or 'regional' perspective is critical. Many of the Dykes had more than a purely village-level significance.

In some ways the tactical considerations are more challenging. That is, 'why dig a dyke just here, rather than a few feet over there?' Their siting and profile are sometimes far more sophisticated than some observers think. Furthermore, sometimes feet matter. Just a few feet 'elsewhere' can make all the difference.

A very good example is what can be termed the 'Streatley Anomaly'. This section, near Goring on Thames, appears to face south. If that is the case, then it clearly is not part of a nation-wide scheme to keep the Anglo-Saxons out of southern England. It can be taken to suggest that the dykes are not fortifications at all. The reason that archaeologists think it faces south is that there is a very deep and steep drop on the south side. It is at the top of a field so steep that only sheep can graze on it.

However, that section runs along a ridge. A hundred yards or so further east, it runs down to the Thames. There, it fairly clearly faces north. A few hundred yards further west, it runs along a forward slope. There, it fairly clearly faces north. The problem which the builder faced was how to link those two sections. If he moved the linking section further north, it would have run along a fairly simple forward slope. However, the defenders would then have had real problems. It would have resulted in a salient or angle which could easily be overlooked from slightly further west. If he moved the dyke further south it would be on a dramatically steep reverse slope. No amount of clever construction would put the defenders in anything other than a very awkward position. What the builder seems to have done was to run the dyke very skilfully along the ridge, accepting a very steep drop behind the home bank. After all, if attackers broke through just there they would be in a very awkward situation. Surviving defenders would be behind and above them. When I first saw it, the siting of that section struck me as incredibly skilful. It was only months afterwards that I discovered that it is considered to be a major anomaly.

We have considered the difficulty of a single warrior trying to cross even quite modest dykes. We have also seen that much of warfare before the gunpowder era depended on charging, to break the defender's cohesion. Even a small dyke of this sort would completely stop the momentum of a charge. Each individual would have to stop and try to scramble over the earthwork. In practice it would be impossible to keep together in the face of even a single line of defenders manning the far bank.

Thus mass and depth would avail the attackers nothing. Like the battle of Thermopylae, it would be a case of a few holding off a multitude without difficulty. (Remember that the Thermopylae position was eventually outflanked, not penetrated.) The battles of Marignano in 1515 and Bicocca in 1522 AD are extremely good examples of how even the best-trained infantry have huge difficulty in crossing earthworks and maintaining their formation. In both cases phalanxes of Swiss pikemen came to grief. They suffered heavily from musket fire from the defending French. Were it not for the earthworks, the Swiss would have swept the French away with ease.

Earthworks made very good defences. Mass and depth would count for every little. A single line of defenders would have a major advantage over any number of attackers who could not outflank them. If the defenders defend with only a single line of defenders on the bank, they could keep reserves to counter any local penetration. The simple trick of counterattacking from the flanks would be devastating. The attackers, exhausted from breaking over the dyke, would be in some disorder and could be attacked from one or both flanks. The flanks of the counterattacking defenders, however, would be protected by the dyke. See Figure 13.3.

To a Roman commander, defending a dyke would be pretty straightforward. One line of soldiers manned the crest of the bank. They took cover by kneeling behind the crest (with their shields in front of them) if the enemy tried to use javelins or arrows. Small parties of reserves were kept at intervals behind the line. If there was any penetration, the nearest reserves counterattacked directly. Adjoining reserves moved up to the back of the bank, turned inwards, and attacked the enemy from flank and rear. That is pretty simple. It would have been complex for, say, a primitive British or Germanic war band. But it would have been well within the abilities of anyone trained by, or who had learned from, the Romans.

At first sight, this requires the dyke to be manned before the attackers arrived. That is where advanced warning, or intelligence, would be important. It might just be news from passing travellers that the enemy are massing for war. It might be bright young lads on shaggy ponies scouting forward of the dyke. It might be *turmae* of late- or post-Roman cavalry. There is no suggestion that these dykes had a permanent garrison. They didn't need one. What they needed was early warning that the enemy

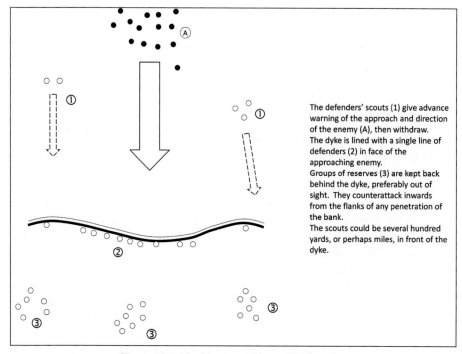

The defenders' scouts (1) give advance warning of the approach and direction of the enemy (A), then withdraw.
The dyke is lined with a single line of defenders (2) in face of the approaching enemy.
Groups of reserves (3) are kept back behind the dyke, preferably out of sight. They counterattack inwards from the flanks of any penetration of the bank.
The scouts could be several hundred yards, or perhaps miles, in front of the dyke.

Figure 13.3 The Tactics of Linear Earthworks.

were approaching. With that, a few men could keep a multitude at bay. Conversely, such dykes were not an Iron Curtain. When they were not manned, scouts or spies could come and go across them fairly easily.

Even if the dyke was not manned, it would give an advantage. The defenders, having built the dyke, would know the ground. The attackers might not. On hearing that the enemy had crossed, the defending commander could divide his forces (*especially* if outnumbered) into two or three groups. One force would go straight towards the attackers and make a demonstration. The others would advance to the dyke on one or both sides of the attackers, turn inwards and attack. Surprise attacks from the flanks are devastating. No-one would want to have to defend with a major earthwork behind them. There would be a massive advantage to the defenders if some of the flanking groups were cavalry, and the attackers had none.

The Romans could successfully attack across earthworks. The tactical articulation which their Centuries gave them, together minor tactics such as the *testudo* or tortoise (in which they attacked with their shields covering themselves front, sides and top), gave them a huge advantage. Yet even the Romans baulked at assaulting manned earthworks. At places such as Masada in Palestine or Maiden Castle in England they declined to do so. They used set-piece siege techniques instead. If the Romans, with their organisation, training and discipline declined to attack well-constructed fortifications, we can be reasonably sure that their successors might be reluctant to do so as well.

Attacking a defended dyke would take more than just an effort of will. It was entirely unambiguous. If an invading leader took his warriors across a dyke he had declared hostile intent. It was difficult to fall back across it, especially with any live-stock or plunder. The defenders might catch him on the dyke. Similarly, he would not want to be caught with a dyke behind him. It left him open to being outflanked quite easily. It was not to be undertaken lightly. Certainly not the second time!

Some of the details of siting are most interesting. The two most important design features seem to be: (a) the total height of the dyke; and (b) to ensure that the home bank is not overlooked locally. The total height is the height difference between the bottom of the ditch and the top of the bank. To some extent the greater the total height is, the harder it is to cross the dyke. The home bank should not be overlooked from within a few yards. Beyond that, relative heights are not too important. There was little missile fire (from javelins or arrows) in the Dark Ages. Certainly it does not seem to be important that the dyke has 'command', to use the Victorian term. Even if the opposing commander could see over it, there was little he could do with the knowledge. In practically any circumstances a defender would be much better off with a dyke, even if it is overlooked from a distance, than without one.

Figure 13.4 gives some representative dimensions of V-shaped dykes. They are typical of the sections I have found across the length and breadth of England. They all assume angles of 45 degrees for the slopes, which is close enough in most cases. Knowing how the dykes were dug helps understand their design. The average man with a spade or shovel can throw spoil up to a height of about six or seven feet. As he digs down, this becomes a problem. Not least, the spoil he has already dug gets in his way. When he has dug about two feet down he is already throwing spoil up four feet or so. After about six or seven feet, the spoil will have to be handled twice. Typically it is put into buckets or barrows which are transported, emptied and returned. Double handling reduces the rate of construction by more than half. Given vast amounts of manpower and plenty of time, one can dig almost anything. The Cambridge dykes are an example. But, more normally, engineers or commanders would have gone to considerable lengths to avoid double handling of spoil.

Depth of Ditch	Height of Bank	Width of Ditch	Width of Bank	Total Height	Total Width
3 ft	3 ft	6 ft	6 ft	6 ft	12 ft
6 ft	6 ft	12 ft	12 ft	12 ft	24 ft
9 ft	9 ft	18 ft	18 ft	18 ft	36 ft
12 ft	12 ft	24 ft	24 ft	24 ft	48 ft
15 ft	15 ft	30 ft	30 ft	30 ft	60 ft

Figure 13.4 Representative Dimensions of Dykes.

If you are reading this you are probably between five and six feet tall. You may be a few inches over six feet tall. Imagine that you are standing in the bottom of one of those ditches and that someone a few feet away, above you, is trying to kill you. Now look at the 'total height' column of Figure 13.4. You will now understand how even quite a small earthwork can be quite a significant obstacle.

Now, if the total height of the dyke is the critical parameter and the far bank should not overlook the home bank, there are several ways of proceeding. One is to dig down about three or four feet, throwing spoil onto the home bank; then dig down an extra foot or so and throwing the spoil onto the far bank. If you have time, you can level that off. If you haven't, it forms what is called a counterscarp bank. As long as it is not higher than the home bank that doesn't matter very much. It might be an advantage. This effect is particularly marked on a forward slope, because even on a mild slope (say, 1 in 8) the home bank starts a foot or so higher than the far bank, even for quite a small dyke.

Reverse slope dykes have to be dug quite carefully, otherwise the far bank will be higher than the home. Double handling might be necessary. Another possibility on a forward slope is to dig a small ditch behind the home bank and use it to top off the bank, as in Figure 13.6.

These details are important because they affect what we see today. For example, at Morgan's Hill the Wansdyke has a profile something like Figure 13.5. No-one would pretend that that faces uphill. Were the hill slightly less steep, and the profile rather more eroded, it might look like Figure 13.7. At that point one could easily convince oneself that it is a reverse slope dyke, or not a fortification at all. Like the Streatley Anomaly, archaeologists have long believed that the section near Ginge near Wantage in Oxfordshire faces south. If so, it is either a reverse-slope fortification and the Goring to Bristol 'line' is not a continuous line; or the earthworks are not fortifications. However, almost nowhere is the north bank of the Ginge section higher than the south, even today. Over most of the visible section the land drops quite steeply:

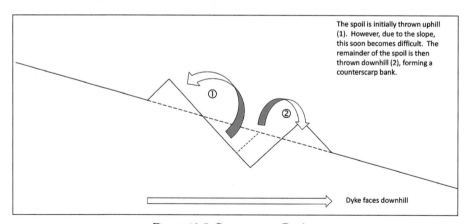

The spoil is initially thrown uphill (1). However, due to the slope, this soon becomes difficult. The remainder of the spoil is then thrown downhill (2), forming a counterscarp bank.

Dyke faces downhill

Figure 13.5 Counterscarp Banks.

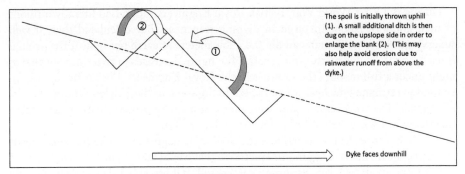

The spoil is initially thrown uphill (1). A small additional ditch is then dug on the upslope side in order to enlarge the bank (2). (This may also help avoid erosion due to rainwater runoff from above the dyke.)

Dyke faces downhill

Figure 13.6 Enlarging the Bank.

about 15 feet in 40. It does seem to be a forward slope earthwork facing north. It does seem to be part of a continuous system from the Thames to the Severn.

A further consideration is the bulking factor. If you pour sugar from a bag into a jar, and then tap the jar, the volume reduces. That happens with most granular material. In general, freshly disturbed material is more bulky than was before it was disturbed. The phenomenon is highly relevant to man-made earthworks. You always get more out of a hole than the hole you made, because the spoil bulks up. So, in general, the cross-sectional area of a bank will be bigger than the area of the dyke it was excavated from. It may be considerably bigger. Some writers are unaware of that. They have invented ideas like 'borrow pits' to explain differences in section. Why would you dig and transport spoil if you can avoid it? Soil weighs between one and two tons per cubic meter if dry, and a ton more if wet. Chalk or stone is even heavier. One cubic metre of spoil doesn't go very far. If you need the bank to be higher, it is easier to dig the ditch a little deeper (or wider) than to transport spoil along the length of the dyke from a 'borrow pit'. Roman engineers would have known that.

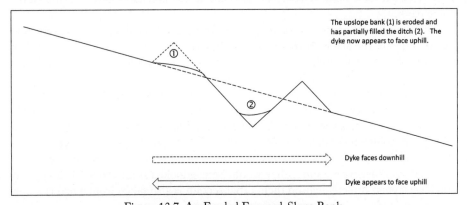

The upslope bank (1) is eroded and has partially filled the ditch (2). The dyke now appears to face uphill.

Dyke faces downhill

Dyke appears to face uphill

Figure 13.7 An Eroded Forward-Slope Bank.

During the First World War, British Royal Engineers supervised literally millions of man-hours of labour involved in digging trenches. They calculated that, if well supervised, the average man can dig 0.4 cubic meters of earth per hour if the ground is hard, and 0.7 cubic metres if it is soft. (The figure decreases to two thirds of that at night under a full moon). The figure is in the Royal Engineers' Pocket Book and can be used to estimate how long it would take to dig some of these dykes. The results are interesting. They correspond quite well with historical figures. We used a calculation like that when we looked at Offa's Dyke in Chapter Ten.

If a ditch is three feet deep and its sides slope at 45 degrees, its cross-sectional area is about one square metre. Digging 100 metres of that would take about 180 man hours, or (say) 10 men about two days, assuming average soil. If it was about six feet deep it would take at least four times as long, since the cross-sectional area would be four times larger. In practice it would take even longer, because of the need for double handling.

At the Siege of Alesia in 52 BC, Caesar's forces dug 18 kilometres of defensive ditch about four metres deep in three weeks. Assuming eight hours a day and a six-day week, that required about three thousand men working in the trenches at any one time. As Caesar had several legions plus auxiliary troops, that seems quite possible. The figures given in works by the Roman writers Hyginus and Vegetius are broadly consistent with the Royal Engineer Pocket Book.

What we see today can be quite impressive. At times, however, it is much less so. In places there is just a gentle ridge in the ground, perhaps thirty feet across but only a foot or so high. Perhaps there is just a slight dip, perhaps only a foot or so deep. Sometimes there is not even that. However, something caught the attention of the Ordnance Survey mapmakers at some stage between 1801, when Ordnance Survey maps were first published, and today.

It is normally fairly easy to identify a dyke where there is a bank and a ditch, but in perhaps ten percent of all cases you can only see one or the other. That makes it impossible to tell directly which way it faced. Sometimes the wider context gives some idea. Some sites must have faced a certain way. That is typically because the site is too steep to be a reverse slope defence. The far bank would inevitably have overlooked the home bank.

Sometimes the alignment gives more away. In Figure 13.8, dyke 'C' clearly faces in the direction of the arrow. If that is the case the stream junction is in front of it. If it were the other way around, a short section of earthwork would have an 'island' ('D') enclosed by two streams behind it. The defenders would not choose to risk being cut off like that. In that instance (it is taken from a real case somewhere in the Scottish Lowlands), whoever laid it out could easily have moved the whole section about 30 yards downstream to avoid that problem (line 'E'). The section at diagram Figure 13.9 also clearly points in the direction of the arrow. That being the case, the defenders are overlooked from about 30 yards away, but have a pond immediately in front of them. If it was the other way around, they would be overlooked from about 10 yards away and have a pond directly behind them. That section is also taken from a real example in the Lowlands.

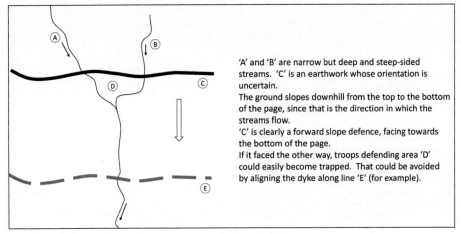

'A' and 'B' are narrow but deep and steep-sided streams. 'C' is an earthwork whose orientation is uncertain.

The ground slopes downhill from the top to the bottom of the page, since that is the direction in which the streams flow.

'C' is clearly a forward slope defence, facing towards the bottom of the page.

If it faced the other way, troops defending area 'D' could easily become trapped. That could be avoided by aligning the dyke along line 'E' (for example).

Figure 13.8 Local Context (1).

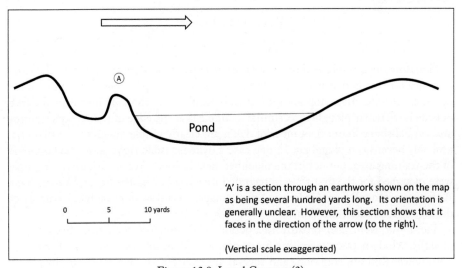

Pond

'A' is a section through an earthwork shown on the map as being several hundred yards long. Its orientation is generally unclear. However, this section shows that it faces in the direction of the arrow (to the right).

(Vertical scale exaggerated)

0   5   10 yards

Figure 13.9 Local Context (2).

Erosion will have had an effect on what we see today. The pattern of soil which an eroded bank makes has been studied in detail. It was actually measured in the 1960s by digging a dyke and letting it erode. Where there is only one bank, the soil forms a set of asymmetric layers. Where there are two, they are more-or-less symmetric. On a slope, the uphill bank may be eroded by rainwater runoff from further uphill. That may erode the bank more than the rest of the section. That could reinforce the perception that a forward slope dyke with a counterscarp ditch is actually a reverse slope position. See Figure 13.10.

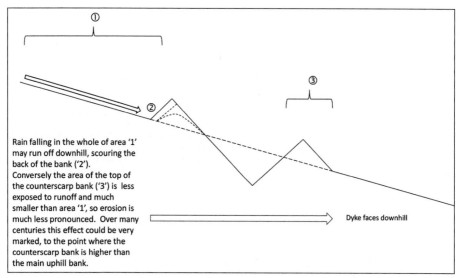

Rain falling in the whole of area '1' may run off downhill, scouring the back of the bank ('2'). Conversely the area of the top of the counterscarp bank ('3') is less exposed to runoff and much smaller than area '1', so erosion is much less pronounced. Over many centuries this effect could be very marked, to the point where the counterscarp bank is higher than the main uphill bank.

Dyke faces downhill

Figure 13.10 Erosion.

Ploughing seems to have destroyed far more earthworks than erosion has. The main evidence for that is that many surviving sections can be easily seen in woodland, but not at all outside. They stop abruptly at the wood's edge. In many instances the field outside is currently ploughed. A similar example is at the edge of the Army's training area on Salisbury Plain. A number of dykes are clearly visible: much of the Plain has probably never been ploughed. In one case a dyke is visible right up to the boundary of the training area, but not in the ploughed field beyond. Across Britain, many areas were ploughed for the first time in recorded memory during the Second World War. As far as we can tell from Ordnance Survey maps, several sections of dyke disappeared during, or soon after, the War.

The 1940s were also broadly the period when tractors took over from horsed ploughs. Modern tractors are far more powerful than horses. Tractors of over 100 horsepower (hp) are common, and several are over 500hp. Tractors can plough out dykes far faster than horses ever could. Some dykes have clearly been bulldozed out. There is, however, clear documentary evidence of dykes being deliberately ploughed out in the 17th, 18th and 19th centuries, possibly because they just got in the way.

Scarp slopes tend to be steeper and seem less likely to have been ploughed. Dip slopes are often quite shallow. In a number of places there are dykes which are quite apparent on the scarp slope but appear to have been grubbed out on the dip slope. The ridgeline itself is often high and remote, so less likely to have been ploughed. Many dykes cross ridges, seemingly because the ridge was the only dry route to avoid the boggy or forested valleys below. On many ridges there are several dykes parallel with each other. Other dykes seem to cut off routes up to the ridge.

Such ridges are also often at, or near, the site of hill forts. The Anglo-Saxons rarely seem to have used them. The Romano-British seem to have taken some back into use, perhaps for a generation or so. Hill forts are often associated with other earthworks for some distance. Some are clearly not fortifications. Some are agricultural terraces called 'strip lynchets'. In some cases nowadays one can see strip lynchets on hillsides above very good farmland. Nowadays there are sheep and crops in the fields below. The lynchets are not necessarily Dark Age, but they tell us that at some stage the land below was not available. The population chose to level off the slopes to create lynchets at great effort. One example is on the south side of the Vale of Pewsey. It supports the idea that much of the Savernake Forest was once a great wooded swamp.

Some earthworks clearly have to be disregarded. Some are strip lynchets. Others are Iron Age. Some may be even older. Some Iron Age earthworks may be linear fortifications, but irrelevant to our discussion. I have generally disregarded the following: any that are clearly not linear fortifications; any that are within a mile or so of a hill fort; and any that are obviously multiple dykes (that is, say, two banks and three ditches in close succession, or similar). A further example of something that is clearly not a linear fortification is a Roman roadbed (or *agger*). You can often indentify them quite easily because they are too wide, have shallow ditches on both sides, and have a fairly flat profile. I have also ignored a number of short dykes which cut ridges and for which there is no other context.

Were they effective? Apparently so. The Anglo-Saxons, and particularly the Romano-British, kept building them for several centuries. Offa's Dyke seems to be the last big one, built in the 780s AD. That is about 350 years after the first ones were dug. In the case of the Cambridge Dykes, whoever dug them kept building them bigger and bigger. He, or they, clearly believed that they were basically a good idea; and that bigger was better.

Dykes may have contributed significantly to keeping the Anglo-Saxons at bay. The Cambridge dykes may have kept the Romano-British back for a generation. The Wansdyke seems to have kept the West Saxons out of south western England from the Battle of Dyrham in about 577 AD to the Battle of Bradford-on-Avon in 642 or so. That is about 65 years, or two or three generations. Offa's Dyke appears to have been peculiarly successful. It kept the people who spoke Welsh apart from those who spoke English for centuries.

At a lower level they seem to have provided real tactical benefits. An attacker could break into an area, dig a dyke and then defend what he had taken. The opposition were then given a stark choice. They could risk attacking the earthwork, or give up the land that had been seized. The land defended by the dyke would be much easier to defend and much harder to seize back. That might almost have been 'siege warfare'. The earthworks around Chichester seem to show this pattern at the lower tactical levels. The earthworks around Chute and Sidbury Hill, then west towards Amesbury, seem to show it over a wider area. During the First World War, General Rawlinson developed 'bite and hold' tactics on the Western Front. General Plumer used them to advantage in the Third Battle of Ypres (Paschendaele). We seem to see the same pattern in Wiltshire and Hampshire, over a thousand years earlier.

The dykes did, however, go out of use. Anglo-Saxon armies moved by land. The Vikings used ships for strategic, operational and tactical mobility. If they came up against a dyke, they could return to their ships and go somewhere else; even Gaul, if need be! The Anglo-Saxons were initially outmanoeuvred. Their eventual response was to increase the operational mobility of their forces by mounting every man on a horse or pony. They also reduced the Vikings' advantage by building bridges across rivers, as close to the sea as possible. The Vikings could not, or would not, sail past them. They were forced either to attack them, or not use the rivers to penetrate inland. In either case, the need for long linear earthworks was over.

'Where they have been dated, they have been shown to be Iron Age'. Is that true? Perhaps it is, apart from the Cambridge Dykes. And the Bokerly Dyke. And the Wansdyke. And, of course, Offa's Dyke. And any dyke that cuts through a Roman road. And almost any other dyke that has been dated. So, 'where they have been dated, they have been shown to be Iron Age'. Except, that is, where they have actually been dated.

The real reason why all this may come as a surprise is that the dykes have been over-looked by academics for decades. The Lines of Brabant tell us that extensive systems of earthworks can be virtually ignored. Writers have not even noticed that there is an elephant in the room.

14

Conjecture

One day in 2003 I was in the Cambridge Tourist Information Office. I was looking at the local Ordnance Survey map on the wall. It showed some enormous earthworks. They stretched for miles across the countryside. I thought that was odd, because Cambridge is a long way inland. (I now don't know why I thought that was relevant.)

A year or so later I was in Cambridge again. I was driving down the road across the Backs. The Backs were once the water meadows of the River Cam. They are now the grounds of some of the older colleges. I turned left at the bottom across the bridge that takes you into the town centre. The road is called the Fen Causeway. 'Odd', I thought. Even this far inland, the land there was marshy in relatively recent times.

At the time I was working on Salisbury Plain and had a copy of the Ordnance Survey Map of Roman Britain. I noticed that the road from Portchester to Cirencester passed within about ten miles of where I was staying. There was a pronounced kink in the road at the Chute Causeway. A while later I got the local 1:25,000 map, which showed the Chute area. I was on the edge of two 1:50,000 maps (that always happens). The northern sheet showed the Wansdyke, about five miles away. Both the Wansdyke and the Causeway provoked my curiosity.

My brother had a copy of John Morris' 'The Age of Arthur'. It was fascinating. However, it raised more questions than it answered. About then I realised that, for example, we knew almost nothing about what happened in East Anglia, from Boudicca's revolt to the point where it was substantially Anglian. I started looking at the period. I didn't know what the main issue was. I was drawn further and further into the period. Eventually, with some blind alleys and some guidance from some exceptionally able academics, I realised that the key question was not 'who was Arthur?' Neither was it 'what are all these dykes?' It was 'how did post-Roman Britain become Anglo-Saxon England?'

I have been lucky to be able to spend a fair amount of effort looking into that question. It has been wonderful. The English countryside is a joy to behold, at almost any time of year. I have visited many places for the first time. I have occasionally been frozen, soaked, stung and (sun)burnt in the process. But despite that, and sometimes because of that, I have come to love the countryside even more. If this book has piqued your curiosity at all, then get a map; drive into the countryside; get out and walk; and look. You may find something quite interesting. You may find something which I have not. But, best of all, you will find that green and pleasant land.

On almost every day I have been out, I have seen rabbits and hares. On most days I have seen buzzards or kites; four kites together, on one occasion. I have often seen deer. I have seen foxes several times. Moments like that are pure magic and sheer joy. You don't experience them sitting at home reading books or watching TV. If this book makes you do one thing, get out into the countryside and look around you.

This book is intended to answer the question 'how did post-Roman Britain become Anglo-Saxon England?' It does not lay out the argument. It is not intended to be a closely-worded academic treatise. It does not show even a fraction of my reasoning. That would take hundreds of thousands of words and be very boring to read. It is intended to describe my findings. That is, it describes my conjecture: not a guess; not proof. Conjecture is 'an opinion or conclusion based on incomplete information'. The contents of this book are not '*mere* conjecture'. They are tentative conclusions based on extensive, but necessarily incomplete, information. I have not used 'certainly' nor 'must have': we cannot be certain. I have generally used 'did', but am quite explicit about the fact that this is conjecture. Any history of the Dark Ages is conjecture.

At any one point in time, the landscape is real. You can go out and touch it. However, when we look back into history we are in practice talking about conceived, or imagined, landscapes. In a sense, this book has proposed a landscape of fifth to ninth century England, together with a series of events that took place in it. Both that landscape and those events differ from previous views. It is important to realise, however, that *whatever* we think of the landscape and the events, they are to some extent imagined. We cannot really know. For some people that landscape contains a place called Camelot. For many people it is shaped by the writings of Thomas Malory or John Leland. It should also, to my mind, reflect the work of archaeologists such as Pitt Rivers, Cyril Fox and Mortimer Wheeler.

The imagined landscape (almost inevitably) shows some trace of Bede. We should consider Bede not only as a historian (monastic, Anglo-Saxon, and Northumbrian) but also as a geographer. A map in a fairly recent book shows places which Bede mentioned. It exposes a glaring anomaly. It shows incredibly few places in the western half of England. A few of them are most probably correct. Malmesbury Abbey in Wiltshire is one. A few are relatively close to where Bede lived, such as Carlisle. The others are Caerwent, Chester, Bangor (on Dee, near Chester) and Oswestry.

The map is wrong. Bede never mentioned those places at all. He named a place called *Urbs Legionis*, 'the city of the legions', twice (hence possibly Caerwent and Chester). He mentioned *a* place called Bangor. He mentioned the place where King (Saint) Oswald was killed. Bede called that 'Maserfelth' and makes no reference to an 'Oswald's Tree' (Oswestry), or similar. Overall, this tells us two things. Firstly, that whatever we think of the real location of *Urbs Legionis*, etc, very few events described by Bede occurred in the western half of England. But, more importantly here: that the imaginary landscape which puts much of the early history of Northumbria and Mercia on the Welsh borders (in Chester, Bangor on Dee and Oswestry) does not come to us from Bede. It actually comes to us from what historians, typically in the eighteenth and nineteenth centuries, *assumed* that Bede meant.

We need to peel all those assumptions away and get back to what we know. We have some original historical sources, which include Bede. That is: what Bede actually wrote, not what people assume he meant when he wrote it. We have some archaeology. That should include a far more rigorous study of dark age earthworks than has been the case. And we also have geography. That should include much, much better toponymy; and more detailed military terrain analysis. Those three elements create the landscape which I have tried to capture and describe.

In the early fifth century, Roman rule in Britain collapsed. About four centuries later, the Anglo-Saxon wars of conquest came to an end. Most, but not all, of England was under the sway of people who spoke a Germanic language and used the common law.

That is over four hundred years of war. It wasn't continuous. In places, and at times, there was peace for decades. But, writ large, it was the longest and most significant conflict which Britain has ever experienced.

There does seem to have been someone called 'Arthur'. He probably wasn't a king. He was a post-Roman British commander who fought the Germanic foreigners for two or perhaps three decades. He was not the only, and perhaps not the most significant, British commander. His name comes to us, in part, due to Breton romantic poetry; in part due to Welsh epic poetry; and in part due to Plantagenet propaganda.

In a sense, Gildas was right; but in a political rather than a religious sense. That is to say, in terms of how power is brokered, not in terms of theology. In the late fifth century, and perhaps under Arthur, it was possible that the British would eventually win. A century or so later that was unlikely. By the 640s, Wessex was well on the way to breaking the resistance in the south. Northumbria had been united (with a few interruptions) for decades. Mercia was established as a major regional power. British resistance was broken and would never recover. So, when Gildas bemoaned the actions of the post-Roman kings who ruled the British kingdoms in the 530s and 540s, he was pointing to their eventual destruction. He was also pointing to the eventual submergence of the British church. As a cleric of his day (he died about 60 years before the first Anglo-Saxon ruler was baptised) he probably had no insight into that.

When Columbus discovered America in 1492, there was perhaps one generation of lawlessness and untrammelled opportunity. Exploration would continue for centuries. South American gold and silver would make (some) Europeans rich for centuries. But by the 1530s or so most of Latin America had been carved up. Spanish and Portuguese governors had been appointed. Religious missions had been established and churches built. Those Spanish and the Portuguese had just spent more than seven centuries reconquering their own lands from the Moors.

Imagine what it was like to live in a country which had been fought over, on and off, for seven centuries. The frontier moved; mostly in one direction, sometimes in another. Kingdoms rose and fell. Some areas may have been entirely untouched by war for decades, or perhaps entirely. But think also what it meant to be in the Americas in that one generation after 1492. It was a world of unlimited opportunity; the chance to become unbelievably rich, and lord of all you surveyed. But also a good chance of dying a violent death.

Both of those pictures apply, in some ways, to the four centuries of what we have called King Arthur's Wars. War was common, but not continuous nor necessarily widespread. Life was often violent but not always so. From time to time, like in the upper Thames valley after Bedcanford, or the lands just west of the Severn in the early eighth century (when Aethelbald of Mercia conquered much of Chester and Shropshire), there would be a wild, unsettled frontier. There would be land to be had for the taking. But within a generation it was to some extent settled.

Writ large, there was a 'Wild West'; just as there was in what is now the United States. Just as in the United States, the frontier moved westwards over generations. Even before the coming of the railways, people in America were calling the states just east of the Mississippi river the 'Old West'. Similarly, if 'Mercia' did mean 'the marches' and did mean 'the borders of Lindsey', the frontier moved west from the lower Trent, to the Tame, to the Severn, and finally into the Cambrian (Welsh) Mountains where it lies today. And the Cambrian Mountains were a wild frontier from before the times of Offa of Mercia to the times of Edward Plantagenet: about 500 years. Ironically, Edward presented himself as an English king. He imported a British legendary hero (Arthur) from Brittany, a province of France, conscious of his French family name.

It had possibly started in Kent, with Hengest's revolt, but that revolt spread no further. It was a king of Kent who was the first Anglo-Saxon ruler to be baptized. East Anglia also revolted, but had been definitively contained; not least by the settlement of Saxons in Essex. The East Anglians may subsequently have enjoyed a generation or so of prominence after the Battle of Bedcanford. Although Bedcanford established the kingdom of the West Saxons, it may also have allowed the East Anglians to expand into the eastern Midlands. They may have ruled Lindsey for a while, until contained by Mercia. It seems to be no coincidence that the one king of East Anglia to be a major figure (Raedwald, possibly the owner of the Sutton Hoo ship) lived during the generation after Bedcanford.

Essex, conversely, never rebelled. The East Saxons were settled by the Romano-British. They were organised to prevent Anglian encroachment into the lower Thames valley. They did what they were originally asked to do, until (and after) the coming of the Vikings. The Vikings never settled in Essex. The success of the settlement of Essex with (East) Saxons may explain why we know practically nothing of London, Surrey, Hertfordshire and Middlesex. There was no revolt. There was no major war. Over the centuries there was a gradual transition from Roman, and British, to English. It may have been as unremarkable as, say, Birmingham electing its first British Asian lord mayor (in 2002). Over the decades things changed, but no-one particularly noticed. No-one particularly minded.

Sussex did rebel. Like Kent, the South Saxons established their independence. They were contained and thereafter did nothing significant. Except, of course, to live largely at peace within their borders for centuries. For the times, that was a good outcome. The Cerdicings, the Gewisse, may have contributed to bottling the South Saxons up on the Downs. It seems that they then rebelled. However, they were suppressed and booted out of south Hampshire fairly unceremoniously. But the legend of Cerdic lived on. Within a generation or so, the Gewisse had established what we can identify as the origins of Wessex in the upper Thames valley. It would still take three centuries to conquer the rest of south-west England. But, after Bedcanford in 571 AD and particularly Deorham in 577, there was no realistic prospect of them being defeated. Their conquest of the south-west was not inevitable and not easy. It may not have been complete. Cornwall is still quite different today.

Indeed the history of Wessex might have been very different had it not had a powerful neighbour, Mercia, to its north. That may have been a factor in orienting Wessex towards the south and west. The rewards may have been greater (or, maybe, just 'achievable') and the costs less.

Mercia seems to have been lucky in being in the right place (in a remote area a long way from centres of Romano-British power) at the right time. That is, at the moment when the death of its ally Cadwallon of Gwynedd, fighting against Northumbria, led to a power vacuum. Lucky or not, a succession of strong kings and long reigns established Mercia as the dominant power in England for a century or so.

Northumbria's early history is dominated by struggles between Deiran and Bernician leaders. Or so we think now. It was not inevitable that there would be one kingdom called Northumbria. It was not inevitable that the area of the east coast from Hadrian's Wall to the Tweed should now be part of England, nor even Anglo-Saxon. Indeed none of what happened was inevitable, and much of it happened as a result of war.

On the British side, urban society largely collapsed in the fifth and early sixth centuries. We can, however, trace the story of the British from the areas around the major roman cities. The areas around London and Lincoln seem to have been quietly Germanicised. York – *Urbs Legionis* – seems to have fallen in about 607 AD. With that, the men of Elmet were displaced west towards Leeds and then conquered. The province around Cirencester was damaged at the battle of Bedcanford and destroyed at Deorham. The Hwicca may have been the remnants of those people, withdrawn into the Cotswolds and the Wych Wood and eventually becoming a part of Mercia. See Figure 14.1.

It seems that the people around Gloucester had a more significant migration. Gloucester was *Glevum* in Latin. The British in that area seem to have called themselves the 'Glevissig' (or similar). Displaced after Deorham, they migrated into the gentle valleys of south Wales and became the Kingdom of Glamorgan. They took their religion with them. Llandaff is in Glamorgan, and seems to be the last surviving Romano-British bishopric. Ironically, it left a gap for centuries: the Bishopric of Gloucester was only established in 1541 (the present Cathedral was originally built as an abbey church). When the Glevissig migrated, they moved past the kingdom of Gwent. The name 'Gwent' has its origins in the Roman city of *Venta Silures*, the Market of the Silures (a tribe; we could call them the Silurians).

Figure 14.1 Regions of Post-Roman Britain.

Venta Silures is the modern Caerwent. Gwent had the almost unique good fortune of being far enough west that the Anglo-Saxons never conquered it. Caerwent is in Monmouthshire, but in the south-west corner where the place-names are mostly Welsh. The next hamlet is called 'Trewen', a British name. Caerwent is about five miles west of Offa's Dyke.

The most significant of the groups further north along the Welsh border was the kingdom of Powys. We saw in Chapter Ten how it had originally occupied the area around Wroxeter, and was then pushed west into the mountains. Wroxeter was the fourth-largest city in Roman Britain, after London, York and Cirencester. It was bigger than places more familiar to us today, like the former colony at Lincoln and the legionary base at Chester. That, and the good farmland of the upper Severn valley, may account for Powys' relative success in resisting Mercia. It was not destroyed. Although it was moved out of its homeland, it did not go far. It moved neither as far as the Glevissig, nor its neighbours to the north, the kingdom of Gwynedd. We also saw how Gwynedd had probably occupied the Cheshire Plain, but was evicted and ended up on the north Welsh coast around Conway.

In what we now know as England the British survivors were, possibly, the kingdom of Rheged and the *Cornovii*. Rheged seems to have survived in some form into the tenth century in Cumbria. 'Cornwall' seems to mean 'the land of the Corn-Welsh'. 'Corn-' is borrowed from *Cornovii*, the name of the pre-roman tribe who live there. However, *'Cornovii'* is a Latin name. *'Cornus'* is a horn and refers to the shape of the peninsula. It is not Celtic. So the names of some of the post-Roman kingdoms that we can identify tell us something in Latin. Elmet comes from the *Dalmatae*. Glevissig comes from *Glevum*. 'Powys' seems to be derived from a Latin term, *'pagenses'*, meaning 'the countrymen'. Gwent comes from *Venta*. Hwicca possibly comes from *Victores (Iuniores Britanniaci)*. One largely discredited theory suggests that pre-Roman kingdoms survived through the whole of the Roman period. However, the people of *Venta Silures* thought it more important to remember their market (*venta*, a Roman creation) than the fact that they were Silurian, for example. The sole exception in this context is Canterbury and the people called the Cantware (the people called the *Cantii*, or perhaps *Cantiaci*). We can be fairly certain that Kent and the Cantware were generally taken over by Jutes. Kent is exceptional, but the exception proves the rule. The Romano-British thought of themselves as *cives* – citizens of the Roman Empire – foremost. The idea that their ancestors had been had been woad-painted Celtic savages four centuries earlier meant little to them.

There is a large amount of circumstantial evidence. It includes place names, archaeology, historical sources, Welsh poetry and Plantagenet propaganda. It all suggests that Roman-British rule survived until the death of the last commander who had the ability, the knowledge and the strategic vision to keep the Germanic newcomers bottled up in their enclaves along the coast. He is known to us today as Arthur. Within a generation of his death, half a dozen small Germanic kingdoms emerged. About 400 years later, in 927 AD, those kingdoms were finally united into what we now recognise as England.

Arthur was probably not a king. Camelot seems to have been Colchester. Lancelot was a French invention. Guinevere was possibly blond (or may have actually have been a French saint, and irrelevant to the story of Arthur). The story of Arthur as we understand it today is at least in part political propaganda. But in a very real sense it doesn't matter. The Arthurian legends are a part of English history which cannot be uninvented. It is part of what has made England English. It was an important part of developing an overall story. Political scientists would call it a 'grand narrative'. That story put British, Anglo Saxon and Norman ingredients into a big melting pot and produced what (for example) the Elizabethans or the Victorians thought was English.

It does seem that post-Roman forces, which included several *alae* of cavalry and some infantry, survived after the end of Imperial Roman rule. Commanders could coordinate their actions over large areas. That capability seems to have largely disappeared early in the sixth century. Some units, possibly including cavalry, may have survived in some identifiable form into the early seventh century. By then the supply of horses, fodder, recruits and equipment had fallen apart. These things may have fallen apart for political rather than military reasons. There was no-one in overall control. As logistics fell apart, the ability to move forces over long distances fell apart as well. Without some form of organised food supply, armies cannot move more than about three days' journey from their homes.

We have looked at a significant period of British history, of which much has been written. Much of that story was made up; especially anything about King Arthur. This book has tried to correct that. It develops some major new findings, largely by looking from a new perspective. That perspective comes from looking at the landscape and the period with a military and a technical eye. That is because, for this period, the only useful record of those wars is written in the landscape.

Researching this book benefitted enormously from cheap, or free, access to mapping. Around the beginning of the work in 2003, digital production techniques had made paper Ordnance Survey maps (particularly in 1:25,000 scale) better and, effectively, cheaper. For most of my research I had relatively cheap 1:50,000 digital mapping of the British mainland on my laptop. Later on I had some 1:25,000 digital mapping as well. I could access some historic map collections in libraries. By the end of my work, many historic Ordnance Survey maps were available on line. That made the process much easier and faster.

To read the relevance of the landscape you generally need the skills of a soldier. It is not just the ability to read a map. Many people can do that, although some just can't. You have to look at the landscape, and the map, and see what a soldier saw. You need to understand the landscape of the time, and what a soldier of the time made of that.

The dykes are a major part of that. More important than the dykes, however, is why they were built. They were dug in a given place for a purpose. Understanding that purpose, particularly at the theatre or strategic level, tells us a lot about what was happening at the time. That is particularly true when you start to integrate individual stretches of earthworks across whole counties or regions.

It is also important to see how the dykes developed. In some ways the engineering deteriorated. After the Chiltern dykes, we rarely see anything laid out with Roman precision. But the West Saxons, and the Deirans, seem to have grasped how to use them offensively, using 'bite and hold' tactics.

Nobody seems to have looked at all of the earthworks in England holistically before. Some archaeologists, particularly Sir Cyril Fox in the 1920s, researched some of them.

Fox proposed what might be called a 'Mercian School' of earthworks. In the 1960s the archaeologists of the Ordnance Survey were broadly aware to some extent of how many, how widely distributed, and how big the dykes were. Unfortunately, they never followed that up with a systematic survey. In conducting this research, the big surprise to me was not the identity of Arthur, but the dykes.

The responsibilities of the Archaeology Division of the Ordnance Survey were transferred to the Royal Commissions for Historic Monuments for England, Scotland and Wales in 1983. Any knowledge of the geospatial distribution of long linear earthworks throughout England seems to have disappeared in that reorganisation. The Survey's 1966 edition of 'Britain in the Dark Ages' was never revised. In the 1920s, and through to the 1960s, archaeologists seem to have known that there was a nation-wide network of dikes. That awareness seems to have then been lost.

This book tells a story which is quite different from what is generally accepted. Having said which, it is hard to know what is generally accepted, because there is no single version of the story. What we can do, however, is to take the general theme from respected works such as the Oxford History series and compare it. It is important to discriminate between differences of fact and differences of interpretation. In this period, there are very few facts. A great deal comes down to interpretation. In this section we shall look at where the contents of the previous chapters vary from currently accepted knowledge. We will do no more than summarise the major issues here. More detail is at Appendix II.

Firstly, the dykes. Most works simply ignore them. A very good book was published recently by a well-respected historian. A glance at the index tells us that he didn't mention 'earthworks', 'dykes', the Wansdyke or the Cambridge dikes at all. Offa's dyke got precisely one short mention. That is entirely typical, and it is staggering. It is worse than writing a book on Roman Britain and not mentioning Hadrian's Wall. Academics clearly don't think that that aspect of the physical record is important. That is despite the fact that many of the largest dykes were without doubt built in the Dark Ages. None of the books in the bibliography treat the dykes in any detail. That means that they overlook the largest and most significant class of evidence about the transition from Roman Britain to Anglo-Saxon England. That means that they all need to be substantially, or radically, revised.

Secondly, Christianity. Bede wrote a book called 'An Ecclesiastical History of the English People'. It is exactly what the title says. But it is not 'a history of England', nor 'a history of post-Roman Britain'. It is definitely not an ecclesiastical history of post-Roman Britain. For our purposes, that has two effects. The first is to almost totally ignore the history, and specifically the ecclesiastical history, of the British. We therefore tend to overlook the fact that Britain had been Christianised, to some extent, decades before the end of Roman Imperial rule. The second effect is that much of Bede's work is irrelevant here.

Perhaps just as important is the alleged Rescript of Honorius. There are copies of the *Notitia Dignatatum*. They exist. Yet Zosimus did not actually say that there was a Rescript. We certainly do not have a copy of it. The *Notitia* points to a substantial garrison in Roman Britain after 410 AD. Yet writers chose to believe in a mythical Rescript. It defies common sense. If we apply Occam's Razor, we can confidently say that there is no good evidence that the Roman Army left Britain in or about 410.

With regard to the progress of the wars of conquest, some writers would agree with much of the broad scope of this book. They would find the treatment of the dykes novel. They would, however, probably find two areas challenging. The first is the issue of Wessex and its origins in the Solent. The key problem, to my mind, is place-name evidence. It is entirely credible to think that the Latin *Sorviodunum* became [Old] Sarum, and we know by the eleventh century Salisbury was called Salesberia, or similar. We also know that the battle in 552 AD was at a place called Searobyrg, or similar. But there is no positive link between the battle and Sarum. When looking for the site of the battle of Beranbyrh, writers and academics identified it with a hill-fort. They found Barbury Castle near Swindon. That was convenient, because Swindon is relatively close to Sarum.

There is a lot of good reason for placing Cerdic in the area of Hampshire and the Solent. But beyond that, the traditional story of Wessex seems to raise more problems than it answered. Probably the biggest is the Wansdyke. The Wansdyke faces north. The attackers were in the upper Thames Valley, and Sarum is well south of the Wansdyke. Then there are the Pinner and the Chiltern Dykes. They face south east and east. And the best site for Bedcanford seems to be Bedford. Wibbandun seems to be associated with Whipsnade. It is on the flanks of the Chiltern Dykes and on a route that would lead to Bedford.

The other aspect of the story of Wessex which writers would probably disagree with is the dating of the conquest of the far west. Chapter 12 sees it not being complete, as far as Devon, until the early to middle ninth century. Many writers have put it as early as the early seventh century. They place the Battle of Beandun in 614 AD at Bindon near Seaton in Devon, rather than at Bampton on the upper Thames. This story depends on three pieces of evidence, two of them being ecclesiastical. The first is Sherborne Abbey. We discussed the issue of its charter and its bishopric in 671. The charter seems to be a fake. Sherborne probably didn't become a bishopric until much later.

Secondly there is Saint Boniface, who lived from roughly 680 to 755 AD. According to his biographer, who was an *English* monk, Boniface: (a) was born in Crediton; (b) entered holy orders in an abbey at Exeter; (c) had an English name before being renamed Boniface; and (d) his Prior also had an English name. All four facts may be true. If so, it seems that Crediton and Exeter, both in Devon, were part of Wessex before 680 or so. There is, however, doubt about all four statements. The fact that his biographer was an English monk raises suspicions. But even if (a), (b), (c) and (d) are all true, it does not prove that Devon was part of Wessex in the late seventh century. All it tells us is that Exeter had an abbey in the late seventh century, and that some people with English names lived in what we now call Devon. Well, some people with Asian names now live in Milton Keynes. Milton Keynes is not currently part of Bangladesh.

As we have seen, Bede does not mention Sherborne. He also does not mention Saint Boniface. Yet they were contemporaries. Bede corresponded with other clerics across much of western Europe. He was active, and writing, until weeks (if not days) before he died on 26 May, 735 AD. Boniface had been appointed Archbishop of Mainz (with responsibility for the whole of Germany) by Pope Gregory the Third in 732. A cleric from Britain appointed archbishop? Saint Wilibrord was an Anglo-Saxon monk and Boniface's former mentor. Wilibrord, like Boniface, also preached on the Continent. Bede mentioned Wilibrord at least six times in his writings. It seems most unlikely that Bede did not know of Boniface. The truth is probably blindingly simple: Bede wrote an ecclesiastical history of the English people, and Boniface was not, in fact, English.

The third major piece of evidence pointing towards an earlier conquest of the south west is the battle of Hengestdun in 838 AD. Several sites have been suggested, the most prominent being Hingston Down in Cornwall. Conveniently, it is near the western end of the enclave of English place names around Callington, just west of the Tamar. The story is that the Vikings brought their ships up the Tamar to a landing at Danescombe (near Calstock). They marched the three miles or so up to Hingston Down on the slopes of Kit Hill. They then met the British and fought against the West Saxons there.

I really doubt it. I have been there. My mother used to live about a mile from Danescombe. Vikings could quite possibly get their ships that far up the Tamar, but not much further. The first crossing was at Gunnislake, about another three or four miles further up the river (but only about a mile and a half away in a straight line). But that is where the story falls apart. To reach Kit Hill the Vikings would have to march west. The West Saxons would have come from across the Tamar. That is, from the east. The Vikings would have to fight with their ships behind the West Saxons. Now, you can think of all sorts of possible scenarios. For example, a Wessex warband returning east towards the Tamar being caught by British and Vikings, who had got between them and the river. How amazingly convenient that the Vikings were sailing past just as the West Saxons were raiding! The real issue, however, is that if the battle was at Hingston Down, the Vikings' ships were at considerable risk. They would have been beached ten miles up the Tamar, and just across the river from West Saxon Devon. It is hard to believe that Vikings would do that.

The name 'Danescombe' probably means 'wooded valley'; nothing to do with Norsemen. 'Hingston Down' is probably named after a family called Hingston. The family comes from south Devon, about ten miles away. So 'Hingston Down' near Callington in Cornwall is probably totally irrelevant. It assumes that Hingston Down was called Hengestdun in 838 AD. Why on earth would a hill ten miles inland be called after a Jute who had died almost four centuries earlier? The nearest Jutish settlements were on the Isle of Wight (or perhaps the New Forest), over a hundred miles east. The name of the site proposed in Chapter 12, Hengistbury Head, may be wrong. But at least the site is on the coast and only ten miles from the Isle of Wight.

You can add the details of St Boniface's early life, the apparent history of Sherborne, and the battle of Hengestdun together in a certain way. If you do, you can easily see

Dorset, Devon and Somerset being conquered by the West Saxons as early as the seventh century. If, however, you look at place name evidence and the dykes; and then hang that evidence around the historical background; a very different picture emerges.

We have been largely concerned with the wars of Anglo-Saxon conquest. Some academics and writers doubt that Roman Britain became England through a process of wars at all, and cite two major pieces of evidence. They are related: population change and language. Most people in England today think of themselves as English and speak English as their first language. War alone does not explain that. These issues are not entirely central to the subject of this book, but deserve some discussion.

When British settlers first arrived in New Zealand, they were greatly outnumbered by Maoris. Today New Zealanders of European descent greatly outnumber the Maoris, and the Maoris speak English. Many place names have Maori origins, but very few other words spoken in New Zealand are of Maori origin. Much the same applies in Australia. The few aboriginal words tend to refer to things largely or exclusively of aboriginal origins, such as 'Didgeridoo', 'Koala' and 'Kangaroo'. These processes, and others, have been studied by anthropologists. They can tell us a lot about what seems to have happened in Dark Age Britain. The process largely comes down to migration, breeding and war.

In the case of New Zealand, the current picture reflects quite a lot of migration; some war; and the fact that European settlers used to breed faster than the Maoris. The Europeans won the wars. For Dark Age Britain, the historical record indicates a lot of fighting, which the Anglo-Saxons generally won. The issues of migration and breeding are less clear.

Geneticists have done some very detailed research into the origin of the English population. Two statistics stand out. The first refers to the absolute number of migrants. Most estimates point to between ten thousand and a hundred thousand migrants from Denmark and Germany in total, over a period of two or three hundred years. One estimate has the number of migrants as high as two hundred and fifty thousand. The native, British population was probably about one million, but perhaps as high as two million. Even if there were as many as two hundred and fifty thousand immigrants, that is only about a thousand a year on average. Critically, however, the second statistic relates to mitochondrial DNA. That is a marker of maternal origin. One particular strain of mitochondrial DNA is characteristic of Denmark and northern Germany. Almost none of it is present in the English population today. In very simple terms, tens (and possibly hundreds) of thousands of Anglo-Saxon men came to Britain: but very few women.

Some did. One Anglo-Saxon skeleton has been shown to be that of a woman who was born in Denmark and came to England after puberty. Bone and teeth analysis can tell us such things quite clearly. Overall, however, it seems that almost all the migrants were male. Therefore they must have interbred with British women.

An entirely separate strand of research involved a computer simulation of demographics. It explored how quickly a minority population can become the majority, by out-breeding the natives. The thinking behind the computer simulation was quite compelling. It presumed that there was a dominant group of higher-status people, mostly males and mostly warriors. It assumed that their offspring would identify themselves as belonging to that group, rather than assimilating into the majority. It also assumed that higher-status people would (on average) produce more children than the lower-status, native population. It also assumed that there was very little intermarriage.

Quite a lot of evidence underpinned the simulation. For example, it looked at the difference in birth rates between native and migrant populations. In New Zealand *today*, the indigenous Maoris have birth rate about 1.3 times higher than people of European descent. Often, however, higher-status migrants have a higher birth rate. We can be fairly sure that there was a difference in status between the initial migrant, warrior Anglo-Saxons and native Britons. Skeletons show quite marked differences in body size between adult males buried with weapons and high-value grave goods and those buried without weapons and goods. That persisted for several generations, from the fifth century into the seventh. Body size is typically a result of better diet, which reflects higher status.

The study also considered intermarriage. If there is little intermarriage, high-status migrants remain identifiably separate, and that status remains desirable. An Anglo-Saxon wouldn't want his daughter to marry a Briton, but a British girl might be quite keen to marry an Anglo-Saxon. If she did, any children would think of themselves as Anglo-Saxon. So any intermarriage that did take place would strongly favour Anglo-Saxon numbers.

Intermarriage rates can be surprisingly low, even where there is no apparent conflict between the different parts of a society. For example, the southern part of Pembrokeshire has historically been called 'little England beyond Wales'. It was settled in Norman times with Flemish merchants and peasants. They often describe themselves as English, not Welsh, even today. They maintained, and surreptitiously maintain, a separate cultural identity from the native Welsh. There has been no fighting between the populations for centuries. Yet, throughout the whole of the 20th century, the intermarriage rate was just four per cent. And, as we have just seen, any intermarriage in the Dark Ages would strongly favour Anglo-Saxon numbers.

The computer simulation looked at how fast a higher-status minority, with little intermarriage but a higher birth rate, could become a majority (that is, become more than 50% of the population). The results were quite compelling. Depending on the circumstances, it could be as little as five generations. That is not much more than a century. It could happen within fifteen generations very easily. That is roughly the period between the end of Imperial Roman rule and the reign of King Alfred. We may never know how quickly it happened in England. However, perhaps surprisingly, the simulation suggested that migration was not the dominant factor. More migration would make a difference, but faster reproduction would have a greater impact in the long run.

Much of this discussion describes how the population came to be, or at least think of itself, as Anglo-Saxon rather than British. It does not explain how it came to speak

English. Some of that is probably related to status and identity. High-status people tend to speak their own language and insist that their children do. However, the twenty or perhaps thirty thousand Norman immigrants didn't manage to impose their language on the English. They did introduce a lot of legal words (such as 'legal' and 'jury'). Everyday words remained Anglo-Saxon, such as 'house', 'cow' and 'plough'.

What seems to have happened in Dark Age England is a combination of population growth and status. The details are concealed by the process of writing. Chaucer wrote his Canterbury Tales in the everyday English in the fourteenth century. Until then English was written only in official, clerical and legal documents. It did not necessarily reflect the way that everyday people spoke. Other evidence suggests that, for example, Cornish largely died out (without much English migration into Cornwall) as late as the twelfth and thirteenth centuries. Gaelic largely died out in Ireland (with very little immigration) by the nineteenth century. By analogy, everyday language in England may have slowly become more and more Anglicised. Fewer and fewer people would have spoken Celtic languages. There would have been fewer and fewer Celtic words in everyday use, right through to the fourteenth century. We simply would not know, however, because the everyday language was not written down.

There were many battles and much slaughter. There is no real evidence of extermination and expulsion. There is evidence of intermarriage, even at the highest levels. The names of Cerdic and Caedwalla of Wessex, and Caedbeth of Lindsey, tell us so. The disappearance of the British language was not the result of the disappearance of the British, but the total political and economic takeover which the English achieved. Ironically, an Anglo-Saxon standing on the banks of the Tamar in the mid-ninth century might be entirely proud to be an Anglo-Saxon, and be unable to speak anything other than English. But, after 15 generations, he might be as little as perhaps 0.003% (that is, $(\frac{1}{2})^{15}$) Germanic by descent.

Is all this right? Is it true? Are the contents of this book anything more than the products of an overactive imagination? The answer, in part, depends on our understanding of 'right' and 'true'. What we know about what happened in the past generally comes to us from history and archaeology. I have looked at both disciplines and interpreted the evidence. In every case I have not tried to find things which are true beyond all reasonable doubt. I have tried to find things which are probably true, in the sense of 'more likely than unlikely'. I have had to come to a judgement over that, in a number of cases and for several reasons.

Several times, particularly during fieldwork (and hence looking at real, physical evidence) I found that my initial assumptions were wrong. That caused me to completely re-shape important parts of the conjecture, particularly in Hampshire and in East Yorkshire. I formed hypotheses and tested them. Some were wrong, typically because a dyke doesn't face the way I thought it would. Sometimes I had formed the wrong mental picture of what had happened. Getting out into the country and looking at the landscape told me that it couldn't be right. Sometimes the resulting picture was just too complex. Occam's Razor told me that there was probably a simpler truth.

In a remarkable number of cases, however, my research seems to have demonstrated that the basic idea is correct. In the early stages of my research I looked for dykes on Ordnance Survey maps. I could soon predict where I would find them. I could find them surprisingly quickly. In some cases there would be nothing on the 1:50,000 scale map, but something turned up on the 1:25,000 version. After a while I found that my work was developing along several interlinked branches. One was how and where the dykes were sited. Another was their design and construction. A third was the use of place-name evidence. More importantly, another was how the wars of Anglo Saxon conquest were fought. In some ways the dykes are not particularly important. On a canvas the size of England, they are a small detail. What is more important are the tactical, operational and strategic reasons as to why anyone would dig dykes at those places.

There are limits to this method, however. Not all aspects of this conjecture will be right. I believe that it is the best interpretation of the evidence I have found. I have looked at some of the old evidence in a different way. I have found some new evidence. I am quite prepared to interpret further evidence, and adjust my findings if appropriate. The whole field, and not just my findings, should be considered to be dynamic.

There is no absolute proof. In this period, archaeology and history cannot provide any.

Some people will not believe this. They are welcome to produce further evidence, which we can then consider. But let us reflect, for a moment, on the history of witchcraft. In the early seventeenth century a Royal Commission looked at subject and came to a deeply insightful observation. In every accusation of witchcraft, you should look first of all at the motivation of the accuser.

⌒—⌒

I would like to leave the reader with a thought. There is an elephant in the room. There is: it is there. There is an earthwork within about 40 miles of wherever you are, if you live in England. You may not believe that the elephant is like the one I have described. That is fine; but please do not just ignore it. If it is not an elephant that I have described, what is it? If these are not fifth- to eighth-century earthworks, what are they? We are reasonably sure that many of them – the ones which have been excavated and dated – are fifth- to eighth-century fortifications. So why do we ignore them?

Appendix I

Arthur and Cerdic

We know very little about either Arthur or Cerdic. They appear to have been contemporaries. Arthur seems to have been a Romano-British commander. He fought against Germanic warriors at Badon in perhaps 509 AD, or perhaps as late as 517. He died at, or after, a battle at Camlann about 20 years later, so perhaps in the period from the 520s to the 530s.

Cerdic seems to have rebelled against the British in 508 AD or so. He established himself as a ruler in about 519, took over the Isle of Wight in 530 and died in 534. Cerdic probably wasn't Germanic. His name seems to be Celtic. He is definitively associated with the south coast around Portsmouth.

A third character to consider is Aelle. He was Saxon. He seems to have arrived in Britain, on the south coast, in about 477 AD. He fought against the British in perhaps 485 and burnt Pevensey in 490.

All these dates are questionable. We have generally assumed that dates are accurate to within about five years or so. In this early part of the period the dating is likely to be less, rather than more, accurate. So perhaps something more than 'about five years or so' would be appropriate. Perhaps ten years?

Addressing all these strands and extrapolating, the picture looks like this. Arthur was the senior British commander. Aelle led a revolt of the South Saxon *Foederati* in about 485 AD. The British, perhaps led by Arthur, managed to bottle him up in the eastern part of the South Downs, as described in Chapter Five. Arthur installed a British leader, Ceretic (Cerdic) to keep a watch over the South Saxons, probably based in the Saxon shore fort at Portchester Castle.

A few years later, in about 508 AD, Cerdic revolted and seized much of the area astride the Solent. The population of Winchester held out against him. That may have been the same year as the Battle of Badon. Cerdic rebelled whilst Arthur was campaigning elsewhere. If so, Arthur would have felt that Cerdic had betrayed him.

It took several years for the British to organise and conduct a counteroffensive. Arthur may have led them. They threw Cerdic and his forces out of the New Forest area, west of the Solent. In about 530 AD they threw him out of the area east of the Solent. Cerdic fled to the Isle of Wight, where he died. It is tempting to think that he and Arthur died in the same year at (or as a result of) the same battle: at Camlann, wherever that may be.

If you read the events that way, Cerdic sounds much like another character of whom we know almost nothing: Mordred. Mordred was Arthur's nemesis in the Arthurian legends. The name 'Mordred' seems to be derived from the Latin adjective '*moderatus*', meaning 'temperate' or 'moderate'. It isn't a name, so much as a soubriquet or perhaps nickname. It implies a 'wise adviser', or similar. So, Cerdic was a British warrior who had been one of Arthur's trusted advisors. He betrayed Arthur by rebelling around the time of the Battle of Badon.

Mordred comes to us through the Welsh Annals: a British source. Cerdic comes to us through the Anglo-Saxon chronicle, a Germanic source. That may explain why he appears to be two different people. Mordred is described in various Welsh and medieval sources as having two sons; always two. Cerdic is described as having two kinsmen, possibly nephews, known to us as Stuf and Wihtgar. Cerdic's son and heir is described as being Cynric, Cynric is, however, also described as being the son of Creoda, an otherwise unknown son of Cerdic.

In Chapter Six we saw how the Gewisse claimed their legitimacy as being the heirs to Cerdic. We also noted a big discontinuity between the activities of Cerdic on the south coast and Cynric and his son, Ceawlin, in the Thames Basin.

All this suggests that:

a.   Cerdic and Mordred are the same person.
b.   Mordred (or Cerdic) had two sons, called something like Stuf and Wihtgar.
c.   Cynric was not related to Cerdic (or Mordred); or, if so, not closely.
d.   The various references in the Anglo-Saxon Chronicle to Cynric being with Cerdic in the period before 530 AD were largely invented. The purpose was to give Cynric and his successors legitimacy through apparent descent from Cerdic.

This is conjecture.

Appendix II

Contention

This Appendix lists some of the more significant differences between the description of events given in 'King Arthur's Wars' and the previously accepted view. That 'previously accepted view' is based largely on the Oxford History of England. This Appendix does not attempt to prove any one issue. It simply lists some of the issues on each side of the discussion and makes some comment. In this period there is no real proof.

In the end, readers will make up their own minds as to which is generally true. That will probably depend on which overall version of the Anglo-Saxon wars of conquest is the most convincing.

Ser	Approx. Date	Issue	Commonly Accepted View	King Arthur's Wars	Comment
(a)	(b)	(c)	(d)	(e)	(f)
1.	409 AD	The Romans lost control of Britain	Dependant on the alleged 'Rescript of Honorius' (Zosimus). In addition, Bede wrote that the Romans lost control of Britain 'after the sack of Rome' (in 410 AD)	There is no good evidence for such a rescript. So there is no firm date for the end of Roman rule. However, it seems that the Imperial government stopped sending officials to govern Britain about this time	Zosimus' remarks about Honorius and Bruttium cannot be relied on in this context. See also 435 AD, below
2.	Early 5th Century	*Notitia Dignatatum*	Cannot be correct, because the Roman Army left Britain in 409 AD or so	Correct, and generally accurate into perhaps the early 420s AD	
3.	418 AD	Roman Treasury	Unclear	The Imperial authorities removed all reserves of coinage from provincial treasuries in Britain	Interpretation of an entry in the Anglo-Saxon chronicle for 418 AD
4.	435 AD	Anglo-Saxon Chronicle: Gothic siege	This is an incorrect entry for 410 AD and the siege, and sack, of Rome.	The entry is partly correct, but the siege was of Narbonne and unsuccessful. The correct date was probably 436 AD. The Romans may well have 'lost control of Britain' soon after this date (see ser. 1).	It is unlikely that the date in the Anglo-Saxon Chronicle was wrong by as much as 25 years. (Most other datable events are much more accurate)
5.	Mid 5th Century	Origins of Gwynedd	A Celtic tribe named for the Roman region of *Venedotia* (in Wales)	Named after Cunedda. Simplest explanation.	
6.	Late 5th Century	Essex	Essex was conquered by Saxons	Essex was settled with Saxons by the Romano-British.	Extensive place-name evidence. No evidence of conquest

Ser	Approx. Date	Issue	Commonly Accepted View	King Arthur's Wars	Comment
(a)	(b)	(c)	(d)	(e)	(f)
7.	Late 5th – early 6th Centuries	Camelot	South Cadbury, because of proximity to River Cam and folk legend	Colchester (Roman *Camulodunum*). Simplest explanation	John Leland considered South Cadbury to have been Camelot in 1542
8.	509 AD	Battle at Badon	Bath	Barton; and probably a Barton near Cambridge. The outcome was a major reason for building the Cambridge dikes	Bath makes no strategic or operational sense
9.	Early 6th Century	Cerdic and Cynric	Hampshire	Hampshire and then the Thames Basin	See also Appendix One
10.	After 534 AD	Wihtgarabyrg	Carisbrooke, Isle of Wight	Near Wippingham, Isle of Wight. The toponymy is much closer	
11.	552 AD	Battle of Searobyrg	Old Sarum (Roman *Sorviodunum*). Became 'Seresburie' in medieval English	St Albans, in the context of: the Pinner dykes; Beranbyrg as Berinhsill; Wibbandun being near Whipsnade; the Chiltern dykes; earthworks near Luton; and the battle of Bedcanford	'Searobyrg' may simply mean 'a walled town', or similar
12.	556 AD	Battle at Beranbyrg	Barbury Castle (near Swindon)	Berins Hill (just north of Goring on Thames)	
13.	577 AD	Battle of Deorham	Dyrham in Gloucestershire	Close to the Derry Brook north east of Swindon.	The hill fort at Dyrham was not called Dyrham in historic times
14.	601 AD	Battle at Catraeth	Catterick (Roman *Cataractonium*)	Near the Catrael (Scottish Borders, south of Hawick). Phonetically closer	

Ser	Approx. Date	Issue	Commonly Accepted View	King Arthur's Wars	Comment
(a)	(b)	(c)	(d)	(e)	(f)
15.	607 AD	Battle of *Urbs Legionis*	Chester	York	If the battle were at Chester, then Elmet would have been bypassed and left far in the Northumbrians' rear as they marched across the Pennines
16.	607 AD	Abbey at Bangor	Bangor on Dee, near Wrexham and hence close to Chester (about 5 miles east of Wat's Dyke)	'Bangor' is simply a British word for 'fenced enclosure'. There may have been several Bangors nearer to York	There were probably many Bangors in post-Roman Britain, but virtually none have survived in England. There are several in Wales
17.	614 AD	Battle at Beandun	Bindon near Seaton in Devon	Bampton on the Thames near Lechlade. Bindon is generally much too far west	Bampton is more appropriate for a king of Wessex fighting against Hwicca
18.	634 AD	Battle of Heavenfield	Near Hadrian's Wall, north of Hexham	Near Slack in the Pennines. Toponymy closer	Slack is more appropriate for a king of Gwynedd invading Northumbria
19.	642 AD	Battle of Maesfeld	Oswestry ('Oswald's Tree'?)	Mexborough near Rotherham. Toponymy closer. Masbrough is another possibility	Mexborough more appropriate for a king of Mercia invading Northumbria
20.	658 AD	Advance to the River Parrett	Cenwalh of Wessex chased the British as far as the Parrett after the battle of *ad Peornum*	That does not demonstrate that Cenwalh could hold the land so far west	An advance to the Parrett at such and early date ignores earthworks such as the Bokerley Dike and Combs Ditch (near Blandford in Dorset)

Ser (a)	Approx. Date (b)	Issue (c)	Commonly Accepted View (d)	King Arthur's Wars (e)	Comment (f)
21.	733 AD	Battle of Somerton	Somerton, former county town of Somerset	Somerton in Oxfordshire. Extensive earthworks	Oxfordshire is more appropriate for a king of Mercia invading Wessex. Somerset would be strategically very difficult if the border between Mercia and Wessex remained on the Thames (cf battles at Burford in 752 and Kempsford in 802)
22.	823 AD	Battle of Ellandun	Wilton near Salisbury	Ullenhall or Hallend near Redditch in Worcestershire. Toponymy much closer	
23.	823 AD	Battle at Gafulford.	Camelford in Cornwall. The poet John Milton suggested that 'Gafulford' was Camelford	A ford over the River Yeo, near Yeovil in Somerset. The River Yeo or Ivel was originally called the 'Gifle', 'Gaful' or similar	Camelford in Cornwall is generally much too far west
24.	838 AD	Battle at Hengestdun	Hingston Down in Cornwall	At or near Hengistbury Head in Dorset	Hingston Hill is generally much too far west

Perhaps the biggest differences relate to the origins of Wessex. Annexes A and B show the 'previously held' view and the revised view, respectively. Shown (carto)graphically, the Edwardian view makes little sense. Note that the arrows indicate the sequence of events, and not necessarily the routes taken.

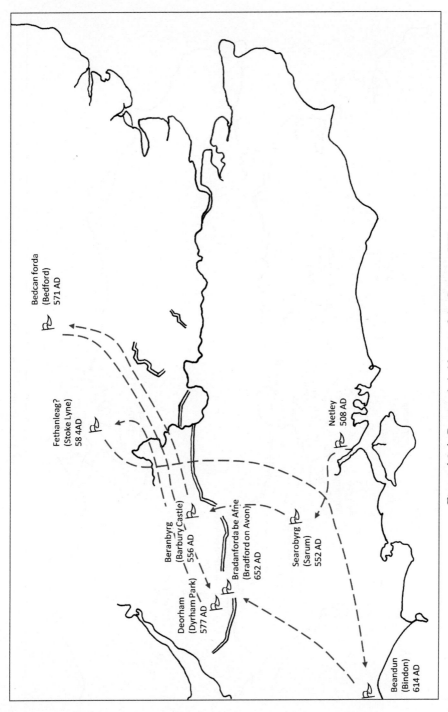

Bedcan forda
(Bedford)
571 AD

Fethanleag?
(Stoke Lyne)
58 4AD

Netley
508 AD

Beranbyrg
(Barbury Castle)
556 AD

Bradanforda be Afne
(Bradford on Avon)
652 AD

Searobyrg
(Sarum)
552 AD

Deorham
(Dyrham Park)
577 AD

Beandun
(Bindon)
614 AD

Figure A2.A Previously held view of the Origins of Wessex.

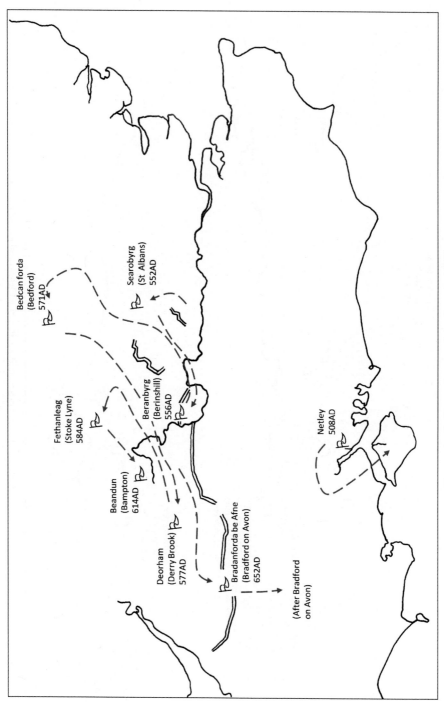

Figure A2.B Revised view of the Origins of Wessex.

Bibliography

Alcock, Leslie, *Economy, Society and Warfare among the Britons and Saxons* (Cardiff, University of Wales Press, 1987)

Alcock, Leslie, *Bede, Eddius and the Forts of the North Britons* The Jarrow Lecture, 1988 (Leicester, The Vaughan Archaeological and Historical Society, 1988)

Alcock, Leslie, *Arthur's Britain. History and Archaeology AD 367-634* (London, Penguin 1971)

Ashley, Mike, *A Brief History of King Arthur* (London, Constable and Robinson, 2005)

Bassett, S., *The Origin of the Anglo-Saxon Kingdoms* (London, Leicester University Press, 1989)

Bede [The Venerable], *The Ecclesiastical History of the English People* (Oxford, Oxford University Press, 1994)

Bishop, M. C. and Coulston, J. C. N., *Roman Military Equipment from the Punic Wars to the Fall of Rome* (Oxford, Oxbow Books, 2nd Edition 2006)

Bowen, H. C. and Eagles, B. N. (eds), *The Archaeology of the Bokerley Dyke* (London, HMSO, 1990)

Cameron, Kenneth (ed), *Place Name Evidence for Anglo-Saxon Invasion and Scandinavian Settlements* (Nottingham, The English Place Name Society, 1975)

Campbell, James (ed), *The Anglo-Saxons* (London, Penguin, 1991)

Castleden, Rodney, *King Arthur. The Truth Behind the Legend* (London, Routledge, 2000)

Codrington, Thomas, *Roman Roads in Britain* (London, The Sheldon Press, 1928)

Colgrave, Bertram and Mynors, R. A. B. (eds), *Bede's Ecclesiastical History* (Oxford, Clarendon Press, 1969)

Cronk, K. A., *Journey Along the Roman Ridge: Explaining the Purpose of South-West Yorkshire's Ancient Dykes* (Rotherham, Clifton and Wellgate Local History Group, 2004)

Dark, Petra, *The Environment of Britain in the First Millennium AD* (London, Gerald Duckworth and Co, 2000)

Divine, David, *The North West Frontier of Rome* (London, Macdonald and Co, 1969)

Dumville, David, *History and Legend* in History, Vol 62 (1977), pp 173-92

Dumville, David and Keynes, Simon (eds) *The Anglo-Saxon Chronicle Collaborative Edition* (Cambridge, D. S. Brewer, 1983)

Dumville, David N., *Britons and Anglo-Saxons in the Early Middle Ages* (Aldershot, Ashgate Publishing Ltd, 1993)

John, Eric, *Reassessing Anglo-Saxon England* (Manchester, Manchester University Press, 1996)

Fisher, D. J. V., *The Anglo-Saxon Age c 400-1042* (London, Longman, 1973)

Fleming, Robin, *Britain After Rome* (London, Penguin, 2011)

Frere, Sheppard, *Britannia. A History of Roman Britain* (London, Book Club Associates, 1974)

Geoffrey of Monmouth, *The History of the Kings of Britain* (London, Penguin Books, 1966)

Halsall, Guy, *Warfare and Society in the Barbarian World, 450-900* (London, Routledge, 2003)

Higham, N. J., *Gildas, Roman Walls and British Dykes* in Cambridge Mediaeval Celtic Studies, Vol 22 (1991), pp363-72

Higham, Nicholas, *Rome, Britain and the Anglo-Saxons* (London, British Archaeological Society Ltd, 1992)

Higham, N. J., *The English Conquest. Gildas and Britain in the Fifth Century* (Manchester, Manchester University Press, 1994)

Higham, N. J. (ed), *Britons in Anglo-Saxon England* (Woodbridge, Suffolk, The Boydell Press, 2007)

Higham, Nicholas J. and Ryan, Martin J. (eds), *Place Names, Language and the Anglo-Saxon Landscape* (Woodbridge, Suffolk, The Boydell Press, 2007)

Gelling, Margaret and Cole, Ann, *The Landscape of Place-Names* (Stamford, Shaun Tyas, 2000)

Haden, D. B. (ed), *Dark Age Britain* (London, Methuen and Co, 1956)

Hill, David, *An Atlas of Anglo-Saxon England* (Oxford, Blackwell Publishers, 1992)

Hills, Catherine, *Blood of the British. From Ice Age to Norman Conquest* (London, Hamlyn, 1986)

Hills, Catherine, *Origins of the English* (London, Gerald Duckworth and Co Ltd, 2003)

Holmes, Michael, *King Arthur: A Military History* (London, Cassell, 1998)

Ingram, James (trans), *The Anglo-Saxon Chronicle* (The Dodo Press, undated) [2007]

Lambert, Malcolm, *Christians and Pagans. The Conversion of Britain from Alban to Bede* (London, Yale University Press, 2010)

Laycock, Stuart, *Britannia, The Failed State* (Stroud, The History Press, 2008)

Lewis, M. J. T., *Surveying Instruments of Greece and Rome* (Cambridge, Cambridge University Press, 2009)

Major, Albany and Burrow, Edward J, *The Mystery of Wansdyke* (Cheltenham, Ed. J. Burrow and Co, 1926)

Malim, Tim et al, *New Evidence on the Cambridgeshire Dykes and Worsted Street Roman Road* in Proceedings of the Cambridge Antiquarian Society. Volume LXXXV (for 1996), pp 27-122

Margary, Ivan D., *Roman Roads in Britain* (2 Vols) (London, Phoenix House Ltd, 1955)

Maxfield, Valerie A. (ed), *The Saxon Shore. A Handbook* (Exeter, Exeter University, 1989)

Morris, John, *The Age of Arthur. A History of the British Isles from 350 to 650* (London, Weidenfield and Nicholson, 1973)

Myres, J. N. L., *The Angles, the Saxons and the Jutes*. The Raleigh Lecture on History. In Proceedings of the British Academy, Vol LVI (London, Oxford University Press, 1970)

Myres, J. N. L., *The English Settlements* (The Oxford History of England) (Oxford, Oxford University Press, 1980)

Newton, Sam, *The Origins of Beowulf and the Pre-Viking Kingdom of East Anglia* (Woodbridge, Surrey, Boydell and Brewer, 1999)

Noble, Frank (ed Gelling, M.), *Offa's Dyke Reviewed* (Oxford, British Archaeological Review, 1983)

Oldfirle, Master Cisbury, Schoolmaster, *The Legend of Devil's Dyke* (Brighton, H & C Treacher Ltd, undated)

Oppenheimer, Stephen, *The Origin of the British* (London, Constable and Robinson, 2006)

Peddie, John, *The Roman War Machine* (Stroud, Alan Sutton Publishing, 1994)

Rackham, Oliver, *Trees and Woodland in the English Landscape* (London, J.M. Dent and Sons, 1983)

Rackham, Oliver, *The History of the Countryside* (London, J.M. Dent and Sons, 1986)

Ryman, Ernest, *Guide to the Devil's Dyke* (Brighton, Dyke Publications, 1984)

Salway, Peter, *Roman Britain* (The Oxford History of England) (Oxford, Oxford University Press, 1981)

Simmons, B. B. and Cope-Faulkner, Paul, *The Car Dyke. Past Work, Current State and Future Possibilities* (Sleaford, Lincs, Heritage Trust of Lincolnshire, 2004)

Simmons, Brian and Cope-Faulkner, Paul, *The Car Dyke* (Sleaford, Lincs, Heritage Trust of Lincolnshire, 2006)

Snyder, Christopher A., *An Age of Tyrants* (Stroud, Sutton, 1998)

Stanton, F. M., *Anglo-Saxon England* (Volume II of the Oxford History of England. 3rd Edition, re-edited posthumously) (Oxford, Clarendon Press, 1971)

Thackray, D., *East Anglia Defensive Linear Earthworks* Doctoral Thesis, Cambridge University, 1980

Unsworth, Walter, *Grimsdyke* (London, Victor Gollancz Ltd, 1974)

Watts, Victor et al (eds), *The Cambridge Dictionary of English Place-Names* (Cambridge, Cambridge University Press, 2010)

Williamson, Tom, *Shaping Medieval Landscapes. Settlement, Society, Environment* (Macclesfield, Windgather Press, 2003)

However, the most important sources of information have been the maps of the Ordnance Survey of Great Britain. The current 1:50,000 scale Landranger mappage of the whole of Great Britain can be bought in digital format at a reasonable price. The current 1:25,000 scale Explorer series is also available in digital format. However, a given area requires four times the mappage of the Landranger series. It is therefore appreciably more expensive.

Some retailers also sell historic editions going back to the nineteenth century, in a variety of scales, both digitally and on paper. The National Library of Scotland has digitised much of its holdings. They can be viewed online at no cost at: http://maps.nls.uk/geo/find/#zoom=5&lat=56.0000&lon=-4.0000&layers=7&b=1&point=0,0. At time of writing (early 2016), they include six inch to one mile coverage for all of Great Britain, and twenty-five inches to one mile coverage for most of southern England and some parts of Scotland.

Paper Ordnance Survey maps are held in a number of libraries, including the Bodleian at Oxford University and Cambridge University Library. My own collection of paper maps includes several hundred Ordnance Survey sheets, of a variety of scales and editions.

Index